BAHÁ'Í REFEREN

JUDAISM, CHRISTIANIT

Bahá'í References
to
Judaism, Christianity and Islám

with other materials for the study of Progressive Revelation

compiled by
James Heggie

GR
GEORGE RONALD
OXFORD

GEORGE RONALD, Publisher
46 High Street, Kidlington, Oxford, OX5 2DN

British Library Cataloguing in Publication Data

Heggie, James
Bahá'í references to Judaism, Christianity and Islám.
1. Bahai Faith—Sacred books—Concordances
I. Title
297'.8982'0321 BP370

ISBN 0-85398-242-2

Printed in Great Britain at the Alden Press, Oxford

Contents

Preface vii

List of Sources ix

Bahá'í References to Judaism, Christianity and Islám I

Appendix Selections from the Holy Qur'án: Translations and Emendations by Shoghi Effendi *compiled by Burl Barer* 247

Page Conversion Tables 253

List of Head Words 257

Dedicated to
Jane Routh
devoted seeker and treasured mentor

Preface

This book of more than two thousand quotations taken from the Bahá'í Writings presents material for the study of the Old and New Testaments and the Qur'án, and also makes mention of the Hindu, Zoroastrian and Buddhist Scriptures. While the head words are alphabetically listed the material is subject orientated to show the evolutionary process of mankind's religious education. The idea of progressive revelation is a new principle which has been expounded in the Bahá'í Writings, and one which gives the key to a universal understanding of the Scriptures of all Faiths. The religions of the world have in the past been generally looked upon as unconnected and even antagonistic towards each other, but investigation shows this idea to be misplaced, resulting in widespread religious misunderstanding.

To study society one must begin with the family, not only the individual. To understand God's purpose for humanity we must investigate the family of religions as a progressive revelation of God to man, and see every aspect presented, every thought, as vitally important to man's spiritual welfare and material guidance. As a child progresses from the primary to the secondary and tertiary grades of schooling, so has man's religious education advanced: in the Old Testament the emphasis is on God and His interest in man; in the New Testament we find spiritual education stressed, and in the Qur'án is found a commentary on the history of the Prophets from Adam to Christ and a prediction of the ultimate and imminent coming of the Promised One of all Faiths. Man has always wanted answers to his questions – but Daniel was told to 'close the books' until the time of the end; Christ said, 'Many things I have to tell you but ye cannot bear them now', and Muḥammad spoke of the coming of the 'explanation' when all things would be made known. And all these were fulfilled with the revelation of the *Bayán* and the *Kitáb-i-Íqán* which at last resolve the abstruse meanings of previous Scriptures.

Students of religion have a tendency to place a literal interpretation upon the many sayings of the Holy Scriptures, and this has led to misunderstandings and controversy among both clergy and seekers after truth. Such perplexing questions are simply resolved by the explanations given throughout the Bahá'í Scriptures, as for instance those concerning the Trinity, the passage of the Israelites through the Red Sea, that story of Christ walking on the waters; prophecies are similarly explained and shown to have a spiritual meaning. Deep spiritual truths are made plain, limited only by the student's capacity to absorb them, for in such a quest it is found that each garden of search leads to a greater garden of knowledge.

This book then offers material for a comprehensive study of the true meanings of all the world's Scriptures. It allows the student to embark on a spiritual journey into the treasurehouse of God, conducted by the three Central Figures of the Faith of God for today – Bahá'u'lláh, the Báb and 'Abdu'l-Bahá – and by its Guardian, Shoghi Effendi. It is a journey which reveals the spiritual truths underlying all religions and explains many details in the lives of the Prophets as well as the attitudes and actions of the people – and where and how they went against the divine intention. These highly concentrated quotations are in the nature of a commentary covering nearly six thousand years of mankind's efforts to understand God's purpose for man, a study of recorded religious history illumined by the Manifestation of God Himself, Bahá'u'lláh, the Universal Manifestation for this age, the Promised One of all Faiths.

James Heggie
Sydney, 1986

List of Sources

Tablets of Bahá'u'lláh revealed after the Kitáb-i-Aqdas. Translated by Habib Taherzadeh with the assistance of a Committee at the Bahá'í World Centre. Haifa: Bahá'í World Centre, 1978. TB

Gleanings from the Writings of Bahá'u'lláh. Translated by Shoghi Effendi. Wilmette, Illinois: Bahá'í Publishing Trust, 1939, 3rd edn. 1976. G

Epistle to the Son of the Wolf. Bahá'u'lláh, translated by Shoghi Effendi. Wilmette, Illinois: Bahá'í Publishing Trust, 1932, rev. edn. 1976. ESW

Kitáb-i-Íqán. The Book of Certitude. Bahá'u'lláh, translated by Shoghi Effendi. Wilmette, Illinois: Bahá'í Publishing Trust, 1931, rev. edn. 1974. KI

'The Hidden Words' revealed in Arabic in *The Hidden Words*. Bahá'u'lláh, translated by Shoghi Effendi with the assistance of some English friends. Wilmette, Illinois: Bahá'í Publishing Trust, rev. edn. 1954. AHW

Selections from the Writings of the Báb. Translated by Habib Taherzadeh with the assistance of a Committee at the Bahá'í World Centre. Haifa: Bahá'í World Centre, 1976. SB

The Secret of Divine Civilization. 'Abdu'l-Bahá, translated by Marzieh Gail. Wilmette, Illinois: Bahá'í Publishing Trust, 2nd edn. 1970, RP 1975. SDC

Selections from the Writings of 'Abdu'l-Bahá. Translated by a Committee at the Bahá'í World Centre and by Marzieh Gail. Haifa: Bahá'í World Centre, 1978. SAB

Some Answered Questions. 'Abdu'l-Bahá, translated by Laura Clifford Barney. Wilmette, Illinois: rev. edn. 1981. SAQ

The Promulgation of Universal Peace. Discourses by 'Abdu'l Bahá Abbas during His Visit to the United States in 1912. Wilmette, Illinois: Bahá'í Publishing Trust, rev. edn. 1982. PUP

Paris Talks. Addresses given by 'Abdu'l-Bahá in Paris in 1911–12. London: Bahá'í Publishing Trust, 11th edn. 1969, RP 1972. PT

Bahá'í World Faith. Selected Writings of Bahá'u'lláh and 'Abdu'l-Bahá. Wilmette, Illinois: 2nd edn. 1953, RP 1976. BWF

Foundations of World Unity. Compiled from FWU

List of Sources

Addresses and Tablets of 'Abdu'l-Bahá. Wilmette, Illinois: Bahá'í Publishing Trust, 1945.	
Tablets of Abdul Baha Abbas. First published 1909–16. New York: Bahá'í Publishing Committee, 1930.	TAB
Star of the West. The Bahai News Service. Chicago: 1910–33. Vols. I–XIV reprinted in *Star of the West*. Oxford: George Ronald, 1978.	SW
God Passes By. Shoghi Effendi. Wilmette, Illinois: Bahá'í Publishing Trust, 1944, 1970.	GPB
The World Order of Bahá'u'lláh. Shoghi Effendi. Wilmette, Illinois: Bahá'í Publishing Trust, 1938, 1980.	WOB
The Advent of Divine Justice. Shoghi Effendi. Wilmette, Illinois: Bahá'í Publishing Trust, 1939, 1971.	ADJ
The Promised Day Is Come. Shoghi Effendi. Wilmette, Illinois: Bahá'í Publishing Trust, rev. edn. 1981.	PDC
Dawn of a New Day. Messages to India: 1923–57. Shoghi Effendi. New Delhi: Bahá'í Publishing Trust, 1970.	DND
Citadel of Faith. Messages to America: 1947–57. Shoghi Effendi. Wilmette, Illinois: Bahá'í Publishing Trust, 1965, RP 1970.	CF
Bahá'í Administration. Selected Messages: 1922–32. Shoghi Effendi. Wilmette, Illinois: Bahá'í Publishing Trust, 1928, 6th rev. edn. 1974.	BA
Tablets of the Divine Plan. 'Abdu'l-Bahá. Wilmette, Illinois: Bahá'í Publishing Trust, 1959, RR 1975.	TDP
Messages to the Bahá'í World: 1950–57. Shoghi Effendi. Wilmette, Illinois: Bahá'í Publishing Trust, 1958.	MBW
Lights of Guidance: A Bahá'í Reference File. Compiled by Helen Hornby. New Delhi: Bahá'í Publishing Trust, 1983.	LG
Bahá'í News. Wilmette, Illinois: National Spiritual Assembly of the Bahá'ís of the United States, nos. 80–313.	BN

In case the reader wishes to refer back to the original books, but does not have access to the editions used in this book, page conversion tables are supplied at the back of the book where there is more than one edition in common use.

Sources cited are the most recent and authoritative translations available. Where a passage occurs in two or more sources, the most original is preferred. Thus ESW and KI are preferred to G, while AHW, G, SAQ, PUP and PT are preferred to BWF, FWU and TAB. Between TAB, now long out of print, and BWF, the latter is preferred as more generally available, and in any case many passages from these two works have been replaced by the new and authoritative translations in SAB.

Abase

'he that is exalted among you shall be abased' *Balál* G 83–4

this abasement and glory, this dominion, power, and the like *Poverty* KI 132

even as it is said: 'The abased amongst you, He shall exalt; and they that are exalted, He shall abase.' And likewise, He hath revealed in the Qur'án: 'And We desire to show favour to those who were brought low in the land, and to make them spiritual leaders among men, and to make of them Our heirs.' It hath been witnessed in this day how many of the divines, owing to their rejection of the Truth, have fallen into, and abide within, the uttermost depths of ignorance, and whose names have been effaced from the scroll of the glorious and learned. And how many of the ignorant who, by reason of their acceptance of the Faith, have soared aloft and attained the high summit of knowledge, and whose names have been inscribed by the Pen of Power upon the Tablet of divine Knowledge. Thus, 'What He pleaseth will God abrogate or confirm: for with Him is the Source of Revelation' 146–7

likewise behold this Revelation. The essences of the people have, through divinely-conceived designs, been set in motion and until the present day three hundred and thirteen disciples have been chosen. In the land of Ṣád (Iṣfáhán), which to outward seeming is a great city, in every corner of whose seminaries are vast numbers of people regarded as divines and doctors, yet when the time came for inmost essences to be drawn forth, only its sifter of wheat donned the robe of discipleship. This is the mystery of what was uttered by the kindred of the Prophet Muḥammad – upon them be the peace of God – concerning this Revelation, saying that the abased shall be exalted and the exalted shall be abased SB 83

remember the Messiah, and His days on earth, and His abasement, and His tribulations, and how the people paid Him no mind SAB 173

'Abdu'lláh Ubayy

'Abdu'lláh Ubayy, a leader among the learned, maliciously strove to oppose Him *Balál* G 83–4

Divines – re: Muḥammad KI 108

'Abdu'ṣ-Ṣaḥib

O 'Abdu'ṣ-Ṣaḥib! . . . Thy vision is obscured by the belief that divine revelation ended with the coming of Muḥammad, and unto this We have borne witness in Our first epistle. Indeed, He Who hath revealed verses unto Muḥammad, the Apostle of God, hath likewise revealed verses unto 'Alí-Muḥammad. For who else but God can reveal to a man such clear and manifest verses as overpower all the learned — SB 31

Abel

the miracle of Abel and Cain, that is, offer a sacrifice, and the fire from heaven consume it; even as they had heard it recounted in the story of Abel, which story is recounted in the scriptures — KI 148

why should Muḥammad, that Essence of truthfulness, have charged the people of His day with the murder of Abel or other Prophets? Thou hast none other alternative except to regard Muḥammad as an impostor or a fool – which God forbid! – or to maintain that those people of wickedness were the self-same people who in every age opposed and caviled at the Prophets and Messengers of God, till they finally caused them all to suffer martyrdom — 149

during the cycle of Adam it was lawful and expedient for a man to marry his own sister, even as Abel, Cain and Seth, the sons of Adam, married their sisters *Adam* — (BWF 274) PUP 365

the criminal act perpetrated by Cain against Abel *Cain* — GPB 163

Abí-'Abdi'lláh

a lengthy tradition is attributed to Abí-'Abdi'lláh *Qá'im* — ESW 112

Abu-Ja'far-i-Ṭúsi hath said: 'I said to Abí-'Abdi'lláh: "You are the Way mentioned in the Book of God, and you are the Impost, and you are the Pilgrimage." He replied: "O man! We are the Way mentioned in the Book of God, – exalted and glorified be He – and We are the Impost, and We are the Fast, and We are the Pilgrimage, and We are the Sacred Month, and We are the Sacred City, and We are the Kaaba of God, and We are the Qiblih of God, and We are the Face of God"' — 112–13

Abject

'none hath followed you except the abject amongst us, those who are worthy of no attention' [see also *Christ* SW IX 10 p112] *Cavil* — KI 222

why dost thou burden thy soul with that which is far more abject than the deeds of Pharaoh, and still call thyself one of the faithful – re: to Muḥammad Sháh — SB 26

and the Children of Israel, through that Mosaic Law, were delivered out of their ignorance and came into the light; they were lifted up from their abjectness and attained to a glory that fadeth not — SAB 52

we need only recall the nineteen hundred years of abject misery and dispersion which they who, only for the short space of three years, persecuted the Son of God have had to endure, and are still enduring – re: Jewish people — PDC 99

Abode

He said, and His Word is the truth: 'And God calleth to the Abode of Peace; and He guideth whom He will into the right way.' 'For them is an Abode of Peace with their Lord! and He shall be their Protector' because of their works — KI 174–5

vain indeed is your dominion, for God hath set aside earthly possessions for such as have denied Him; for unto Him Who is your Lord shall be the most excellent abode, He Who is, in truth, the Ancient of Days — SB 43 in that city, described in Islamic traditions as 'Ẓahru'l-Kúfih,' designated for centuries as the 'Abode of Peace,' and immortalized by Bahá'u'lláh as the 'City of God,' He, except for His two year retirement to the mountains of Kurdistán . . . continued to reside until His banishment to Constantinople. To that city the Qur'án had alluded as 'Abode of Peace' to which God Himself 'calleth.' To it, in that same Book, further allusion had been made in the verse 'For them is a Dwelling of Peace with their Lord . . . on the Day whereon God shall gather them all together [see also *Father* 110] GPB 109–10

Abolish

briefly, this Man, Who, apparently, and in the eyes of all, was lowly, arose with such great power that he abolished a religion that had lasted fifteen hundred years, at a time when the slightest deviation from it exposed the offender to danger or to death – re: Christ and Israel SAQ 16

Abomination of Desolation see *Daniel*

Abraham

that which thou hast heard concerning Abraham, the Friend of the All-Merciful, is the truth, and no doubt is there about it. The Voice of God commanded Him to offer up Ishmael as a sacrifice, so that His steadfastness in the Faith of God and His detachment from all else but Him may be demonstrated unto men. The purpose of God, moreover, was to sacrifice him as a ransom for the sins and iniquities of all the peoples of the earth. This same honour, Jesus, the Son of Mary, besought the one true God, exalted be His name and glory, to confer upon Him. For the same reason was Ḥusayn offered up as a sacrifice by Muḥammad, the Apostle of God G 75–6

later, Abraham, the Friend of God, appeared and shed upon the world the light of Divine Revelation. The language He spoke while He crossed the Jordan became known as Hebrew (Ibrání) which meaneth 'the language of the crossing'. The Books of God and the Sacred Scriptures were revealed in that tongue 173

later, the beauty of the countenance of the Friend of God appeared from behind the veil, and another standard of divine guidance was hoisted. He invited the people of the earth to the light of righteousness. The more passionately He exhorted them, the fiercer waxed the envy and waywardness of the people, except those who wholly detached themselves from all save God, and ascended on the wings of certainty to the station which God hath exalted beyond the comprehension of men. It is well known what a host of enemies besieged Him, until at last the fires of envy and rebellion were kindled against Him. And after the episode of the fire came to pass, He, the lamp of God amongst men, was, as recorded in all the books and chronicles, expelled from His city KI 10–11

among the Prophets was Abraham, the Friend of God. Ere He manifested Himself, Nimrod dreamed a dream. Thereupon, he summoned the soothsayers, who informed him of the rise of a star in the heaven. Likewise, there appeared a herald who announced throughout the land the coming of Abraham 62–3

some, who are not sufficiently informed as to the meaning of the divine Texts and the contents of traditional and written history, will aver that these customs of the Days of Ignorance were laws which had come down from His Holiness Abraham and had been retained by the idolaters. In this connection they will cite the Qur'ánic verse: 'Follow the religion of Abraham, the sound in faith.' Nevertheless it is a fact attested by SDC 29–30 writings of all the Islamic schools that the months of truce, the lunar calendar, and the cutting off of the right hand as punishment for theft, formed no part of Abraham's Law. In any case, the Pentateuch is extant and available today, and contains the laws of Abraham. Let them refer to it. They will then, of course, insist that the Torah has been tampered with, and in proof will quote the Qur'ánic verse: 'They pervert the text of the Word of God.' It is, however, known where such distortion has occurred, and is a matter of record in critical texts and commentaries

the Founder of monotheism was Abraham; it is to Him that this concept can be traced, and the belief was current among the Children of Israel, even in the days of Socrates SAB 55

Abraham's migration from His native land caused the bountiful gifts of the All-Glorious to be made manifest 281

one of those Who possessed this power and was assisted by it was Abraham. And the proof of it was that He was born in Mesopotamia, and of a family who were ignorant of the Oneness of God. He opposed His own nation and people, and even His own family, by rejecting all their gods. Alone and without help He resisted a powerful tribe, a task which is neither simple nor easy. It is as if in this day someone were to go to a Christian people who are attached to the Bible, and deny Christ; or in the Papal Court – God forbid! – if such a one were in the most powerful manner to blaspheme against Christ and oppose the people. These people believed not in one God but in many gods, to whom they ascribed miracles; therefore, they all arose against Him, and no one supported Him except Lot, His brother's son, and one or two other people of no importance. At last, reduced to the utmost distress by the opposition of His enemies, He was obliged to leave His native land. In reality they banished Him in order that He might be crushed and destroyed, and that no trace of Him might be left. SAQ 12–13

Abraham then came into the region of the Holy Land. His enemies considered that His exile would lead to His destruction and ruin, as it seemed impossible that a man banished from His native land, deprived of His rights and oppressed on all sides – even though He were a king – could escape extermination. But Abraham stood fast and showed forth extraordinary firmness – and God made this exile to be His eternal honour until He established the Unity of God in the midst of a polytheistic generation. This exile became the cause of the progress of the descendants of Abraham, and the Holy Land was given to them. As a result the teachings of Abraham were spread abroad, a Jacob appeared among His posterity, and a Joseph who became ruler in Egypt. In consequence of His exile a Moses and a being like Christ were manifested from His posterity, and Hagar was found from whom Ishmael was born, one of whose descendants was Muḥammad. In consequence of His Exile the Báb appeared from His posterity, and the Prophets of Israel were numbered among the descendants of Abraham. And so it will continue for ever and ever. Finally, in consequence of His exile the whole of Europe and Asia came under the protecting shadow of the God of Israel

besides this, an especial blessing is conferred on some families and some generations. Thus it is an especial blessing that from among the descendants of Abraham should have come all the Prophets of the children of Israel. This is a blessing that God has granted to this descent: to Moses from His father and mother, to Christ from His mother's line; also to Muḥammad and the Báb, and to all the Prophets and the Holy Manifestations of Israel (BWF 319) 213 some souls were lovers of the name Abraham, loving the lantern instead of the light and when they saw this same light shining from another lantern, they were so attached to the former lantern that they did not recognize its later appearance and illumination. Therefore, those who were attached and held tenaciously to the name Abraham were deprived when the Abrahamic virtues reappeared in Moses (FWU 16) PUP 152

among the great Prophets was Abraham, Who, being an iconoclast and a Herald of the oneness of God, was banished from His native land. He founded a family upon which the blessing of God descended, and it was owing to this religious basis and ordination that the Abrahamic house progressed and advanced. Through the divine benediction noteworthy and luminous prophets issued from His lineage (BWF 271) 362

during the time of the Abrahamic Prophethood *Law* (BWF 274) 365

look how Abraham strove to bring faith and love among the people; how Moses tried to unite the people by sound laws; how the Lord Christ suffered unto death to bring the light of love and truth into a darkened world; how Muḥammad sought to bring unity and peace between the various uncivilized tribes among whom he dwelt. And last of all, Bahá'u'lláh has suffered forty years for the same cause – the single noble purpose of spreading love among the children of men – and for the peace and unity of the world the Báb gave up His life PT 171

His Holiness Abraham, on Him be peace, made a covenant concerning His Holiness Moses and gave the glad-tidings of His coming. His Holiness Moses made a covenant concerning the Promised One i.e. His Holiness Christ, and announced the good news of His Manifestation to the world. His Holiness Christ made a covenant concerning the Paraclete and gave the tidings of His coming. His Holiness the Prophet Muḥammad made a covenant concerning His Holiness the Báb and the Báb was the One promised by Muḥammad, for Muḥammad gave the tidings of His coming BWF 358

He called to remembrance the triumph of Abraham over Nimrod, of Moses over Pharaoh, of Jesus over the Jewish people, and of Muḥammad over the tribes of Arabia, and asserted the inevitability and ultimate ascendancy of His own Revelation – re: Báb's address to Letters of the Living GPB 8

He derived His descent, on the one hand, from Abraham (the Father of the Faithful) through his wife Katurah, and on the other from Zoroaster, as well as from Yazdigird, the last king of the Sásáníyán dynasty – re: Bahá'u'lláh 94

and above all the banishment of Abraham from Ur of the Chaldees to the Promised Land – a banishment which, in the multitudinous benefits it conferred upon so many divers peoples, faiths and nations, constitutes the nearest historical approach to the incalculable blessings destined to be vouchsafed in this day, and in future ages, to the whole human race, in direct consequence of the exile suffered by Him Whose Cause is the flower and fruit of all previous Revelations 107

'Abdu'l-Bahá, after enumerating in His 'Some Answered Questions' the far-reaching consequences of Abraham's banishment, significantly affirms that 'since the exile of Abraham from Ur to Aleppo in Syria produced this result, we must consider what will be the effect of the exile of Bahá'u'lláh in His several removes from Ṭihrán to Baghdád, from thence to Constantinople, to Rumelia and to the Holy Land 107–8

the 'transgression' of Pharaoh in the days of Moses, and of the 'impiety' of Nimrod in the days of Abraham 174

in a highly significant prayer, revealed by Bahá'u'lláh in memory of His son 188

Abraham

– a prayer that exalts his death to the rank of those great acts of atonement associated with Abraham's intended sacrifice of His son, with the crucifixion of Jesus Christ and the martyrdom of the Imám Ḥusayn – we read the following: 'I have, O my Lord, offered up that which Thou hast given Me, that Thy servants may be quickened, and all that dwell on earth be united.' And, likewise, these prophetic words addressed to His martyred son: 'Thou art the Trust of God and His Treasure in this Land. Erelong will God reveal through thee that which He hath desired'

had Muḥammad, the Apostle of God, attained this Day,' Bahá'u'lláh writes in a Tablet revealed on the eve of His banishment to the penal colony of 'Akká, 'He would have exclaimed: "I have truly recognized Thee, O Thou the Desire of the Divine Messengers!" Had Abraham attained it, He too, falling prostrate upon the ground, and in the utmost lowliness before the Lord thy God, would have cried: "Mine heart is filled with peace, O Thou God of all that is in heaven and on earth! I testify that Thou hast unveiled before mine eyes all the glory of Thy power and the full majesty of Thy law — WOB 105

'the leaders of men,' He [Bahá'u'lláh] has likewise asserted, 'have, from time immemorial, prevented the people from turning unto the Most Great Ocean. The Friend of God (Abraham) was cast into fire through the sentence pronounced by the divines of the age, and lies and calumnies were imputed to Him Who discoursed with God (Moses) — PDC 80

concerning the passage in the Old Testament in which Abraham is reported to have addressed his wife as his sister, the interpretation given it by some Christians cannot hold, as it implies that the Messengers of God are all sinners. A much more plausible explanation would be, that in doing so Abraham wished to emphasize the superiority of the spiritual relationship binding him with his wife to the purely physical and material one — DND 197–8

Abú-Jahl

Hamzih – re: verse of the Qur'án — KI 121

Accept

for instance, if the Apostle of God – may divine blessings rest upon Him – accepted a certain deed, in truth God accepted it; otherwise it hath remained within the selfish desires of the person who wrought it, and did not reach the presence of God *Exponent* — SB 81

should a Christian contend, 'How can I deem the Qur'án a testimony while I am unable to understand it?' such a contention would not be acceptable. Likewise the people of the Qur'án disdainfully observe, 'We are unable to comprehend the eloquence of the verses in the Bayán, how can we regard it as a testimony?' — 120

Access

the contingent world hath no other access unto the presence of the Ancient of Days *Exponent* — SB 81

if ye entertain any doubts in this matter consider the people unto whom the Gospel was given. Having no access to the apostles of Jesus, they sought the pleasure of the Lord in their churches, hoping to learn that which would be acceptable unto God, but they found therein no path unto Him — 137

Adam

contemplate with thine inward eye the chain of successive Revelations that hath linked the Manifestation of Adam with that of the Báb. I testify before God that each one of these Manifestations hath been sent down — G 74 through the operation of the Divine Will and Purpose, that each hath been the bearer of a specific Message, that each hath been entrusted with a divinely-revealed Book and been commissioned to unravel the mysteries of a mighty Tablet. The measure of the Revelation with which every one of them hath been identified had been definitely fore-ordained

and now regarding thy question, 'How is it that no records are to be found concerning the Prophets that have preceded Adam, the Father of Mankind, or of the kings that lived in the days of those Prophets?' Know thou that the absence of any reference to them is no proof that they did not actually exist. That no records concerning them are now available, should be attributed to their extreme remoteness, as well as to the vast changes which the earth hath undergone since their time. 172–3

Moreover such forms and modes of writing as are now current amongst men were unknown to the generations that were before Adam. There was even a time when men were wholly ignorant of the art of writing, and had adopted a system entirely different from the one which they now use

dust-made Adam was raised up, through the Word of God, to the heavenly throne, and a mere fisherman was made the repository of Divine wisdom, and Abú-Dhar, the shepherd, became a prince of the nations ESW 19

thus hath Muḥammad, the Point of the Qur'án revealed: 'I am all the Prophets.' Likewise, He saith: 'I am the first Adam, Noah, Moses, and Jesus' KI 152–3

hath not Muḥammad, Himself, declared: 'I am all the Prophets'? Hath He not said as We have already mentioned: 'I am Adam, Noah, Moses, and Jesus'? Why should Muḥammad, that immortal Beauty, Who hath said: 'I am the first Adam' be incapable of saying also: 'I am the last Adam'? 162

Ḥusayn, son of 'Alí, who, addressing Salmán, spoke words such as these: 'I was with a thousand Adams, the interval between each and the next Adam was fifty thousand years, and to each one of these I declared the Successorship conferred upon my father' 167–8

consider; He hath declared Knowledge to consist of twenty and seven letters, and regarded all the Prophets, from Adam even unto the 'Seal,' as Expounders of only two letters thereof and of having been sent down with these two letters. He also saith that the Qá'im will reveal all the remaining twenty and five letters 243–4

it behooveth man, upon reaching the age of nineteen, to render thanksgiving for the day of his conception as an embryo. For had the embryo not existed, how could he have reached his present state? Likewise had the religion taught by Adam not existed, this Faith would not have attained its present stage. Thus consider thou the development of God's Faith until the end that hath no end SB 89

therefore, this verse in Corinthians, 'As in Adam all die, even so in Christ shall all be made alive,' means, according to this terminology, that Adam is the father of man – that is to say, He is the cause of the physical life of mankind; His was the physical fatherhood. He is a living soul, but He is not the giver of spiritual life, whereas Christ is the cause of the spiritual life of man, and with regard to the spirit, His was the spiritual fatherhood. Adam is a living soul; Christ is a quickening spirit SAQ 119

[story of Adam] 122

therefore, this story of Adam and Eve who ate from the tree, and their expulsion from Paradise, must be thought of simply as a symbol. It contains divine mysteries and universal meanings, and is capable of marvelous explanations. Only those who are initiated into mysteries, 123 and those who are near the Court of the All-Powerful, are aware of these secrets. Hence these verses of the Bible have numerous meanings.

We will explain one of them, and we will say: Adam signifies the heavenly spirit of Adam, and Eve His human soul. For in some passages in the Holy Books where women are mentioned, they represent the soul of man. The tree of good and evil signifies the human world; for the spiritual and divine world is purely good and absolutely luminous, but in the human world light and darkness, good and evil, exist as opposite conditions

the meaning of the serpent is attachment to the human world. This attachment of the spirit to the human world led the soul and spirit of Adam from the world of freedom to the world of bondage and caused Him to turn from the Kingdom of Unity to the human world. When the soul and spirit of Adam entered the human world, He came out from the paradise of freedom and fell into the world of bondage. From the height of purity and absolute goodness, He entered into the world of good and evil 123–4

from the days of Adam until the days of Christ, They spoke little of eternal life and the heavenly universal perfections. This tree of life was the position of the Reality of Christ; through His manifestation it was planted and adorned with everlasting fruits 124

Sin Tree – re: story of Adam 124

for the spirit and the soul of Adam, when they were attached to the human world, passed from the world of freedom into the world of bondage, and His descendants continued in bondage. This attachment of the soul and spirit to the human world, which is sin, was inherited by the descendants of Adam . . . That enmity continues and endures. For attachment of the world has become the cause of the bondage of spirits, and this bondage is identical with sin, which has been transmitted from Adam to His posterity. It is because of this attachment that men have been deprived of essential spirituality and exalted position 124–5

during the cycle of Adam it was lawful and expedient for a man to marry his own sister, even as Abel, Cain and Seth the sons of Adam, married their sisters. But in the law of the Pentateuch revealed by Moses these marriages were forbidden and their custom and sanction abrogated (BWF 274) PUP 365

all men are the leaves and fruit of one same tree, they are all branches of the tree of Adam, they all have the same origin. The same rain has fallen upon them all, the same warm sun makes them grow, they are all refreshed by the same breeze. The only differences that exist and that keep them apart are these: there are the children who need guidance, the ignorant to be instructed, the sick to be tended and healed; thus, I say that the whole of humanity is enveloped by the Mercy and Grace of God. As the Holy Writings tell us: All men are equal before God. He is no respecter of persons PT 129–30

evil is imperfection. Sin is the state of man in the world of the baser nature, for in nature exist defects such as injustice, tyranny, hatred, hostility, strife: these are characteristics of the lower plane of nature. These are the sins of the world, the fruits of the tree from which Adam did eat. Through education we must free ourselves from these imperfections. The Prophets of God have been sent, the Holy Books have been written, so that man may be made free. Just as he is born into this world of imperfection from the womb of his earthly mother, so is he born into the world of spirit through divine education. When a man is born into the world of phenomena he finds the universe; when he is born from this world to the world of the spirit, he finds the Kingdom 177–8

His Holiness Bahá'u'lláh addressing all humanity, said that Adam the parent of mankind may be likened to the tree of nativity upon which you are the leaves and blossoms. Inasmuch as your origin was one, you must now be united and agreed; you must consort with each other in joy and fragrance BWF 233

we are in the cycle which began with Adam, and its universal Manifestation is Bahá'u'lláh FWU 54

thank thou God for He hath guided thee to the path of His Kingdom and provided thee with the fruit of the Tree of Life, which is planted in the middle of the Ferdowce (i.e., the highest Paradise). Yea, this fruit is the knowing God and love for God, and reliance upon God and is the virtue with which the reality of man is adorned, and it is the perfections which are the great gift for the child of Adam (i.e., mankind) in this first creation TAB 516

thus ended a life which posterity will recognize as standing at the confluence of two universal prophetic cycles, the Adamic Cycle stretching back as far as the first dawnings of the world's recorded religious history and the Bahá'í Cycle destined to propel itself across the unborn reaches of time for a period of no less than five thousand centuries GPB 54–5

'the whole world,' is Bahá'u'lláh's matchless testimony in the Kitáb-i-Íqán, 'marveled at the manner of their sacrifice . . . The mind is bewildered at their deeds, and the soul marveleth at their fortitude and bodily endurance . . . Hath any age witnessed such momentous happenings?' And again: 'Hath the world, since the days of Adam, witnessed such tumult, such violent commotion? . . . Methinks, patience was revealed only by virtue of their fortitude, and faithfulness itself was begotten only by their deeds – re: Bábí martyrs 79–80

a Revelation, hailed as the promise and crowning glory of past ages and centuries, as the consummation of all the Dispensations within the Adamic Cycle, inaugurating an era of at least a thousand years' duration, and a cycle destined to last no less than five thousand centuries, signalizing the end of the Prophetic Era and the beginning of the Era of Fulfillment – re: Bahá'í Revelation 100

the Faith of Bahá'u'lláh should indeed be regarded, if we wish to be faithful to the tremendous implications of its message, as the culmination of a cycle, the final stage in a series of successive, of preliminary and progressive revelations. These, beginning with Adam and ending with the Báb, have paved the way and anticipated with an ever-increasing emphasis the advent of that Day of Days in which He Who is the Promise of All Ages should be made manifest WOB 103

feelings of profound emotion evoked by this historic occasion of the worldwide commemoration of the First Centenary of the Martyrdom of the Blessed Báb, Prophet and Herald of the Faith of Bahá'u'lláh, Founder of the Dispensation marking the culmination of the six thousand year old Adamic Cycle, Inaugurator of the five thousand century Bahá'í Cycle CF 80

Á<u>dh</u>irbáyján

if it were My will, I would disclose to Your Majesty all things; but I have not done this, nor will I do it . . . and this prophecy uttered by the Imám Báqir – may peace rest upon Him – be fully realized: 'What must needs befall us in Á<u>dh</u>irbáyján is inevitable and without parallel. When this happeneth, rest ye in your homes and remain patient as we have remained patient. As soon as the Mover moveth make ye haste to attain unto Him, even though ye have to crawl over the snow' SB 16–17

Admittance

indeed, the essential prerequisites of admittance into the Bahá'í fold of Jews, Zoroastrians, Hindus, Buddhists, and the followers of other ancient faiths, as well as of agnostics and even atheists, is the whole-hearted and unqualified acceptance by them all of the Divine origin of both Islám and Christianity, of the Prophetic functions of both Muḥammad and Jesus Christ, of the legitimacy of the institution of the Imamate, and of the primacy of St. Peter, the Prince of the Apostles PDC 110

Admonition

notwithstanding the divinely-inspired admonitions of all the Prophets, the Saints, and Chosen ones of God, enjoining the people to see with their own eyes and hear with their own ears, they have disdainfully rejected their counsels and have blindly followed, and will continue to follow, the leaders of their Faith KI 164–5

O brother, we should open our eyes, meditate upon His Word, and seek the sheltering shadow of the Manifestations of God, that perchance we may be warned by the unmistakable counsels of the Book, and give heed to the admonitions recorded in the holy Tablets; that we may not cavil at the Revealer of the verses, that we may resign ourselves wholly to His Cause, and embrace whole-heartedly His law, that haply we may enter the court of His mercy, and dwell upon the shore of His grace. He, verily, is merciful, and forgiving towards His servants 217

Advent

they failed to attain His presence, notwithstanding that His advent had been promised them in the Book of Isaiah as well as in the Books of the Prophets and the Messengers – re: the Pharisees *Spirit* TB 9–10

they clamoured that He Whose advent the Bible had foretold must needs promulgate and fulfil the laws of Moses *Annul* KI 18

and finally, in several passages addressed to the entire body of the followers of Jesus Christ He identifies Himself with the 'Father' spoken of by Isaiah, with the 'Comforter' Whose Covenant He Who is the Spirit (Jesus) had Himself established, and with the 'Spirit of Truth' Who will guide them 'into all truth'; proclaims His Day to be the Day of God GPB 210

'the Father hath come. That which ye were promised in the Kingdom of God is fulfilled. This is the Word which the Son veiled when He said to those around Him that at that time they could not bear it . . . Verily the Spirit of Truth is come to guide you unto all truth . . . He is the One Who glorified the Son and exalted His Cause . . .' 'The Comforter Whose advent all the scriptures have promised is now come that He may reveal unto you all knowledge and wisdom. Seek Him over the entire surface of the earth, haply ye may find Him' [words of Bahá'u'lláh] WOB 104–5

Affliction

these two most great afflictions, brought on by Nebuchadnezzar and Titus, are referred to in the glorious Qur'án: 'And We solemnly declared to the children of Israel in the Book, "Twice surely will ye commit evil in the earth, and with great loftiness of pride will ye surely be uplifted"' SDC 79

'Akká

thereupon, a Voice was raised from the direction of Ḥijáz, calling aloud and saying: 'Great is thy blessedness, O 'Akká, in that God hath made thee the dayspring of His Most Sweet Voice, and the dawn of His most mighty signs. Happy art thou in that the Throne of Justice hath been established upon thee, and the Day-Star of God's loving-kindness and ESW 79 bounty hath shone forth above thy horizon. Well is it with every fair-minded person that hath judged fairly Him Who is the Most Great Remembrance, and woe betide him that hath erred and doubted'

the Sun of Truth shineth resplendently, at the bidding of the Lord of the kingdom of utterance, and the King of the heaven of knowledge, above the horizon of the prison-city of 'Akká. Repudiation hath not veiled it, and ten thousand hosts arrayed against it were powerless to withhold it from shining. Thou canst excuse thyself no longer. Either thou must recognize it, or – God forbid – arise and deny all the Prophets 119

lend an ear unto the song of David. He saith: 'Who will bring me into the Strong City?' The Strong City is 'Akká, which hath been named the Most Great Prison, and which possesseth a fortress and mighty ramparts 144

peruse that which Isaiah hath spoken in His Book. He saith: 'Get thee up into the high mountain, O Zion, that bringest good tidings; lift up Thy Voice with strength, O Jerusalem, that bringest good tidings. Lift it up, be not afraid; say unto the cities of Judah: "Behold your God! Behold the Lord God will come with strong hand, and His arm shall rule for Him."' This Day all the signs have appeared. A Great City hath descended from heaven, and Zion trembleth and exulteth with joy at the Revelation of God, for it hath heard the Voice of God on every side. This Day Jerusalem hath attained unto a new Evangel, for in the stead of the sycamore standeth the cedar. Jerusalem is the place of pilgrimage for all the peoples of the world, and hath been named the Holy City. Together with Zion and Palestine, they are all included within these regions. Wherefore, hath it been said: 'Blessed is the man that hath migrated to 'Akká' 144–5

'I bring you tidings of a city betwixt two mountains in Syria, in the middle of a meadow, which is called 'Akká. Verily, he that entereth therein longing for it and eager to visit it, God will forgive his sins, both of the past and of the future. And he that departeth from it, other than as a pilgrim, God will not bless his departure. In it is a spring called the Spring of the Cow. Whoso drinketh a draught therefrom, God will fill his heart with light, and will protect him from the most great terror on the Day of Resurrection' 178

'by the shore of the sea is a city, suspended beneath the Throne, and named 'Akká. He that dwelleth therein, firm and expecting a reward from God – exalted be He – God will write down for him, until the Day of Resurrection, the recompense of such as have been patient, and have stood up, and knelt down, and prostrated themselves, before Him' 178–9

'Akká, itself, flanked by the 'glory of Lebanon,' and lying in full view of the 'splendour of Carmel,' at the foot of the hills which enclose the home of Jesus Christ Himself, had been described by David as 'the Strong City,' designated by Hosea as 'a door of hope,' and alluded to by Ezekiel as 'the gate that looketh towards the East,' whereunto 'the glory of the God of Israel came from the way of the East,' His voice 'like a noise of many waters' GPB 184

'Alí

the Commander of the Faithful (Imám 'Alí) – peace be upon him – moreover, saith in the Khuṭbiy-i-Ṭutujíyyih: 'Anticipate ye the Revelation of Him Who conversed with Moses from the Burning Bush on Sinai' ESW 42

Divinity – re: saying of 'Alí 111–12

the Commander of the Faithful (Imám 'Alí) hath said: 'I am He Who can neither be named, nor described.' And likewise He hath said: 112

'Alí

'Outwardly I am an Imám; inwardly I am the Unseen, the Unknowable'

moreover, the Commander of the Faithful (Imám 'Alí) – peace be upon him – hath said: 'How can I worship a Lord Whom I have not seen?' And, in another connection, he saith: 'Nothing have I perceived except that I perceived God before it, God after it, or God with it' 113

and, now, strive thou to comprehend the meaning of this saying of 'Alí, the Commander of the Faithful: 'Piercing the veils of glory, unaided.' Among these 'veils of glory' are the divines and doctors living in the days of the Manifestation of God, who, because of their want of discernment and their love and eagerness for leadership, have failed to submit to the Cause of God, nay, have even refused to incline their ears unto the divine Melody. 'They have thrust their fingers into their ears' KI 164

have they not heard the melody of that bird of Heaven, uttering this mystery: 'A thousand Fátimihs I have espoused, all of whom were the daughters of Muḥammad, Son of 'Abdu'lláh, the "Seal of the Prophets"'? 166–7

as to those who have put the kindred of 'Alí to death, ere long they shall realize to what depths of perdition they have descended SB 5

Ḥusayn – re: waged war against 70

compare His manifestation with that of the Point of the Qur'án. How vast the number of the Letters of the Gospel who eagerly expected Him, yet from the time of His declaration up to five years no one became an inmate of Paradise, except the Commander of the Faithful (Imám 'Alí), and those who secretly believed in Him. All the rest were accounted as inmates of the fire, though they considered themselves as dwellers in Paradise 83

Qur'án – re: recognition by 'Alí 90

it is said they 'are clothed in sackcloth' *Sackcloth* SAQ 48–9

Witness – re: one of the two witnesses 48–9

Lamp – re: two olive trees, two candlesticks 49

Servant – re: standing in the service of God 49

they also would have the power and the material force necessary *Power* 50

Testimony – re: and when they shall have finished their testimony 51

Law – re: two witnesses 51

Beast – re: the beast made war against these two witnesses 51

Alpha and Omega

the Lord God Omnipotent hath been enthroned in His Kingdom and hath made all things new. This is the truth and what truth can be greater than that announced by the Revelation of St. John the Divine?
He is Alpha and Omega. He is the One that will give unto him that is athirst of the fountain of the water of life and bestow upon the sick the remedy of true salvation SAB 12–13

to Him the Author of the Apocalypse had alluded as the 'Glory of God,' as 'Alpha and Omega,' 'the Beginning and the End,' 'the First and the Last' – re: Bahá'u'lláh GPB 95

Amos

Amos saith: 'The Lord will roar from Zion, and utter His Voice from Jerusalem; and the habitations of the shepherds shall mourn, and the top of Carmel shall wither' ESW 145

reflect upon these words addressed by Him Who is the Desire of the world to Amos. He saith: 'Prepare to meet thy God, O Israel, for, lo, He that formeth the mountains and createth the wind, and declareth unto man 145–6 what is his thought, that maketh the morning darkness, and treadeth upon the high places of the earth, the Lord, the God of Hosts, is His name.' He saith that He maketh the morning darkness. By this is meant that if, at the time of the Manifestation of Him Who conversed on Sinai anyone were to regard himself as the true morn, he will, through the might and power of God, be turned into darkness. He truly is the false dawn, though believing himself to be the true one. Woe unto him, and woe unto such as follow him without a clear token from God, the Lord of the worlds

Ancient of Days

this is indeed the eternal Truth which God, the Ancient of Days, hath revealed *Truth* SB 41

He Who is, in truth, the Ancient of Days *Abode* 43

will ye not fear the One true God, He Who is your Lord, the Ancient of Days? *Gate* 51–2

at one time I hear His Voice as He acclaimeth Him Who is the Ever-Living, the Ancient of Days, and at another time as He speaketh of the mystery of His most august Name. And when He intoneth the anthems of the greatness of God all Paradise waileth in its longing to gaze on His Beauty, and when He chanteth words of praise and glorification of God all Paradise becomes motionless like unto ice locked in the heart of a frost-bound mountain 54

the Lord hath, in truth, inspired Me: Verily, verily, I am God, He besides Whom there is none other God, and I am indeed the Ancient of Days 58

the contingent world hath no other access unto the presence of the Ancient of Days *Exponent* 81

the Ancient of Days Whom none can ever describe *Beloved* 212

Angel

the heaven of every religion hath been rent, and the earth of human understanding been cleft asunder, and the angels of God are seen descending G 45

We see men drunken in this Day, the Day in which men and angels have been gathered together 45

and now, concerning His words: 'And He shall send His angels . . .' By 'angels' is meant those who, reinforced by the power of the spirit, have consumed, with the fire of the love of God, all human traits and limitations, and have clothed themselves with the attributes of the most exalted Beings and of the Cherubim KI 78–9

and now, inasmuch as these holy beings have sanctified themselves from every human limitation, have become endowed with the attributes of the spiritual, and have been adorned with the noble traits of the blessed, they therefore have been designated as 'angels' 79–80

were the prophecies recorded in the Gospel to be literally fulfilled; were Jesus, Son of Mary, accompanied by angels, to descend from the visible heaven upon the clouds; who would dare to disbelieve, who would dare to reject the truth, and wax disdainful? 80–81

protest in such words: 'If Thou art in truth the promised Prophet, why then art Thou not accompanied by those angels our sacred Books foretold, and which must needs descend with the promised Beauty to assist Him in His Revelation and act as warners unto His people?' *Christianity* 81

hath not the Seraph himself, the angel of the Judgment Day, and his like been ordained by Muḥammad's own utterance 116

Angel

the meaning of 'angels' is the confirmations of God and His celestial powers. Likewise angels are blessed beings who have severed all ties with this nether world, have been released from the chains of self and the desires of the flesh, and anchored their hearts to the heavenly realms of the Lord — SAB 81

'and the seventh angel sounded; and there were great voices in heaven, saying, The kingdoms of this world are become the kingdoms of our Lord, and of His Christ; and He shall reign for ever and ever.' — SAQ 56

The seventh angel is a man qualified with heavenly attributes, who will arise with heavenly qualities and character. Voices will be raised, so that the appearance of the Divine Manifestation will be proclaimed and diffused

ye are the angels, if your feet be firm, your spirits rejoiced, your secret thoughts pure, your eyes consoled, your ears opened — BWF 360

Annas see *Caiaphas*

Announcement

likewise, in the Qur'án He saith: 'Of what ask they of one another? Of the Great Announcement.' This is the Announcement, the greatness of which hath been mentioned in most of the Books of old and of more recent times. This is the Announcement that hath caused the limbs of mankind to quake, except such as God, the Protector, the Helper, the Succorer, hath willed to exempt. Men have indeed with their own eyes witnessed how all men and all things have been thrown into confusion and been sore perplexed, save those whom God hath chosen to exempt [see also *Father Joel*] — ESW 143–4

O Qurratu'l-'Ayn! I recognize in Thee none other except the 'Great Announcement' – the Announcement voiced by the Concourse on high. By this name, I bear witness, they that circle the Throne of Glory have ever known Thee — SB 72

O Qurratu'l-'Ayn! Say: Verily I am the One Who is hailed in the Mother Book as the 'Great Announcement'. Say: The people have grievously differed over Me, whereas in truth there is no difference between Me and the Báb — 74

Annul

they clamoured that He Whose advent the Bible had foretold must needs promulgate and fulfil the laws of Moses, whereas this youthful Nazarene, who laid claim to the station of the divine Messiah, had annulled the law of divorce and of the sabbath day – the most weighty of all the laws of Moses — KI 18

thus it is that the adherents of Jesus maintained that the law of the Gospel shall never be annulled . . . This is their fundamental belief — 27

hence, it is clear and manifest that by the words 'the sun shall be darkened, and the moon shall not give her light, and the stars shall fall from heaven' is intended the waywardness of the divines, and the annulment of laws firmly established by divine Revelation, all of which, in symbolic language, have been foreshadowed by the Manifestation of God — 41

by 'cloven asunder' is meant that the former Dispensation is superseded and annulled — 44

these 'clouds' signify, in one sense, the annulment of laws, the abrogation of former Dispensations, the repeal of rituals and customs current amongst men, the exalting of the illiterate faithful above the learned opposers of the Faith — 71–2

Muḥammad observed: 'Why is it then that this law is annulled and hath ceased to operate among the Jews?' [see also *Jews*] 85

even as the Christian divines who, holding fast to the verse of the Gospel to which We have already referred, have sought to explain that the law of the Gospel shall at no time be annulled, and that no independent Prophet shall again be made manifest, unless He confirmeth the law of the Gospel. Most of the people have become afflicted with the same spiritual disease 213

it is evident that the reason for such behaviour is none other than the annulment of those rules, customs, habits, and ceremonials to which they have been subjected – re: the wretched behaviour of the people 238

Apocalypse see *John, Beast, Bride, Child, Daniel, Dead, Dragon, Elders, Rod, Servant, Storm, Sword, Witness, Woe, Woman*

Apostle of God [see also *Muḥammad*]

there can be no doubt whatever that had these Apostles appeared, in bygone ages and cycles, in accordance with the vain imaginations which the hearts of men had devised, no one would have repudiated the truth of these sanctified Beings G 82

nay, all the Prophets of God, His well-favoured, His holy, and chosen Messengers, are, without exception, the bearers of His names, and the embodiments of His attributes. They only differ in the intensity of their revelation, and the comparative potency of their light. Even as He hath revealed: 'Some of the Apostles We have caused to excel the others' KI 103–4

'already have Apostles before me come to you with sure testimonies, and with that of which ye speak. Wherefore slew ye them? Tell me, if ye are men of truth' *Sacrifice* 148–9

'some of the Apostles We have caused to excel the others. To some God hath spoken, some He hath raised and exalted. And to Jesus, Son of Mary, We gave manifest signs, and We strengthened Him with the Holy Spirit' 176–7

Apostleship or Servitude *Voice* 180–81

when the Apostle of God (Muḥammad) appeared, He did not announce unto the unbelievers that the Resurrection had come, for they could not bear the news. That Day is indeed an infinitely mighty Day, for in it the Divine Tree proclaimeth from eternity unto eternity, 'Verily, I am God. No God is there but Me'. Yet those who are veiled believe that He is one like unto them, and they refuse even to call Him a believer, although such a title in the realm of his Heavenly Kingdom is conferred everlastingly upon the most insignificant follower of His previous Dispensation. Thus, had the people in the days of the Apostle of God regarded Him at least as a believer of their time how would they have debarred Him, for seven years while He was in the mountain, from access to His Holy House (Ka'bah)? SB 78–9

in the case of the Apostle of God – may the blessings of God rest upon Him – before the revelation of the Qur'án everyone bore witness to His piety and noble virtues. Behold Him then after the revelation of the Qur'án. What outrageous insults were levelled against Him, as indeed the pen is ashamed to recount. Likewise behold the Point of the Bayán. His behaviour prior to the declaration of His mission is clearly evident unto those who knew Him. Now, following His manifestation, although He hath, up to the present, revealed no less than five hundred thousand verses on different subjects, behold what calumnies are uttered, so unseemly that the pen is stricken with shame at the mention of them. But 96–7

Apostle of God

if all men were to observe the ordinances of God no sadness would befall that heavenly Tree

even as the pious deeds of the Christian monks profited them not, inasmuch as at the time of the manifestation of the Apostle of God – may the blessings of God rest upon Him – they contented themselves with the standard set forth in the Gospel 102

and from the inception of the Revelation of the Apostle of God – may the blessings of God be upon Him – till the day of His ascension was the Resurrection of Jesus – peace be upon Him – wherein the Tree of divine Reality appeared in the person of Muḥammad, rewarding by His Word everyone who was a believer in Jesus, and punishing by His Word everyone who was not a believer in Him 107

for instance, if all those who were expecting the fulfilment of the promise of Jesus had been assured of the manifestation of Muḥammad, the Apostle of God, not one would have turned aside from the sayings of Jesus 110

it is recorded in a tradition that of the entire concourse of the Christians no more than seventy people embraced the Faith of the Apostle of God. The blame falleth upon their doctors, for if these had believed, they would have been followed by the mass of their countrymen 123

Apostles of Christ [see also *Disciple*]

if ye entertain any doubts in this matter consider the people unto whom the Gospel was given. Having no access to the apostles of Jesus, they sought the pleasure of the Lord in their churches, hoping to learn that which would be acceptable unto God, but they found therein no path unto Him SB 137

fifteen centuries after Christ, Luther . . . opposed the Pope on certain points of doctrine such as the prohibition of monastic marriage, the revering and bowing down before images of the Apostles and Christian leaders of the past, and various other religious practices and ceremonies which were accretional to the ordinances of the Gospel SDC 41–2

consider how at the beginning of the Christian era the Apostles were afflicted, and what torments they endured in the pathway of Christ. Every day of their lives they were targets for the Pharisees' darts of mockery, vilification and abuse. They bore great hardship; they saw prison; and most of them carried to their lips the sweet cup of martyrdom SAB 238

Christ, in His blessed day, in reality only educated eleven men: the greatest of them was Peter, who, nevertheless, when he was tested, thrice denied Christ SAQ 35

after the death of Christ the disciples were troubled, and their ideas and thoughts were discordant and contradictory; later they became firm and united *Disciple* 106

so the descent of the Holy Spirit upon the Apostles means their attraction by the Christ Spirit, whereby they acquired stability and firmness. Through the spirit of the love of God they gained a new life, and they saw Christ living, helping and protecting them. They were like drops, and they became seas; they were like feeble insects, and they became majestic eagles; they were weak and became powerful. They were like mirrors facing the sun; verily, some of the light became manifest in them 106–7

for example, Peter cannot become Christ. All that he can do is, in the condition of servitude, to attain endless perfections (BWF 329) 231

other sufferings there are, which come upon the Faithful of God. Consider the great sorrows endured by Christ and by His apostles! PT 50 the apostles of Christ who steadfastly bore all their trials and sufferings – did they not prove their faithfulness? Was not their endurance the best proof? *Suffer* 50

Disciple – re: were just as other men are 61

on the other hand, Paul, the Apostle, was in his early life an enemy of Christ, whilst later he became His most faithful servant 147

be not like Thomas; be thou like Peter BWF 384

the Supper of the Lord which His Highness the Spirit ate with the apostles was a heavenly supper and not one of material bread and water, for material objects have no connection with spiritual objects 390

the apostles upon many occasions partook of material food with His Highness Christ, yet the supper of that night became designated as the 'Lord's Supper.' From this designation it is plain and evident that they ate heavenly food at that supper 391

after the crucifixion the apostles had not in the beginning the capacity and ability of witnessing the Messianic reality. For they were agitated. But when they found firmness and steadfastness, their inner sight became opened, and they saw the reality of the Messiah as manifest. For the body of Christ was crucified and vanished, but the Spirit of Christ is always pouring upon the contingent world, and is manifest before the insight of the people of assurance TAB 193–4

Israel – re: calumny, slander, cruelty, oppression 361

this is self-evident that the letter is an organic member of the word. This membership denotes subordination; that is, the letter draws its life from the word and hath spiritual relationship with it and is accounted a part of it. The apostles were the Letters and His Highness Christ the Essence of the Word; and the significance of the Word, which is the Everlasting Outpouring, cast a splendour upon those Letters. Since a Letter is part of the Word itself, it is intrinsically identical with the Word 539

to labour tirelessly and to follow the heroic example of the Apostles of Jesus Christ GPB 328

could Peter, the admitted chief of the Apostles, or the Imám 'Alí, the cousin and legitimate successor of the Prophet, produce in support of the primacy with which both had been invested written and explicit affirmations from Christ and Muḥammad that could have silenced those who either among their contemporaries or in a later age have repudiated their authority and, by their action, precipitated the schisms that persist until the present day? WOB 145

the indwelling Spirit of God which, in the Apostolic Age of the Church, animated its members, the pristine purity of its teachings, the primitive brilliancy of its light, will, no doubt, be reborn and revived as the inevitable consequence of this redefinition of its fundamental verities, and the clarification of its original purpose 185

if the Son of Man was capable of infusing into apparently so crude and helpless an instrument such potency . . . how much more can the Father, Who is Bahá'u'lláh, empower the most puny and insignificant among His followers to achieve, for the execution of His purpose, such wonders as would dwarf the mightiest achievements of even the first apostle of Jesus Christ ADJ 38

as to the position of Christianity, let it be stated without any hesitation or equivocation that . . . the primacy of Peter, the Prince of the Apostles, is upheld and defended *Christianity* PDC 109

the initial clash between the forces of darkness and the army of light, as CF 26

Apostles of Christ

unnoticed as the landing, two millenniums ago, of the apostles of Christ on the southern shores of the European continent, is being registered by the denizens of the Abhá Kingdom

Ark

the statement in 'Seven Days of Creation' certainly cannot be considered authoritative or correct. The Ark and the Flood we believe are symbolical LG 378

Ascendancy

how then could the ascendancy of the sovereignty of these Lamps be explained? *Lamp* KI 127

but the purpose of these verses is not what they have imagined. Nay, the terms 'ascendancy,' 'power,' and 'authority' imply a totally different station and meaning. For instance, consider the pervading power of those drops of the blood of Ḥusayn which besprinkled the earth. What ascendancy and influence hath the dust itself, through the sacredness and potency of that blood, exercised over the bodies and souls of men! So much so, that he who sought deliverance from his ills, was healed by touching the dust of that holy ground, and whosoever, wishing to protect his property, treasured with absolute faith and understanding, a little of that holy earth within his house, safeguarded all his possessions. These are the outward manifestations of its potency. And were We to recount its hidden virtues they would assuredly say: 'He verily hath considered the dust to be the Lord of Lords, and hath utterly forsaken the Faith of God [see also *Ḥusayn*] 127–8

say, God hath, according to that which is revealed in the Book, taken upon Himself the task of ensuring the ascendancy of any one of the followers of the Truth, over and above one hundred other souls, and the supremacy of one hundred believers over one thousand non-believers and the domination of one thousand of the faithful over all the peoples and kindreds of the earth; inasmuch as God calleth into being whatsoever He willeth by virtue of His behest. Verily He is potent over all things SB 153

Ascension

for example, from the inception of the mission of Jesus – may peace be upon Him – till the day of His ascension was the Resurrection of Moses SB 107

after the ascension of Jesus to the Realm of Glory *Jesus Christ* SDC 45

the individual realities of the Divine Manifestations have no separation from the Bounty of God and the Lordly Splendour. In the same way, the orb of the sun has no separation from the light. Therefore, it may be said that the ascension of the Holy Manifestation is simply the leaving of this elemental form. For example, if a lamp illumines this niche, and if its light ceases to illuminate it because the niche is destroyed, the bounty of the lamp is not cut off SAQ 155

Ásíyih

the name Aseyeh is acceptable in the Threshold of Oneness, for the daughter of Pharaoh had this name, who, when (Moses) the Light of Guidance dawned, became confirmed by the Merciful One, left the court of Pharaoh with its grandeur and sovereignty and became perfumed with the fragrances of holiness. Then she assisted in the service of His Holiness (Moses) – upon Him be peace! Also, Aseyeh was the name of my mother TAB 218

those immortal heroines such as Sarah, Ásíyih, the Virgin Mary, Fáṭimih GPB 347 and Ṭáhirih, each of whom has outshone every member of her sex in previous Dispensations – re: Greatest Holy Leaf

Ask

dost thou not realize that by 'asking is not meant asking by tongue or speech, even as the verse itself doth indicate and prove it'? *Qur'án* KI 173

Assemblage

Disciple – re: meeting of disciples at Pentecost SAQ 106

for instance, consider how many thousand assemblages – religious, political and literary – have been organized in India, Persia, Turkestan, Chinese countries and, in a word, in every part of Asia. All these gave no result except that assemblage of the disciples of Christ on the mount fifty days after Christ's ascension. All that hath since been effected along the line of diffusing the holy fragrances of Christ, uplifting the Word of God, spreading the Gospel, training souls and guiding the people, hath been wholly from the result of the effects produced by that assemblage of the disciples. Those effects are continual even in the present time TAB 301

Astray

consider likewise, how numerous at this time are the monks who have secluded themselves in their churches, calling upon the Spirit, but when He appeared through the power of Truth, they failed to draw nigh unto Him and are numbered with those that have gone far astray TB 10

they have gone astray and have caused the people to go astray, yet perceive it not. They worship vain imaginings but know it not. They have taken idle fancies for their lords and have neglected God, yet understand not – re: people of tyranny 107

those who have rejected God and firmly cling to Nature as it is in itself are, verily, bereft of knowledge and wisdom. They are truly of them that are far astray 144

on that Day ye will continue to rove distraught, even as camels, seeking a drop of the water of life. God will cause oceans of living water to stream forth from the presence of Him Whom God shall make manifest, while ye will refuse to quench your thirst therefrom, notwithstanding that ye regard yourselves as the God-fearing witnesses of your Faith. Nay, and yet again, nay! Ye will go astray far beyond the peoples unto whom the Gospel, or the Qur'án or any other Scripture was given SB 141

glorified, immeasurably glorified art Thou, O Lord! Every man of insight is far astray in his attempt to recognize Thee, and every man of consummate learning is sore perplexed in his search after Thee 207–8

O army of God! Today, in this world, every people is wandering astray in its own desert, moving here and there according to the dictates of its fancies and whims, pursuing its own particular caprice SAB 70

Atonement

know thou that when the Son of Man yielded up His breath to God, the whole creation wept with a great weeping. By sacrificing Himself, however, a fresh capacity was infused into all created things. Its evidences, as witnessed in all the peoples of the earth, are now manifest before thee. The deepest wisdom which the sages have uttered, the profoundest learning which any mind hath unfolded, the arts which the ablest hands have produced, the influence exerted by the most potent of rulers, are but manifestations of the quickening power released by His transcendent, His all-pervasive, and resplendent Spirit G 85

Atonement

as to the souls who are born into this world radiant entities and who through excessive difficulty are deprived of great benefits and thus leave the world – they are worthy of all sympathy, for in reality this is worthy of regret. It is for this purpose (that is, it is with regard to this wisdom) that the great Manifestations (of God) unveil themselves in this world, bear every difficulty and ordeal – to make these ready souls dawnings of light and confer upon them eternal life. This is the real atonement that His Holiness Christ made – He sacrificed Himself for the life of the world TAB 543

Abraham – re: intended sacrifice of his son GPB 188

Attain

leaders of religion, in every age, have hindered their people from attaining the shores of eternal salvation KI 15

only those will attain to the knowledge of the Word of God that have turned unto Him, and repudiated the manifestations of Satan 122–3

also He saith: 'They who bear in mind that they shall attain unto the Presence of their Lord, and that unto Him shall they return.' Also in another instance He saith: 'They who held it as certain that they must meet God, said, "How oft, by God's will, hath a small host vanquished a numerous host!"' In yet another instance He revealeth: 'Let him then who hopeth to attain the presence of his Lord work a righteous work.' And also He saith: 'He ordereth all things. He maketh His signs clear, that ye may have firm faith in attaining the presence of your Lord.' 138–9

this people have repudiated all these verses, that unmistakably testify to the reality of 'attainment unto the divine Presence.' No theme hath been more emphatically asserted in the holy scriptures 139

attainment unto the Divine Presence *Resurrection* 139

within every garden they will behold the mystic bride of inner meaning enshrined within the chambers of utterance in the utmost grace and fullest adornment. Most of the verses of the Qur'án indicate, and bear witness to, this spiritual theme. The verse: 'Neither is there aught which doth not celebrate His praise' is eloquent testimony thereto; and 'We noted all things and wrote them down,' a faithful witness thereof. Now, if by 'attainment unto the Presence of God' is meant attainment unto the knowledge of such revelation, it is evident that all men have already attained unto the presence of the unchangeable Countenance of that peerless King. Why, then, restrict such revelation to the Day of Resurrection? 140–41

Essence – re: Day of Resurrection 142–3

attainment unto the Divine Presence *Qur'án* 169

Resurrection – re: presence of His Beauty in the person of His Manifestation 170

Authority

authority lieth in the grasp of God, the Fountainhead of revelation and inspiration and the Lord of the Day of Resurrection TB 58

know assuredly that just as thou firmly believest that the Word of God, exalted be His glory, endureth for ever, thou must, likewise, believe with undoubting faith that its meaning can never be exhausted. They who are its appointed interpreters, they whose hearts are the repositories of its secrets, are, however, the only ones who can comprehend its manifold wisdom. Whoso, while reading the Sacred Scriptures, is tempted to choose therefrom whatever may suit him with which to challenge the authority of the Representative of God among men, is, indeed, as one G 175 dead, though to outward seeming he may walk and converse with his neighbours, and share with them their food and their drink

verily, Christ is Our Word which We communicated unto Mary; and let no one say what the Christians term as 'the third of three', inasmuch as it would amount to slandering the Remembrance Who, as decreed in the Mother Book, is invested with supreme authority. Indeed God is but one God, and far be it from His glory that there should be aught else besides Him — SB 60–61

'Aválim

in the "Aválim,' an authoritative and well-known book, it is recorded: 'A Youth from Baní-Háshim shall be made manifest, Who will reveal a new Book and promulgate a new law;' then follow these words: 'Most of His enemies will be the divines' — KI 241

Báb

Gate — SB 50

for indeed the mandate of the Báb hath befittingly been proclaimed unto you in the Qur'án aforetime *Qur'án* — 67

O concourse of the believers! Do ye harbour any doubt as to that whereunto the Remembrance of God doth summon you? By the righteousness of the One true God, He is none other than the sovereign Truth Who hath been made manifest through the power of Truth. Are ye in doubt concerning the Báb? Verily He is the One Who holdeth, by Our leave, the kingdoms of earth and heaven in His grasp, and the Lord is in truth fully aware of what ye are doing — 72–3

God, of a truth, revealed unto Me in the sacred house of the Ka'bah, 'Verily, I am God, no God is there but Me. I have singled Thee out for Myself and have chosen Thee as the Remembrance. Indeed, whosoever beareth allegiance unto Thee by walking in the way of the Báb, for him the recompense of the next world hath surely been prescribed . . .' It is ordained in the Book that upon the realization of the Cause of the Remembrance, the Most Great Event will have come to pass according to the dispensation of Providence, and God, truly, is potent over all things — 73

say: The people have grievously differed over Me, whereas in truth there is no difference between Me and the Báb – re: Great Announcement *Announcement* — 74

He is none other but the Apostle of God Himself *Mecca* — 105

Promised One – re: dissertation on — 119

the child Who is referred to is the Báb, the Primal Point *Child* — SAQ 68–9

Babel

consider the differences that have arisen since the days of Adam. The divers and widely-known languages now spoken by the peoples of the earth were originally unknown, as were the varied rules and customs now prevailing amongst them. The people of those times spoke a language different from those now known. Diversities of language arose in a later age, in a land known as Babel. It was given the name Babel, because the term signifieth 'the place where the confusion of tongues arose' — G 172

Baghdád

Abode – re: mentioned in Qur'án — GPB 109–10

Bahá'u'lláh

'they shall not hurt nor destroy in all My holy mountain: for the earth shall be full of the knowledge of the Lord, as the waters cover the sea' . . . but these verses apply word for word to Bahá'u'lláh. Likewise in this marvellous cycle the earth will be transformed, and the world of humanity arrayed in tranquillity and beauty. Disputes, quarrels and murders will be replaced by peace, truth and concord; among the nations, peoples, races and countries, love and amity will appear SAQ 63

this is He whom God promised in all His Books and Scriptures, such as the Bible, the Gospels and the Qur'án *Promise* TAB 613–14

He was formally designated Bahá'u'lláh, an appellation specifically recorded in the Persian Bayán, signifying at once the glory, the light and the splendour of God, and was styled the 'Lord of Lords,' the 'Most Great Name,' the 'Ancient Beauty' *Names* GPB 94

to Him Isaiah, the greatest of the Jewish prophets, had alluded as the 'Glory of the Lord,' the 'Everlasting Father,' the 'Prince of Peace,' the 'Wonderful,' the 'Counsellor,' . . . Of Him David had sung in his Psalms, acclaiming Him as the 'Lord of Hosts' and the 'King of Glory.' To Him Haggai had referred as the 'Desire of all nations,' and Zachariah as the 'Branch' Who 'shall grow up out of His place,' and 'shall build the Temple of the Lord.' Ezekiel had extolled Him as the 'Lord' Who 'shall be king over all the earth,' while to His day Joel and Zephania had both referred as the 'day of Jehovah,' . . . 94–5

He alone is meant by the prophecy attributed to Gautama Buddha Himself, that 'a Buddha named Maitreye, the Buddha of universal fellowship' should, in the fullness of time, arise and reveal 'His boundless glory.' To Him the Bhagavad-Gita of the Hindus had referred as the 'Most Great Spirit,' the 'Tenth Avatar,' the 'Immaculate Manifestation of Krishna'

as to the third Dispensation – the Revelation proclaimed by Bahá'u'lláh – inasmuch as the Sun of Truth when attaining that station shineth in the plenitude of its meridian splendour its duration hath been fixed for the period of one whole month, which is the maximum time taken by the sun to pass through the sign of the Zodiac. From this thou canst imagine the magnitude of the Bahá'í cycle – a cycle that must extend over a period of at least five hundred thousand years [words of 'Abdu'l-Bahá] – re: Zoroastrian prophecy WOB 102

'In this most mighty Revelation,' He [Bahá'u'lláh] unequivocally announces, 'all the Dispensations of the past have attained their highest, their final consummation' 103

'Be fair, ye peoples of the world,' He thus appeals to mankind, 'is it meet and seemly for you to question the authority of one Whose presence "He Who conversed with God" (Moses) hath longed to attain, the beauty of Whose countenance "God's Well-beloved" (Muḥammad) had yearned to behold, through the potency of Whose love the "Spirit of God" (Jesus) ascended to heaven, for Whose sake the "Primal Point" (the Báb) offered up His life?' 106–7

Balál

consider how Balál, the Ethiopian, unlettered though he was, ascended into the heaven of faith and certitude, whilst 'Abdu'lláh Ubayy, a leader among the learned, maliciously strove to oppose Him. Behold, how a mere shepherd was so carried away by the ecstasy of the words of God that he was able to gain admittance into the habitation of his Best-Beloved, and was united to Him Who is the Lord of Mankind, G 83–4 whilst they who prided themselves on their knowledge and wisdom strayed far from His path and remained deprived of His grace. For this reason He hath written: 'He that is exalted among you shall be abased, and he that is abased shall be exalted'

Balance

He is the Lord of the Day of Resurrection, of Regeneration and of Reckoning, and His revealed Word is the Balance *Lord* SB 157

Banquet-Hall of God

moreover, in a remarkable tradition, which is contained in Shaykh Ibnu'l-'Arabí's work, entitled 'Futúḥát-i-Makkíyyih,' and which is recognized as an authentic utterance of Muḥammad, and is quoted by Mírzá Abu'l-Faḍl in his 'Fará'id,' this significant prediction has been made: 'All of them (the companions of the Qá'im) shall be slain except One Who shall reach the plain of 'Akká, the Banquet-Hall of God' GPB 184

Baptism

John, son of Zacharias, said what My Forerunner hath said: 'Saying, repent ye, for the Kingdom of heaven is at hand. I indeed baptize you with water unto repentance, but He that cometh after Me is mightier than I, Whose shoes I am not worthy to bear' ESW 158

the principle of baptism is purification by repentance. John admonished and exhorted the people, and caused them to repent; then he baptized them. Therefore, it is apparent that this baptism is a symbol of repentance from all sin: its meaning is expressed in these words: 'O God! as my body has become purified and cleansed from physical impurities, in the same way purify and sanctify my spirit from the impurities of the world of nature, which are not worthy of the Threshold of Thy Unity!' Repentance is the return from disobedience to obedience. Man, after remoteness and deprivation from God, repents and undergoes purification: and this is a symbol signifying 'O God! make my heart good and pure, freed and sanctified from all save Thy love' SAQ 91

as Christ desired that this institution of John should be used at that time by all, He Himself conformed to it in order to awaken the people and to complete the law of the former religion. Although the ablution of repentance was the institution of John, it was in reality formerly practiced in the religion of God 91–2

Christ was not in need of baptism; but as at that time it was an acceptable and praiseworthy action, and a sign of the glad tidings of the Kingdom, therefore, He confirmed it. However, afterward He said the true baptism is not with material water, but it must be with spirit and with water. In this case water does not signify material water, for elsewhere it is explicitly said baptism is with spirit and with fire, from which it is clear that the reference is not to material fire and material water, for baptism with fire is impossible 92

therefore, the spirit is the bounty of God, the water is knowledge and life, and the fire is the love of God. For material water does not purify the heart of man; no, it cleanses his body. But the heavenly water and spirit, which are knowledge and life, make the human heart good and pure; the heart which receives a portion of the bounty of the Spirit becomes sanctified, good and pure – that is to say, the reality of man becomes purified and sanctified from the impurities of the world of nature. These natural impurities are evil qualities: anger, lust, worldliness, pride, lying, hypocrisy, fraud, self-love, etc. 92

no, this baptism with water was a symbol of repentance, and of seeking forgiveness of sins *Symbol* 92 other peoples are amazed and wonder why the infant is plunged into the water, since this is neither the cause of the spiritual awakening of the child, nor of its faith or conversion, but it is only a custom which is followed. In the time of John the Baptist it was not so; no, at first John used to exhort the people, and to guide them to repentance from sin, and to fill them with the desire to await the manifestation of Christ. Whoever received the ablution of baptism, and repented of sins in absolute humility and meekness, would also purify and cleanse his body from outward impurities. With perfect yearning, night and day, he would constantly wait for the manifestation of Christ, and the entrance to the Kingdom of the Spirit of God 95

in the Gospel according to St. John, Christ has said: 'Except a man be born of water and the Spirit, he cannot enter into the Kingdom of Heaven.' The priests have interpreted this into meaning that baptism is necessary for salvation. In another Gospel it is said: 'He shall baptize you with the Holy Ghost and with fire' [John 3:5; Matt. 3:11] PT 81

thus the water of baptism and the fire are one! It cannot mean that the 'water' spoken of is *physical* water, for it is the direct opposite of 'fire', and one destroys the other. When in the Gospels, Christ speaks of 'water', He means *that which causes life*, for without water no worldly creature can live – mineral, vegetable, animal and man, one and all, depend upon water for their very being 82

water is the cause of life, and when Christ speaks of water, He is symbolizing that which is the cause of *Everlasting Life*. 82

This life-giving water of which He speaks is like unto fire, for it is none other than the Love of God, and this love means life to our souls

those alone who are baptized by the Divine Spirit will be enabled to bring all peoples into the bond of unity. It is by the power of the Spirit that the Eastern World of spiritual thought can intermingle with the Western realm of action, so that the world of matter may become Divine 85

the performance of baptismal celebration would cleanse the body, but the spirit hath no share; but the divine teachings and the exhortations of the Beauty of Abhá will baptize the soul. This is the real baptism BWF 390

so, in the Qur'án it is said, 'and we have caused a pure water to descend from heaven;' and in the Gospel, 'Except a man hath received the baptism of water and of spirit, he cannot enter the Kingdom of God.' Then it is evident that the divine teachings are the heavenly grace and the showers of the mercy of God, which purify the hearts of men TAB 581

the people have not understood the meaning of baptism. In one place in the Gospels it is commanded that one must be baptized by water and spirit, and also by fire, and from these commands we can understand that the meaning is spiritual and not material. The baptism of Christians as practiced today is not the teachings of Christ! The Christians in the beginning used to baptize as a symbol of the purification of the spirit. SW IX 9, p103

When the time drew near for the Manifestation of Christ, John the Baptist appeared and called the people to repentance, and when they repented they were baptized as a symbol that their hearts were purified and ready to accept the truth and teachings which would soon appear, for John was declaring the coming of Jesus. But these people were not children; they were men and women. And Jesus himself was baptized by John, but he was thirty years old when he was baptized. After he was baptized he said: 'John has baptized you with water, but I shall baptize you with the Spirit!' Water symbolizes the knowledge of God which gives eternal life, because all forms of life had their beginning in the water.

Fire is the symbol of love, and the baptism by fire means the love of God which descends in the hearts that are turned unto him! Now as fire is used to symbolize love, be sure that water is used also as a symbol, for would it be possible for one to be put into the fire as one is put into the water for baptism? Many who have not understood what Christ meant by baptism think that if a child dies without passing through this ceremony its soul is lost! But this is not true, for the child has not sinned and goes from this world quite free from faults and defects! And ofttimes baptism of infants is attended by great danger to the child [words of 'Abdu'l-Bahá]

Barter

even as the people of Israel, in the time of Moses, bartered away the bread of heaven for the sordid things of the earth, these people, likewise, sought to exchange the divinely-revealed verses for their foul, their vile, and idle desires KI 208

Bayán

Abí-'Abdi'lláh ESW 112–13

Jábir hath said that Abú-Ja'far – peace be upon him – spoke to him as follows: 'O Jábir! Give heed unto the Bayán (Exposition) and the Ma'ání (Significances).' He – peace be upon him – added: 'As to the Bayán, it consisteth in thy recognition of God – glorified be He – as the One Who hath no equal, and in thy adoration of Him, and in thy refusal to join partners with Him [see also *Ma'ání*] 113

Proof – re: proofs from the Qur'án SB 35

likewise in this Dispensation of the Point of the Bayán, if the people had not refused to concede the name believer unto Him, how could they have incarcerated Him on this mountain, without realizing that the quintessence of belief oweth its existence to a word from Him? Their hearts are deprived of the power of true insight, and thus they cannot see, while those endowed with the eyes of the spirit circle like moths round the Light of Truth until they are consumed. It is for this reason that the Day of Resurrection is said to be the greatest of all days, yet it is like unto any other day [see also *Apostle of God*] 79

know thou of a certainty that whenever thou makest mention of Him Whom God shall make manifest, only then art thou making mention of God. In like manner shouldst thou hearken unto the verses of the Bayán and acknowledge its truth, only then would the revealed verses of God profit thee. Otherwise what benefit canst thou derive therefrom? 80–81

likewise behold the Point of the Bayán. His behaviour prior to the declaration of His mission is clearly evident unto those who knew Him *Apostle of God* 96

the Bayán shall constitute God's unerring balance till the Day of Resurrection which is the Day of Him Whom God will make manifest. Whoso acteth in conformity with that which is revealed therein will abide in Paradise, under the shadow of His affirmation and reckoned among the most sublime Letters in the presence of God; while whoso deviateth, were it even so much as the tip of a grain of barley, will be consigned to the fire and will be assembled neath the shadow of negation. This truth hath likewise been laid bare in the Qur'án where in numerous instances God hath set down that whoever should pass judgement contrary to the bounds fixed by Him, would be deemed an infidel 102

and from the moment when the Tree of the Bayán appeared until it disappeareth is the Resurrection of the Apostle of God, as is divinely foretold in the Qur'án *Qur'án* 107

Bayán

He Who hath revealed the Qur'án unto Muḥammad, the Apostle of God, ordaining in the Faith of Islám that which was pleasing unto Him, hath likewise revealed the Bayán, in the manner ye have been promised, unto Him Who is your Qá'im, your Guide, your Mihdí, your Lord, Him Whom ye acclaim as the manifestation of God's most excellent titles. Verily the equivalent of that which God revealed unto Muḥammad during twenty-three years, hath been revealed unto Me within the space of two days and two nights. However, as ordained by God, no distinction is to be drawn between the two. He, in truth, hath power over all things 139

Truth – re: according to that which hath been revealed in the Bayán 143

the Bayán is in truth Our conclusive proof for all created things, and all the peoples of the world are powerless before the revelation of its verses. It enshrineth the sum total of all the Scriptures, whether of the past or of the future, even as Thou art the Repository of all Our proofs in this Day. We cause whomsoever We desire to be admitted into the garden of our most holy, most sublime Paradise. Thus is divine revelation inaugurated in each Dispensation at Our behest. We are truly the supreme Ruler. Indeed no religion shall We ever inaugurate unless it be renewed in the days to come. This is a promise We solemnly have made. Verily We are supreme over all things 159

this Book at once abrogated the laws and ceremonials enjoined by the Qur'án regarding prayer, fasting, marriage, divorce and inheritance, and upheld, in its integrity, the belief in the prophetic mission of Muḥammad, even as the Prophet of Islám before Him had annulled the ordinances of the Gospel and yet recognized the Divine origin of the Faith of Jesus Christ. It moreover interpreted in a masterly fashion the meaning of certain terms frequently occurring in the sacred Books of previous Dispensations such as Paradise, Hell, Death, Resurrection, the Return, the Balance, the Hour, the Last Judgment, and the like GPB 25

Beast

'the beast that ascendeth out of the bottomless pit shall war against them, and shall overcome them, and kill them': this beast means the Umayyads who attacked them from the pit of error, and who rose against the religion of Muḥammad and against the reality of 'Alí – in other words, the love of God. SAQ 51

It is said, 'The beast made war against these two witnesses' – that is to say, a spiritual war, meaning that the beast would act in entire opposition to the teachings, customs and institutions of these two witnesses, to such an extent that the virtues and perfections which were diffused by the power of these two witnesses among the peoples and tribes would be entirely dispelled, and the animal nature and carnal desires would conquer. Therefore, this beast making war against them would gain the victory – meaning that the darkness of error coming from this beast was to have ascendancy over the horizons of the world, and kill those two witnesses – in other words, that it would destroy the spiritual life which they spread abroad in the midst of the nation, and entirely remove the divine laws and teachings, treading under foot the Religion of God. Nothing would thereafter remain but a lifeless body without spirit

Beginning

concerning the prejudice of race: it is an illusion, a superstition pure and simple! For God created us all of one race. There were no differences in the beginning, for we are all descendants of Adam. In the beginning, also, there were no limits and boundaries between the different lands; no part of the earth belonged more to one people than to another. In the PT 148 sight of God there is no difference between the various races. Why should man invent such a prejudice? How can we uphold war caused by an illusion?

Belief

it instructed the companions of Muḥammad to declare the following unto the infidels and idolators: 'Ye oppress and persecute us, and yet, what else have we done except that we have believed in God and in the verses sent down unto us through the tongue of Muḥammad, and in those which descended upon the Prophets of old?' – see also Qur'án 5:64 *Companions* KI 218

for example, from the inception of the mission of Jesus – may peace be upon Him – till the day of His ascension was the resurrection of Moses. For during that period the Revelation of God shone forth through the appearance of that divine Reality, Who rewarded by His Word everyone who believed in Moses, and punished by His Word everyone who did not believe; inasmuch as God's Testimony for that Day was that which He had solemnly affirmed in the Gospel SB 107

Beloved

if, on the day of His Revelation, all that are on earth bear Him allegiance, Mine inmost being will rejoice, inasmuch as all will have attained the summit of their existence, and will have been brought face to face with their Beloved, and will have recognized, to the fullest extent attainable in the world of being, the splendour of Him Who is the Desire of their hearts SB 156

End – re: Best Beloved 159

magnified be Thy Name, Thou art the Best Beloved Who hast enabled me to know Thee and Thou art that All-Renowned One Who hast graciously favoured me with Thy love. Thou art the Ancient of Days Whom none can ever describe through the evidences of Thy glory and majesty 212

Bible

all the people of Israel arose in protest against Him. They clamoured that He Whose advent the Bible had foretold must needs promulgate and fulfil the laws of Moses, whereas this youthful Nazarene, who laid claim to the station of the divine Messiah, had annulled the law of divorce and of the sabbath day – the most weighty of all the laws of Moses. Moreover, what of the signs of the Manifestation yet to come? These people of Israel are even unto the present day still expecting that Manifestation which the Bible hath foretold! KI 18

Israel refused to apprehend the meaning of such words as have been revealed in the Bible concerning the signs of the coming Revelation. As she never grasped their true significance, and, to outward seeming, such events never came to pass, she, therefore, remained deprived of recognizing the beauty of Jesus and of beholding the face of God. And they still await His coming! 18–19

verily by 'perverting' the text is not meant that which these foolish and abject souls have fancied, even as some maintain that Jewish and Christian divines have effaced from the Book such verses as extol and magnify the countenance of Muḥammad, and instead thereof have inserted the contrary. How utterly vain and false are these words! Can a man who believeth in a book, and deemeth it to be inspired by God, mutilate it? . . . And as the Jews, in the time of Muḥammad, interpreted those verses of the Pentateuch, that referred to His Manifestation, after 86–7 their own fancy, and refused to be satisfied with His holy utterance, the charge of 'perverting' the text was therefore pronounced against them

thou hast written that thou lovest the Bible. Undoubtedly, the friends and the maid-servants of the Merciful should know the value of the Bible, for they are the ones who have discovered its real significances and have become cognizant of the hidden mystery of the Holy Book — TAB 218

as to thy question concerning the additions to the Old and New Testament: Know thou, verily, as people could not understand the words, nor could they apprehend the realities therein, therefore they have translated them according to their own understanding and interpreted the verses after their own ideas and thus the text fell into confusion. This is undoubtedly true. As to an intentional addition: This is something uncertain. But they have made great mistakes as to the understanding of the texts and the comprehending of the references and have therefore fallen into doubts, especially in regard to the symbolical verses — 609

Biḥár

mention of the sorrows, the imprisonment and afflictions inflicted upon that Essence of divine virtue hath been made in the former traditions. In the 'Biḥár' it is recorded: 'In our Qá'im there shall be four signs from four Prophets, Moses, Jesus, Joseph, and Muḥammad. The sign from Moses, is fear and expectation; from Jesus, that which was spoken of Him; from Joseph, imprisonment and dissimulation; from Muḥammad, the revelation of a Book similar to the Qur'án.' Notwithstanding such a conclusive tradition, which in such unmistakable language hath foreshadowed the happenings of the present day, none hath been found to heed its prophecy, and methinks none will do so in the future, except him whom thy Lord willeth. 'God indeed shall make whom He will to hearken, but We shall not make those who are in their graves to hearken' — KI 254

Birth of Jesus [see also *Jesse* n.]

in the light of what Bahá'u'lláh and 'Abdu'l-Bahá have stated concerning this subject it is evident that Jesus came into the world through the direct intervention of the Holy Spirit and that consequently His birth was quite miraculous. This is an established fact, and the friends need not feel at all surprised, as the belief in the possibility of miracles has never been rejected in the Teachings. Their importance, however, has been minimized — LG 366

regarding the point you have raised concerning the Virgin Birth of Jesus; it would be sacrilege for a Bahá'í to believe that the parents of Jesus were illegally married and that the latter was subsequently the fruit of an illegal union. Such a possibility cannot even be conceived by a believer who recognizes the high station of Jesus Christ. It is this same false accusation which the people of His Day attributed to Mary that Bahá'u'lláh indirectly repudiated in the Íqán — 367

Blind

wherever in the Holy Books they speak of raising the dead, the meaning is that the dead were blessed by eternal life; where it is said that the blind received sight, the signification is that he obtained the true perception; where it is said a deaf man received hearing, the meaning is that he acquired spiritual and heavenly hearing. This is ascertained from the text of the Gospel where Christ said: 'These are like those of whom Isaiah said, They have eyes and see not, they have ears and hear not; and I healed them.' — SAQ 101–2

Blood

Ascendancy – re: blood of Ḥusayn KI 127–8

if they wished, they could turn the water of the Nile into blood, so far as the Egyptians and those who denied them were concerned – re: Muḥammad and 'Alí *Witness* SAQ 50

Body

'and their dead bodies shall lie in the street of the great city, which spiritually is called Sodom and Egypt, where also our Lord was crucified' *Dead* SAQ 51–2

Qur'án – re: twelve hundred and sixty years 52

the body of the Law of God, like a corpse, has been exposed to public view for twelve hundred and sixty days, each day being counted as a year, and this period is the cycle of Muḥammad *Law* 53

Book

His own Book – the Book unto which all the Books of former Dispensations must needs be referred, the Book that standeth amongst them all transcendent and supreme *Word* G 269

in all sacred books mention hath been made of the divines of every age. Thus He saith: 'O people of the Book! Why disbelieve the signs of God to which ye yourselves have been witnesses?' And also He saith: 'O people of the Book! Why clothe ye the truth with falsehood? Why wittingly hide the truth?' Again, He saith: 'Say, O people of the Book, Why repel believers from the way of God?' It is evident that by 'people of the Book,' who have repelled their fellow-men from the straight path of God, is meant none other than the divines of that age, whose names and character have been revealed in the sacred books, and alluded to in the verses and traditions recorded therein, were you to observe with the eye of God KI 16

every discerning believer will recognize that in the Dispensation of the Qur'án both the Book and the Cause of Jesus were confirmed 20

again in another instance, He saith: 'Woe unto those who, with their own hands, transcribe the Book corruptly, and then say: "This is from God," that they may sell it for some mean price.' This verse was revealed with reference to the divines and leaders of the Jewish Faith. These divines, in order to please the rich, acquire worldly emoluments, and give vent to their envy and misbelief, wrote a number of treatises, refuting the claims of Muḥammad, supporting their arguments with such evidences as it would be improper to mention, and claimed that these arguments were derived from the text of the Pentateuch. 87–8

The same may be witnessed today. Consider how abundant are the denunciations written by the foolish divines of this age against this most wondrous Cause! How vain their imaginings that these calumnies are in conformity with the verses of God's sacred Book, and in consonance with the utterances of men of discernment!

Gospel – re: His most great testimony amongst His creatures 89

and if thou dwellest in the land of testimony, content thyself with that which He, Himself, hath revealed: 'Is it not enough for them that We have sent down unto Thee the Book?' This is the testimony which He, Himself, hath ordained; greater proof than this there is none, nor ever will be: 'This proof is His Word; His own Self, the testimony of His truth' 91–2

were these people, wholly for the sake of God and with no desire but His good-pleasure, to ponder the verses of the Book in their heart, they 174 would of a certainty find whatsoever they seek. In its verses would they find revealed and manifest all the things, be they great or small, that have come to pass in this Dispensation. They would even recognize in them references unto the departure of the Manifestations of the names and attributes of God from out their native land; to the opposition and disdainful arrogance of government and people; and to the dwelling and establishment of the Universal Manifestation in an appointed and specially designated land. No man, however, can comprehend this except he who is possessed of an understanding heart

all the things that people required in connection with the Revelation of Muḥammad and His laws were to be found revealed and manifest in that Riḍván of resplendent glory. That Book constitutes an abiding testimony to its people after Muḥammad, inasmuch as its decrees are indisputable, and its promise unfailing. All have been enjoined to follow the precepts of that Book until 'the year sixty' – the year of the advent of God's wondrous Manifestation. That Book is the Book which unfailingly leadeth the seeker unto the Riḍván of the divine Presence, and causeth him that hath forsaken his country and is treading the seeker's path to enter the Tabernacle of everlasting reunion – re: Qur'án 200–201

Muḥammad, Himself, as the end of His mission drew nigh, spoke these words: 'Verily, I leave amongst you My twin weighty testimonies: The Book of God and My Family.' Although many traditions have been revealed by that Source of Prophethood and Mine of divine Guidance, yet He mentioned only that Book, thereby appointing it as the mightiest instrument and surest testimony for the seekers; a guide for the people until the Day of Resurrection 201–2

with unswerving vision, with pure heart, and sanctified spirit, consider attentively what God hath established as the testimony of guidance for His people in His Book, which is recognized as authentic by both the high and lowly. To this testimony we both, as well as all the peoples of the world, must cling, that through its light we may know and distinguish between truth and falsehood, guidance and error. Inasmuch as Muḥammad hath confined His testimonies to His Book and to His Family, and whereas the latter hath passed away, there remaineth His Book only as His one testimony amongst the people 202

in the beginning of His Book He saith: 'Alif, Lám. Mim. No doubt is there about this Book: It is a guidance unto the God-fearing' [discourse] 202

Qur'án 202–3

'say, O people of the Book! do ye not disavow us' *Islám* 217

and likewise, He saith: 'And had We sent down unto Thee a Book written on parchment, and they had touched it with their hands, the infidels would surely have said "This is naught but palpable sorcery."' Most of the verses of the Qur'án are indicative of this theme 219

His Book, the Qur'án, which is free from error *Qur'án* SB 46

whenever the faithful hear the verses of this Book being recited *Faith* 62–3

this Book which We have sent down is indeed abounding in blessings and beareth witness to the Truth, so that the people may realize that the conclusive Proof of God in favour of His Remembrance is similar to the one wherewith Muḥammad, the Seal of the Prophets, was invested, and verily great is the Cause as ordained in the Mother Book – re: Bayán 70–71

ponder a while and observe that everything in Islám hath its ultimate and eventual beginning in the Book of God. Consider likewise the Day of the Revelation of Him Whom God shall make manifest, He in Whose grasp 104 lieth the source of proofs, and let not erroneous considerations shut thee out from Him, for He is immeasurably exalted above them, inasmuch as every proof proceedeth from the Book of God which is itself the supreme testimony as all men are powerless to produce its like

this is the divinely-inscribed Book. This is the outspread Tablet *Face* 154

people of the Book *Christianity* SDC 26

People – re: compulsion in religion 43

shouldst thou come with the whole of thy being to God and be attracted to the lights of the Kingdom of God and be enkindled by the fire of the love of God, then wilt thou see that which thou canst not see today, wilt comprehend the inner significance of the Word of God and thoroughly understand the mysteries contained in the holy Books. BWF 391

But as to the Jewish doctors, Christian priests and monks who read those Books, verily, they know the letter only and they utter the words, as parrots, without understanding their inner meanings. They comprehend them not, because they are engrossed in worldly desires and lusts and their hearts are attached to mundane allurements. Verily, are they not heedless of God and understand nothing and find not the right path?

Elders – re: mentioned in the Revelation of St. John GPB 7–8

the 'Book' had been 'set,' and the 'Bridge' had been 'laid out,' and the 'Balance' had been 'set up,' and the 'mountains scattered in dust' – re: Báb – prophetic fulfillment 58

the Day 'when the earth shall shine with the light of her Lord, and the Book shall be set, and the Prophets shall be brought up, and the witnesses; and judgment shall be given between them with equity; and none shall be wronged – re: Bahá'u'lláh 96

revealed on the eve of the declaration of His Mission, it proffered to mankind the 'Choice Sealed Wine,' whose seal is of 'musk,' and broke the 'seals' of the 'Book' referred to by Daniel, and disclosed the meaning of the 'words' destined to remain 'closed up' till the 'time of the end' – re: Kitáb-i-Íqán 139

nor can we fail to note the progressive deterioration in the authority, wielded by the ecclesiastical leaders of the Jewish and Zoroastrian Faiths, ever since the voice of Bahá'u'lláh was raised, announcing, in no uncertain terms, that the 'Most Great Law is come,' that the Ancient Beauty 'ruleth upon the throne of David,' and that 'whatsoever hath been announced in the Books (Zoroastrian Holy Writ) hath been revealed and made clear' 230

Branch [see also *Jesse*]

this Divine Banner, which is no other than the Lordly Branch itself *Standard* SAQ 65

Bread

We ask for neither meed nor reward. 'We nourish your souls for the sake of God; we seek from you neither recompense nor thanks.' This is the food that conferreth everlasting life upon the pure in heart and the illumined in spirit. This is the bread of which it is said: 'Lord, send down upon us Thy bread from heaven.' This bread shall never be withheld from them that deserve it, nor can it ever be exhausted. It groweth everlastingly from the tree of grace; it descendeth at all seasons from the heavens of justice and mercy KI 22–3

then strive thou with all thy might to guide the people, and eat thou of the SAB 57 bread that hath come down from heaven. For this is the meaning of Christ's words: 'I am the living bread which came down from heaven . . . he that eateth of this bread shall live forever'

the disciples had taken many meals from the hand of Christ; why was the last supper distinguished from the others? It is evident that the heavenly bread did not signify this material bread, but rather the divine nourishment of the spiritual body of Christ, the divine graces and heavenly perfections of which His disciples partook, and with which they became filled. . . SAQ 99

Then it is clear that the bread and wine were symbols which signified: I have given you My bounties and perfections, and when you have received this bounty, you have gained eternal life and have partaken of your share and your portion of the heavenly nourishment

'I am the bread which descended from heaven' *Jesus Christ* 121

the Spirit breathing through the Holy Scriptures is food for all who hunger. God Who has given the revelation to His Prophets will surely give of His abundance daily bread to all those who ask Him faithfully PT 57

the Supper of the Lord which His Highness the Spirit ate with the apostles was a heavenly supper and not one of material bread and water, for material objects have no connection with spiritual objects BWF 390

the apostles upon many occasions partook of material food with His Highness Christ, yet the supper of that night became designated as the 'Lord's supper.' From this designation it is plain and evident that they ate heavenly food at that supper 391

thank God that thou wert fed from the table which hath descended from heaven. That food is the 'I am the bread which descended from heaven,' recorded in the Gospel. That is faith, certainty, love and knowledge TAB 677

Bride

what is most frequently meant by the Holy City, the Jerusalem of God, which is mentioned in the Holy Book, is the Law of God. It is compared sometimes to a bride, and sometimes to Jerusalem, and again to the new heaven and earth. So in chapter 21, verses 1, 2 and 3 of the Revelation of St. John, it is said SAQ 67

the Law of God is also compared to an adorned bride who appears with most beautiful ornaments, as it has been said in chapter 21 of the Revelation of St. John 68

as the 'Bride,' the 'New Jerusalem coming down from God' *Kitáb-i-Aqdas* GPB 213

Bridge

for on the Day of Resurrection ye shall, upon the Bridge, be, in very truth, held answerable for the position ye occupied *Divines* SB 44

take ye good heed that ye may all, under the leadership of Him Who is the Source of Divine Guidance, be enabled to direct your steps aright upon the Bridge, which is sharper than the sword and finer than a hair 96

Brother

consider this text of the New Testament: the brothers of His Holiness Christ, came to Him and they said: 'These are your brothers.' He answered that His brothers were those who believed in God, and refused to associate with His own brothers BWF 437

to whom else could these significant words of Muḥammad, the Apostle of God, quoted by Quddús while addressing his companions in the Fort of Shaykh Ṭabarsí, apply if not to those heroes of God who, with their GPB 80 life-blood, ushered in the Promised Day? 'O how I long to behold the countenance of My brethren, my brethren who will appear at the end of the world! Blessed are We, blessed are they; greater is their blessedness than ours'

Muḥammad n. – re: explanation of Deut. 18:18 by Shoghi Effendi

Buddha

Buddha also established a new religion, and Confucius renewed morals and ancient virtues, but their institutions have been entirely destroyed. The beliefs and rites of the Buddhists and Confucianists have not continued in accordance with their fundamental teachings. The founder of Buddhism was a wonderful soul. He established the Oneness of God, but later the original principles of His doctrines gradually disappeared, and ignorant customs and ceremonials arose and increased until they finally ended in the worship of statues and images SAQ 165

the meaning is that the Buddhists and Confucianists now worship images and statues. They are entirely heedless of the Oneness of God and believe in imaginary gods like the ancient Greeks. But in the beginning it was not so; there were different principles and other ordinances 166

thou hast written regarding Buddha and Confucius. Buddha was an illustrious personage. Confucius became the cause of civilization, advancement and prosperity for the people of China TAB 469

there are prophecies concerning this Manifestation in the Buddhistic books, but they are in symbols and metaphors, and some spiritual conditions are mentioned therein, but the leaders of religion do not understand. They think these prophecies are material things; yet those signs are foreshadowing spiritual occurrences 565

to the Zoroastrians the promised Sháh-Bahrám; to the Hindus the reincarnation of Krishna; to the Buddhists the fifth Buddha – re: Bahá'u'lláh GPB 94

the Buddha was a Manifestation of God, like Christ, but his followers do not possess His authentic writings LG 369

Bugle

Ṭáhirih GPB 32–3

on that memorable day the 'Bugle' mentioned in the Qur'án was sounded, the 'stunning trumpet-blast' was loudly raised, and the 'Catastrophe' came to pass. The days immediately following so startling a departure from the time-honoured traditions of Islám witnessed a veritable revolution in the outlooks, habits, ceremonials and manners of worship of these hitherto zealous and devout upholders of the Muḥammadan Law – re: Conference at Badasht 33

Burning Bush

and every attentive ear can recognize the Voice that was heard from the Burning Bush *Revelation* G 270

He Who hath been raised up from the midst of the Burning Bush *Truth* SB 41

the Path of Truth amidst the Burning Bush *Call* 69

indeed We conversed with Moses by the leave of God from the midst of the Burning Bush in the Sinai and revealed an infinitesimal glimmer of Thy Light upon the Mystic Mount and its dwellers, whereupon the Mount shook to its foundations and was crushed into dust 72

I am the Mystic Fane which the Hand of Omnipotence hath reared. I am the Lamp which the Finger of God hath lit within its niche and caused to 74 shine with deathless splendour. I am the Flame of that supernal Light that glowed upon Sinai in the gladsome Spot, and lay concealed in the midst of the Burning Bush

Most Great Spirit – re: symbolism of Burning Bush GPB 101

'whilst from the Burning Bush breaketh forth the cry: "Lo, the Desire of the world is made manifest in His transcendent glory!" The Father hath come. That which ye were promised in the Kingdom of God is fulfilled' [words of Bahá'u'lláh] WOB 104

'the Blessed Beauty is the One promised by the sacred books of the past, the revelation of the Source of light that shone upon Mount Sinai, Whose fire glowed in the midst of the Burning Bush' [words of 'Abdu'l-Bahá] 127

Caiaphas

consider the Dispensation of Jesus Christ. Behold, how all the learned men of that generation, though eagerly anticipating the coming of the Promised One, have nevertheless denied Him. Both Annas, the most learned among the divines of His day, and Caiaphas, the high priest, denounced Him and pronounced the sentence of His death G 82–3

then, they led Him away, He Who was the Day-star of the heaven of divine Revelation, unto Pilate and Caiaphas, who was the leading divine of that age. The chief priests were all assembled in the palace, also a multitude of people who had gathered to witness His sufferings, to deride and injure Him KI 132

Caiaphas lived a comfortable and happy life while Peter's life was full of sorrow and trial; which of these two is the more enviable? Assuredly we should choose the present state of Peter, for he possesses immortal life whilst Caiaphas has won eternal shame. The trials of Peter tested his fidelity PT 50

Caiaphas and Annas were the colossal pillars of the Mosaic Dispensation in the day of His Highness the Spirit; but as they did not acknowledge the Word of God, they fell from the apex of glory to the bottom of the pit of the greatest abasement. But Peter was a catcher of fish; as he turned his face toward the Word of God, the fame of his imperishable, deathless and immortal glory encircled East and West; and he found in the sovereignty of the Kingdom, eternal and everlasting majesty. It is the same in these days TAB 223

Cain

the miracle of Abel and Cain *Abel* KI 148

Adam – re: marriage of Cain PUP 365

the criminal act perpetrated by Cain against Abel GPB 163

deep-seated as that which had blazed in the bosom of Cain and prompted him to slay his brother Abel – re: envy 246

Calamity

the formal assumption by the Báb of the authority of the promised Qá'im, in such dramatic circumstances and in so challenging a tone, before a distinguished gathering of eminent Shí'ah ecclesiastics, powerful, jealous, alarmed and hostile, was the explosive force that loosed a veritable avalanche of calamities which swept down upon the Faith and the people among whom it was born GPB 35–6

'in the latter days a grievous calamity shall befall My people at the hands of their ruler, a calamity such as no man ever heard to surpass it. So fierce will it be that none can find a shelter. God will then send down One of WOB 179

My descendants, One sprung from My family, Who will fill the earth with equity and justice, even as it hath been filled with injustice and tyranny' – re: Tradition of Muḥammad

Caliphate

thirteen hundred years had to elapse from the death of the Prophet Muḥammad ere the illegitimacy of the institution of the Caliphate, the founders of which had usurped the authority of the lawful successors of the Apostle of God, could be fully and publicly demonstrated. An institution which in its inception had trampled upon so sacred a right and unchained the forces of so distressful a schism, an institution which, in the latter days, had dealt so grievous a blow to a Faith Whose Forerunner was Himself a descendant of the very Imáms whose authority that institution had repudiated, deserved full well the chastisement that had sealed its fate — WOB 178

Call

Messenger — KI 179

they claimed their utterance to be the Voice of divinity, the Call of God Himself *Voice* — 180

O ye that circle the throne of glory! Hearken unto My Call which is raised from the midst of the Burning Bush, 'Verily I am God and there is none other God but Me. Hence worship Me, and for the sake of Him Who is the Most Great Remembrance, offer ye prayers purged from the insinuations of the people, for verily your Lord, the One true God, is none other than the Sovereign Truth. Indeed such as invoke others besides Him are deservedly numbered among the inmates of the fire, while He Who is the Remembrance of God verily abideth, firm and undeviating, on the Path of Truth amidst the Burning Bush' — SB 69

Calumny

how well and true is the saying: 'Flingest thou thy calumnies unto the face of Them Whom the one true God hath made the Trustees of the treasures of His seventh sphere?' — KI 186

although that Essence of lovingkindness and bounty caused those evanescent beings to step into the realm of immortality, and guided those destitute souls to the sacred river of wealth, yet some denounced Him as 'a calumniator of God, the Lord of all creatures,' others accused Him of being 'the one that withholdeth the people from the path of faith and true belief,' and still others declared Him to be 'a lunatic' and the like – re: Muḥammad — 215

Canaan

Israel – re: and came to Canaan and Philistia — SDC 76

Noah's grandson, Canaan, was detested in the sight of Noah and others were accepted — BWF 438

Canons

they argued with force and justification that the canons promulgated by the Councils of the Church were not divinely-appointed laws, but were merely human devices which did not even rest upon the actual utterances of Jesus — WOB 20–21

Carmel

Carmel, in the Book of God, hath been designated as the Hill of God, and His Vineyard — ESW 145

Carmel

all the prophets have been on Mt. Carmel, but in the mountains of Lebanon there were no prophets. It is strange that all the world is one, yet this part has become especially blessed. Palestine has been mentioned by God continually. But Sumal, Lebanon, and Damascus have never been mentioned. There was a magnificent temple of the sun at Baalbek. Its ruins still exist. It is written in the Qur'án: 'God gives His bounty and favour to whomsoever He willeth.' So it is with this land. SW XI 16, pp269–70

The heart is attracted here. His Holiness Elijah dwelt in a cave below this spot. At that time all the children of Israel were opposed to the religion of God. They were engaged in their own passions and pursuits. Only their name indicated that they were the people of His Holiness Moses. If His Holiness Moses had come among them at that time He would not have recognized them. He would have said: 'I do not consider them as my own, for they have entirely forsaken the religion of God. They are deprived of the law of God. There is no light at all remaining in them. They are like a negro servant whose name is Diamond. His name is Diamond but he is a black servant.' Such was their condition.

Then His Holiness Elijah educated certain souls in this cave. He educated pure and sincere souls as they ought to be and sent them among the children of Israel. They began to teach and call the children of Israel back to God. They called them back to the law of God. His Holiness Elijah gathered all their chief men together and brought them to the top of this mountain. There were three hundred and sixty of these chief men. But however much he taught and counselled them he obtained no result. He tried to guide them, but it was no use. For several years he worked to educate them. At the end no result was apparent. He realized that they would corrupt other souls. Then he had these three hundred and sixty men put to death. Then the rest of the children of Israel returned to their original spiritual morals and behaviour. Then they regained their spiritual life. The everlasting glory again became apparent. They overcame the neighbouring tribes. They rebuilt the Holy Temple. The laws of God were put into effect

Bahá'u'lláh's tent, the 'Tabernacle of Glory,' was raised on Mt. Carmel, 'the Hill of God and His Vineyard,' the home of Elijah, extolled by Isaiah as the 'mountain of the Lord,' to which 'all nations shall flow' GPB 194

– re: Mírzá Abu'l-Faḍl's explanation SW VII 3, pp17–19, 22–4

Catastrophe

on that memorable day the 'Bugle' mentioned in the Qur'án was sounded, the 'stunning trumpet-blast' was loudly raised, and the 'Catastrophe' came to pass – re: declaration of Ṭáhirih at Badas͟ht *Bugle* GPB 33

Cause

thus He saith: 'Our Cause is but one.' Inasmuch as the Cause is one and the same, the Exponents thereof also must needs be one and the same – re: Muḥammad *Imám* KI 153

the Cause of Bahá'u'lláh is the same as the Cause of Christ. It is the same Temple and the same Foundation. Both of these are spiritual springtimes and seasons of the soul-refreshing awakening and the cause of the renovation of the life of mankind . . . In the coming of Christ, the divine teachings were given in accordance with the infancy of the human race. The teachings of Bahá'u'lláh have the same basic principles, but are according to the stage of the maturity of the world and the requirements of this illumined age BWF 400

Cavil

such consternation of soul, such despondency, could have been caused by no other than the censure of the enemy and the cavillings of the infidel and perverse *Mary* — KI 56–7

and the cavillings which they heaped upon the Beauty of Muḥammad, the same have in this day been upheld by the people of the Qur'án *Muḥammad* — 135

among the cavils which the Jewish divines raised against Him was that after Moses no Prophet should be sent of God *Muḥammad* — 135

even as He hath revealed concerning them that erred: 'Then said the chiefs of His people who believed not, "We see in Thee but a man like ourselves; and we see not any who have followed Thee except our meanest ones of hasty judgment, nor see we any excellence in you above ourselves: nay, we deem you liars."' They cavilled at those holy Manifestations, and protested saying: 'None hath followed you except the abject amongst us, those who are worthy of no attention.' Their aim was to show that no one amongst the learned, the wealthy, and the renowned believed in them. By this and similar proofs they sought to demonstrate the falsity of Him that speaketh naught but the truth — 222

'and the Jewish doctors cavilled at Him, until they committed what made the Holy Spirit to lament' [words of Bahá'u'lláh] — PDC 101

Ceremony

it is evident that the reason for such behaviour is none other than the annulment of those rules, customs, habits, and ceremonials to which they have been subjected. Otherwise, were the Beauty of the Merciful to comply with those same rules and customs, which are current amongst the people, and were He to sanction their observances, such conflict and mischief would in no wise be made manifest in the world — KI 238

opposed the Pope on certain points of doctrine such as the prohibition of monastic marriage, the revering and bowing down before images of the Apostles and Christian leaders of the past, and various other religious practices and ceremonies which were accretional to the ordinances of the Gospel – re: Luther — SDC 41–2

religion which consists only of rites and ceremonies of prejudice is not the truth. Let us earnestly endeavour to be the means of uniting religion and science — PT 131

the practical part of religion deals with exterior forms and ceremonies, and with modes of punishment for certain offences. This is the material side of the law, and guides the customs and manners of the people — 142

Chain

'the hand of God,' say the Jews, 'is chained up' *Muḥammad* — KI 136

Champion

in this sense, neither the person of Jesus nor His writings hath differed from that of Muḥammad and of His holy Book, inasmuch as both have championed the Cause of God, uttered His praise, and revealed His commandments. Thus it is that Jesus, Himself, declared: 'I go away and come again unto you' — KI 21

Change

in like manner, endeavor to comprehend the meaning of the 'changing of the earth.' Know thou, that upon whatever hearts the bountiful showers of mercy, raining from the 'heaven' of divine Revelation, have fallen, the — KI 46 earth of those hearts hath verily been changed into the earth of divine knowledge and wisdom

it is evident that the changes brought about in every Dispensation constitute the dark clouds that intervene between the eye of man's understanding and the divine Luminary which shineth forth from the dayspring of the divine Essence. Consider how men for generations have been blindly imitating their fathers, and have been trained according to . . . the dictates of their Faith 73–4

for if the character of mankind be not changed, the futility of God's universal Manifestations would be apparent *Character* 240–41

the spiritual part never changes. All the Manifestations of God and His Prophets have taught the same truths and given the same spiritual law. They all teach the one code of morality. There is no division in the truth PT 142

reality does not admit of multiplicity although each of the divine religions is separable into two divisions. One concerns the world of morality and ethical training of human nature . . . This is ideal and spiritual teaching, the essential quality of divine religion and not subject to change or transformation. It is the one foundation of all the religions of God BWF 274

Character

they idly contend that the laws formerly revealed, must in no wise be altered. And yet, is not the object of every Revelation to effect a transformation in the whole character of mankind, a transformation that shall manifest itself both outwardly and inwardly, that shall affect both its inner life and external conditions? For if the character of mankind be not changed, the futility of God's universal Manifestations would be apparent KI 240–41

in this way the primary purpose of revealing the Divine Law – which is to bring about happiness in the after life and civilization and the refinement of character in this – will be realized SDC 46

a good character is in the sight of God and His chosen ones and the possessors of insight, the most excellent and praiseworthy of all things, but always on condition that its center of emanation should be reason and knowledge and its base should be true moderation 60

Jesus, then, founded the sacred Law on a basis of moral character and complete spirituality, and for those who believed in Him He delineated a special way of life which constitutes the highest type of action on earth 82

what a firm foundation of excellent character was laid down in those days, thanks to the training of holy souls who arose to promote the teachings of the Gospel. How many primary schools, colleges, hospitals, were established, and institutions where fatherless and indigent children received their education. How many were the individuals who sacrificed their own personal advantages and 'out of desire to please the Lord' devoted the days of their lives to teaching the masses 85

universal benefits derive from the grace of the Divine religions, for they lead their true followers to sincerity of intent, to high purpose, to purity and spotless honor, to surpassing kindness and compassion, to the keeping of their covenants when they have covenanted, to concern for the rights of others, to liberality, to justice in every aspect of life, to humanity and philanthropy, to valor and to unflagging efforts in the service of mankind. It is religion, to sum up, which produces all human virtues, and it is these virtues which are the bright candles of civilization. If a man is not characterized by these excellent qualities, it is certain that he has never attained to so much as a drop out of the fathomless river of the waters of life 98

Chastise

if God should chastise men for their perverse doings, He would not leave upon earth a moving thing! But to an appointed time doth He respite them *Seal* KI 170

Child

the newborn Child is the Beauty of the Adored One [the Báb] come forth out of the Law of God – re: Rev. 12:2 *John* SAB 172

then it is said in the second verse: 'and she being with child cried,' meaning that this Law fell into the greatest difficulties and endured great troubles and afflictions until a perfect offspring was produced – that is, the coming Manifestation, the Promised One, Who is the perfect offspring, and Who was reared in the bosom of this Law, which is as its mother. The child Who is referred to is the Báb, the Primal Point, Who was in truth born from the Law of Muḥammad – that is to say, the Holy Reality, Who is the child and outcome of the Law of God, His mother, and Who is promised by that religion, finds a reality in the kingdom of that Law; but because of the despotism of the dragon the child was carried up to God. After twelve hundred and sixty days the dragon was destroyed, and the child of the Law of God, the Promised One, became manifest – re: Rev. 12:2 [see also *Woman* 68, 70] SAQ 68–9

'and she brought forth a man child, Who was to rule all nations with a rod of iron.' This great son is the promised Manifestation Who was born of the Law of God and reared in the bosom of the divine teachings. The iron rod is a symbol of power and might – it is not a sword – and means that with divine power and might He will shepherd all the nations of the earth. This son is the Báb. 70

'And her child was caught up unto God, and to His throne.' This is a prophecy of the Báb, Who ascended to the heavenly realm, to the Throne of God, and to the center of His Kingdom. Consider how all this corresponds to what happened – re: Rev. 12:5

Jesus Christ – re: children of the Kingdom TAB 605–6

the 'Man Child,' mentioned in the Book of Revelation, destined to 'rule all nations with a rod of iron,' had released, through His coming, the creative energies which, reinforced by the effusions of a swiftly succeeding and infinitely mightier Revelation, were to instill into the entire human race the capacity to achieve its organic unification, attain maturity and thereby reach the final stage in its age-long evolution – re: Báb GPB 58

Chosen

in the Gospel He saith: 'For many are called, but few are chosen.' That is, to many is it offered, but rare is the soul who is singled out to receive the great bestowal of guidance SAB 9

Question. – In the Gospel Christ said: 'Many are called, but few are chosen,' and in the Qur'án it is written: 'He will confer particular mercy on whom He pleaseth.' What is the wisdom of this? SAQ 129

it is from the bounty of God that man is selected for the highest degree; and the differences which exist between men in regard to spiritual progress and heavenly perfections are also due to the choice of the Compassionate One. For faith, which is life eternal, is the sign of bounty, and not the result of justice. The flame of the fire of love, in this world of earth and water, comes through the power of attraction and not by effort and striving. Nevertheless, by effort and perseverance, knowledge, science and other perfections can be acquired; but only the light of the 130

Chosen

Divine Beauty can transport and move the spirits through the force of attraction. Therefore, it is said: 'Many are called, but few are chosen'

but the discerning faith that consists of true knowledge of God and the comprehension of divine words, of such faith there is very little in any age. That is why His Holiness Christ said to His followers, 'Many are called but few are chosen' BWF 364

consider how there are thousands of heedless souls who are asleep, while there is one who is conscious and awake! Even as His Holiness Christ has said, the friends of God are the salt of the earth, and the salt is but a little part of the whole. Undoubtedly the friends of God have been endowed with ability and capacity, on which account they became of the 'chosen' and not of the 'called' TAB 109

His Holiness Christ – may my spirit be His sacrifice! – saith in the Gospel, 'Many are called, but few chosen.' That is, many have been invited to faith, but few chosen for guidance 306

Christ see *Jesus Christ*

Christianity

Jesus Christ – re: Christian divines and literal interpretation KI 26

the ignorant among the Christian community, following the example of the leaders of their faith, were likewise prevented from beholding the beauty of the King of glory, inasmuch as those signs which were to accompany the dawn of the sun of the Muḥammadan Dispensation did not actually come to pass *Muḥammad* 26

it was owing to their misunderstanding of these truths that many a Christian divine hath objected to Muḥammad, and voiced his protest in such words: 'If Thou art in truth the promised Prophet, why then art Thou not accompanied by those angels our sacred Books foretold, and which must needs descend with the promised Beauty to assist Him in His Revelation and act as warners unto His people?' Even as the All-Glorious hath recorded their statement: 'Why hath not an angel been sent down to him, so that he should have been a warner with Him?' 81

Trinity – re: the third of three SB 60–61

even as the pious deeds of the Christian monks profited them not, inasmuch as at the time of the manifestation of the Apostle of God – may the blessings of God rest upon Him – they contented themselves with the standard set forth in the Gospel *Qur'án* 102

Testimony – re: unable to understand the Qur'án 120

it is recorded in a tradition that of the entire concourse of the Christians no more than seventy people embraced the Faith of the Apostle of God. The blame falleth upon their doctors, for if these had believed, they would have been followed by the mass of their countrymen. Behold, then, that which hath come to pass! The learned men of Christendom are held to be learned by virtue of their safeguarding the teaching of Christ, and yet consider how they themselves have been the cause of men's failure to accept the Faith and attain unto salvation! Is it still thy wish to follow in their footsteps? The followers of Jesus submitted to their clerics to be saved on the Day of Resurrection, and as a result of their obedience they eventually entered into the fire, and on the Day when the Apostle of God appeared they shut themselves out from the recognition of His exalted Person. Dost thou desire to follow such divines? 123–4

Tradition – re: China SDC 26

the Europeans are at least 'Peoples of the Book,' and believers in God and 26 specifically referred to in the sacred verse, 'Thou shalt certainly find those to be nearest in affection to the believers, who say, "We are Christians."' It is therefore quite permissible and indeed more appropriate to acquire knowledge from Christian countries. How could seeking after knowledge among the heathen be acceptable to God, and seeking it among the People of the Book he repugnant to Him?

under the fiercest tortures, they did every one of these holy souls to death; with butchers' cleavers, they chopped the pure and undefiled bodies of some of them to pieces and burned them in furnaces, and they stretched some of the followers on the rack and then buried them alive. In spite of this agonizing requital, the Christians continued to teach the Cause of God, and they never drew sword from its scabbard or even so much as grazed a cheek. Then in the end the Faith of Christ encompassed the whole earth, so that in Europe and America no traces of other religions were left, and today in Asia and Africa and Oceania, large masses of people are living within the sanctuary of the Four Gospels 45–6

at that time the peoples of the world were utterly ignorant, fanatical and idolatrous. Only a small group of Jews professed belief in the oneness of God and they were wretched outcasts. These holy Christian souls now stood up to promulgate a Cause which was diametrically opposed and repugnant to the beliefs of the entire human race 83

one demonstration of the excellent character of the Christians in those days was their dedication to charity and good works, and the fact that they founded hospitals and philanthropic institutions 85

the control of Christian affairs passed into the hands of ignorant priests *Priests* 85–6

thou didst begin thy letter with a blessed phrase, saying: 'I am a Christian.' O would that all were truly Christian! It is easy to be a Christian on the tongue, but hard to be a true one. Today some five hundred million souls are Christian, but the real Christian is very rare: he is that soul from whose comely face there shineth the splendour of Christ, and who showeth forth the perfections of the Kingdom; this is a matter of great moment, for to be a Christian is to embody every excellence there is SAB 29–30

Congregations – re: have given up the ground of their belief 174

all religions have gradually become bound by tradition and dogma *Dogma* PT 135

if a Christian sets aside traditionary forms and blind imitation of ceremonials and investigates the reality of the gospels, he will discover that the foundation principles of the teachings of His Holiness Christ were mercy, love, fellowship, benevolence, altruism, the resplendence or radiance of divine bestowals, acquisition of the breaths of the Holy Spirit and oneness with God FWU 105

the gradual infiltration into Christian doctrine of the principles of the Mithraic cult, of the Alexandrian school of thought, of the precepts of Zoroastrianism and of Grecian philosophy WOB 56–7

Dogma – re: obscured the purpose of the Christian Faith 138

the great variety of popular cults, of fashionable and evasive philosophies which flourished in the opening centuries of the Christian Era, and which attempted to absorb and pervert the state religion of the Roman people 184

as to the position of Christianity, let it be stated without any hesitation or equivocation that its divine origin is unconditionally acknowledged, that the Sonship and Divinity of Jesus Christ are fearlessly asserted, that the divine inspiration of the Gospel is fully recognized, that the reality of the mystery of the Immaculacy of the Virgin Mary is confessed, and the PDC 109 primacy of Peter, the Prince of the Apostles, is upheld and defended. The Founder of the Christian Faith is designated by Bahá'u'lláh as the 'Spirit of God,' is proclaimed as the One Who 'appeared out of the breath of the Holy Ghost,' and is even extolled as the 'Essence of the Spirit'

the Revelation associated with the Faith of Jesus Christ focused attention primarily on the redemption of the individual and the moulding of his conduct, and stressed, as its central theme, the necessity of inculcating a high standard of morality and discipline into man, as the fundamental unit in human society 119

it is only from dogmas and creeds of the churches that we dissociate ourselves, not from the Spirit of Christianity (Letter) LG 121

Christmas

as regards the celebration of the Christian Holidays by the believers; it is surely preferable and even highly advisable that the friends should in their relation to each other discontinue observing such holidays as Christmas and New Year, and to have their festival gatherings of this nature instead during the intercalary days and Naw-Rúz [words of Shoghi Effendi] BN 134, p2

Church

having no access to the apostles of Jesus, they sought the pleasure of the Lord in their churches, hoping to learn that which would be acceptable unto God, but they found therein no path unto Him. Then when God manifested Muḥammad as His Messenger and as the Repository of His good-pleasure, they neglected to quicken their souls from the Fountain of living waters which streamed forth from the presence of their Lord and continued to rove distraught upon the earth seeking a mere droplet of water and believing that they were doing righteous deeds. They behaved as the people unto whom the Qur'án was given are now behaving SB 137

and upon this belief the foundation of the church of God – which is the Law of God – shall be established *Peter* SAQ 135

therefore, turn thou thy face to the Church of God which consists in divine instructions and merciful exhortations. For what similarity is there between the church of stone and cement and the celestial Holy of Holies BWF 390

the fundamental reason why the unity of the Church of Christ was irretrievably shattered, and its influence was in the course of time undermined, was that the Edifice which the Fathers of the Church reared after the passing of His First Apostle was an Edifice that rested in nowise upon the explicit directions of Christ WOB 20

not one of the sacraments of the Church; not one of the rites and ceremonies which the Christian Fathers have elaborately devised and ostentatiously observed; . . . Not one of these did Christ conceive, none did He specifically invest with sufficient authority to either interpret His Word, or to add to what He had not specifically enjoined 20

Canons – re: promulgated by Councils of the Church 20

those who, in the first two centuries of the Christian era, 'purchased an ignominious life by betraying the holy Scriptures into the hands of the infidels,' the scandalous conduct of those bishops who were thereby branded as traditors, the discord of the African Church, the gradual infiltration into Christian doctrine of the principles of the Mithraic cult, of the Alexandrian school of thought, of the precepts of Zoroastrianism and of Grecian philosophy, and the adoption by the churches of Greece 56–7 and Asia of the institutions of provincial synods of a model which they borrowed from the representative councils of their respective countries

were not the first fifteen bishops of Jerusalem all circumcised Jews, and had not the congregation over which they presided united the laws of Moses with the doctrines of Christ? 57

the indwelling Spirit of God which, in the Apostolic Age of the Church, animated its members, the pristine purity of its teachings, the primitive brilliancy of its light, will, no doubt, be reborn and revived as the inevitable consequence of this redefinition of its fundamental verities, and the clarification of its original purpose 185

such is the pass to which the Christian clergy have come – a clergy that have interposed themselves between their flock and the Christ returned in the glory of the Father. As the Faith of this Promised One penetrates farther and farther into the heart of Christendom, as its recruits from the garrisons which its spirit is assailing multiply, and provoke a concerted and determined action in defence of the strongholds of Christian orthodoxy, and as the forces of nationalism, paganism, secularism and racialism move jointly towards a climax, might we not expect that the decline in the power, the authority, and the prestige of these ecclesiastics will be accentuated, and further demonstrate the truth, and more fully unfold the implications, of Bahá'u'lláh's pronouncement predicting the eclipse of the luminaries of the Church of Jesus Christ PDC 106–7

City

hasten forth and circumambulate the City of God that hath descended from heaven G 16

'Akká – re: Strong City ESW 144

that city is none other than the Word of God revealed in every age and dispensation *Word* KI 199

we are told in the Holy Scriptures that the New Jerusalem shall appear on earth. Now it is evident that this celestial city is not built of material stones and mortar, but that it is a city not made with hands, eternal in the Heavens. PT 84

This is a prophetic symbol, meaning the coming again of the Divine Teaching to enlighten the hearts of men

but now, at last, the Holy City of the New Jerusalem has come again to the world, it has appeared anew under an Eastern sky; from the horizon of Persia has its effulgence arisen to be a light to lighten the whole world. We see in these days the fulfilment of the Divine Prophecy. Jerusalem had disappeared. The heavenly city was destroyed, now it is rebuilt; it was razed to the ground, but now its walls and pinnacles have been restored, and are towering aloft in their renewed and glorious beauty 84

'Akká – re: Biblical prophecies concerning GPB 184

Clean

We bear witness that through the power of the Word of God every leper was cleansed, every sickness was healed, every human infirmity was banished G 86

observe how pleasing is cleanliness in the sight of God, and how specifically it is emphasized in the Holy Books of the Prophets; for the Scriptures forbid the eating or the use of any unclean thing. Some of these prohibitions were absolute, and binding upon all, and whoso transgressed the given law was abhorred of God and anathematized by the believers SAB 147

Cleaving of the Heaven

the 'cleaving of the heaven' – one of the signs that must needs herald the coming of the last Hour, the Day of Resurrection. As He hath said: 'When the heaven shall be cloven asunder.' By 'heaven' is meant the heaven of divine Revelation, which is elevated with every Manifestation, and rent asunder with every subsequent one. By 'cloven asunder' is meant that the former Dispensation is superseded and annulled. I swear by God! That this heaven being cloven asunder is, to the discerning, an act mightier than the cleaving of the skies! [see also *Revelation* 44–5] KI 44

Clerics [see also *Divines, Leaders, Priests, Prelates*]

not one Prophet of God was made manifest Who did not fall a victim to the relentless hate, to the denunciation, denial, and execration of the clerics of His day *Veil* KI 165–6

the followers of Jesus submitted to their clerics to be saved on the Day of Resurrection, and as a result of their obedience they eventually entered into the fire *Christianity* SB 123–4

the arrogant, fanatical, perfidious, and retrograde clericals – re: Shí'ih clergy *Prelates* PDC 92–3

a clergy that have interposed themselves between their flock and the Christ returned in the glory of the Father 106

Cloud

and now regarding His words, that the Son of man shall 'come in the clouds of heaven.' By the term 'clouds' is meant those things that are contrary to the ways and desires of men . . . These 'clouds' signify, in one sense, the annulment of laws, the abrogation of former Dispensations, the repeal of rituals and customs current amongst men KI 71–2

the changes brought about in every Dispensation constitute the dark clouds that intervene *Change* 73–4

to descend from the visible heaven upon the clouds – re: Jesus 80–81

what can such expect but that God should come down to them overshadowed with clouds [see also *Qur'án* 75–6] *Qá'im* 144

and they are waiting for Him to come down from there again, riding upon a cloud, and they imagine that there are clouds in that infinite space and that He will ride thereon and by that means He will descend. Whereas the truth is that a cloud is but vapour that riseth out of the earth, and it doth not come down from heaven. Rather, the cloud referred to in the Gospel is the human body, so called because the body is as a veil to man, which, even as a cloud, preventeth him from beholding the Sun of Truth that shineth from the horizon of Christ SAB 168

let us not, with the dark clouds of our illusions, our selfish interests, blot out the glory that streameth from the Abhá Realm 264

Comforter

for this reason did Christ say: 'I have yet many things to say unto you, matters needing to be told, but ye cannot bear to hear them now. Howbeit when that Comforting Spirit, Whom the Father will send, shall come, He will make plain unto you the truth' SAB 59

He identifies Himself with the 'Father' spoken of by Isaiah, with the 'Comforter' Whose Covenant He Who is the Spirit (Jesus) had Himself established – re: Bahá'u'lláh GPB 210

'the Comforter Whose advent all the scriptures have promised is now come that He may reveal unto you all knowledge and wisdom' [words of Bahá'u'lláh] WOB 104–5

Commentary on the Súrih of Joseph see *Qur'án*

Communion see *Lord's Supper*

Community

the ignorant among the Christian community, following the example of the leaders of their faith, were likewise prevented from beholding the beauty of the King of glory, inasmuch as those signs which were to accompany the dawn of the sun of the Muḥammadan Dispensation did not actually come to pass KI 26

in like manner, have such false imaginings caused other communities to stray from the Kawthar of the infinite mercy of Providence, and to be busied with their own idle thoughts 27

Christianity – re: and acceptance of Islám SB 123–4

the constitution of the communities depends upon justice, not upon forgiveness. Then what Christ meant by forgiveness and pardon is not that, when nations attack you, burn your homes, plunder your goods, assault your wives, children and relatives, and violate your honour, you should be submissive in the presence of these tyrannical foes and allow them to perform all their cruelties and oppressions. No, the words of Christ refer to the conduct of two individuals toward each other: if one person assaults another, the injured one should forgive him. But the communities must protect the rights of man SAQ 270–71

Companions

and now, with fixed gaze and steady wings enter thou the way of certitude and truth. 'Say: It is God; then leave them to entertain themselves with their cavillings.' Thus, wilt thou be accounted of those companions of whom He saith: 'They that say "Our Lord is God," and continue steadfast in His way, upon them, verily, shall the angels descend.' Then shalt thou witness all these mysteries with thine own eyes KI 42–3

causing the companions of the Prophet to waver *Qiblih* 52

you must undoubtedly have been informed of the tribulations, the poverty, the ills, and the degradation that have befallen every Prophet of God and His companions. You must have heard how the heads of their followers were sent as presents unto different cities, how grievously they were hindered from that whereunto they were commanded. Each and every one of them fell a prey to the hands of the enemies of His Cause, and had to suffer whatsoever they decreed 73

the more they observe the indomitable strength,the sublime renunciation, the unwavering constancy of God's noble companions, who, by the aid of God, are growing nobler and more glorious every day, the deeper the dismay which ravageth their souls. In these days, praise be to God, the power of His Word hath obtained such ascendancy over men, that they dare breathe no word. Were they to encounter one of the companions of God who, if he could, would freely and joyously, offer up ten thousand lives as a sacrifice for his Beloved, so great would be their fear, that they forthwith would profess their faith in Him, whilst privily they would vilify and execrate His name! Even as He hath revealed: 'And when they meet you, they say, "We believe"; but when they are apart, they bite their fingers' ends at you, out of wrath. Say: "Die in your wrath!" God truly knoweth the very recesses of your breasts' 77–8

nay, the contrary hath come to pass. Have not His disciples and companions been afflicted of men? – re: Qá'im *Sovereignty* 106

Muḥammad – re: all ceased to hold intercourse with Him and His companions 109

Companions

it is related that on a certain day, one of the companions of Ṣádiq complained of his poverty before him — 131

His Companions must likewise be the ‘return’ of the bygone Companions – re: Muḥammad *Return* — 151

reflect for a while upon the behaviour of the companions of the Muḥammadan Dispensation *Muḥammad* — 159

and now, observe the ‘return’ of the self-same determination, the self-same constancy and renunciation, manifested by the companions of the Point of the Bayán — 160

when the Companions of Muḥammad were denounced as repudiators of God and as followers of a lying sorcerer *Islám* — 218

at such a time this blessed verse was sent down from the heaven of divine Revelation. It revealed an irrefutable evidence, and brought the light of an unfailing guidance. It instructed the companions of Muḥammad to declare the following unto the infidels and idolators: ‘Ye oppress and persecute us, and yet, what else have we done except that we have believed in God and in the verses sent down unto us through the tongue of Muḥammad, and in those which descended upon the Prophets of old?’ By this is meant that their only guilt was to have recognized that the new and wondrous verses of God, which had descended upon Muḥammad, as well as those which had been revealed unto the Prophets of old, were all of God, and to have acknowledged and embraced their truth – re: Qur’án 5:64 — 218

that all the divines and doctors sentence Him and His companions to death – re: Qá’im *Tradition* — 245

in that place His companions have been with great suffering put to death – re: martyrdoms – Rayy *Tradition* — 247

‘and whoso shall withdraw from the remembrance of the Merciful, We will chain a Satan unto him, and he shall be his fast companion’ — 257

Brother – re: address by Quddús at Shaykh Ṭabarsí — GPB 80

Conduct

the noble conduct of the Prophets and Holy Ones of God is widely known, and it is indeed, until the coming of the Hour, in every aspect of life an excellent pattern for all mankind to follow — SDC 53–4

Confederates

furthermore, in the Battle of the Confederates, Abú Sufyán enlisted the aid of the Baní Kinánih, the Baní Qahtán, and the Jewish Baní Qurayzih and rose up with all the tribes of the Quraysh to put out the Divine Light that flamed in the lamp of Yathrib (Medina). In those days the great winds of trials and tribulations were blowing from every direction, as it is written: ‘Do men think when they say “We believe” they shall be let alone and not be put to proof?’ The believers were few and the enemy attacking in force, seeking to blot out the new-risen Sun of Truth with the dust of oppression and tyranny. Then Salmán (the Persian) came into the presence of the Prophet – the Dawning-Point of revelation, the Focus of the endless splendours of grace – and he said that in Persia to protect themselves from an encroaching host they would dig a moat or trench about their lands, and that this had proved a highly efficient safeguard against surprise attacks — SDC 26–7

Confucius

Buddha [discourse on beliefs] — SAQ 165, 166, TAB 469–70

Confucius was not a Prophet. It is quite correct to say he is the founder of a moral system and a great reformer LG 369

Congregations

the diverse congregations have given up the ground of their belief, and adopted doctrines that are of no account in the sight of God. They are even as the Pharisees who both prayed and fasted, and then did sentence Jesus Christ to death. By the life of God! This thing is passing strange SAB 174

Consummation

take heed, and be watchful; and remember that all things have their consummation in belief in Him, in attainment unto His day, and in the realization of His divine presence. 'There is no piety in turning your faces toward the east or toward the west, but he is pious who believeth in God and the Last Day' KI 92–3

Contrary

the All-Glorious hath decreed these very things, that are contrary to the desires of wicked men, to be the touchstone and standard whereby He proveth His servants, that the just may be known from the wicked, and the faithful distinguished from the infidel *Smoke* KI 76

and should the Essence of Truth reveal that which is contrary to their inclinations and desires, they will straightway denounce Him as an infidel, and will protest saying: 'This is contrary to the sayings of the Imáms of the Faith and of the resplendent lights. No such thing hath been provided by our inviolable Law.' Even so in this day such worthless statements have been and are being made by these poor mortals *Tradition* 242

Corruption of the Text

verily I say, throughout all this period they have utterly failed to comprehend what is meant by corrupting the text *Sign* KI 84

verily by 'perverting' the text is not meant that which these foolish and abject souls have fancied, even as some maintain that Jewish and Christian divines have effaced from the Book such verses as extol and magnify the countenance of Muḥammad, and instead thereof have inserted the contrary. How utterly vain and false are these words! Can a man who believeth in a book, and deemeth it to be inspired by God, mutilate it? . . . Nay, rather, by corruption of the text is meant that in which all Muslim divines are engaged today, that is the interpretation of God's holy Book in accordance with their idle imaginings and vain desires. And as the Jews, in the time of Muḥammad, interpreted those verses of the Pentateuch, that referred to His Manifestation, after their own fancy, and refused to be satisfied with His holy utterance, the charge of 'perverting' the text was therefore pronounced against them. Likewise, it is clear, how in this day, the people of the Qur'án have perverted the text of God's holy Book, concerning the signs of the expected Manifestation, and interpreted it according to their inclination and desires 86–7

again in another instance, He saith: 'Woe unto those who, with their own hands, transcribe the Book corruptly – re: divines and leaders of the Jewish Faith *Book* 87–8

yea 'corruption' of the text, in the sense We have referred to, hath been actually effected in particular instances. A few of these We have mentioned, that it may become manifest to every discerning observer that unto a few untutored holy Men hath been given the mastery of 88–9

Corruption of the Text

human learning, so that the malevolent opposer may cease to contend that a certain verse doth indicate 'corruption' of the text, and insinuate that We, through lack of knowledge, have made mention of such things. Moreover, most of the verses that indicate 'corruption' of the text have been revealed with reference to the Jewish people, were ye to explore the isles of the Qur'ánic Revelation

Countenance

by their countenance shall the sinners be known, and they shall be seized KI 173
by their forelocks and their feet *Reckoning*

thus the peoples of the world are judged by their countenance. By it, their 173–4
misbelief, their faith, and their iniquity are all made manifest. Even as it is evident in this day how the people of error are, by their countenance, known and distinguished from the followers of divine Guidance

Covenant

verily, God hath entered into a covenant with us that we are not to credit KI 148
an apostle until he present us a sacrifice which fire out of heaven shall devour *Sacrifice*

Gate – re: Most Great Remembrance SB 46

O Qurratu'l-'Ayn! Deliver the summons of the most exalted Word unto the 52
handmaids among Thy kindred, caution them against the Most Great Fire and announce unto them the joyful tidings that following this mighty Covenant there shall be everlasting reunion with God in the Paradise of His good-pleasure, nigh unto the Seat of Holiness. Verily God, the Lord of creation, is potent over all things

verily We have taken a covenant from every created thing upon its coming 65
into being concerning the Remembrance of God, and there shall be none to avert the binding command of God for the purification of mankind, as ordained in the Book which is written by the hand of the Báb

the Lord of the universe hath never raised up a prophet nor hath He sent 87
down a Book unless He hath established His covenant with all men, calling for their acceptance of the next Revelation and of the next Book; inasmuch as the outpourings of His bounty are ceaseless and without limit

praise be to Thee, O Lord, my Best Beloved! Make me steadfast in Thy 215
Cause and grant that I may be reckoned among those who have not violated Thy Covenant nor followed the gods of their own idle fancy

as for the reference in *The Hidden Words* regarding the Covenant entered SAB 207
into on Mount Párán, this signifieth that in the sight of God the past, the present and the future are all one and the same – whereas, relative to man, the past is gone and forgotten, the present is fleeting, and the future is within the realm of hope

Sinai – re: a Covenant regarding the Messiah 207

today, the Lord of Hosts is the defender of the Covenant, the forces of the 228
Kingdom protect it, heavenly souls tender their services, and heavenly angels promulgate and spread it broadcast. If it is considered with insight, it will be seen that all the forces of the universe, in the last analysis serve the Covenant

the Báb made a Covenant concerning the Blessed Beauty of Bahá'u'lláh BWF 358
and gave the glad-tidings of His coming for the Blessed Beauty was the One promised by His Holiness the Báb. Bahá'u'lláh made a covenant concerning a promised One who will become manifest after one thousand or thousands of years *Abraham*

Creation

as regards thine assertions about the beginning of creation, this is a matter on which conceptions vary by reason of the divergences in men's thoughts and opinions. Wert thou to assert that it hath ever existed and shall continue to exist, it would be true; or wert thou to affirm the same concept as is mentioned in the sacred Scriptures, no doubt would there be about it, for it hath been revealed by God, the Lord of the worlds. Indeed He was a hidden treasure. This is a station that can never be described nor even alluded to — TB 140

God's creation hath existed from eternity and will continue to exist forever *Existence* — G 150

thus hath He, the Spirit of God, recorded, as spoken by the infidels: 'And if thou shouldst say, "After death ye shall surely be raised again," the infidels will certainly exclaim, "This is nothing but manifest sorcery."' Again He speaketh: 'If ever thou dost marvel, marvellous surely is their saying, "What! When we have become dust, shall we be restored in a new creation?"' Thus, in another passage, He wrathfully exclaimeth: 'Are We wearied out with the first creation? Yet are they in doubt with regard to a new creation!' — KI 114–15

all praise be unto God Who was Ever-Existent ere created things were called into being, when there was no one else besides Him — SB 196

this supreme emblem of God stands first in the order of creation and first in rank, taking precedence over all created things. Witness to it is the Holy Tradition, 'Before all else, God created the mind.' From the dawn of creation, it was made to be revealed in the temple of man — SDC 1

consider then, how all the peoples of the world are bowing the knee to a fancy of their own contriving, how they have created a creator within their own minds, and they call it the Fashioner of all that is – whereas in truth it is but an illusion. Thus are the people worshipping only an error of perception — SAB 53–4

and if a human life, with its spiritual being, were limited to this earthly span, then what would be the harvest of creation? Indeed, what would be the effects and the outcomes of Divinity Itself? Were such a notion true, all created things, all contingent realities, and this whole world of being – all would be meaningless — 184–5

supreme importance should be attached, therefore, not to this first creation but rather to the future life — 197

Cross [see also *Crucifixion*]

He regarded the cross as a throne, the wound as a balm – re: Christ *Sacrifice* — SAQ 120

Crown

it is thus that you see even in the kingdom of this world – that is to say, in the realm of souls and countries – that the glory and the grandeur of Christ appeared in this earth after His ascension. When in the world of the body He was subject to the contempt and jeers of the weakest nation of the world, the Jews, who thought it fitting to set a crown of thorns upon His sacred head. But after His ascension the bejeweled crowns of all the kings were humbled and bowed before the crown of thorns — SAQ 117

Crucifixion

[of Christ] — G 75

[significance of sacrifice of Christ] — 85

they crucified the Word of God *Spirit* — SAB 45

Crucifixion

Christ's intention was to represent and promote a Cause which was to educate the human world . . . meant that He would be killed and crucified, so Christ in proclaiming His mission sacrificed His life *Sacrifice* SAQ 120–21

after the crucifixion the apostles had not in the beginning the capacity and ability of witnessing the Messianic reality. For they were agitated. But when they found firmness and steadfastness, their inner sight became opened, and they saw the reality of the Messiah as manifest. For the body of Christ was crucified and vanished, but the Spirit of Christ is always pouring upon the contingent world, and is manifest before the insight of the people of assurance TAB 193–4

Cult

the great variety of popular cults, of fashionable and evasive philosophies which flourished in the opening centuries of the Christian Era *Christianity* WOB 57, 184

Customs

the annulment of those rules, customs, habits and ceremonials *Ceremony* KI 238

Abraham – re: Days of Ignorance SDC 29–30

Cycle see *Adam, Prophetic Cycle*

Daniel

Jerusalem – re: rebuilding of Temple SAQ 40

but Daniel refers especially to the third edict which was issued in the year 457 B.C. . . . Each day, according to the text of the Holy Book, is a year. For in the Bible it is said: 'The day of the Lord is one year.' Therefore, four hundred and ninety days are four hundred and ninety years. The third edict of Artaxerxes was issued four hundred and fifty seven years before the birth of Christ, and Christ when He was martyred and ascended was thirty-three years of age. When you add thirty-three to four hundred and fifty seven, the result is four hundred and ninety, which is the time announced by Daniel for the manifestation of Christ 40

– re: explanation of the sixty-two weeks and the seven weeks, and the ascension of Christ 41

in the eighth chapter of the Book of Daniel, verse thirteen, it is said: 'Then I heard one saint speaking, and another saint said unto that certain saint which spake, How long shall be the vision concerning the daily sacrifice, and the transgression of desolation, to give both the sanctuary and the host to be trodden under foot?' Then he answered (V. 14): 'Unto two thousand and three hundred days; then shall the sanctuary be cleansed'; (V. 17) 'But he said unto me . . . at the time of the end shall be the vision.' That is to say, how long will this misfortune, this ruin, this abasement and degradation last? meaning, when will be the dawn of the Manifestation? Then he answered, 'Two thousand and three hundred days; then shall the sanctuary be cleansed.' Briefly, the purport of this passage is that he appoints two thousand three hundred years, for in the text of the Bible each day is a year. Then from the date of the issuing of the edict of Artaxerxes to rebuild Jerusalem until the day of the birth of Christ there are 456 years, and from the birth of Christ until the day of the manifestation of the Báb there are 1844 years. When you add 456 years to this number it makes 2300 years. That is to say, the fulfillment of the vision of Daniel took place in the year A.D. 1844, and this is the year of the Báb's manifestation according to the actual text of the Book of Daniel 41–2 in Matthew, chapter 24, verse 3, Christ clearly says what Daniel meant by this prophecy was the date of the manifestation, and this is the verse: 'As He sat upon the mount of Olives, the disciples came unto Him privately, saying, Tell us, when shall these things be? and what shall be the sign of Thy coming, and of the end of the world?' One of the explanations He gave them in reply was this (v. 15): 'When ye therefore shall see the abomination of desolation, spoken of by Daniel the prophet, stand in the holy place, (whoso readeth, let him understand).' In this answer He referred them to the eighth chapter of the Book of Daniel, saying that everyone who reads it will understand that it is this time that is spoken of. Consider how clearly the manifestation of the Báb is spoken of in the Old Testament and in the Gospel 42–3

in Daniel, chapter 12, verse 6, it is said: 'And one said to the man clothed in linen, which was upon the waters of the river, How long shall it be to the end of these wonders? And I heard the man clothed in linen, which was upon the waters of the river, when he held up his right hand and his left hand unto heaven, and sware by Him that liveth for ever that it shall be for a time, times, and a half; and that when He shall have accomplished to scatter the power of the holy people, all these things shall be finished.' . . . Thus three years and a half make forty-two months, and forty-two months are twelve hundred and sixty days. The Báb, the precursor of Bahá'u'lláh, appeared in the year 1260 from the Hejira of Muḥammad, by the reckoning of Islám. 43–4

Afterward, in verse 11, it is said: 'And from the time that the daily sacrifice shall be taken away, and the abomination that maketh desolation be set up, there shall be a thousand two hundred and ninety days. Blessed is he that waiteth, and cometh to the thousand three hundred and five and thirty days!'

The beginning of this lunar reckoning is from the day of the proclamation of the prophethood of Muḥammad in the country of Ḥijáz; and that was three years after His mission, because in the beginning the prophethood of Muḥammad was kept secret, and no one knew it save Khadíjah and Ibn Nawfal. After three years it was announced. And Bahá'u'lláh, in the year 1290 from the proclamation of the Mission of Muḥammad, caused His manifestation to be known

the 'Second Woe,' spoken of in the Apocalypse of St. John the Divine, had, at long last, appeared, and the first of the two 'Messengers,' Whose appearance had been prophesied in the Qur'án, had been sent down . . . The 'cleansing of the Sanctuary,' prophesied by Daniel and confirmed by Jesus Christ in His reference to the 'Abomination of desolation,' had been accomplished [see also GPB 151] GPB 58

His Day Ezekiel and Daniel had, moreover, both acclaimed as the 'day of the Lord,' and Malachi described as 'the great and dreadful day of the Lord' when 'the Sun of Righteousness' will 'arise, with healing in His wings,' whilst Daniel had pronounced His advent as signalizing the end of the 'abomination that maketh desolate' – re: Bahá'u'lláh 95

out of it went forth the earliest tidings of the Message of Salvation which, as prophesied by Daniel, was to mark, after the lapse of 'a thousand two hundred and ninety days' (1290 A.H.), the end of 'the abomination that maketh desolate' – re: Baghdád period 110

and broke the 'seals' of the 'Book' referred to by Daniel, and disclosed the meaning of the 'words' destined to remain 'closed up' till the 'time of the end' – re: Kitáb-i-Íqán *Book* 139

the 'thousand two hundred and ninety days,' fixed by Daniel in the last chapter of His Book, as the duration of the 'abomination that maketh 151 desolate' had now elapsed. The 'hundred lunar years,' destined to immediately precede that blissful consummation (1335 days), announced by Daniel in that same chapter, had commenced – re: Declaration of Bahá'u'lláh, Riḍván 1863

the prophecy mentioned by Daniel in the last chapter of His Book, related to the year 1335, and associated by 'Abdu'l-Bahá with the world triumph of the Faith of His Father — CF 32

now concerning the verse in Daniel, the interpretation whereof thou didst ask, namely, 'Blessed is he who cometh unto the thousand three hundred and thirty-five days.' These days must be reckoned as solar and not lunar years. For according to this calculation a century will have elapsed from the dawn of the Sun of Truth, then will the teachings of God be firmly established upon the earth, and the Divine Light shall flood the world from the East even unto the West. Then, on this day, will the faithful rejoice [words of 'Abdu'l-Bahá] — LG 323–4

the 1335 days is figured according to the solar calendar, but in adjusting the 1335 days, one must take into consideration the time at which the prophecies were given and change them into solar time, which would bring the date to 1963. — 324

There is one thing of importance for the Bahá'ís to understand; and that is, that this prophecy refers to happenings within the Faith, not occurrences outside the Faith (Letter Dec. 53)

sometimes people strive all their lives to render outstanding service. Here is the time and opportunity to render historic services; in fact the most unique in history, aiding in the fulfilment of Daniel's prophecies of the Last Day, and the 1335 days, when men are to be blessed by the Glory of the Lord, covering the entire globe – which is the real goal of the Ten Year Crusade. — BN 313, p7

In other words, when we fulfil the Ten Year Crusade we will have brought into fulfilment Daniel's great prophecy of 'Blessed is he who waits and comes to the 1335 days.' What could be more wonderful than taking part in the fulfilment of religious prophecy of over 3,000 years

[see also *Nebuchadnezzar* n.]

David

'Akká – re: Strong City — ESW 144

how many men and women awaited the manifestation of the Messiah after Moses? Yet when His beauty shone forth and His face appeared, they (the people) did not recognize Him, but continued to follow the superstitions of the Pharisees, who used to say: 'Where is the authority of the Messiah? Where is the throne of David, the Glorious? Where is his iron rod? Where are his innumerable hosts? Where are his attacking armies? Where are the angels of heaven? — TAB 230

of Him David had sung in his Psalms, acclaiming Him as the 'Lord of Hosts' and the 'King of Glory' — GPB 95

David, in his Psalms, had predicted: 'Lift up your heads, O ye gates; even lift them up, ye everlasting doors; and the King of Glory shall come in. Who is this King of Glory? The Lord of Hosts, He is the King of Glory.' 'Out of Zion, the perfection of beauty, God hath shined. Our God shall come, and shall not keep silence' — 184

addressing the Jewish people Bahá'u'lláh has written: 'The Most Great Law is come, and the Ancient Beauty ruleth upon the throne of David' — PDC 76

Day

Isaiah – re: the exalted character of this Day – the Day of God Himself G 13

say: O people! The Day, promised unto you in all the Scriptures, is now come 314

the voice of the true Faith calleth aloud, at this moment, and saith: O people! Verily, the Day is come, and My Lord hath made Me to shine forth with a light whose splendour hath eclipsed the suns of utterance ESW 29

the day when mankind shall stand before the Lord of the worlds *Seal* 114

hearken with thine inner ear unto the Voice of Jeremiah, Who saith: 'Oh, for great is that Day, and it hath no equal' 144

therefore, whosoever, and in whatever Dispensation, hath recognized and attained unto the presence of these glorious, these resplendent and most excellent Luminaries, hath verily attained unto the 'Presence of God' Himself, and entered the city of eternal and immortal life. Attainment unto such presence is possible only in the Day of Resurrection, which is the Day of the rise of God Himself through His all-embracing Revelation KI 143

Moses – re: meaning of Resurrection SB 107

when God sent forth His Prophet Muḥammad, on that day the termination of the prophetic cycle was foreordained in the knowledge of God. Yea, that promise hath indeed come true and the decree of God hath been accomplished as He hath ordained . . . These are the glorious days on the like of which the sun hath never risen in the past. These are the days which the people in bygone times eagerly expected. What hath then befallen you that ye are fast asleep? These are the days wherein God hath caused the Day-Star of Truth to shine resplendent. What hath then caused you to keep your silence? These are the appointed days which ye have been yearningly awaiting in the past – the days of the advent of divine justice 161

it is certain that the day of woe is the day of the Lord . . . This third woe is the day of the manifestation of Bahá'u'lláh, the day of God; and it is near to the day of the appearance of the Báb *Lord* [see also *Woe*] SAQ 56

this is the day of God, for the Sun of Reality will arise in it with the utmost warmth and splendour *God* 57

the 'day of whose length shall be a thousand years,' foretold by the Apostle of God in His Book, had terminated – re: Declaration of the Báb GPB 58

the cloud of despondency that had momentarily settled on the disconsolate lovers of the Cause of Bahá'u'lláh was lifted. The continuity of that unerring guidance vouchsafed to it since its birth was now assured. The significance of the solemn affirmation that this is 'the Day which shall not be followed by night' was now clearly apprehended 245

'a day shall be witnessed by My people whereon there will have remained of Islám naught but a name, and of the Qur'án naught but a mere appearance' – re: tradition WOB 179

the promised day is come, the day when tormenting trials will have surged above your heads, and beneath your feet, saying: "Taste ye what your hands have wrought!"' 'Soon shall the blasts of His chastisement beat upon you, and the dust of hell enshroud you' PDC 3

'the day will soon come,' He, referring to the foolish one of the earth, has written, 'whereon they will cry out for help and receive no answer' 3

in the spiritual realm they have also reached the point where God could leave, in human hands, guided directly by the Báb and Bahá'u'lláh, as the Master states in His Will, the affairs of His Faith for this LG 231–2

Dispensation. This is what is meant by 'this is the day which will not be followed by night' *Night* 232, p8

in the Sacred Scriptures of various religions there are to be found frequent references to days, but these have to be considered as indicating different periods of time, as for instance in the Qur'án a day is reckoned as one thousand lunar years 353

Dead

in another passage of the Gospel it is written: 'And it came to pass that on a certain day the father of one of the disciples of Jesus had died. That disciple reporting the death of his father unto Jesus, asked for leave to go and bury him. Whereupon, Jesus, that Essence of detachment, answered and said: 'Let the dead bury their dead' KI 119

'shall the dead, whom We have quickened, and for whom We have ordained a light whereby he may walk among men, be like him, whose likeness is in the darkness, whence he will not come forth?' – re: Abú-Jahl *Hamzih* 121

while the hearts of them that associate partners with God are impotent, devoid of life on this earth, for assuredly they are dead SB 153

'and their dead bodies shall lie in the street of the great city, which spiritually is called Sodom and Egypt, where also our Lord was crucified.' 'Their bodies' means the Religion of God, and 'the street' means in public view. The meaning of 'Sodom and Egypt,' the place 'where also our Lord was crucified,' is this region of Syria, and especially Jerusalem, where the Umayyads then had their dominions; and it was here that the Religion of God and the divine teachings first disappeared, and a body without spirit remained. 'Their bodies' represents the Religion of God,which remained like a dead body without spirit. SAQ 51–2

'And they of the people and kindreds and tongues and nations shall see their dead bodies three days and a half, and shall not suffer their dead bodies to be put in graves' [see *Qur'án*] – re: 1260 years

the people forfeited all that these two persons had established, which was the foundation of the Law of God, and destroyed the virtues of the world of humanity, which are the divine gifts and the spirit of this religion, to such a degree that truthfulness, justice, love, union, purity, sanctity, detachment and all the divine qualities departed from among them. In the religion only prayers and fasting persisted; this condition lasted for twelve hundred and sixty years, which is the duration of the cycle of the Furqán. It was as if these two persons were dead, and their bodies were remaining without spirit [see also *Islám* 53–4] 53

Blind – re: meaning; also raising the dead 102

there is, however, another Spirit which may be termed the Divine, to which Jesus Christ refers when He declares that man must be born of its quickening and baptized with its living fire. Souls deprived of that Spirit are accounted as dead, though they are possessed of the human spirit. Jesus Christ has pronounced them dead inasmuch as they have no portion of the Divine Spirit PUP 58

those souls who are not vivified and attracted by the Holy Spirit, are accounted among the dead, because their souls are deprived of the breath of the Holy Spirit, and these persons after physical death are in a certain condition, having feeling and discernment in their environment, but in comparison with the pure souls who have been vivified by the Holy Spirit, they are as dead and deprived TAB 670

Deaf

where it is said a deaf man received hearing, the meaning is that he acquired spiritual and heavenly hearing. This is ascertained from the text of the Gospel where Christ said: 'These are like those of whom Isaiah said, They have eyes and see not, they have ears and hear not; and I healed them' *Blind* — SAQ 102

Death

true life is not the life of the flesh but the life of the spirit. For the life of the flesh is common to both men and animals, whereas the life of the spirit is possessed only by the pure in heart who have quaffed from the ocean of faith and partaken of the fruit of certitude. This life knoweth no death, and this existence is crowned by immortality. Even as it hath been said: 'He who is a true believer liveth both in this world and in the world to come.' If by 'life' be meant this earthly life, it is evident that death must needs overtake it — KI 120–21

'wish for death, if ye are men of truth' *Touchstone* — 227

for example, there is in the Pentateuch a law that if anyone break the Sabbath, he shall be put to death. Moreover, there are ten sentences of death in the Pentateuch. Would it be possible to keep these laws in our time? *Pentateuch* — SAQ 96

Deed

thy purpose in performing thy deeds is that God may graciously accept them; and divine acceptance can in no wise be achieved except through the acceptance of Him Who is the Exponent of His Revelation *Exponent* — SB 81

at the time of the appearance of Him Whom God shall make manifest, wert thou to perform thy deeds for the sake of the Point of the Bayán, they would be regarded as performed for one other than God, inasmuch as on that Day the Point of the Bayán is none other than Him Whom God shall make manifest. — 95

It is for this reason that at the beginning of every Dispensation a vast multitude, who fondly imagine that their deeds are for God, become drowned and ungodly, and perceive this not, except such as He guideth at His behest

Degradation

and Israel had fallen into a state of the utmost degradation, misery and bondage *Israel* — SAQ 16

Deluge

mention hath been made in certain books of a deluge which caused all that existed on earth, historical records as well as other things, to be destroyed — G 174

Ark — LG 378

Deny

and whensoever the portals of grace did open, and the clouds of divine bounty did rain upon mankind, and the light of the Unseen did shine above the horizon of celestial might, they all denied Him, and turned away from His face – the face of God Himself. Refer ye, to verify this truth, to that which hath been recorded in every sacred Book — KI 4

moreover, the more closely you observe the denials of those who have opposed the Manifestations of the divine attributes, the firmer will be your faith in the Cause of God — 6

whatever in days gone by hath been the cause of the denial and opposition — 13–14 of those people hath now led to the perversity of the people of this age. To maintain that the testimony of Providence was incomplete, that it hath therefore been the cause of the denial of the people, is but open blasphemy

not one Prophet of God was made manifest Who did not fall a victim to the relentless hate, to the denunciation, denial, and execration of the clerics of His day — 165–6

deny not My servant should he ask anything from thee, for his face is My face; be then abashed before Me — AHW 30

and deny thyself that which thou desirest if thou seekest My pleasure — 38

say, how dare ye flagrantly deny the verses sent down from the heaven of justice, yet ye read the Books of God revealed in the past? How do ye repudiate the meeting with your Lord which was appointed with you aforetime, and fail in this Day to heed His warning? — SB 162

as for the deniers, they are veiled from God: they see not, they hear not, neither do they understand. 'Leave them to entertain themselves with their cavillings.' Abandon them to their wanderings along river beds where no stream flows [see also *Jesus Christ* 42–3] — SAB 43

Christ, in His blessed day, in reality only educated eleven men: the greatest of them was Peter, who, nevertheless, when he was tested, thrice denied Christ. In spite of this, the Cause of Christ subsequently permeated the world — SAQ 35

but failing justice, the people attack, dispute and openly deny the evidence, like the Pharisees who, at the manifestation of Christ, denied with the greatest obstinacy the explanations of Christ and of His disciples — 71

in that time no one but a certain few persons believed in Him; and the great one among them was Peter the disciple, who, through the burning of the fire of test and persecution, was in great fear and denied Christ three times — TAB 528

Deprive

they therefore became deprived of the streaming grace of the Muḥammadan Revelation and its showering bounties – re: Christian divines *Jesus Christ* — KI 26

as they have literally interpreted the Word of God, and the sayings and traditions of the Letters of Unity, and expounded them according to their own deficient understanding, they have therefore deprived themselves and all their people of the bountiful showers of the grace and mercies of God – re: the divines — 82

Descent

thereupon, they will behold the countenance of the promised One, the adored Beauty, descending from heaven and riding upon the clouds. By this is meant that the divine Beauty will be made manifest from the heaven of the will of God, and will appear in the form of the human temple — KI 66–7

these ancient Beings, though delivered from the womb of their mother, have in reality descended from the heaven of the will of God. Though they be dwelling on this earth, yet their true habitations are the retreats of glory in the realms above. Whilst walking amongst mortals, they soar in the heaven of the divine presence — 67

were the prophecies recorded in the Gospel to be literally fulfilled; were Jesus, Son of Mary, accompanied by angels, to descend from the visible heaven upon the clouds; who would dare to disbelieve, who would dare to reject the truth, and wax disdainful? — 80–81 and they are waiting for Him to come down from there again, riding upon a cloud, and they imagine that there are clouds in that infinite space and that He will ride thereon and by that means he will descend *Cloud* SAB 168

afterward Christ came, saying, 'I am born of the Holy Spirit.' Though it is now very easy for the Christians to believe this assertion, at that time it was very difficult. According to the text of the Gospel the Pharisees said, 'Is not this the son of Joseph of Nazareth Whom we know? How can He say, therefore, I came down from heaven?' SAQ 16

then it is evident that the dove which descended upon Christ was not a material dove, but it was a spiritual state, which, that it might be comprehensible, was expressed by a sensible figure 85

'I am the bread which descended from heaven; whosoever shall eat of this bread will not die' – that is to say, that whosoever shall partake of this divine food will attain unto eternal life: that is, every one who partakes of this bounty and receives these perfections will find eternal life, will obtain preexistent favours, will be freed from the darkness of error, and will be illuminated by the light of His guidance 121

thank God that thou wert fed from the table which hath descended from heaven. That food is the 'I am the bread which descended from heaven,' recorded in the Gospel. That is faith, certainty, love and knowledge TAB 677

the Christians believe that after Christ, no prophet with Laws will come, but that Christ himself will descend from heaven *Jesus Christ* SW IX 10, p111

Disaster

a disaster that razed to its foundations the Temple of Solomon, destroyed the Holy of Holies, laid waste the city of David, uprooted the Jewish hierarchy in Jerusalem, massacred thousands of the Jewish people – the persecutors of the religion of Jesus Christ . . . and reared a pagan colony on Zion PDC 96

Disavow

and likewise, He [Muḥammad] saith: 'Say, O people of the Book! do ye not disavow us only because we believe in God and in what He hath sent down to us, and in what He hath sent down aforetime, and because most of you are doers of ill?' How explicitly doth this verse reveal Our purpose *Islám* KI 217

Disbelieve

by the righteousness of Him Who hath called thee into being and unto Whom ere long thou shalt return, if thou remainest, at the moment of death, a disbeliever in the signs of thy Lord thou shalt surely enter the gates of hell, and none of the deeds thy hands have wrought will profit thee, nor shalt thou find a patron nor anyone to plead for thee – re: Epistle to Muḥammad Sh̲áh SB 19

at the time of the manifestation of Him Whom God shall make manifest everyone should be well trained in the teachings of the Bayán, so that none of the followers may outwardly cling to the Bayán and thus forfeit their allegiance unto Him. If anyone does so, the verdict of 'disbeliever in God' shall be passed upon him 85

Disciple [see also *Apostles of Christ*]

Solomon – re: Greek philosophers SDC 77

after Christ four disciples, among whom were Peter and Paul, permitted the use of animal food forbidden by the Bible, except the eating of those animals which had been strangled, or which were sacrificed to idols, and of blood SAQ 93

Disciple

after the death of Christ the disciples were troubled, and their ideas and thoughts were discordant and contradictory; later they became firm and united, and at the feast of Pentecost they gathered together and detached themselves from the things of this world. Disregarding themselves, they renounced their comfort and worldly happiness, sacrificing their body and soul to the Beloved, abandoning their houses, and becoming wanderers and homeless, even forgetting their own existence. Then they received the help of God, and the power of the Holy Spirit became manifested; the spirituality of Christ triumphed, and the love of God reigned. They were given help at that time and dispersed in different directions, teaching the Cause of God, and giving forth proofs and evidences 106

when the disciples were calling in the name of Christ, the Jews scoffed, scorned and laughed at them. They were saying, 'They are taken with madness, and madness is made an art.' They even beat them with whips, threw stones at them, prevented the people from approaching them, and were saying, 'This man is naught but a sorcerer, blasphemeth God and is possessed of a devil' BWF 394

the first institute by the disciples was a Temple. They planned a church in every country *Temple* 418

observe the gatherings of the disciples after Christ: Their light is still shining, their power is still revealing and their trumpets still resounding throughout the ages. Such is the spiritual meeting TAB 69

Crucifixion – re: after the crucifixion 193–4

Assemblage – re: Pentecost 301

the injunction of 'Abdu'l-Bahá bequeathed in His Will to follow in the footsteps of the disciples of Jesus Christ GPB 389

'the disciples of Christ forgot themselves and all earthly things, forsook all their cares and belongings, purged themselves of self and passion, and with absolute detachment scattered far and wide and engaged in calling the peoples of the world to the divine guidance; till at last they made the world another world, illumined the surface of the earth, and even to their last hour proved self-sacrificing in the pathway of that beloved One of God. Finally in various lands they suffered glorious martyrdom. Let them that are men of action follow in their footsteps' BA 69

Divine Physician

the Prophets of God should be regarded as physicians *Prophet* G 79

no man, however acute his perception, can ever hope to reach the heights which the wisdom and understanding of the Divine Physician have attained. Little wonder, then, if the treatment prescribed by the physician in this day should not be found to be identical with that which he prescribed before. How could it be otherwise when the ills affecting the sufferer necessitate at every stage of his sickness a special remedy 79–80

Divines

respect ye the divines and learned amongst you, they whose conduct accord with their professions G 128

they who disregard and neglect the divines and learned that live amongst them – these have truly changed the favour with which God hath favoured them 128

those divines, however, who are truly adorned with the ornament of knowledge and of a goodly character are, verily, as a head to the body of the world, and as eyes to the nations ESW 16–17 for this reason, in all sacred books mention hath been made of the divines of every age. Thus He saith: 'O people of the Book! Why disbelieve the signs of God to which ye yourselves have been witnesses?' And also He saith: 'O people of the Book! Why clothe ye the truth with falsehood? Why wittingly hide the truth?' Again, He saith: 'Say, O people of the Book, Why repel believers from the way of God?' It is evident that by the 'people of the Book,' who have repelled their fellowmen from the straight path of God, is meant none other than the divines of that age, whose names and character have been revealed in the sacred books, and alluded to in the verses and traditions recorded therein, were you to observe with the eye of God — KI 16

they therefore became deprived of the streaming grace of the Muḥammadan Revelation and its showering bounties – re: Christian divines *Muḥammad* — 26

as most of the divines have failed to apprehend the meaning of these verses, and have not grasped the significance of the Day of Resurrection, they therefore have foolishly interpreted these verses according to their idle and faulty conception — 78

it was owing to their misunderstanding of these truths that many a Christian divine hath objected to Muḥammad, and voiced his protest in such words: 'If thou art in truth the promised Prophet, why then art Thou not accompanied by those angels our sacred Books foretold, and which must needs descend with the promised Beauty to assist Him in His Revelation and act as warners unto His people?' — 81

Corruption of the Text – re: perverting the text — 86

these divines, in order to please the rich, acquire worldly emoluments, and give vent to their envy and misbelief, wrote a number of treatises, refuting the claims of Muḥammad, supporting their arguments with such evidences as it would be improper to mention, and claimed that these arguments were derived from the text of the Pentateuch — 87–8

it is evident that wretched generation, in their wicked and satanic fancy, regarded every injury to that immortal Being as a means to the attainment of an abiding felicity; inasmuch as the recognized divines of that age, such as 'Abdu'lláh-i-Ubayy, Abú 'Ámir, the hermit, Ka'b-Ibn-i-As͟hraf, and Naḍr-Ibn-i-Ḥárit͟h, all treated Him as an imposter, and pronounced Him a lunatic and a calumniator – re: Muḥammad — 108

how many of the divines, owing to their rejection of the Truth, have fallen into, and abide within, the uttermost depths of ignorance, and whose names have been effaced from the scroll of the glorious and learned *Abase* — 146

among these 'veils of glory' are the divines and doctors living in the days of the Manifestation of God, who, because of their want of discernment and their love and eagerness for leadership, have failed to submit to the Cause of God, nay, have even refused to incline their ears unto the divine Melody. 'They have thrust their fingers into their ears' — 164

it is clear and evident that whenever the Manifestations of Holiness were revealed, the divines of their day have hindered the people from attaining unto the way of truth. To this testify the records of all the scriptures and heavenly books — 165

for such, today, is the manner of the divines and doctors of the age, who occupy the seats of knowledge and learning, and who have named ignorance knowledge, and called oppression justice *Word* — 182 and now behold the divines of the age who, because of their being honoured by His name, and finding that their fathers have acknowledged His Revelation, have blindly submitted to His truth *Muḥammad* 183

although the outward meaning of 'Whom God causeth to err through a knowledge' is what hath been revealed, yet to Us it signifieth those divines of the age who have turned away from the Beauty of God, and who, clinging unto their own learning, as fashioned by their own fancies and desires, have denounced God's divine Message and Revelation *Knowledge* 214

even as in this Dispensation, not one amongst the renowned divines, in the grasp of whose authority were held the reins of the people, hath embraced the Faith. Nay, they have striven against it with such animosity and determination that no ear hath heard and no eye hath seen the like 229

'out of Baní-Há<u>sh</u>im there shall come forth a Youth Who shall reveal new laws. He shall summon the people unto Him, but none will heed His call. Most of His enemies will be the divines' *Tradition* 242

O concourse of divines! Fear God from this day onwards in the views ye advance, for He Who is Our Remembrance in your midst, and Who cometh from Us, is, in very truth, the Judge and Witness. Turn away from that which ye lay hold of, and which the Book of God, the True One, hath not sanctioned, for on the Day of Resurrection ye shall, upon the Bridge, be, in very truth, held answerable for the position ye occupied SB 44

if the Muslim divines have cause for pride in understanding the meaning of the Holy Writings, His glory is in revealing the Writings, that none of them may hesitate to believe in His words *Writings* 118–19

nay, by God, be thou neither a divine without discernment nor a follower without discernment, for both of these shall perish on the Day of Resurrection. Rather it behooveth thee to be a discerning divine, or to walk with insight in the way of God by obeying a true leader of religion 124

stresses the responsibilities, and censures the conduct, of the Christian divines of a former age who, had they recognized the truth of Muḥammad's mission, He contends, would have been followed by the mass of their co-religionists – re: Báb in His 'Seven Proofs' GPB 26

'the divines of Persia,' He [Bahá'u'lláh] affirms, 'committed that which no people amongst the peoples of the world hath committed.' And again: '. . . The divines of Persia . . . have perpetrated what the Jews have not perpetrated during the Revelation of Him Who is the Spirit (Jesus) 231

'the Friend of God (Abraham) was cast into fire through the sentence pronounced by the divines of the age' [words of Bahá'u'lláh] PDC 80

'the foolish divines,' another Tablet declares, 'have laid aside the Book of God, and are occupied with that which they themselves have fashioned. The Ocean of Knowledge is revealed, and the shrill of the Pen of the Most High is raised, and yet they, even as earth-worms, are afflicted with the clay of their fancies and imaginings. They are exalted by reason of their relationship to the one true God, and yet they have turned aside from Him! Because of Him they have become famous, and yet they are shut off as by a veil from Him!' 81

'the pagan priests,' in yet another Tablet is written, 'and the Jewish and Christian divines, have committed the very things which the divines of the age, in this Dispensation, have committed, and are still committing. Nay, these have displayed a more grievous cruelty and a fiercer malice. Every atom beareth witness unto that which I say' 81 through the actions of Muslim and Christian divines – 'idols,' whom Bahá'u'lláh has stigmatized as constituting the majority of His enemies – who failed, as commanded by Him, to lay aside their pens and fling away their fancies, and who, as He Himself testified, had they believed in Him would have brought about the conversion of the masses, Islám and Christianity have, it would be no exaggeration to say, entered the most critical phase of their history 107

'the divine whose conduct is upright, and the sage who is just, are as the spirit unto the body of the world. Well is it with that divine whose head is attired with the crown of justice, and whose temple is adorned with the ornament of equity' [words of Bahá'u'lláh] 111

Divinity

the whole universe reflecteth His glory, while He is Himself independent of, and transcendeth His creatures. This is the true meaning of Divine unity *Unity* G 165

such references as have been made to Divinity and Godhead by the holy ones and chosen ones of God have been made a cause for denial and repudiation. The Imám Ṣádiq hath said: 'Servitude is a substance, the essence of which is Divinity.' The Commander of the Faithful (Imám 'Alí) answered an Arab, who had questioned him concerning the soul, as follows: 'The third is the soul which is divine and celestial. It is a divine energy, a substance, simple, and self-subsistent.' And further He – peace be upon him – said: 'Therefore it is the Most Sublime Essence of God, the Tree of Blessedness, the Lote-Tree beyond which there is no passing, the Garden of Repose ESW 111–12

alone the Jews believed in the divinity and oneness of God SDC 44

consequently, the Divinity of God, which is the sum of all perfections, reflects itself in the reality of man – that is to say, the Essence of Oneness is the gathering of all perfections, and from this unity He casts a reflection upon the human reality SAQ 196

the more the world of humanity develops, the more the effulgences or emanations of Divinity will become revealed, just as the stone when it becomes polished and pure as a mirror will reflect in fuller degree the glory and splendour of the sun PUP 59

concerning the essence of Divinity: in truth it is on no account determined by anything apart from its own nature, and can in no wise be comprehended . . . Thus man cannot grasp the Essence of Divinity, but can, by his reasoning power, by observation, by his intuitive faculties and the revealing power of his faith, believe in God, discover the bounties of His Grace BWF 341

that Essence of the Divine Entity and the Unseen of the unseen is holy above imagination and is beyond thought. Consciousness doth not reach It. Within the capacity of comprehension of a produced reality that Ancient Reality cannot be contained. It is a different world; from it there is no information; arrival thereat is impossible; attainment thereto is prohibited and inaccessible. This much is known: It exists and Its existence is certain and proven – but the condition is unknown 382

His Holiness Christ announced, 'That which is born of flesh is flesh and that which is born of spirit is spirit,' meaning that man must be born again. As the babe is born into the light of this physical world so must the physical and intellectual man be born into the light of the world of divinity FWU 59

Divorce

had annulled the law of divorce and of the sabbath day – re: Christ *Annul* KI 18

He abolished certain unimportant laws and forms which were no longer compatible with the exigencies of the time, such as divorce and plurality of wives *Jesus Christ* FWU 75

Dogma

gradually these heavenly teachings and foundations of reality have been beclouded by human interpretations and dogmatic imitations of ancestral beliefs PUP 141

just as the thoughts and hypotheses of past ages are fruitless today, likewise dogmas and codes of human invention are obsolete and barren of product in religion . . . For if we remain fettered and restricted by human inventions and dogmas, day by day the world of mankind will be degraded, day by day warfare and strife will increase and satanic forces converge toward the destruction of the human race 144

if a man would succeed in his search after truth, he must, in the first place, shut his eyes to all the traditional superstitions of the past. PT 135
The Jews have traditional superstitions, the Buddhists and the Zoroastrians are not free from them, neither are the Christians! All religions have gradually become bound by tradition and dogma

unless we make a distinction in our minds between dogma, superstition and prejudice on the one hand, and truth on the other, we cannot succeed. When we are in earnest in our search for anything we look for it everywhere. This principle we must carry out in our search for truth 136–7

when religion, shorn of its superstitions, traditions, and unintelligent dogmas, shows its conformity with science, then will there be a great unifying, cleansing force in the world which will sweep before it all wars, disagreements, discords and struggles – and then will mankind be united in the power of the Love of God 146

the differences which have arisen between us are due to blind imitations of dogmatic beliefs and adherence to ancestral forms of worship FWU 92

to those irrational and superstitious beliefs which have insensibly crept, in the first century of the Christian era, into the teachings of Jesus Christ, and by crystallizing into accepted dogmas have impaired the effectiveness and obscured the purpose of the Christian Faith WOB 138

it is only from dogmas and creeds of the churches that we dissociate ourselves, not from the Spirit of Christianity (Letter) LG 121

Dove

then it is evident that the dove which descended upon Christ was not a material dove, but it was a spiritual state, which, that it might be comprehensible, was expressed by a sensible figure SAQ 85

how much better if they would live like a flock of doves in peace and harmony, instead of being like wolves and tearing each other to pieces PT 115

Most Great Spirit – re: symbolism of dove GPB 101

Dragon

Beast – re: Umayyads SAQ 51

'and there appeared a great wonder in heaven; and behold a great red dragon, having seven heads and ten horns, and seven crowns upon his heads. And his tail drew the third part of the stars of heaven, and did cast them to the earth.' These signs are an allusion to the dynasty of the Umayyads who dominated the Muḥammadan religion. Seven heads and 69–70 seven crowns mean seven countries and dominions over which the Umayyads had power: they were the Roman dominion around Damascus; and the Persian, Arabian and Egyptian dominions, together with the dominion of Africa – that is to say, Tunis, Morocco and Algeria; the dominion of Andalusia, which is now Spain; and the dominion of the Turks of Transoxania. The Umayyads had power over these countries. The ten horns mean the names of the Umayyad rulers – that is, without repetition, there were ten names of rulers, meaning ten names of commanders and chiefs – the first is Abú Sufyán and the last Marván – but several of them bear the same name. So there are two Mu'ávíya, three Yazíd, two Valíd, and two Marván; but if the names were counted without repetition there would be ten. The Umayyads, of whom the first was Abú Sufyán, Amír of Mecca and chief of the dynasty of the Umayyads, and the last was Marván, destroyed the third part of the holy and saintly people of the lineage of Muḥammad who were like the stars of heaven – re: Rev. 12:3–4

Earth

'the whole earth shall on the Resurrection Day be but His handful' *Resurrection* KI 47

I swear by God! But for the divine Decree, and the inscrutable dispensations of Providence, the earth itself would have utterly destroyed all this people *People* 172

East

this is the meaning of the sacred verse: 'But nay! I swear by the Lord of the Easts and the Wests' *Lord* KI 43

in the books of the prophets certain glad-tidings are recorded which are absolutely true and free from doubt. The East has ever been the dawning-point of the Sun of Reality. All the prophets of God have appeared there. The religions of God have been promulgated, the teachings of God have been spread and the law of God founded in the East. The Orient has always been the centre of lights. The West has acquired illumination from the East but in some respects the reflection of the light has been greater in the Occident. This is especially true of Christianity FWU 72

Educator

this Wronged One exhorteth the peoples of the world to observe tolerance and righteousness, which are two lights amidst the darkness of the world and two educators for the edification of mankind TB 36

were there no educator, all souls would remain savage, and were it not for the teacher, the children would be ignorant creatures SAB 126

it therefore becometh manifest that amity and cohesion are indicative of the training of the Real Educator, and dispersion and separation a proof of savagery and deprivation of divine education 290

the prophets of God are the first educators. They bestow universal education upon man and cause him to rise from the lowest levels of savagery to the highest pinnacles of spiritual development PUP 84–5

Jesus Christ was an Educator of humanity *Jesus Christ* 85

it is self-evident that the prophets are the educators of men and the teachers of the human race. They come to bestow universal education upon humanity, to give humanity training, to uplift the human race from the abyss of despair and desolation and enable man to attain the apogee of advancement and glory FWU 94

Educator

these holy Manifestations of God are the educators and trainers of the world of existence, the teachers of the world of humanity *Manifestation* 110

Egypt

'and their dead bodies shall lie in the street of the great city, which spiritually is called Sodom and Egypt, where also our Lord was crucified' – re: Umayyads *Dead* SAQ 51–2

Elders

and the four and twenty elders, which sat before God on their seats, fell upon their faces, and worshipped God. SAQ 57

'Saying, We give Thee thanks, O Lord God Almighty, Which art, and wast, and art to come; because Thou hast taken to Thee Thy great power, and hast reigned' [see also *Jacob*]

but in this glorious manifestation there are twenty-four, double the number of all the others, for the greatness of this manifestation requires it. These holy souls are in the presence of God seated on their own thrones, meaning that they reign eternally. 57–8

These twenty-four great persons, though they are seated on the thrones of everlasting rule, yet are worshippers of the appearance of the universal Manifestation, and they are humble and submissive, saying, 'We give thanks to Thee, O Lord God Almighty, Which art, and wast, and art to come, because Thou hast taken to Thee Thy great power and hast reigned' – that is to say, Thou wilt issue all Thy teachings, Thou wilt gather all the people of the earth under Thy shadow, and Thou wilt bring all men under the shadow of one tent

these 'first Letters generated from the Primal Point,' this 'company of angels arrayed before God on the Day of His coming,' these 'Repositories of His Mystery,' these 'Springs that have welled out from the Source of His Revelation,' these first companions who, in the words of the Persian Bayán, 'enjoy nearest access to God,' these 'Luminaries that have, from everlasting, bowed down, and will everlastingly continue to bow down, before the Celestial Throne,' and lastly these 'elders' mentioned in the Book of Revelation as 'sitting before God on their seats,' 'clothed in white raiment' and wearing on their heads 'crowns of gold' – these were, ere their dispersal, summoned to the Báb's presence GPB 7–8

regarding the four and twenty elders: The Master, in a Tablet, stated that they are the Báb, the eighteen Letters of the Living and five others who would be known in the future. So far we do not know who these five others are (Letter 22.7.43) LG 377

Elias

so, having regard to this state and station, Christ announced that John the Baptist was Elias, who was to come before Christ. And the likeness of this station is as that of lamps kindled: for these in respect to their glasses and oil-holders, are different, but in respect to their light, One, and in respect to their illumination, One; nay, each one is identical with the other, without imputation of plurality, or diversity or multiplicity or separateness. This is the Truth and beyond the Truth there is only error BWF 371

Elijah

in the Gospel the return of Christ and Elijah is promised *Jews* SAQ 39

the 'Return of Elijah' anticipated by the Jews, Whose Revelation was to show forth 'the signs and tokens of all the Prophets', Who was to 'manifest the perfection of Moses, the radiance of Jesus and the patience of Job' had appeared – re: the Báb [see *Carmel*] GPB 58 within this Most Holy Land rises the Mountain of God of immemorial sanctity, the Vineyard of the Lord, the Retreat of Elijah, Whose return the Báb Himself symbolizes CF 95

Emmanuel

in reality Emmanuel was the forerunner of the second coming of His Highness the Christ and the herald of the path of the Kingdom [see SAB 60] TAB 539

End

endeavour now to apprehend from these two traditions the mysteries of 'end,' 'return,' and 'creation without beginning or end' *Ḥusayn* KI 168

and yet, feeble souls, through lack of understanding, reject these abstruse utterances, and question the truth of such traditions. Nay, none can comprehend them save those that are possessed of an understanding heart. Say, He is that End for Whom no end in all the universe can be imagined, and for Whom no beginning in the world of creation can be conceived. Behold, O concourse of the earth, the splendours of the End, revealed in the Manifestations of the Beginning 168

in truth I have created Thee through Thyself, then at My Own behest I have fashioned all things through the creative power of Thy Word. We are All-Powerful. I have appointed Thee to be the Beginning and the End, the Seen and the Hidden. Verily We are the All-Knowing. SB 159

No one hath been or will ever be invested with prophethood other than Thee, nor hath any sacred Book been or will be revealed unto any one except Thee. Such is the decree ordained by Him Who is the All-Encompassing, the Best-Beloved [see *Essence* SB 112]

Enemy

'most of His enemies will be the divines' *Tradition* KI 242

Error

'whom God causeth to err through a knowledge' *Divines* KI 214

if ye wish to distinguish truth from error *Essence* SB 142

Essence

through the manifold attributes of these Essences of Detachment, Who are both the first and the last, the seen and the hidden, it is made evident that He Who is the Sun of Truth is 'the First and the Last, the Seen, and the Hidden.' Likewise the other lofty names and exalted attributes of God. Therefore, whosoever, and in whatever Dispensation, hath recognized and attained unto the presence of these glorious, these resplendent and most excellent Luminaries, hath verily attained unto the 'Presence of God' Himself, and entered the city of eternal and immortal life. Attainment unto such presence is possible only in the Day of Resurrection, which is the Day of the rise of God Himself through His all-embracing Revelation. KI 142–3

This is the meaning of the 'Day of Resurrection,' spoken of in all the scriptures, and announced unto all people

essence of existence *Gate* SB 57

this Religion is indeed, in the sight of God, the essence of the Faith of Muḥammad *Religion* 71

fire and paradise both bow down and prostrate themselves before God. That which is worthy of His Essence is to worship Him for His sake, without fear of fire, or hope of paradise 78

it is not permissible to ask questions from Him Whom God will make 101 manifest, except that which well beseemeth Him. For His station is that of the Essence of divine Revelation . . . Whatever evidence of bounty is witnessed in the world, is but an image of His bounty; and every thing owes its existence to His Being

every revelation of His divine Essence betokens the sublimity of His glory, the loftiness of His sanctity, the inaccessible height of His oneness and the exaltation of His majesty and power. His beginning hath had no beginning other than His Own firstness and His end knoweth no end save His Own lastness 112

if ye wish to distinguish truth from error, consider those who believe in Him Whom God shall make manifest and those who disbelieve Him at the time of His appearance. The former represent the essence of truth, as attested in the Book of God, while the latter the essence of error, as attested in that same Book 142

Evangel

they read the Evangel and yet refuse to acknowledge the All-Glorious Lord, notwithstanding that He hath come through the potency of His exalted, His mighty and glorious dominion. We, verily, have come for your sakes, and have borne the misfortunes of the world for your salvation TB 10

and the laws of the great Evangel, the rock-foundation on which the civilization of the world was based, turned barren of results *Priests* SDC 86

at another, We address the people of the Evangel and say: 'The All-Glorious is come in this Name whereby the Breeze of God hath wafted over all regions' PDC 76

Eve

therefore, this story of Adam and Eve who ate from the tree, and their expulsion from Paradise, must be thought of simply as a symbol SAQ 123

Adam signifies the heavenly spirit of Adam, and Eve His human soul. For in some passages in the Holy Books where women are mentioned, they represent the soul of man. The tree of good and evil signifies the human world; for the spiritual and divine world is purely good and absolutely luminous, but in the human world light and darkness, good and evil, exist as opposite conditions [see also *Serpent* 123–4, 126] 123

Evolution

God, the Vigilant, the Just, the Loving, the All-Wise Ordainer, can, in this supreme Dispensation, neither allow the sins of an unregenerate humanity, whether of omission or of commission, to go unpunished, nor will He be willing to abandon His children to their fate, and refuse them that culminating and blissful stage in their long, their slow and painful evolution throughout the ages, which is at once their inalienable right and their true destiny PDC 4–5

just as the organic evolution of mankind has been slow and gradual, and involved successively the unification of the family, the tribe, the city-state, and the nation, so has the light vouchsafed by the Revelation of God, at various stages in the evolution of religion, and reflected in the successive Dispensations of the past, been slow and progressive. Indeed the measure of Divine Revelation, in every age, has been adapted to, and commensurate with, the degree of social progress achieved in that age by a constantly-evolving humanity 118

Existence

know assuredly that God's creation hath existed from eternity, and will continue to exist forever. Its beginning hath had no beginning, and its end knoweth no end. His name, the Creator, presupposeth a creation, even as His title, the Lord of Men, must involve the existence of a servant G 149–50

Exponent

First – re: as both are the Exponents of one and the same Cause KI 161

thy purpose in performing thy deeds is that God may graciously accept them; and divine acceptance can in no wise be achieved except through the acceptance of Him Who is the Exponent of His Revelation. For instance, if the Apostle of God – may divine blessings rest upon Him – accepted a certain deed, in truth God accepted it; otherwise it hath remained within the selfish desires of the person who wrought it, and did not reach the presence of God. Likewise, any act which is accepted by the Point of the Bayán is accepted by God, inasmuch as the contingent world hath no other access unto the presence of the Ancient of Days. Whatever is sent down cometh through the Exponent of His Revelation, and whatever ascendeth, ascendeth unto the Exponent of His Revelation SB 81

Extinguish

so much so that Pharaoh and his people finally arose and exerted their utmost endeavour to extinguish with the waters of falsehood and denial the fire of that sacred Tree, oblivious of the truth that no earthly water can quench the flame of divine wisdom, nor mortal blasts extinguish the lamp of everlasting dominion. Nay, rather, such water cannot but intensify the burning of the flame, and such blasts cannot but ensure the preservation of the lamp KI 11–12

thus hath God laid hold of them for their sins, hath extinguished in them the spirit of faith, and tormented them with the flames of the nethermost fire. And this for no other reason except that Israel refused to apprehend the meaning of such words as have been revealed in the Bible concerning the signs of the coming Revelation 18

Face

Face of God *Primal Point* SB 36

this is the divinely-inscribed Book. This is the outspread Tablet. Say, this indeed is the Frequented Fane, the sweet-scented Leaf, the Tree of divine Revelation, the surging Ocean, the Utterance which lay concealed, the Light above every light . . . Indeed every light is generated by God through the power of His behest. He of a truth is the Light of the kingdom of heaven and earth and whatever is between them. Through the radiance of His light God imparteth illumination to your hearts and maketh firm your steps, that perchance ye may yield praise unto Him. 154–5

Say, this of a certainty is the Garden of Repose, the loftiest Point of adoration, the Tree beyond which there is no passing, the blessed Lote-Tree, the Most Mighty Sign, the most beauteous Countenance and the most comely Face

will have attained the summit of their existence, and will have been brought face to face with their Beloved *Beloved* 156

Faith

as soon as they drank the immortal draught of faith, from the cup of certitude, at the hand of the Manifestation of the All-Glorious *Transform* KI 155

Faith

if ye fail to believe in Him, then your faith in Muḥammad and His Book which was revealed in the past will indeed be treated as false in the estimation of God – re: Bayán *Qur'án* SB 46

whenever the faithful hear the verses of this Book being recited, their eyes will overflow with tears and their hearts will be deeply touched by Him Who is the Most Great Remembrance for the love they cherish for God, the All-Praised. He is God, the All-knowing, the Eternal. They are indeed the inmates of the all-highest Paradise wherein they will abide for ever. Verily they will see naught therein save that which hath proceeded from God, nothing that will lie beyond the compass of their understanding. There they will meet the believers in Paradise, who will address them with the words 'Peace, Peace' lingering on their lips 62–3

this Religion is indeed, in the sight of God, the essence of the Faith of Muḥammad – re: Bábí Religion *Religion* 71

today, however, when only belief in this Faith truly profiteth you, ye have debarred yourselves therefrom by reason of the things which are disadvantageous unto you and will inflict harm upon you, whereas He Who is the Manifestation of My Self hath been and shall ever remain immune from any harm whatever, and any loss that hath appeared or will appear shall eventually revert unto yourselves 88

well versed in every science, yet it is their adherence to the holy Word of God which will determine their faith *Word* 88

man's highest station, however, is attained through faith in God in every Dispensation and by acceptance of what hath been revealed by Him, and not through learning *Station* 89

say, verily any one follower of this Faith can, by the leave of God, prevail over all who dwell in heaven and earth and in whatever lieth between them; for indeed this is, beyond the shadow of a doubt, the one true Faith. Therefore fear ye not, neither be ye grieved 153

for the Faith of Bahá'u'lláh – if we would faithfully appraise it – can never, and in no aspect of its teachings, be at variance, much less in conflict, with the purpose animating, or the authority invested in, the Faith of Jesus Christ WOB 185

is not faith but another word for implicit obedience, whole-hearted allegiance, uncompromising adherence to that which we believe is the revealed and express will of God BA 62–3

Islám attained a very high spiritual state, but western scholars are prone to judging it by Christian standards. One cannot call one world Faith superior to another, as they all come from God; they are progressive, each suited to certain needs of the times (Letter 19.11.45) LG 371

Father

say, Lo! The Father is come, and that which ye were promised in the Kingdom is fulfilled! This is the Word which the Son concealed, when to those around Him He said: 'Ye cannot bear it now.' And when the appointed time was fulfilled and the Hour had struck, the Word shone forth above the horizon of the Will of God. Beware, O followers of the Son, that ye cast it not behind your backs TB 11

hearken unto the melodies of the Gospel with the ear of fairness. He saith – glorified be His utterance – prophesying the things that are to come: 'But of that Day and Hour knoweth no man, no, not the angels of heaven, nor the Son, but the Father.' By Father in this connection is meant God – exalted be His glory. He, verily, is the True Educator, and the Spiritual Teacher ESW 143 how could she claim that a Babe Whose father was unknown had been conceived of the Holy Ghost? *Mary* KI 56–7

God conferred upon that essence of the Spirit, Who was known amongst the people as fatherless, the glory of Prophethood *Spirit* 57

'verily we found our fathers with a faith, and verily, in their footsteps we follow' 155

and when Our clear verses are recited to them, their only argument is to say, 'Bring back our fathers, if ye speak the truth!' *Verse* 209

'this is merely a man who would fain pervert you from your father's worship' *Knowledge* 214–15

Messiah – re: Son and Father SAB 40

this is the meaning of the Messiah's words, that the Father is in the Son. Dost thou not see that should a stainless mirror proclaim, 'Verily is the sun ashine within me, together with all its qualities, tokens and signs', such an utterance by such a mirror would be neither deceptive nor false? 42

for this reason did Christ say: 'I have yet many things to say unto you, matters needing to be told, but ye cannot bear to hear them now. Howbeit when that Comforting Spirit, Whom the Father will send, shall come, He will make plain unto you the truth' 59

the Sun of Reality, as we have said, has always been in one condition; it has no change, no alteration, no transformation and no vicissitude. It is eternal and everlasting. But the Holy Reality of the Word of God is in the condition of the pure, fine and shining mirror; the heat, the light, the image and likeness – that is to say, the perfections of the Sun of Reality – appear in it. That is why Christ says in the Gospel, 'The Father is in the Son' – that is to say, the Sun of Reality appears in the mirror SAQ 207

the Lord Christ said, 'He that hath seen Me hath seen the Father' – God manifested in man PT 26

why is it thus? Why do we not love one another and live in unity?
It is because we have shut our eyes to the underlying principle of all religions, that God is one, that He is the Father of us all, that we are all immersed in the ocean of His mercy and sheltered and protected by His loving care 120

the Word which the Son concealed is made manifest. It hath been sent down in the form of the human temple in this day. Blessed be the Lord Who is the Father – re: Tablet to the Pope BWF 62

in it the Tabernacle of the promised 'Lord of Hosts' was first erected, and the foundations of the long-awaited Kingdom of the 'Father' unassailably established. Out of it went forth the earliest tidings of the Message of Salvation which, as prophesied by Daniel, was to mark, after the lapse of 'a thousand two hundred and ninety days' (1290 AH), the end of 'the abomination that maketh desolate' – re: Baghdád – the 'Abode of Peace' GPB 110

in several passages addressed to the entire body of the followers of Jesus Christ He identifies Himself with the 'Father' spoken of by Isaiah – re: Bahá'u'lláh 210

such is the pass to which the Christian clergy have come – a clergy that have interposed themselves between their flock and the Christ returned in the glory of the Father [see GPB 230] PDC 106

Fealty

and also He saith: 'In truth, they who plighted fealty unto thee, really plighted that fealty unto God' *God* KI 178–9

Fidelity

Job proved the fidelity of his love for God by being faithful through his great adversity, as well as during the prosperity of his life *Job* PT 50

the trials of Peter tested his fidelity *Peter* 50

Fire

there He heard the soul-stirring Voice of the Spirit speaking from out of the kindled Fire, bidding Him to shed upon Pharaohic souls the light of divine guidance *Moses* KI 54

thus in every Dispensation a number of souls enter the fire by reason of their following in the footsteps of others *Judge* SB 91

this judgment of God, as viewed by those who have recognized Bahá'u'lláh as His Mouthpiece and His greatest Messenger on earth, is both a retributory calamity and an act of holy and supreme discipline. It is at once a visitation from God and a cleansing process for all mankind. Its fires punish the perversity of the human race, and weld its component parts into one organic, indivisible, world-embracing community. Mankind, in these fateful years, which at once signalize the passing of the first century of the Bahá'í Era and proclaim the opening of a new one, is, as ordained by Him Who is both the Judge and the Redeemer of the human race, being simultaneously called upon to give account of its past actions, and is being purged and prepared for its future mission PDC 4

God, however, as has been pointed out in the very beginning of these pages, does not only punish the wrong-doings of His children. He chastises because He is just, and He chastens because He loves. Having chastened them, He cannot, in His great mercy, leave them to their fate. Indeed, by the very act of chastening them He prepares them for the mission for which He has created them. 'My calamity is My providence,' He, by the mouth of Bahá'u'lláh, has assured them, 'outwardly it is fire and vengeance, but inwardly it is light and mercy' 115–16

Sacred fire – re: symbol *Most Great Spirit* GPB 101

First

the First and the Last, the Seen, and the Hidden *Essence* KI 142–3

from these statements therefore it hath been made evident and manifest that should a Soul in the 'End that knoweth no end' be made manifest, and arise to proclaim and uphold a Cause which in 'the Beginning that hath no beginning' another Soul had proclaimed and upheld, it can be truly declared of Him Who is the Last and of Him Who was the First that they are one and the same, inasmuch as both are the Exponents of one and the same Cause 161

even as in the 'Beginning that hath no beginning' the term 'last' is truly applicable unto Him Who is the Educator of the visible and of the invisible, in like manner, are the terms 'first' and 'last' applicable unto His Manifestations. They are at the same time the Exponents of both the 'first' and the 'last'. Whilst established upon the seat of the 'first,' they occupy the throne of the 'last.' Were a discerning eye to be found, it will readily perceive that the exponents of the 'first' and the 'last,' of the 'manifest' and the 'hidden,' of the 'beginning' and the 'seal' are none other than these holy Beings, these Essences of Detachment, these divine Souls 163

Follow

dost thou desire to follow such divines *Christianity* SB 124

be thou neither a divine without discernment nor a follower without 124

discernment, for both of these shall perish on the Day of Resurrection *Divines*
consider the followers of Jesus *Good-Pleasure* 124

Food

permitted the use of animal food forbidden by the Bible *Disciple* SAQ 93
the Spirit breathing through the Holy Scriptures is food for all who hunger. God Who has given the revelation to His Prophets will surely give of His abundance daily bread to all those who ask Him faithfully PT 57
Apostles of Christ – re: Lord's Supper as heavenly food BWF 391
make ye an effort in every meeting that the Lord's Supper may become realized and the heavenly food descend. This heavenly food is knowledge, understanding, faith, assurance, love, affinity, kindness, purity of purpose, attraction of hearts and the union of souls. It was this manner of the Lord's Supper which descended from the heavenly kingdom in the day of Christ 407–8
thank God that thou wert fed from the table which hath descended from heaven. That food is the 'I am the bread which descended from heaven,' recorded in the Gospel. That is faith, certainty, love and knowledge TAB 677
the manna which came from heaven for the disciples, was neither cress, onion, lentil, garlic nor leek. It was bounty and knowledge; it was faith and assurance; it was love and attraction; it was attachment and enkindlement by the fire of the love of God. These spiritual foods were present upon that table. As the disciples ate from these bounties of His Holiness Christ, they became filled with the love of Christ; they hastened to all parts of the world and heralded the Kingdom of God SW XI 16, p275

Footsteps

'verily we found our fathers with a faith, and verily, in their footsteps we follow' *Tradition* KI 155
thus on the Day of Resurrection God will ask everyone of his understanding and not of his following in the footsteps of others *Truth* SB 90
thus in every Dispensation a number of souls enter the fire by reason of their following in the footsteps of others *Judge* 91
the learned men of Christendom are held to be learned by virtue of their safeguarding the teaching of Christ, and yet consider how they themselves have been the cause of men's failure to accept the Faith and attain unto salvation! Is it still thy wish to follow in their footsteps? *Christianity* 123
how great hath been the number of those who have falsely laid claim to a cause within Islám, and ye followed in their footsteps without having witnessed a single proof. What evidence can ye then produce in the presence of your Lord, if ye do but meditate a while? 134

Forerunner

the sign of the invisible heaven must needs be revealed in the person of that perfect man who, before each Manifestation appeareth, educateth, and prepareth the souls of men for the advent of the divine Luminary, the Light of the unity of God amongst men [discourse on, 64–6] KI 66

Foundation

Christ ratified and proclaimed the foundation of the law of Moses. Muḥammad and all the Prophets have revoiced that same foundation of reality. Therefore, the purposes and accomplishments of the divine Messengers have been one and the same. They were the source of PUP 366 advancement to the body politic and the cause of the honour and divine civilization of humanity, the foundation of which is one and the same in every dispensation

Frequented Fane

say, this indeed is the Frequented Fane, the sweet-scented Leaf, the Tree of divine Revelation *Face* SB 154

Gabriel

Most Great Spirit – re: symbol GPB 101

Garden

today, to this melody of the Company on high, the world will leap and dance: 'Glory be to my Lord, the All-Glorious!' But know ye this:. . . save for this nightingale-cry of truth from the Garden of God, no melody will lure away the heart. 'Whence cometh this Singer Who speaketh the Beloved's name?' SAB 93

the Lord of all mankind hath fashioned this human realm to be a Garden of Eden, an earthly paradise. If, as it must, it findeth the way to harmony and peace, to love and mutual trust, it will become a true abode of bliss, a place of manifold blessings and unending delights. Therein shall be revealed the excellence of humankind, therein shall the rays of the Sun of Truth shine forth on every hand 275

the gardeners of the world of humanity are the Prophets of God SAQ 194

know that in every home where God is praised and prayed to, and His Kingdom proclaimed, that home is a garden of God and a paradise of His happiness TAB 69

Gate

fear ye God and breathe not a word concerning His Most Great Remembrance other than what hath been ordained by God, inasmuch as We have established a separate covenant regarding Him with every Prophet and His followers. Indeed, We have not sent any Messenger without this binding covenant and We do not, of a truth, pass judgement upon anything except after the covenant of Him Who is the Supreme Gate hath been established. Ere long the veil shall be lifted from your eyes at the appointed time. Ye shall then behold the sublime Remembrance of God, unclouded and vivid SB 46

the angels and the spirits, arrayed rank upon rank, descend, by the leave of God, upon this Gate and circle round this Focal Point in a far-stretching line. Greet them with salutations, O Qurratu'l-'Ayn, for the dawn hath indeed broken; then proclaim unto the concourse of the faithful: 'Is not the rising of the Morn, foreshadowed in the Mother Book, to be near at hand?. . .' 50

O Qurratu'l-'Ayn! Say: Verily I am the 'Gate of God' and I give you to drink, by the leave of God, the sovereign Truth, of the crystal-pure waters of His Revelation which are gushing out from the incorruptible Fountain situate upon the Holy Mount. And those who earnestly strive after the One True God, let them then strive to attain this Gate. Verily God is potent over all things 50

O ye peoples of the earth! During the time of My absence I sent down the Gates unto you. However the believers, except for a handful, obeyed them not. Formerly I sent forth unto you Aḥmad and more recently Káẓim, but apart from the pure in heart amongst you no one followed them. What hath befallen you, O people of the Book? Will ye not fear the One true God, He Who is your Lord, the Ancient of Days? . . . O ye 51–2 who profess belief in God! I adjure you by Him Who is the Eternal Truth, have ye discerned among the precepts of these Gates anything inconsistent with the commandments of God as set forth in this Book? Hath your learning deluded you by reason of your impiety? Take ye heed then, for verily your God, the Lord of Eternal Truth, is with you and in very truth is watchful over you

O ye peoples of the earth! Hearken unto My call, ringing forth from the precincts of this sacred Tree – a Tree set ablaze by the pre-existent Fire: There is no God but Him; He is the Exalted, the All-Wise. O ye the servants of the Merciful One! Enter ye, one and all, through this Gate and follow not the steps of the Evil One, for he prompteth you to walk in the ways of impiety and wickedness; he is, in truth, your declared enemy 56–7

indeed God hath created everywhere around this Gate oceans of divine elixir, tinged crimson with the essence of existence and vitalized through the animating power of the desired fruit; and for them God hath provided Arks of ruby, tender, crimson-coloured, wherein none shall sail but the people of Bahá, by the leave of God, the Most Exalted; and verily He is the All-Glorious, the All-Wise 57–8

Gems of Holiness

hath caused those luminous Gems of Holiness to appear out of the realm of the spirit, in the noble form of the human temple, and be made manifest unto all men, that they may impart unto the world the mysteries of the unchangeable Being, and tell of the subleties of His imperishable Essence. These sanctified Mirrors, these Day-springs of ancient glory are one and all the Exponents on earth of Him Who is the central Orb of the universe, its Essence and ultimate Purpose. From Him proceed their knowledge and power; from Him is derived their sovereignty. The beauty of their countenance is but a reflection of His image, and their revelation is a sign of His deathless glory. They are the Treasuries of divine knowledge, and the Repositories of celestial wisdom. Through them is transmitted a grace that is infinite, and by them is revealed the light that can never fade. Even as He hath said: 'There is no distinction whatsoever between Thee and Them; except that they are Thy servants, and are created of Thee.' This is the significance of the tradition: 'I am He, Himself, and He is I, myself.' KI 99–100

Glad-Tidings

truly, I say, complete capacity and ability is the cause of the appearance of the divine gifts. Souls are many who in the years gone by have listened to the glad-tidings, but up to this time they have remained veiled, deprived and unmoved. But, through the bounty of the Beauty of Abhá, as soon as thou didst hear the call, thou didst turn thy face toward the Lord of Hosts and became a believer in God and assured of His divine verses. Immediately the Most Great Name made an impression upon thee TAB 639

God

through their appearance the Revelation of God is made manifest, and by their countenance the Beauty of God is revealed. Thus it is that the accents of God Himself have been heard uttered by these Manifestations of the Divine Being G 53

that which He hath reserved for Himself are the cities of men's hearts; and of these the loved ones of Him Who is the Sovereign Truth are, in this Day, as the keys. Please God they may, one and all, be enabled to unlock, through the power of the Most Great Name, the gates of these cities. This is what is meant by aiding the one true God 240–41

to every discerning and illumined heart it is evident that God, the KI 98
unknowable Essence, the divine Being, is immensely exalted beyond
every human attribute, such as corporeal existence, ascent and descent,
egress and regress. Far be it from His glory that human tongue should
adequately recount His praise, or that human heart comprehend His
fathomless mystery. He is and hath ever been veiled in the ancient
eternity of His Essence, and will remain in His Reality everlastingly
hidden from the sight of men. 'No vision taketh in Him, but He taketh in
all vision; He is the Subtile, the All-Perceiving.' No tie of direct
intercourse can possibly bind Him to His creatures

gracious God! How could there be conceived any existing relationship or 98–9
possible connection between His Word and they that are created of it?
The verse: 'God would have you beware of Himself' unmistakably
beareth witness to the reality of Our argument, and the words: 'God was
alone; there was none else beside Him' are a sure testimony of its truth

manifold are the verses that have been repeatedly revealed in all the 101–2
heavenly Books and the holy Scriptures, expressive of this most subtle
and lofty theme. Even as He hath revealed: 'We will surely show them
Our signs in the world and within themselves.' Again He saith: 'And also
in your own selves: will ye not then behold the signs of God?' And yet
again He revealeth: 'And be ye not like those who forget God, and
whom He hath therefore caused to forget their own selves.' In this
connection, He Who is the eternal King – may the souls of all that dwell
within the mystic Tabernacle be a sacrifice unto Him – hath spoken: 'He
hath known God who hath known himself'

'no thing have I perceived, except that I perceived God within it, God 102
before it, or God after it' *Revelation*

what He pleaseth will God abrogate or confirm: for with Him is the Source 147
of Revelation *Proof*

and wert thou to soar in the holy realm of 'God was alone, there was none 163–4
else besides Him,' thou wilt find in that Court all these names utterly
non-existent and completely forgotten. Then will thine eyes no longer be
obscured by these veils, these terms, and allusions. How ethereal and
lofty is this station, unto which even Gabriel, unshepherded, can never
attain, and the Bird of Heaven, unassisted, can never reach

the Cause of God, all deeds and words, are held within the grasp of His 170–71
power. 'All things lie imprisoned within the hollow of His mighty Hand;
all things are easy and possible unto Him.' He accomplisheth whatsoever
He willeth, and doeth all that He desireth. 'Whoso sayeth "why" or
"wherefore" hath spoken blasphemy!' Were these people to shake off
the slumber of negligence and realize that which their hands have
wrought, they would surely perish, and would of their own accord cast
themselves into fire – their end and real abode. Have they not heard that
which He hath revealed: 'He shall not be asked of His doings?' In the
light of these utterances, how can man be so bold as to question Him, and
busy himself with idle sayings?

nothing whatsoever is possible without His permission; no power can 176
endure save through His power, and there is none other God but He. His
is the world of creation, and His the Cause of God. All proclaim His
Revelation, and all unfold the mysteries of His Spirit

were any of the all-embracing Manifestations of God to declare: 'I am 178–9
God!' He verily speaketh the truth, and no doubt attacheth thereto. For
it hath been repeatedly demonstrated that through their Revelation,
their attributes and names, the Revelation of God, His name and His

attributes, are made manifest in the world. Thus, He hath revealed: 'Those shafts were God's, not Thine!' And also He saith: 'In truth, they who plighted fealty unto thee, really plighted that fealty unto God'

'what thinkest thou? He who hath made a God of his passions, and whom God hath caused to err through a knowledge' *Leaders* 214

Face of God *Primal Point* SB 36

whoso obeyeth the Remembrance of God and His Book hath in truth obeyed God and His chosen ones and he will, in the life to come, be reckoned in the presence of God among the inmates of the Paradise of His good-pleasure 43

verily I am the 'Gate of God' *Gate* 50

fire and paradise both bow down and prostrate themselves before God. That which is worthy of His Essence is to worship Him for His sake, without fear of fire, or hope of paradise 78

since all men have issued forth from the shadow of the signs of His Divinity and Lordship, they always tend to take a path, lofty and high. And because they are bereft of a discerning eye to recognize their Beloved, they fall short of their duty to manifest meekness and humility towards Him. Nevertheless, from the beginning of their lives till the end thereof, in conformity with the laws established in the previous religion, they worship God, piously adore Him, bow themselves before His divine Reality and show submissiveness toward His exalted Essence. At the hour of His manifestation, however, they all turn their gaze toward their own selves and are thus shut out from Him, inasmuch as they fancifully regard Him as one like unto themselves. Far from the glory of God is such a comparison. Indeed that august Being resembleth the physical sun, His verses are like its rays, and all believers, should they truly believe in Him, are as mirrors wherein the sun is reflected. Their light is thus a mere reflection 92

Proof – re: verses, a proof which hath proceeded from God 109

however, seek not proofs and evidences after thine idle fancy; but rather base thy proofs upon what God hath appointed *Proof* 124

Good-Pleasure – re: beware lest thou regard as an idle fancy 124

shouldst thou, however, gain a true understanding of God in thine heart of hearts, ere He hath manifested Himself, thou wouldst be able to recognize Him, visible and resplendent, when He unveileth Himself before the eyes of all men 145

Faith – re: prevalence of followers 153

Ascendancy – re: followers of the Truth 153

say, the power of God is in the hearts of those who believe in the unity of God and bear witness that no God is there but Him, while the hearts of them that associate partners with God are impotent, devoid of life on this earth, for assuredly they are dead. 153–4

The Day is approaching when God will render the hosts of Truth victorious, and He will purge the whole earth in such wise that within the compass of His knowledge not a single soul shall remain unless he truly believeth in God, worshippeth none other God but Him, boweth down by day and by night in His adoration, and is reckoned among such as are well assured

all men have proceeded from God and unto Him shall all return *Lord* 157

such is the day of God. For all the days which have come and gone were the days of Abraham, Moses and Christ, or of the other Prophets; but this day is the day of God, for the Sun of Reality will arise in it with the utmost warmth and splendour SAQ 57 know that nothing will benefit thee in this life save supplication and invocation unto God, service in His vineyard, and, with a heart full of love, be in constant servitude unto Him — BWF 375

the good pleasure of God consists in the welfare of all the individual members of mankind — FWU 41

as the divine entity is eternal, the divine attributes are co-existent, co-eternal. The divine bestowals are therefore without beginning, without end. God is infinite; the works of God are infinite; the bestowals of God are infinite. As His divinity is eternal, His Lordship and perfections are without end. As the bounty of the Holy Spirit is eternal, we can never say that His bestowals terminate, else He terminates — 102

within a compass of two hundred pages it proclaims unequivocally the existence and oneness of a personal God, unknowable, inaccessible, the source of all Revelation, eternal, omniscient, omnipresent and almighty – re: Kitáb-i-Íqán — GPB 139

that spirit which is born of God, and on which all success, wherever and however it be sought, must ultimately depend — WOB 52

who, contemplating the helplessness, the fears and miseries of humanity in this day, can any longer question the necessity for a fresh revelation of the quickening power of God's redemptive love and guidance? — 60

does not the very operation of the world-unifying forces that are at work in this age necessitate that He Who is the Bearer of the Message of God in this day should not only reaffirm that self-same exalted standard of individual conduct inculcated by the Prophets gone before Him, but embody in His appeal, to all governments and peoples, the essentials of that social code, that Divine Economy, which must guide humanity's concerted efforts in establishing that all-embracing federation which is to signalize the advent of the Kingdom of God on this earth? — 61

that God-born Force, irresistible in its sweeping power, incalculable in its potency, unpredictable in its course, mysterious in its workings, and awe-inspiring in its manifestations – a Force which, as the Báb has written, 'vibrates within the innermost being of all created things,' and which, according to Bahá'u'lláh, has through its 'vibrating influence,' 'upset the equilibrium of the world and revolutionized its ordered life,' – such a Force, acting even as a two-edged sword, is, under our very eyes, sundering, on the one hand, the age-old ties which for centuries have held together the fabric of civilized society, and is unloosing, on the other, the bonds that still fetter the infant and as yet unemancipated Faith of Bahá'u'lláh — ADJ 39

'the Breath hath been wafted, and the Breeze hath blown, and from Zion hath appeared that which was hidden, and from Jerusalem is heard the Voice of God, the One, the Incomparable, the Omniscient' [words of Bahá'u'lláh] — PDC 77

'the face of the world,' Bahá'u'lláh laments, 'hath altered. The way of God and the religion of God have ceased to be of any worth in the eyes of men.' 'The vitality of men's belief in God,' He also has written, 'is dying out in every land . . . The corrosion of ungodliness is eating into the vitals of human society' — 112–13

the flames which His Divine justice have kindled cleanse an unregenerate humanity, and fuse its discordant, its warring elements as no other agency can cleanse or fuse them. It is not only a retributory and destructive fire, but a disciplinary and creative process, whose aim is the salvation, through unification, of the entire planet. Mysteriously, slowly, and resistlessly God accomplishes His design, though the sight — 116 that meets our eyes in this day be the spectacle of a world hopelessly entangled in its own meshes, utterly careless of the Voice which, for a century, has been calling it to God, and miserably subservient to the siren voices which are attempting to lure it into the vast abyss

are we to doubt that the ways of God are not necessarily the ways of man? BA 62–3
Is not faith but another word for implicit obedience, whole-hearted allegiance, uncompromising adherence to that which we believe is the revealed and express will of God, however perplexing it might first appear, however at variance with the shadowy views, the impotent doctrines, the crude theories, the idle imaginings, the fashionable conceptions of a transient and troublous age? If we are to falter or hesitate, if our love for Him should fail to direct us and keep us within His path, if we desert Divine and emphatic principles, what hope can we any more cherish for healing the ills and sicknesses of this world

what is meant by a personal God is a God who is conscious of His creation, LG 419
Who has a Mind, a Will, a Purpose, and not, as many scientists and materialists believe, an unconscious and determined force operating in the universe. Such conception of Divine Being, as the Supreme and ever present Reality in the world, is not anthropomorphic, for it transcends all human limitations and forms, and does by no means attempt to define the essence of Divinity which is beyond any human comprehension. To say that God is a personal Reality does not mean that He has a physical form, or does in any way resemble a human being. To entertain such belief would be sheer blasphemy (Letter 2.4.39)

Good-Pleasure

moreover, know thou that neither being a man of learning nor being a SB 124
follower is in itself a source of glory. If thou art a man of learning, thy knowledge becometh an honour, and if thou art a follower, thine adherence unto leadership becometh an honour, only when these conform to the good-pleasure of God. And beware lest thou regard as an idle fancy the good-pleasure of God; it is the same as the good-pleasure of His Messenger. Consider the followers of Jesus. They were eagerly seeking the good-pleasure of God, yet none of them attained the good-pleasure of His Apostle which is identical with God's good-pleasure, except such as embraced His Faith

Muḥammad – re: good-pleasure of God 136

then when God manifested Muḥammad as His Messenger and as the 137
Repository of His good-pleasure, they neglected to quicken their souls *Gospel*

the good-pleasure of God consists in the welfare of all the individual FWU 41
members of mankind

Gospel

hearken unto the melodies of the Gospel with the ear of fairness *Father* ESW 143

Joel – re: none aware of the time of the Revelation 143

these are the melodies, sung by Jesus, Son of Mary, in accents of majestic KI 24
power in the Riḍván of the Gospel, revealing those signs that must needs herald the advent of the Manifestation after Him. In the first Gospel according to Matthew it is recorded

there is yet another verse in the Gospel wherein He saith: 'Heaven and 27
earth shall pass away: but My words shall not pass away.' Thus it is that the adherents of Jesus maintained that the law of the Gospel shall never be annulled, and that whensoever the promised Beauty is made manifest and all the signs are revealed, He must needs re-affirm and establish the

law proclaimed in the Gospel, so that there may remain in the world no faith but His faith. This is their fundamental belief

consider now, had the people of the Gospel recognized the meaning of the symbolic terms 'sun' and 'moon' *Symbol* 41–2

were the prophecies recorded in the Gospel to be literally fulfilled *Heaven* 80–81

Our purpose in relating these things is to warn you that were they to maintain that those verses wherein the signs referred to in the Gospel are mentioned have been perverted, were they to reject them, and cling instead to other verses and traditions, you should know that their words were utter falsehood and sheer calumny 88

We have also heard a number of the foolish of the earth assert that the genuine text of the heavenly Gospel doth not exist among the Christians, that it hath ascended unto heaven. How grievously they have erred! How oblivious of the fact that such a statement imputeth the gravest injustice and tyranny to a gracious and loving Providence! How could God, when once the Day-star of the beauty of Jesus had disappeared from the sight of His people, and ascended unto the fourth heaven, cause His holy Book, His most great testimony amongst His creatures, to disappear also? 89

that city is none other than the Word of God revealed in every age and dispensation. In the days of Moses it was the Pentateuch; in the days of Jesus the Gospel 199

even as the Christian divines who, holding fast to the verse of the Gospel to which We have already referred, have sought to explain that the law of the Gospel shall at no time be annulled, and that no independent Prophet shall again be made manifest, unless He confirmeth the law of the Gospel. Most of the people have become afflicted with the same spiritual disease 213

how vast the number of the Letters of the Gospel who eagerly expected Him, yet from the time of His declaration up to five years no one became an inmate of Paradise, except the Commander of the Faithful (Imám 'Alí), and those who secretly believed in Him. All the rest were accounted as inmates of the fire, though they considered themselves as dwellers in Paradise – re: Muḥammad – Point of the Qur'án SB 83

even as the pious deeds of the Christian monks profited them not, inasmuch as at the time of the manifestation of the Apostle of God – may the blessings of God rest upon Him – they contented themselves with the standard set forth in the Gospel 102

from the inception of the mission of Jesus – may peace be upon Him – till the day of His ascension was the Resurrection of Moses. For during that period the Revelation of God shone forth through the appearance of that divine Reality, Who rewarded by His Word everyone who believed in Moses, and punished by His Word everyone who did not believe; inasmuch as God's Testimony for that Day was that which He had solemnly affirmed in the Gospel 107

this is what happened to the monarchs that held fast unto the Gospel. They awaited the coming of the Prophet of God (Muḥammad), and when He did appear, they failed to recognize Him. Behold how great are the sums which these sovereigns expend without even the slightest thought of appointing an official charged with the task of acquainting them in their own realms with the Manifestation of God! They would thereby have fulfilled the purpose for which they had been created. All their desires have been and are still fixed upon leaving behind them traces of their names 117

consider the people unto whom the Gospel was given *Church* 137

ponder upon the people unto whom the Gospel was given. Their religious leaders were considered as the true Guides of the Gospel, yet when they shut themselves out from Muḥammad, the Apostle of God, they turned into guides of error, notwithstanding that all their lives they had faithfully observed the precepts of their religion in order to attain unto Paradise; then when God made Paradise known unto them, they would not enter therein 143

and the wondrous melodies of the Gospel were sounding in the ears of the spiritually illumined *Christ* SDC 44

then the solemn Gospel song rose up till it rang in the ears of those who dwell in the chambers of heaven, and at the touch of Jesus' breath the unmindful dead that lay in the graves of their ignorance lifted up their heads to receive eternal life 80

what a firm foundation of excellent character was laid down in those days, thanks to the training of holy souls who arose to promote the teachings of the Gospel 85

had given up the abiding glory that comes from obedience to the sacred commandments and heavenly teachings of the Gospel *Monk* 86

thou didst ask as to chapter 14, verse 30 of the Gospel of John, where the Lord Christ saith, 'Hereafter I will not talk much with you: for the Prince of this world cometh, and hath nothing in Me.' The Prince of this world is the Blessed Beauty; and 'hath nothing in Me' signifieth: after Me all will draw grace from Me, but He is independent of Me, and will draw no grace from Me. That is, He is rich beyond any grace of Mine SAB 170

how wide is the discrepancy between such acts and the clear Gospel text *Sword* 247–8

Jesus Christ – re: martyrdom of Christ when darkness prevailed SAQ 37–8

this is ascertained from the text of the Gospel where Christ said: 'These are like those of whom Isaiah said, They have eyes and see not, they have ears and hear not; and I healed them' [see *Holy Books*] 102

in the Gospel it is said that a man came to Christ and called Him 'Good Master.' Christ answered, 'Why callest thou Me Good? there is none good but One, that is, God.' This did not mean – God forbid! – that Christ was a sinner; but the intention was to teach submission, humility, meekness and modesty to the man to whom He spoke. These Holy Beings are lights, and light does not unite itself with darkness . . . They are the essence of obedience, and obedience cannot exist with rebellion 170

when in the Gospels, Christ speaks of 'water', He means that which causes life, for without water no worldly creature can live – mineral, vegetable, animal and man, one and all, depend upon water for their very being PT 82

the reality of the gospels *Christianity* FWU 105

Assemblage –re: meeting at Pentecost TAB 301

but there are, in the Gospels, clear expressions indicative of the Trinity; among them: 'The Father is in the Son and the Son is in the Father.' As the Christians did not understand the meaning of this expression, their thoughts were scattered 513

this is why, in the heavenly Books, the divine counsels and commands have been compared to water. So, in the Qur'án it is said, 'and we have caused a pure water to descend from heaven;' and in the Gospel, 'Except a man hath received the baptism of water and of the spirit, he cannot enter into the Kingdom of God' 581

Gospel

which He identified, when addressing the followers of the Gospel in one of His Tablets, with the 'Temple' mentioned by the Prophet Zechariah – re: Bahá'u'lláh about Pentacle GPB 212–13

for this reason, in later generations, voices were raised in protest against the self-appointed Authority which arrogated to itself privileges and powers which did not emanate from the clear text of the Gospel of Jesus Christ, and which constituted a grave departure from the spirit which that Gospel did inculcate. They argued with force and justification that the canons promulgated by the Councils of the Church were not divinely-appointed laws, but were merely human devices which did not even rest upon the actual utterances of Jesus WOB 20–21

the Gospel, however, the only repository of the utterances of Christ, afforded no such shelter to these harassed leaders of the Church, who found themselves helpless in the face of the pitiless onslaught of their enemy, and who eventually had to submit to the forces of schism which invaded their ranks 21

during the lifetime of Jesus Christ the believing, firm souls were few and numbered, but the heavenly blessings descended so plentifully that in a number of years countless souls entered beneath the shadow of the Gospel ADJ 47

that the divine inspiration of the Gospel is fully recognized –re: by the Bahá'í Faith *Christianity* PDC 109

nowhere in the Gospels do we find any reference to the unity of nations or the unification of mankind as a whole 119

words, addressed specifically by Bahá'u'lláh to the followers of the Gospel, in which the fundamental distinction between the Mission of Jesus Christ, concerning primarily the individual, and His own Message, directed more particularly to mankind as a whole, has been definitely established: 'Verily, He (Jesus) said: "Come ye after Me, and I will make you to become fishers of men." In this day, however, We say: "Come ye after Me, that We may make you to become the quickeners of mankind"' 119–20

Grace

for the highest and most excelling grace bestowed upon men is the grace of 'attaining unto the Presence of God' and of His recognition, which has been promised unto all people. This is the utmost degree of grace vouchsafed unto man by the All-Bountiful, the Ancient of Days, and the fulness of His absolute bounty upon His creatures KI 138

Guard

'he must guard himself, defend his faith, oppose his passions and obey the commands of his Lord . . .' *Learned* SDC 34

the first of these requirements is to guard one's own self. It is obvious that this does not refer to protecting oneself from calamities and material tests, for the Prophets and saints were, each and every one, subjected to the bitterest afflictions that the world has to offer, and were targets for all the cruelties and aggressions of mankind. They sacrificed their lives for the welfare of the people, and with all their hearts they hastened to the place of their martyrdom; and with their inward and outward perfections they arrayed humanity in new garments of excellent qualities, both acquired and inborn. The primary meaning of this guarding of oneself is to acquire the attributes of spiritual and material perfection 34–5

Hamzih

moreover, this verse of the Qur'án, revealed concerning Hamzih, the 'Prince of Martyrs,' and Abú-Jahl, is a luminous evidence and sure testimony of the truth of Our saying: 'Shall the dead, whom We have quickened, and for whom We have ordained a light whereby he may walk among men, be like him, whose likeness is in the darkness, whence he will not come forth?' This verse descended from the heaven of the Primal Will at a time when Hamzih had already been invested with the sacred mantle of faith, and Abú-Jahl had waxed relentless in his opposition and unbelief. From the Wellspring of omnipotence and the Source of eternal holiness, there came the judgment that conferred everlasting life upon Hamzih, and condemned Abú-Jahl to eternal damnation — KI 121

Heart

say, the power of God is in the hearts of those who believe in the unity of God and bear witness that no God is there but Him, while the hearts of them that associate partners with God are impotent, devoid of life on this earth, for assuredly they are dead *God* — SB 153

Christ has addressed the world, saying, 'Except ye . . . become as little children, ye shall not enter into the kingdom of heaven' – that is, men must become pure in heart to know God — PUP 53

Heaven

'Lord, send down upon us Thy bread from heaven' *Bread* — KI 22–3

'heaven and earth shall pass away: but My words shall not pass away' *Gospel* — 27

as He hath said: 'When the heaven shall be cloven asunder.' By 'heaven' is meant the heaven of divine Revelation, which is elevated with every Manifestation, and rent asunder with every subsequent one — 44

I swear by God! That this heaven being cloven asunder is, to the discerning, an act mightier than the cleaving of the skies *Cleaving of the Heaven* — 44

as to the signs of the invisible heaven – re: time of Muḥammad *Rúz-bih* — 65

the term 'heaven' denoteth loftiness and exaltation, inasmuch as it is the seat of the revelation of those Manifestations of Holiness, the Day-springs of ancient glory — 67

were the prophecies recorded in the Gospel to be literally fulfilled; were Jesus, Son of Mary, accompanied by angels, to descend from the visible heaven upon the clouds; who would dare to disbelieve, who would dare to reject the truth, and wax disdainful? — 80–81

verily the heaven into which the Messiah rose up was not this unending sky, rather was His heaven the Kingdom of His beneficent Lord. Even as He Himself hath said, 'I came down from heaven,' . . . Hence it is clear that His heaven is beyond all directional points; it encircleth all existence, and is raised up for those who worship God — SAB 167–8

'for the first heaven and the first earth were passed away; and there was no more sea' *Tabernacle* — SAQ 67

from the days of Adam until the days of Christ, They spoke little of eternal life and the heavenly universal perfections — 124

this heavenly food is knowledge, understanding, faith, assurance, love, affinity, kindness, purity of purpose, attraction of hearts and the union of souls – re: the 'Lord's Supper' *Food* — BWF 408

it was this manner of the Lord's Supper which descended from the heavenly kingdom in the day of Christ — 408

Heaven

by heavenly armies those souls are intended who are entirely freed from the human world, transformed into celestial spirits and have become divine angels (BWF 423–4) TDP 17

likewise the address of the angels to the people of Galilee, 'That this Christ will return in the same way and that He will descend from heaven,' is a spiritual address. For when Christ appeared, He came from heaven, although He was outwardly born from the womb of Mary. For He said: 'No man hath ascended up to heaven, but that he came down from heaven.' TAB 192

He said: 'I came down from heaven and likewise will I go to heaven.' By 'heaven' is not meant this infinite phenomenal space, but 'heaven' signifies the world of the divine kingdom which is the supreme station and seat of the Sun of Truth

Hebrew [see also *Israel*]

the enslavement, wretchedness and helplessness of the Hebrews reached such a pitch that they were never, day or night, secure in their own persons nor able to provide any defense for their wives and families against the tyranny of their Pharaohic captors. Then their food was the fragments of their own broken hearts, and their drink a river of tears. They continued on in this anguish until suddenly Moses, the All-Beauteous, beheld the Divine Light streaming out of the blessed Vale SDC 75–6

Heir

'and We desire to show favour to those who were brought low in the land, and to make them spiritual leaders among men, and to make of them Our heirs' *Abase* KI 146

Hezekiah

then Hezekiah and Ezra reestablished in their midst the fundamental principles of the Holy Book, and day by day the Israelites advanced, and the morning-brightness of their earlier ages dawned again SDC 78

Hidden Words

thou hast asked about the statement in the Hidden Words, which reads: 'O Son of Spirit! Turn thy face so that thou mayest find Me within thee, Powerful, Mighty and Supreme.' This is the statement to which His Holiness, the Christ, referred His apostles in the Gospel, saying, 'The Father is in the Son, and the Son is in you.' SW II 7–8, pp11–12

This is evident that, when the hearts are purified and through divine education and heavenly teachings become the manifestors of infinite perfections, they are like clear mirrors, and the Sun of Truth will reflect with might, power and omnipotence in such a mirror, and to such an extent that whatever is brought before it is illumined and ignited

that marvellous collection of gem-like utterances, the 'Hidden Words' with which Bahá'u'lláh was inspired, as He paced, wrapped in His meditations, the banks of the Tigris. Revealed in the year 1274 AH, partly in Persian, partly in Arabic, it was originally . . . identified by its Author with the Book of that same name, believed by Shí'ah Islám to be in the possession of the promised Qá'im, and to consist of words of consolation addressed by the angel Gabriel, at God's command, to Fáṭimih, and dictated to the Imám 'Alí, for the sole purpose of comforting her in her hour of bitter anguish after the death of her illustrious Father. The significance of this dynamic spiritual leaven cast into the life of the world for the reorientation of the minds of men, the edification of their souls GPB 140 and the rectification of their conduct can best be judged by the description of its character given in the opening passage by its Author

might not the following passage of the Hidden Words be, likewise, construed as an allegorical allusion to the progressiveness of Divine Revelation and an admission by its Author that the Message with which He has been entrusted is not the final and ultimate expression of the will and guidance of the Almighty? 'O Son of Justice! In the night-season the beauty of the immortal Being . . . "Thus far and no farther." Verily We bear witness to that which they have done and are now doing' WOB 116

High Priest

to the priestly caste, holding sacerdotal supremacy over the followers of the Faith of Zoroaster, that same Voice, identifying itself with the voice of the promised Sháh-Bahrám, has declared: 'O high priests! Ears have been given you that they may hearken unto the mystery of Him Who is the Self-Dependent, and eyes that they may behold Him. Wherefore flee ye? The Incomparable Friend is manifest. He speaketh that wherein lieth salvation. Were ye, O high priests, to discover the perfume of the rose-garden of understanding, ye would seek none other but Him, and would recognize, in His new vesture, the All-Wise and Peerless One, and would turn your eyes from the world and all who seek it, and would arise to help Him' PDC 77

'whatsoever hath been announced in the Books,' Bahá'u'lláh, replying to a Zoroastrian who had inquired regarding the promised Sháh-Bahrám, has written, 'hath been revealed and made clear. From every direction the signs have been manifested. The Omnipotent One is calling, in this Day, and announcing the appearance of the Supreme Heaven' 77

'this is not the day,' He, in another Tablet declares, 'whereon the high priests can command and exercise their authority. In your Book it is stated that the high priests will, on that Day, lead men far astray, and will prevent them from drawing nigh unto Him. He indeed is a high priest who hath seen the light and hastened unto the way leading to the Beloved' 77

'say, O high priests!' He again addresses them, 'The Hand of Omnipotence is stretched forth from behind the clouds; behold ye it with new eyes. The tokens of His majesty and greatness are unveiled; gaze ye on them with pure eyes . . . Say, O high priests! Ye are held in reverence because of My Name, and yet ye flee Me! Ye are the high priests of the Temple. Had ye been the high priests of the Omnipotent One, ye would have been united with Him, and would have recognized Him . . . Say, O high priests! No man's acts shall be acceptable, in this Day, unless he forsaketh mankind and all that men possess, and setteth his face towards the Omnipotent One' 77–8

Histories

Prophet – re: advent of, not adequately set down in authoritative histories SDC 74–5

the above, however, cannot be found in the Jewish histories; there are many facts which are not included in Jewish history. Not all the events of the life of Christ are set forth in the history of Josephus, a Jew, although it was he who wrote the history of the times of Christ. One may not, therefore, refuse to believe in events of Christ's day on the ground that they are not to be found in the history of Josephus SAB 55

Holy Books

and have been prevented from attaining to the inner significances of the Holy Books *Neglect* SDC 54 observe: those who in appearance were physically alive, Christ considered dead; for life is the eternal life, and existence is the real existence. Wherever in the Holy Books they speak of raising the dead, the meaning is that the dead were blessed by eternal life; where it is said that the blind received sight, the signification is that he obtained the true perception; where it is said a deaf man received hearing, the meaning is that he acquired spiritual and heavenly hearing SAQ 101–2

Holy City

and the Holy City means the material Law which may be abrogated *Holy of Holies* SAQ 48

which the writer of the Apocalypse had described *Kitáb-i-Aqdas* GPB 213

Holy of Holies

'Thou shalt bear the iniquity of the house of Judah forty days: I have appointed thee each day for a year.' SAQ 46–7

This prophesies the duration of the Dispensation of Islám when Jerusalem was trodden under foot, which means that it lost its glory – but the Holy of Holies was preserved, guarded and respected – until the year 1260. This twelve hundred and sixty years is a prophecy of the manifestation of the Báb, the 'Gate' of Bahá'u'lláh, which took place in the year 1260 of the Hejira of Muḥammad, and as the period of twelve hundred and sixty years has expired, Jerusalem, the Holy City, is now beginning to become prosperous, populous and flourishing. Anyone who saw Jerusalem sixty years ago, and who sees it now, will recognize how populous and flourishing it has become, and how it is again honoured.

This is the outward meaning of these verses of the Revelation of St. John; but they have another explanation and a symbolic sense, which is as follows

the Law of God is divided into two parts. One is the fundamental basis which comprises all spiritual things – that is to say, it refers to the spiritual virtues and divine qualities; this does not change nor alter: it is the Holy of Holies, which is the essence of the Law of Adam, Noah, Abraham, Moses, Christ, Muḥammad, the Báb and Bahá'u'lláh, and which lasts and is established in all the prophetic cycles. It will never be abrogated, for it is spiritual and not material truth; it is faith, knowledge, certitude, justice, piety, righteousness, trustworthiness, love of God, benevolence, purity, detachment, humility, meekness, patience and constancy. It shows mercy to the poor, defends the oppressed, gives to the wretched and uplifts the fallen 47

thus among the Jews, at the end of the cycle of Moses, which coincides with the Christian manifestation, the Law of God disappeared, only a form without spirit remaining. The Holy of Holies departed from among them, but the outer court of Jerusalem – which is the expression used for the form of the religion – fell into the hands of the Gentiles. In the same way, the fundamental principles of the religion of Christ, which are the greatest virtues of humanity, have disappeared; and its form has remained in the hands of the clergy and the priests. Likewise, the foundation of the religion of Muḥammad has disappeared, but its form remains in the hands of the official 'ulamá 47–8

briefly, what is meant by the term Holy of Holies is that spiritual Law which will never be modified, altered or abrogated; and the Holy City means the material Law which may be abrogated; and this material Law, which is described as the Holy City, was to be trodden under foot for twelve hundred and sixty years 48 'and the temple of God was opened in heaven' means that the divine Jerusalem is found, and the Holy of Holies has become visible. The Holy of Holies, according to the terminology of the people of wisdom, is the essence of the Divine Law, and the heavenly and true teachings of the Lord, which have not changed in the cycle of any Prophet, as it was before explained. The sanctuary of Jerusalem is likened to the reality of the Law of God, which is the Holy of Holies; and all the laws, conventions, rites and material regulations are the city of Jerusalem – this is why it is called the heavenly Jerusalem 59–60

Holy Land

this Holy Land hath been mentioned and extolled in all the sacred Scriptures. In it have appeared the Prophets of God and His chosen Ones. This is the wilderness in which all the Messengers of God have wandered, from which their cry, 'Here am I, here am I, O my God' was raised. This is the promised Land in which He Who is the Revelation of God was destined to be made manifest. This is the Vale of God's unsearchable decree, the snow-white Spot, the Land of unfading splendour. Whatever hath come to pass in this Day hath been foretold in the Scriptures of old G 343

the Holy Land – the Land promised by God to Abraham, sanctified by the Revelation of Moses, honoured by the lives and labours of the Hebrew patriarchs, judges, kings and prophets, revered as the cradle of Christianity, and as the place where Zoroaster, according to 'Abdu'l-Bahá's testimony, had 'held converse with some of the Prophets of Israel' GPB 183

Holy Spirit

the Holy Spirit is the Bounty of God and the luminous rays which emanate from the Manifestations; . . . The descent of the Holy Spirit upon the Apostles signifies that the glorious divine bounties reflected and appeared in their reality . . . it is evident and clear that the intellectual realities do not enter and descend, and it is absolutely impossible that the Holy Spirit should ascend and descend, enter, come out or penetrate, it can only be that the Holy Spirit appears in splendour, as the sun appears in the mirror SAQ 108

Jesus Christ – re: dissertation on Holy Spirit 118, 118–19

in the human plane and kingdom man is a captive of nature and ignorant of the divine world until born of the breaths of the Holy Spirit out of physical conditions of limitation and deprivation FWU 59

Lament – re: Jewish doctors . . . made the Holy Spirit to lament PDC 101

the world is full of ideas but they are either fleeting or profitless or impractical or limited in their influence or confined within a narrow scope. The beaming shafts of the light of cosmic ideals must pierce through the hearts of men and the power of the Holy Spirit is necessary to carry into execution these noble thoughts of the age. Human power is limited in its influence. It can unite two persons, or two tribes, or two communities, or at the utmost two nations. At the same time it confesses that this unity is temporal and may be abrogated by the whim of either of the contracting parties. SW VIII 8, p101

But the divine power unites nations and peoples and cements them together in the bond of brotherhood and peace for ages and cycles. His Holiness Christ was one person, without any worldly assistance and help, but through the effect of the Holy Spirit he was enabled to unite many nations and religions under the standard of Christianity. Likewise

Holy Spirit

Muḥammad unified the wild, savage tribes of Arabs and made them the conquerors of Asia. Consequently there must needs be divine power for the accomplishment of this universal aim. Human power fails in this undertaking

spiritual education consists in the inculcation of the ideals of divine morality and promotes high thoughts. This spiritual education is made possible through the power of the Holy Spirit. As long as the breaths of the Holy Spirit do not display any influence, spiritual education is not obtained; whereas if a soul is inspired by the Holy Spirit he will be enabled to educate a nation. VIII 8, pp101–2

Consider the records of bygone philosophers; the utmost that they could do was to educate themselves. The circle of their influence was very limited. All that they could do was to instruct a few pupils. Of such a type was the influence of Plato and Aristotle. These philosophers were only able to train a limited number of people. But those souls who are assisted by the breath of the Holy Spirit can educate a nation. The prophets of God were neither philosophers nor celebrated for their genius. Outwardly, they belong to the common people, but as they were encircled with the all-comprehending power of the Holy Spirit they were thus enabled to impart a general education to all men. For instance, His Holiness Christ and His Holiness Muḥammad were not among the thinkers of the age neither were they counted great geniuses; but through the power of the Holy Spirit they were able to confer universal instruction upon many nations.

They illumined the world of morality. They laid the foundation of a spiritual sovereignty which is everlasting. It is the same with those souls who have entered the tabernacle of the Cause of God. Although not important in appearance, yet everyone is confirmed in stimulating the cause of general moral instruction. Therefore it has become evident that real spiritual universal education cannot be realized save through the breath of the Holy Spirit. Man must not look at his own capabilities, but think of the power of the Holy Spirit

Jesus Christ – re: power of Holy Spirit VIII 8, p102

Hour

to the hour of His advent St. Paul had alluded as the hour of the 'last trump,' the 'trump of God,' whilst St. Peter had spoken of it as the 'Day of God, wherein the heavens being on fire shall be dissolved, and the elements shall melt with fervent heat.' His Day he, furthermore, had described as 'the times of refreshing,' 'the times of restitution of all things, which God hath spoken by the mouth of all His holy Prophets since the world began!' – re: Bahá'u'lláh GPB 96

Ḥusayn [see also *Imám*]

consider the eagerness with which certain peoples and nations have anticipated the return of Imám Ḥusayn, whose coming, after the appearance of the Qá'im, hath been prophesied, in days past, by the chosen ones of God, exalted be His glory. These holy ones have, moreover, announced that when He Who is the Day Spring of the manifold grace of God manifesteth Himself, all the Prophets and Messengers, including the Qá'im, will gather together beneath the shadow of the sacred Standard which the Promised One will raise. That hour is now come. The world is illumined with the effulgent glory of His countenance G 12

the purpose of God, moreover, was to sacrifice him as a ransom for the sins and iniquities of all the peoples of the earth. This same honour, Jesus, 75 the Son of Mary, besought the one true God, exalted be His name and glory, to confer upon Him. For the same reason was Ḥusayn offered up as a sacrifice by Muḥammad, the Apostle of God

Ḥusayn, the son of 'Alí – peace be upon him – likewise saith: 'Will there be vouchsafed unto anyone besides Thee a Revelation which hath not been vouchsafed unto Thyself – a Revelation Whose Revealer will be He Who revealed Thee. Blind be the eye that seeth Thee not!' ESW 42

for no warrior could be found on earth more excellent and nearer to God than Ḥusayn, son of 'Alí, so peerless and incomparable was he. 'There was none to equal or to match him in the world.' Yet, thou must have heard what befell him. God's malison on the head of the people of tyranny KI 126

were the verse 'And verily Our host shall conquer' to be literally interpreted, it is evident that it would in no wise be applicable to the chosen Ones of God and His hosts, inasmuch as Ḥusayn, whose heroism was manifest as the sun, crushed and subjugated, quaffed at last the cup of martyrdom in Karbilá, the land of Ṭaff 126

Ascendancy – re: blood of Ḥusayn 127–8

furthermore, call to mind the shameful circumstances that have attended the martyrdom of Ḥusayn. Reflect upon his loneliness, how to outer seeming, none could be found to aid him, none to take up his body and bury it. And yet, behold how numerous, in this day, are those who from the uttermost corners of the earth don the garb of pilgrimage, seeking the site of his martyrdom, that there they may lay their heads upon the threshold of his shrine! Such is the ascendancy and power of God! Such is the glory of His dominion and majesty 128–9

think not that because these things have come to pass after Ḥusayn's martyrdom, therefore all this glory has been of no profit unto him. For that soul is immortal, liveth the life of God, and abideth within the retreats of celestial glory upon the Sadrih of heavenly reunion. These Essences of being are the shining Exemplars of sacrifice 129

likewise, strive thou to comprehend the meaning of the melody of that eternal beauty, Ḥusayn, son of 'Alí, who, addressing Salmán, spoke words such as these: 'I was with a thousand Adams, the interval between each and the next Adam was fifty thousand years, and to each one of these I declared the Successorship conferred upon my father.' He then recounteth certain details, until he saith: 'I have fought one thousand battles in the path of God, the least and most insignificant of which was like the battle of Khaybar, in which battle my father fought and contended against the infidels.' Endeavour now to apprehend from these two traditions the mysteries of 'end,' 'return,' and 'creation without beginning or end' 167–8

were not the happenings of the life of the 'Prince of Martyrs' regarded as the greatest of all events, as the supreme evidence of his truth? Did not the people of old declare those happenings to be unprecedented? Did they not maintain that no manifestation of truth hath ever evinced such constancy, such conspicuous glory? And yet, that episode of his life, commencing as it did in the morning, was brought to a close by the middle of the same day, whereas, these holy lights have, for eighteen years, heroically endured the showers of afflictions which, from every side, have rained upon them 225–6

erelong We will, in very truth, torment such as waged war against Ḥusayn (Imám Ḥusayn), in the Land of the Euphrates, with the most afflictive torment, and the most dire and exemplary punishment . . . SB 70

Ḥusayn

. . . God knoweth well the heart of Ḥusayn, the heat of His burning thirst and His long-suffering for the sake of God, the Incomparable, the Ancient of Days; and unto Him God is verily a witness

the Imám Ḥusayn, the most illustrious of the successors of the Apostle of God – the brightest 'star' shining in the 'crown' mentioned in the Revelation of St. John GPB 94

to Shí'ah Islám the return of the Imám Ḥusayn – re: Bahá'u'lláh 94

glorifies the Imáms of the Faith of Muḥammad; celebrates the martyrdom, and lauds the spiritual sovereignty, of the Imám Ḥusayn – re: Kitáb-i-Íqán 139

in the prayer mentioned above [Abraham, Moses, Joseph, John the Baptist, Christ, Muḥammad, Imám Ḥusayn, the Báb, and Bahá'u'lláh] Bahá'u'lláh identifies Himself with Imám Ḥusayn. This does not make Him a Prophet, but his position was very unique, and we know Bahá'u'lláh claims to be the 'return' of the Imám Ḥusayn. He, in other words, identifies His Spirit with these Holy Souls gone before, that does not, of course, make Him in any way their re-incarnation. Nor does it mean all of them were Prophets [see WOB 118–9] (Letter 8.2.49) LG 374

Ibn-i-Súríyá

when the people of Khaybar asked the focal centre of the Muḥammadan Revelation concerning the penalty of adultery committed between a married man and a married woman, Muḥammad answered and said: 'The law of God is death by stoning.' Whereupon they protested saying: 'No such law hath been revealed in the Pentateuch.' Muḥammad answered and said: 'Whom do ye regard among your rabbis as being a recognized authority and having a sure knowledge of the truth?' They agreed upon Ibn-i-Súríyá. Thereupon Muḥammad summoned him . . . He made reply: 'O Muḥammad! death by stoning is the law' *Jew* KI 84–5

Idol

that haply the whole earth may be freed and sanctified from its servitude to the gods of its idle fancies – gods that have inflicted such loss upon, and are responsible for the misery of their wretched worshippers. These idols form the obstacle that impedeth man in his efforts to advance in the path of perfection TB 86

what could have been the evidence produced by the Pharisees and the idolatrous priests to justify their denial of Muḥammad ESW 81

in the days of Rehoboam, the son of Solomon, terrible dissension broke out among them; one of their number, Jeroboam, plotted to get the throne, and it was he who introduced the worship of idols SDC 77

therefore, reflect that different peoples of the world are revolving around imaginations and are worshippers of the idols of thoughts and conjectures. They are not aware of this; they consider their imaginations to be the Reality which is withdrawn from all comprehension and purified from all descriptions. They regard themselves as the people of Unity, and the others as worshippers of idols; but idols at least have a mineral existence, while the idols of thoughts and the imaginations of man are but fancies; they have not even mineral existence SAQ 149

Buddha – re: followers worship statues and images 165

the chief idols in the desecrated temple of mankind are none other than the triple gods of Nationalism, Racialism and Communism, at whose altars governments and peoples, whether democratic or totalitarian, at peace or at war, of the East or of the West, Christian or Islamic, are, in various PDC 113 forms and in different degrees, now worshipping. Their high priests are the politicians and the worldly-wise

Ignorance

and how many are the ignorant who, by reason of their acceptance of the Faith, have soared aloft and attained the high summit of knowledge, and whose names have been inscribed by the Pen of Power upon the Tablet of divine Knowledge *Abase* KI 146

Tradition – re: days of ignorance SDC 43–4

Imám

the Imáms, those unquenchable lights of divine guidance *Qá'im* KI 144

these Countenances are the recipients of the Divine Command, and the day-springs of His Revelation. This Revelation is exalted above the veil of plurality and the exigencies of number. Thus He saith: 'Our Cause is but one.' Inasmuch as the Cause is one and the same, the Exponents thereof also must needs be one and the same. Likewise, the Imáms of the Muḥammadan Faith, those lamps of certitude, have said: 'Muḥammad is our first, Muḥammad is our last, Muḥammad our all' 153

how well have they followed the directions of the Imáms of the Faith and Lamps of certitude! Although it is clearly stated: 'Were ye to hear that a Youth from Baní-Há<u>sh</u>im hath appeared, summoning the people unto a new and Divine Book, and to new and Divine laws, hasten unto Him,' yet have they all declared that Lord of being an infidel, and pronounced Him a heretic. They hasteneth not unto that Há<u>sh</u>imite Light, that divine Manifestation, except with drawn swords, and hearts filled with malice 241

if we ponder a while over the Qur'ánic verses and proofs, and the traditional accounts which have come down to us from those stars of the heaven of Divine Unity, the Holy Imáms, we shall be convinced of the fact that if a soul is endowed with the attributes of true faith and characterized with spiritual qualities he will become to all mankind an emblem of the outstretched mercies of God SDC 55

'are we,' they noisily remonstrated, 'are we to account as a dead letter the indubitable, the unnumbered traditions of our holy Imáms, or are we to extinguish with fire and sword this brazen heresy that has dared to lift its head in our land – re: the <u>Sh</u>í'ih clergy upon the coming of the Qá'im GPB 36

the validity of the Imamate is, moreover, implicitly recognized in these same passages – that divinely-appointed institution of whose most distinguished member the Báb Himself was a lineal descendant, and which continued for a period of no less than two hundred and sixty years to be the chosen recipient of the guidance of the Almighty and the repository of one of the two most precious legacies of Islám WOB 102

<u>Sh</u>áhs of Persia who ruled the kingdom as temporary trustees for the expected Imám PDC 78

such a revolution did not signalize the disestablishment of a state-church. It indeed was tantamount to the disruption of what may be called a church-state – a state that had been hopefully awaiting, even up till the moment of its expiry, the gladsome advent of the Hidden Imám, who would not only seize the reins of authority from the <u>sh</u>áh, the chief magistrate who was merely representing him, but would also assume dominion over the whole earth – re: Constitutional Revolution in Írán 91

Imitation [see also *Dogma*]

not the dogmas and blind imitations which have gradually encrusted it and which are the cause of the decline and effacement of a nation *Religion* PUP 363

Infidel

when the verses of this Book are recited to the infidels they say: 'Give us a book like the Qur'án and make changes in the verses' – re: Bayán *Qur'án* SB 66

this truth hath likewise been laid bare in the Qur'án where in numerous instances God hath set down that whoever should pass judgement contrary to the bounds fixed by Him, would be deemed an infidel *Bayán* 102

Interpret

inasmuch as the Christian divines have failed to apprehend the meaning of these words, and did not recognize their object and purpose, and have clung to the literal interpretation of the words of Jesus, they therefore became deprived of the streaming grace of the Muḥammadan Revelation and its showering bounties KI 26

as they have literally interpreted the Word of God *Leader* 82

those words uttered by the Luminaries of Truth must needs be pondered, and should their significance be not grasped, enlightenment should be sought from the Trustees of the depositories of Knowledge, that these may expound their meaning, and unravel their mystery. For it behooveth no man to interpret the holy words according to his own imperfect understanding, nor, having found them to be contrary to his inclination and desires, to reject and repudiate their truth 181–2

'none knoweth the interpretation thereof but God and they that are well-grounded in knowledge' *Qur'án* 213

these statements and attitudes of the Jews were inherited from their fathers; blind allegiance to literal expectations which did not come to pass during the time of Jesus Christ FWU 75

Isaiah

they failed to attain His presence, notwithstanding that His advent had been promised them in the Book of Isaiah as well as in the Books of the Prophets and the Messengers – re: the Pharisees *Spirit* TB 9–10

in the Book of Isaiah it is written: 'Enter into the rock, and hide thee in the dust, for fear of the Lord, and for the glory of His majesty.' No man that meditateth upon this verse can fail to recognize the greatness of this Cause, or doubt the exalted character of this Day – the Day of God Himself. This same verse is followed by these words: 'And the Lord alone shall be exalted in that Day.' This is the Day which the Pen of the Most High hath glorified in all the Holy Scriptures G 13

Isaiah saith: 'The Lord alone shall be exalted in that Day.' Concerning the greatness of the Revelation He saith: 'Enter into the rock, and hide thee in the dust, for fear of the Lord, and for the glory of His majesty.' And in another connection He saith: 'The wilderness and the solitary place shall be glad for them; and the desert shall rejoice, and blossom as the rose. It shall blossom abundantly, and rejoice even with joy and singing: the glory of Lebanon shall be given unto it, the splendour of Carmel and Sharon, they shall see the glory of the Lord, and the splendour of our God.' ESW 146

These passages stand in need of no commentary. They are shining and manifest as the sun, and glowing and luminous as light itself

'say to them that are of a fearful heart: be strong, fear not, behold your God' *Trumpet* 147

the Book of Isaiah announces that the Messiah will conquer the East and the West, and all nations of the world will come under His shadow, that SAQ 111

His Kingdom will be established, that He will come from an unknown place, that the sinners will be judged, and that justice will prevail to such a degree that the wolf and the lamb, the leopard and the kid, the sucking child and the asp, shall all gather at one spring, and in one meadow, and one dwelling. The first coming was also under these conditions, though outwardly none of them came to pass. Therefore, the Jews rejected Christ, and, God forbid! called the Messiah masíkh, considered Him to be the destroyer of the edifice of God, regarded Him as the breaker of the Sabbath and the Law, and sentenced Him to death. Nevertheless, each one of these conditions had a signification that the Jews did not understand; therefore, they were debarred from perceiving the truth of Christ

then, according to the prophecy of Isaiah, the wolf and the lamb will drink from the same stream, the owl and the vulture will nest together in the same branches, and the lion and the calf pasture in the same meadow. What does this mean? It means that fierce and contending religions, hostile creeds and divergent beliefs will reconcile and associate, notwithstanding their former hatreds and antagonism — PUP 369

as to thy question concerning the 54th chapter of Isaiah: This chapter refers to the Exalted Leaf, the mother of 'Abdu'l-Bahá. As a proof of this it is said: 'For more are the children of the desolate, than the children of the married wife.' Reflect upon this statement and then upon the following: 'And thy seed shall inherit the Gentiles and make the desolate cities to be inhabited.' And truly the humiliation and reproach which she suffered in the path of God is a fact which no one can refute. For the calamities and afflictions mentioned in the whole chapter are such afflictions which she suffered in the path of God, all of which she endured with patience and thanked God therefor and praised Him, because He had enabled her to endure afflictions for the sake of Bahá — TAB 107

Isaiah had, in this connection, announced in his Book: 'Get thee up into the high mountain, O Zion that bringest good tidings; lift up thy voice with strength, O Jerusalem, that bringest good tidings. Lift it up, be not afraid; say unto the cities of Judah: "Behold your God! Behold the Lord God will come with strong hand, and His arm shall rule for Him"' — GPB 183–4

the principal repository of the Law which the Prophet Isaiah had anticipated – re: Kitáb-i-Aqdas — 213

she to whose dire afflictions, as attested by 'Abdu'l-Bahá in a Tablet, the 54th chapter of the Book of Isaiah has, in its entirety, borne witness – re: Navváb, wife of Bahá'u'lláh — 348

'naught can be seen in Me except God and His Cause, could ye but perceive it. I am the One Whom the tongue of Isaiah hath extolled, the One with Whose name both the Torah and the Evangel were adorned' [words of Bahá'u'lláh] – re: Tablet to the Czar of Russia — PDC 34

Ishmael

the Voice of God commanded Him to offer up Ishmael as a sacrifice, so that His steadfastness in the Faith of God and His detachment from all else but Him may be demonstrated unto men. The purpose of God, moreover, was to sacrifice him as a ransom for the sins and iniquities of all the peoples of the earth *Abraham* — G 75–6

Islám [see also *Muḥammad, Qur'án*]

behold, O Muḥammad, how the sayings and doings of the followers of Shí'ih Islám have dulled the joy and fervour of its early days, and tarnished the pristine brilliancy of its light. In its primitive days, whilst — G 68–9 they still adhered to the precepts associated with the name of their Prophet, the Lord of mankind, their career was marked by an unbroken chain of victories and triumphs. As they gradually strayed from the path of their Ideal Leader and Master, as they turned away from the Light of God and corrupted the principle of His Divine unity, and as they increasingly centred their attention upon them who were only the revealers of the potency of His Word, their power was turned into weakness, their glory into shame, their courage into fear. Thou dost witness to what a pass they have come. Behold, how they have joined partners with Him Who is the Focal Point of Divine unity. Behold how their evil doings have hindered them from recognizing, in the Day of Resurrection, the Word of Truth, exalted be His glory

because of you the Apostle (Muḥammad) lamented, and the Chaste One (Fáṭimih) cried out, and the countries were laid waste, and darkness fell upon all regions. O concourse of divines! Because of you the people were abased, and the banner of Islám was hauled down, and its mighty throne subverted. Every time a man of discernment hath sought to hold fast unto that which would exalt Islám, you raised a clamour, and thereby was he deterred from achieving his purpose, while the land remained fallen in clear ruin ESW 99–100

Muḥammad, the Seal of the Prophets, and the most distinguished of God's chosen Ones, hath likened the Dispensation of the Qur'án unto heaven, by reason of its loftiness, its paramount influence, its majesty, and the fact that it comprehendeth all religions. And as the sun and moon constitute the brightest and most prominent luminaries in the heavens, similarly in the heaven of the religion of God two shining orbs have been ordained – fasting and prayer. Islám is heaven; fasting is its sun, prayer, its moon KI 40

and likewise, He saith: 'Say, O people of the Book! do ye not disavow us only because we believe in God and in what He hath sent down to us, and in what He hath sent down aforetime, and because most of you are doers of ill?' How explicitly doth this verse reveal Our purpose, and how clearly it demonstrates the truth of the testimony of the verses of God! This verse was revealed at a time when Islám was assailed by the infidels, and its followers were accused of misbelief, when the Companions of Muḥammad were denounced as repudiators of God and as followers of a lying sorcerer. In its early days, when Islám was still to outward seeming devoid of authority and power, the friends of the Prophet, who had turned their face toward God, wherever they went, were harassed, persecuted, stoned and vilified 217–18

Companions 218

thou hast set thyself up as one of the learned in the Faith of Islám, that thou mightest save the believers, yet thou didst cause thy followers to descend into the fire, for when the verses of God were sent forth thou didst deprive thyself therefrom and yet reckoned thyself to be of the righteous – re: address to 'Abdu'ṣ-Ṣáḥib [see also *Christianity* 123–4] SB 32

ponder a while and observe that everything in Islám hath its ultimate and eventual beginning in the Book of God *Book* 104

but it is not seen that any one of the followers of <u>Sh</u>í'ih Islám hath understood the meaning of the Day of Resurrection; rather have they fancifully imagined a thing which with God hath no reality *Resurrection* 106

the stage of perfection of everything is reached when its resurrection occurreth. The perfection of the religion of Islám was consummated at the beginning of this Revelation; and from the rise of this Revelation 107 until its setting, the fruits of the Tree of Islám, whatever they are, will become apparent

the fruits of Islám cannot be gathered except through allegiance unto Him (the Qá'im) and by believing in Him *Qá'im* 108

gracious God! Within the domains of Islám there are at present seven powerful sovereigns ruling the world. None of them hath been informed of His (the Báb's) Manifestation, and if informed, none hath believed in Him. Who knoweth, they may leave this world below full of desire, and without having realized that the thing for which they were waiting had come to pass. This is what happened to the monarchs that held fast unto the Gospel. They awaited the coming of the Prophet of God (Muḥammad), and when He did appear, they failed to recognize Him 117

all deeds which in the Islámic Dispensation began with Muḥammad should find their consummation through the appearance of the Qá'im *Qá'im* 118

Promised One – re: bounty for followers of Islám 119

whoever uttereth such words, say unto him, 'O thou untutored one! By what proof hast thou embraced the Religion of Islám? *Testimony* 120

how great hath been the number of those who have falsely laid claim to a cause within Islám, and ye followed in their footsteps without having witnessed a single proof. What evidence can ye then produce in the presence of your Lord, if ye do but meditate a while? 134

He Who hath revealed the Qur'án unto Muḥammad, the Apostle of God, ordaining in the Faith of Islám that which was pleasing unto Him, hath likewise revealed the Bayán, in the manner ye have been promised *Bayán* 139

nor have they obtained the slightest notion of the Faith of Islám 140

the people of the Days of Ignorance engaged in many practices which the Law of Islám later confirmed SDC 28

in the early ages of Islám the peoples of Europe acquired the sciences and arts of civilization from Islám as practiced by the inhabitants of Andalusia 89

a careful and thorough investigation of the historical record will establish the fact that the major part of the civilization of Europe is derived from Islám; for all the writings of Muslim scholars and divines and philosophers were gradually collected in Europe and were with the most painstaking care weighed and debated at academic gatherings and in the centers of learning, after which their valued contents would be put to use 89

furthermore, the laws and principles current in all European countries are derived to a considerable degree and indeed virtually in their entirety from the works on jurisprudence and the legal decision of Muslim theologians 89

those European intellectuals who are well-informed as to the facts of Europe's past, and are characterized by truthfulness and a sense of justice, unanimously acknowledge that in every particular the basic elements of their civilization are derived from Islám 92

for example Draper, the well-known French authority, a writer whose accuracy, ability and learning are attested by all European scholars, in one of his best-known works, *The Intellectual Development of Europe*, has written a detailed account in this connection, that is, with reference to the derivation by the peoples of Europe of the fundamentals of civilization and the bases of progress and well-being from Islám 92–3

Witness – re: Muḥammad and 'Alí SAQ 48–9

Islám

'and they that dwell upon the earth shall rejoice over them, and make merry, and shall send gifts to one another, because these two prophets tormented them that dwell on earth.' 'Those who dwelt upon the earth' means the other nations and races, such as the peoples of Europe and distant Asia, who, when they saw that the character of Islám was entirely changed, the Law of God forsaken – that virtues, zeal and honour had departed from among them, and that their qualities were changed – became happy, and rejoiced that corruption of morals had infected the people of Islám, and that they would in consequence be overcome by other nations. So this thing has come to pass. Witness this people which had attained the summit of power, how degraded and downtrodden it is now 53–4

the call she sounded was the death-knell of the twelve hundred year old law of Islám – re: Ṭáhirih at Badas͟ht GPB 34

interpreting in a masterly fashion the obscure, the designedly allegorical and abstruse traditions, verses and prophecies in the Islámic holy Writ – re: the Báb's disciples 37

Day – re: whereon there will have remained of Islám naught but a name WOB 179

Islám attained a very high spiritual state, but western scholars are prone to judging it by Christian standards. One cannot call one world Faith superior to another, as they all come from God; they are progressive, each suited to certain needs of the times (Letter 19.11.45) LG 371

Israel

Jesus Christ – re: Israel remained deprived of recognizing the beauty of Jesus G 20–21

how many Manifestations of Holiness, how many Revealers of the light everlasting, have appeared since the time of Moses, and yet Israel, wrapt in the densest veils of satanic fancy and false imaginings, is still expectant that the idol of her own handiwork will appear with such signs as she herself hath conceived KI 18

even as the people of Israel, in the time of Moses, bartered away the bread of heaven for the sordid things of the earth, these people, likewise, sought to exchange the divinely-revealed verses for their foul, their vile, and idle desires 208

at a time when the Israelites had multiplied in Egypt and were spread throughout the whole country, the Coptic Pharaohs of Egypt determined to strengthen and favour their own Coptic peoples and to degrade and dishonour the children of Israel, whom they regarded as foreigners. Over a long period, the Israelites, divided and scattered, were captive in the hands of the tyrannical Copts, and were scorned and despised by all, so that the meanest of the Copts would freely persecute and lord it over the noblest of the Israelites SDC 75

He gathered Israel's scattered tribes into the shelter of the unifying and universal Word of God – re: Moses 76

they emigrated from Egypt, set out for Israel's original homeland, and came to Canaan and Philistia 76

they first conquered the shores of the River Jordan, and Jericho, and settled in that area, and ultimately all the neighbouring regions, such as Phoenicia, Edom and Ammon, came under their sway. In Joshua's time there were thirty-one governments in the hands of the Israelites, and in every noble human attribute – learning, stability, determination, courage, honour, generosity – this people came to surpass all the nations 76–7 of the earth. When in those days an Israelite would enter a gathering, he was immediately singled out for his many virtues

Philosophy – re: Socrates journeyed to meet Israel's most illustrious scholars and divines 77

after the Israelites had advanced along every level of civilization, and had achieved success in the highest possible degree, they began little by little to forget the root-principles of the Mosaic Law and Faith, to busy themselves with rites and ceremonials and to show forth unbecoming conduct 77

the strife between Rehoboam and Jeroboam led to centuries of warfare between their descendants, with the result that the tribes of Israel were scattered and disrupted 77–8

Hezekiah – re: Hezekiah and Ezra 78

Jesus Christ 80

Moses, for example, was sent forth to man and He established a Law, and the Children of Israel, through that Mosaic Law, were delivered out of their ignorance and came into the light; they were lifted up from their abjectness and attained to a glory that fadeth not SAB 52

the Founder of monotheism was Abraham; it is to Him that this concept can be traced, and the belief was current among the Children of Israel, even in the days of Socrates 55

moreover, in the days of Christ the morals of the whole world and the condition of the Israelites had become completely confused and corrupted, and Israel had fallen into a state of the utmost degradation, misery and bondage. At one time they had been taken captive by the Chaldeans and Persians; at another time they were reduced to slavery to the Assyrians; then they became the subjects and vassals of the Greeks; and finally they were ruled over and despised by the Romans SAQ 16

this young Man, Christ, by the help of a supernatural power, abrogated the ancient Mosaic Law, reformed the general morals, and once again laid the foundation of eternal glory for the Israelites. Moreover, He brought to humanity the glad tidings of universal peace, and spread abroad teachings which were not for Israel alone but were for the general happiness of the whole human race 16

those who first strove to do away with Him were the Israelites, His own kindred *Jesus Christ* 17

Peace – re: signifying that in this cycle Israel will be gathered in the Holy Land 65

now see: these events did not take place in the Christian cycle, for the nations did not come under the One Standard which is the Divine Branch. But in this cycle of the Lord of Hosts all the nations and peoples will enter under the shadow of this Flag. In the same way, Israel, scattered all over the world, was not reassembled in the Holy Land in the Christian cycle; but in the beginning of the cycle of Bahá'u'lláh this divine promise, as is clearly stated in all the Books of the Prophets, has begun to be manifest. You can see that from all the parts of the world tribes of Jews are coming to the Holy Land; they live in villages and lands which they make their own, and day by day they are increasing to such an extent that all Palestine will become their home 65–6

thus it is an especial blessing that from among the descendants of Abraham should have come all the Prophets of the children of Israel. This is a blessing that God has granted to this descent: to Moses from His father and mother, to Christ from His mother's line; also to Muḥammad and 213 the Báb, and to all the Prophets and the Holy Manifestations of Israel

the children of Israel were in bondage and captivity in the land of Egypt four hundred years. They were in an extreme state of degradation and slavery under the tyranny and oppression of the Egyptians. While they were in the condition of abject poverty, in the lowest degree of abasement, ignorance and servility, Moses suddenly appeared among them . . . This unique Personage, single and alone, rescued the children of Israel from bondage through the power of religious training and discipline PUP 362

after their conquest by the Babylonians the Jews were successively subjugated by the Greeks and Romans. Under the Roman general Titus in AD 70 the Holy Land was stripped and pillaged, Jerusalem razed to its foundations and the Israelites scattered broadcast throughout the world 363–4

through the instrumentality of Christ, through the translation of the New Testament, the little volume of the Gospel, the Old Testament, the Torah, has been translated into six hundred languages and spread everywhere in the world. The names of the Hebrew prophets became household words among the nations, who believed that the children of Israel were, verily, the chosen people of God, a holy nation under the especial blessing and protection of God, and that, therefore, the prophets who had arisen in Israel were the daysprings of revelation and brilliant stars in the heaven of the will of God *Jesus Christ* 366–7

what calumny, slander, cruelty and oppression were brought down upon the apostles by the Israelites for the sake of faith and assurance! They unlocked the hands of pillage, persecuted and tortured those sanctified souls TAB 361

regarding the word Israel, this is the title of Jacob himself and not that of his children. Then from the word of 'Bani Israel' Bani (descendants) was dropped and they sufficed with the word 'Israel.' In Encyclopaedia there are many such examples. The descendants of Ham, for example, are called 'Ham,' the descendants of Yafes are called 'Yafes.' The descendants of the Turks are named 'Turks,' and those of Yaarub are called 'Arab.' Examples such as these are many. Afterward the word Israel was used to denote the 'people of God' as is mentioned in the Bible, i.e., the nations of God. Thus it was gradually generalized as to denote all the souls who accepted the religion of God SW XII 3, p58

to Israel He was neither more nor less than the incarnation of the 'Everlasting Father,' the 'Lord of Hosts' come down 'with ten thousands of saints' – re: Bahá'u'lláh GPB 94

the meaning of the Qur'ánic verse 'All food was allowed to the children of Israel,' . . . Turning to Bahá'u'lláh and repeating his request, he was honoured by a Tablet, in which Israel and his children were identified with the Báb and His followers respectively 116–17

furthermore, it produced those revolutionary changes which, on the one hand, fulfilled the ominous predictions made by Bahá'u'lláh in the Kitáb-i-Aqdas, and enabled, according to Scriptural prophecy, so large an element of the 'outcasts of Israel,' the 'remnant' of the 'flock,' to 'assemble' in the Holy Land, and to be brought back to 'their folds' and 'their own border,' beneath the shadow of the 'Incomparable Branch,' referred to by 'Abdu'l-Bahá in His 'Some Answered Questions' 305

the unfortunate episodes that have, admittedly, and to a very great extent, marred the early history of both Judaism and Islám. Nor is it necessary to stress the damaging effect of the excesses, the rivalries and divisions, the fanatical outbursts and acts of ingratitude that are associated with the WOB 56 early development of the people of Israel and with the militant career of the ruthless pioneers of the Faith of Muḥammad

the appalling misery and wretchedness to which the Israelites had sunk, under the debasing and tyrannical rule of the Pharaohs, in the days preceding their exodus from Egypt under the leadership of Moses; the decline that had set in in the religious, the spiritual, the cultural, and the moral life of the Jewish people, at the time of the appearance of Jesus Christ — ADJ 14

'praise be to God,' writes 'Abdu'l-Bahá, 'that whatsoever hath been announced in the Blessed Tablets unto the Israelites, and the things explicitly written in the letters of 'Abdu'l-Bahá, are all being fulfilled. Some have come to pass; others will be revealed in the future. The Ancient Beauty hath in His sacred Tablets explicitly written that the day of their abasement is over. His bounty will overshadow them, and this race will day by day progress, and be delivered from its age-long obscurity and degradation — 46

the gathering of Israel at Jerusalem means, therefore, and prophesies, that Israel as a whole is gathering beneath the banner of God and will enter the Kingdom of the Ancient of Days [from a Tablet of 'Abdu'l-Bahá] *Prophecy* — LG 383

Jacob

in each cycle the guardians and holy souls have been twelve. So Jacob had twelve sons; in the time of Moses there were twelve heads or chiefs of the tribes; in the time of Christ there were twelve Apostles; and in the time of Muḥammad there were twelve Imáms. But in this glorious manifestation there are twenty-four, double the number of all the others, for the greatness of this manifestation requires it [see also *Elders* 57, 57–8] — SAQ 57

for example, in the Old Testament it is said in the Book of Isaiah, chapter 48, verse 12: 'Hearken unto Me, O Jacob and Israel, My called; I am He; I am the first, I am also the last.' It is evident that it does not mean Jacob who was Israel, but the people of Israel. Also in the Book of Isaiah, chapter 43, verse 1, it is said: 'But now thus saith the Lord that created thee, O Jacob, and He that formed thee, O Israel, Fear not: for I have redeemed thee, I have called thee by thy name; thou art Mine' – re: apparent rebuke to the Prophet — 168–9

Israel – re: this is the title of Jacob himself — SW XII 3, p58

Jehovah

while to His day Joel and Zephania had both referred as the 'day of Jehovah,' the latter describing it as 'a day of wrath, a day of trouble and distress, a day of wasteness and desolation, a day of darkness and gloominess, a day of clouds and thick darkness, a day of the trumpet and alarm against the fenced cities, and against the high towers' – re: Bahá'u'lláh — GPB 95

'He it is,' referring to Himself He further proclaims, 'Who in the Old Testament hath been named Jehovah, Who in the Gospel hath been designated as the Spirit of Truth, and in the Qur'án acclaimed as the Great Announcement' – re: Bahá'u'lláh — WOB 104

Jeremiah

hearken with thine inner ear unto the Voice of Jeremiah, Who saith: 'Oh, for great is that Day, and it hath no equal' — ESW 144

Jerusalem

Zion – re: prophecies in Old Testament ESW 144, 145

Jerusalem is the place of pilgrimage for all the peoples of the world, and hath been named the Holy City 145

this Day Jerusalem hath attained unto a new Evangel, for in the stead of the sycamore standeth the cedar . . . Together with Zion and Palestine, they are all included within these regions. Wherefore, hath it been said: 'Blessed is the man that hath migrated to 'Akká' 145

He continued to turn His face, while praying, unto Jerusalem, the holy city, until the time when the Jews began to utter unseemly words against Him *Qiblih* KI 50

otherwise, He, the ideal King [God], could easily have left the Qiblih unchanged, and could have caused Jerusalem to remain the Point of Adoration unto His Dispensation, thereby withholding not from that holy city the distinction of acceptance which had been conferred upon it *Test* 50–51

Jesus Christ – re: in the regions around Jerusalem SDC 44, 80–81

the descent of the New Jerusalem denoteth a heavenly Law, that Law which is the guarantor of human happiness and the effulgence of the world of God SAB 59

in the Book of Daniel, from the rebuilding of Jerusalem to the martyrdom of Christ, seventy weeks are appointed; for by the martyrdom of Christ the sacrifice is accomplished and the altar destroyed. This is a prophecy of the manifestation of Christ. These seventy weeks begin with the restoration and the rebuilding of Jerusalem, concerning which four edicts were issued by three kings. SAQ 40

The first was issued by Cyrus in the year 536 B.C.; this is recorded in the first chapter of the Book of Ezra. The second edict, with reference to the rebuilding of Jerusalem, is that of Darius of Persia in the year 519 B.C.; this is recorded in the sixth chapter of Ezra. The third is that of Artaxerxes in the seventh year of his reign – that is, in 457 B.C.; this is recorded in the seventh chapter of Ezra. The fourth is that of Artaxerxes in the year 444 B.C.; this is recorded in the second chapter of Nehemiah.

But Daniel refers especially to the third edict which was issued in the year 457 B.C. [see also *Daniel*]

the Holy of Holies departed from among them, but the outer court of Jerusalem – which is the expression used for the form of religion – fell into the hands of the Gentiles *Holy of Holies* 47–8

'and the temple of God was opened in heaven' means that the divine Jerusalem is found, and the Holy of Holies has become visible *Holy of Holies* 59

the sanctuary of Jerusalem is likened to the reality of the Law of God, which is the Holy of Holies; and all the laws, conventions, rites and material regulations are the city of Jerusalem – this is why it is called the heavenly Jerusalem 59–60

the Law of God is also described as the Holy City, the New Jerusalem *Law* 68

but now, at last, the Holy City of the New Jerusalem has come again to the world, it has appeared anew under an Eastern sky PT 84

the holy City, new Jerusalem, hath come down from on high in the form of a maid of heaven, veiled, beauteous, and unique, and prepared for reunion with her lovers on earth BWF 350

identifying His Revelation with the 'third woe,' he, moreover, had extolled His Law as 'a new heaven and a new earth,' as the 'Tabernacle of God,' GPB 95–6 as the 'Holy City,' as the 'New Jerusalem, coming down from God out of heaven, prepared as a bride adorned for her husband' – re: Bahá'u'lláh

as the 'tabernacle of God,' as the 'Holy City,' as the 'Bride,' the 'New Jerusalem coming down from God' *Kitáb-i-Aqdas* 213

Persecution – re: of Jewish people in first century of Christian era 228

were not the first fifteen bishops of Jerusalem all circumcised Jews, and had not the congregation over which they presided united the laws of Moses with the doctrines of Christ? WOB 57

compare, moreover, these words which the persecuted Christ, as witnessed by the Gospel, addressed to Jerusalem, with Bahá'u'lláh's apostrophe to Constantinople, revealed while He lay in His far-off Prison, and recorded in His Most Holy Book: 'O Jerusalem, Jerusalem, thou that killest the Prophets and stonest them which are sent unto thee, how often would I have gathered thy children together, even as a hen gathereth her chickens under her wings!' And again, as He wept over the city: 'If thou hadst known, even thou, at least in this thy day, the things which belong unto thy peace! but now they are hid from thine eyes. For the days shall come upon thee, that thine enemies shall cast a trench about thee, and compass thee round, and keep thee in on every side, and shall lay thee even with the ground, and thy children within thee; and they shall not leave in thee one stone upon another; because thou knowest not the time of thy visitation' 176

and again: 'The Breath hath been wafted, and the Breeze hath blown, and from Zion hath appeared that which was hidden, and from Jerusalem is heard the Voice of God, the One, the Incomparable, the Omniscient [words of Bahá'u'lláh] PDC 77

Jesse*

'and there shall come forth a rod out of the stem of Jesse, and a Branch shall grow out of his roots' . . . this rod out of the stem of Jesse might be correctly applied to Christ, for Joseph was of the descendants of Jesse, the father of David; but as Christ found existence through the Spirit of God, he called Himself the Son of God. If He had not done so, this description would refer to Him SAQ 62–3

* *Some Answered Questions*, [page 62], Chapter XII: 'And there shall come forth a rod out of the stem of Jesse and a Branch shall grow out of his roots': The words 'rod' and 'Branch' are one and the same thing in this sentence, it is a repetition of the same thing and refers to only one thing and this is Bahá'u'lláh. There are Tablets revealed by Bahá'u'lláh (not yet translated), in which He refers to Himself as the Branch, but He means by this the Branch of the Tree of Divinity. This chapter in Isaiah does not refer to the Master at all but to Bahá'u'lláh. The Manifestations are all branches that grow out of the Tree of Divinity, as They are all the Rays of the Sun. When Bahá'u'lláh refers to Himself as a Tree, then the Master is the Branch of that Tree, 'Verily the Branch of Command hath sprung from this Root.' On page 76 [65], in Chapter XII of *Some Answered Questions*, the Master says: 'Universal peace and concord will be realized between all the nations, and that incomparable Branch will gather . . .' etc. Surely the friends must see that He, 'Abdu'l-Bahá, could not refer to Himself as 'that incomparable Branch' . . . The term 'Lordly Branch' refers to Bahá'u'lláh. This means the Branch of Divinity, 'Abdu'l-Bahá is the Branch of the Manifestation. The friends read the writings but they do not ponder them enough.

In *Some Answered Questions*, Chapter XII, page 73 [62–3], we find that the Master shows that the prophecy of Isaiah, Chapter II, verses 1–10, not only proves that the 'Branch' from the stem of Jesse did not refer to Christ but to Bahá'u'lláh, but also states the immaculate conception: 'This rod out of the stem of Jesse might be correctly applied to Christ, for Joseph was of the descendants of Jesse, the Father of David: but as Christ found existence through the Spirit of God, He called Himself the Son of God. If He had not done so, this description would refer to Him.'

Jesse

He was moreover a descendant of Jesse – re: Bahá'u'lláh GPB 94

the 'Rod come forth out of the stem of Jesse' and the 'Branch grown out of his roots,' Who 'shall be established upon the throne of David' – re: Bahá'u'lláh 94

Jesus Christ [see also *Spirit*]

moreover, call thou to mind the one who sentenced Jesus to death. He was the most learned of His age in His own country, whilst he who was only a fisherman believed in Him. Take good heed and be of them that observe the warning TB 10

and when the days of Moses were ended, and the light of Jesus, shining forth from the Day Spring of the Spirit, encompassed the world, all the people of Israel arose in protest against Him G 20

as she never grasped their true significance, and, to outward seeming, such events never came to pass, she, therefore, remained deprived of recognizing the beauty of Jesus and of beholding the Face of God. And they still await His coming – re: Israel 20–21

as to the matter of names, Muḥammad, Himself, declared: 'I am Jesus' *Muḥammad* 21–2

this same honour, Jesus, the Son of Mary, besought the one true God, exalted be His name and glory, to confer upon Him – re: sacrifice of Ishmael *Abraham Sacrifice* 75–6

know thou that when the Son of Man yielded up His breath to God, the whole creation wept with a great weeping. By sacrificing Himself, however, a fresh capacity was infused into all created things. Its evidences, as witnessed in all the peoples of the earth, are now manifest before thee. The deepest wisdom which the sages have uttered, the profoundest learning which any mind hath unfolded, the arts which the ablest hands have produced, the influence exerted by the most potent of rulers, are but manifestations of the quickening power released by His transcendent, His all-pervasive, and resplendent Spirit 85

O Jews! If ye be intent on crucifying once again Jesus, the Spirit of God, put Me to death, for He hath once more, in My person, been made manifest unto you. Deal with Me as ye wish, for I have vowed to lay down My life in the path of God 100

in the sayings of Him Who is the Spirit (Jesus) unnumbered significances lie concealed. Unto many things did He refer, but as He found none possessed of a hearing ear or a seeing eye He chose to conceal most of these things. Even as He saith: 'But ye cannot bear them now.' That Dawning-Place of Revelation saith that on that Day He Who is the Promised One will reveal the things which are to come. Accordingly in ESW 148

Moreover, the prophecies were not fulfilled at that time. Universal peace did not come into existence at the time of Christ. In the word 'but' the Master makes the immaculate conception quite clear. In a Tablet that has not yet been translated from the original Persian, the Master says the conception of Christ was extraordinary, against the natural law. He defines the natural law and says it was not according to this law. The Bahá'ís must accept the immaculate conception. Every religion has its mysteries. The Virgin Mary's perplexity was not due to shame, but because she could not explain her condition. The Íqán, where Bahá'u'lláh refers to Mary as 'that mild and immortal countenance,' if she were not blameless, how could He refer to her in such terms? 'Mild' here means the essence of chastity. But even if Bahá'u'lláh and the Master had not said these things about the immaculate conception, to a Bahá'í the mention of it in the Qur'án would be quite sufficient proof. (Shoghi Effendi, quoted by May Maxwell and Mary Maxwell, *Haifa Notes of Shoghi Effendi's Words*, 1937. Approved by Shoghi Effendi.)

the Kitáb-i-Aqdas, and in the Tablets to the Kings, and in the Lawḥ-i-Ra'ís, and in the Lawḥ-i-Fu'ád, most of the things which have come to pass on this earth have been announced and prophesied by the Most Sublime Pen

the purpose of the Most Exalted One (the Báb) was to insure that the proximity of the Revelation should not withhold men from the Divine and everlasting Law, even as the companions of John (the Baptist) were prevented from acknowledging Him Who is the Spirit (Jesus) 171

Annul – re: divorce and the sabbath day KI 18

it is clear and manifest that when the fire of the love of Jesus consumed the veils of Jewish limitations, and His authority was made apparent and partially enforced, He the Revealer of the unseen Beauty, addressing one day His disciples, referred unto His passing, and, kindling in their hearts the fire of bereavement, said unto them: . . . 'I go and another will come Who will tell you all that I have not told you, and will fulfil all that I have said.' Both these sayings have but one meaning 20

every discerning observer will recognize that in the Dispensation of the Qur'án both the Book and the Cause of Jesus were confirmed 20

afterwards, the companions and disciples of Jesus asked Him concerning those signs that must needs signalize the return of His manifestation. When, they asked, shall these things be? Several times they questioned that peerless Beauty, and, every time He made reply, He set forth a special sign that should herald the advent of the promised Dispensation. To this testify the records of the four Gospels 22

and when they asked Jesus concerning the signs of His coming, He said unto them: 'Immediately after the oppression of those days shall the sun be darkened, and the moon shall not give her light, and the stars shall fall from heaven, . . . and then shall appear the sign of the Son of man in heaven: and then shall all the tribes of the earth mourn, and they shall see the Son of man coming in the clouds of heaven with power and great glory 24–5

inasmuch as the Christian divines have failed to apprehend the meaning of these words, and did not recognize their object and purpose, and have clung to literal interpretation of the words of Jesus, they therefore became deprived of the streaming grace of the Muḥammadan Revelation and its showering bounties 26

there is yet another verse in the Gospel wherein He saith: 'Heaven and earth shall pass away: but My words shall not pass away.' Thus it is that the adherents of Jesus maintained that the law of the Gospel shall never be annulled, and that whensoever the promised Beauty is made manifest and all the signs are revealed, He must needs reaffirm and establish the law proclaimed in the Gospel, so that there may remain in the world no faith but His faith. This is their fundamental belief. And their conviction is such that were a person to be made manifest with all the promised signs and to promulgate that which is contrary to the letter of the law of the Gospel, they must assuredly renounce him, refuse to submit to his law, declare him an infidel, and laugh him to scorn 27–8

Spirit – re: that essence of the Spirit, Who was known amongst the people as fatherless 57

a few of the Magi, aware that the star of Jesus had appeared in heaven, sought and followed it *Magi* 64

it was Yaḥyá, son of Zachariah, who gave unto the people the tidings of the Manifestation of Jesus. Even as He hath revealed: 'God announceth Yaḥyá to thee, who shall bear witness unto the Word from God, and a 64–5 great one and chaste.' By the term 'Word' is meant Jesus, Whose coming Yaḥyá foretold. Moreover, in the heavenly Scriptures it is written: 'John the Baptist was preaching in the wilderness of Judea, and saying, Repent ye: for the Kingdom of heaven is at hand.' By John is meant Yaḥyá

as the adherents of Jesus have never understood the hidden meaning of these words, and as the signs which they and the leaders of their Faith have expected have failed to appear, they therefore refused to acknowledge, even until now, the truth of those Manifestations of Holiness that have since the days of Jesus been made manifest. They have thus deprived themselves of the outpourings of God's holy grace, and of the wonders of His divine utterance 80

were Jesus, Son of Mary, accompanied by angels, to descend from the visible heaven upon the clouds *Angel* 81

thus Jesus, Son of Mary, whilst seated one day and speaking in the strain of the Holy Spirit, uttered words such as these: 'O people! My food is the grass of the field, wherewith I satisfy my hunger. My bed is the dust, my lamp in the night the light of the moon, and my steed my own feet. Behold, who on earth is richer than I?' By the righteousness of God! Thousands of treasures circle round this poverty, and a myriad kingdoms of glory yearn for such abasement 130–31

similarly, call thou to mind the day when the Jews, who had surrounded Jesus, Son of Mary, were pressing Him to confess His claim of being the Messiah and Prophet of God, so that they might declare Him an infidel and sentence Him to death . . . Though they repeatedly questioned Him, hoping that He would confess His claim, yet Jesus held His peace and spake not . . . Thereupon Jesus lifted up His head and said: 'Beholdest thou not the Son of Man sitting on the right hand of power and might?' These were His words, and yet consider how to outward seeming He was devoid of all power except that inner power which was of God and which had encompassed all that is in heaven and on earth 132–3

Jesus said unto him: 'Arise from thy bed; thy sins are forgiven thee.' Certain of the Jews, standing by, protested saying: 'Who can forgive sins, but God alone?' And immediately He perceived their thoughts, Jesus answering said unto them: 'Whether is it easier to say to the sick of the palsy, arise, and take up thy bed, and walk; or to say, thy sins are forgiven thee? that ye may know that the Son of Man hath power on earth to forgive sins.' This is the real sovereignty, and such is the power of God's chosen Ones! 133–4

'and to Jesus, Son of Mary, We gave manifest signs' *Apostle of God* 176–7

verily, Christ is Our Word which We communicated unto Mary *Trinity* SB 60

and from the inception of the Revelation of the Apostle of God – may the blessings of God be upon Him – till the day of His ascension was the Resurrection of Jesus – peace be upon Him – wherein the Tree of divine Reality appeared in the person of Muḥammad, rewarding by His Word everyone who was a believer in Jesus, and punishing by His Word everyone who was not a believer in Him 107

for instance, if all those who were expecting the fulfilment of the promise of Jesus had been assured of the manifestation of Muḥammad, the Apostle of God, not one would have turned aside from the sayings of Jesus 110

the learned men of Christendom are held to be learned by virtue of their safeguarding the teaching of Christ, and yet consider how they themselves have been the cause of men's failure to accept the Faith and attain unto salvation 123

the followers of Jesus submitted to their clerics to be saved on the Day of Resurrection, and as a result of this obedience they eventually entered into the fire, and on the Day when the Apostle of God appeared they shut themselves out from the recognition of His exalted Person 123–4
Christianity

remember when the holy breaths of the Spirit of God (Jesus) were shedding their sweetness over Palestine and Galilee, over the shores of Jordan and the regions around Jerusalem, and the wondrous melodies of the Gospel were sounding in the ears of the spiritually illumined, all the peoples of Asia and Europe, of Africa and America, of Oceania, which comprises the islands and archipelagoes of the Pacific and Indian Oceans, were fireworshippers and pagans, ignorant of the Divine Voice that spoke out on the Day of the Covenant SDC 44

following the declaration of Jesus, the pure and reviving breath of His mouth conferred eternal life on the inhabitants of those regions for a period of three years, and through Divine Revelation the Law of Christ, at that time the vital remedy for the ailing body of the world, was established 44–5

in the days of Jesus only a few individuals turned their faces toward God; in fact only the twelve disciples and a few women truly became believers, and one of the disciples, Judas Iscariot apostatized from his Faith, leaving eleven. After the ascension of Jesus to the Realm of Glory, these few souls stood up with their spiritual qualities and with deeds that were pure and holy, and they arose by the power of God and the life-giving breaths of the Messiah to save all the peoples of the earth 45

when for the second time the unmistakable signs of Israel's disintegration, abasement, subjection and annihilation had become apparent, then the sweet and holy breathings of the Spirit of God (Jesus) were shed across Jordan and the land of Galilee; the cloud of Divine pity overspread those skies, and rained down the copious waters of the spirit, and after those swelling showers that came from the most great Sea, the Holy Land put forth its perfume and blossomed with the knowledge of God 80

and at the touch of Jesus' breath the unmindful dead that lay in the graves of their ignorance lifted up their heads to receive eternal life. For the space of three years, that Luminary of perfections walked about the fields of Palestine and in the neighbourhood of Jerusalem, leading all men into the dawn of redemption, teaching them how to acquire spiritual qualities and attributes well-pleasing to God. Had the people of Israel believed in that beauteous Countenance, they would have girded themselves to serve and obey Him heart and soul, and through the quickening fragrance of His Spirit they would have regained their lost vitality and gone on to new victories 80–81

alas, of what avail was it; they turned away and opposed Him. They rose up and tormented that Source of Divine knowledge, that Point where the Revelation had come down – all except for a handful who, turning their faces toward God, were cleansed of the stain of this world and found their way to the heights of the placeless Realm. They inflicted every agony on that Well-spring of grace until it became impossible for Him to live in the towns, and still He lifted up the flag of salvation and solidly established the fundamentals of human righteousness, that essential basis of true civilization 81

Jesus, then, founded the sacred Law on a basis of moral character and complete spirituality, and for those who believed in Him He delineated a special way of life which constitutes the highest type of action on earth 82 observe how those souls who drank the living waters of redemption at the gracious hands of Jesus, the Spirit of God, and came into the sheltering shade of the Gospel, attained to such a high plane of moral conduct that Galen, the celebrated physician, although not himself a Christian, in his summary of Plato's *Republic* extolled their actions 84

it will be even as was said by the Lord Christ: they shall persecute you for My name's sake SAB 39–40

therefore they passed the sentence upon Him, decreeing that His blood be shed, and they hanged Him on the cross, where He cried out, 'O My beloved Lord, how long wilt Thou abandon Me to them? Lift Me up unto Thee, shelter Me close to Thee, make Me a dwelling by Thy throne of glory 40

such were the words uttered by Christ. On account of these words they cavilled at and assailed Him when He said unto them, 'Verily the Son is in the Father, and the Father is in the Son.' Be thou informed of this, and learn thou the secrets of thy Lord. As for the deniers, they are veiled from God: they see not, they hear not, neither do they understand. 'Leave them to entertain themselves with their cavillings.' Abandon them to their wanderings along river beds where no stream flows. Like grazing beasts they cannot tell paste from pearl. Are they not shut away from the mysteries of thy Lord, the Clement, the Merciful? 42–3

when Christ appeared, twenty centuries ago, although the Jews were eagerly awaiting His Coming, and prayed every day, with tears, saying: 'O God, hasten the Revelation of the Messiah,' yet when the Sun of Truth dawned, they denied Him and rose against Him with the greatest enmity 44

the reason for this was that they said: 'The Revelation of Christ, according to the clear text of the Torah, will be attested by certain signs, and so long as these signs have not appeared, whoso layeth claim to be a Messiah is an impostor 44

now the Bahá'ís hold that the recorded signs did come to pass in the Manifestation of Christ, although not in the sense which the Jews understood, the description in the Torah being allegorical 45

Histories – re: Josephus; many events of the life of Christ not included 55

Father – re: the Comforter 59

the Apostles were even as Letters, and Christ was the essence of the Word Itself; and the meaning of the Word, which is grace everlasting, cast a splendour on those Letters. Again, since the Letter is a member of the Word, it therefore, in its inner meaning, is consonant with the Word 60

when the Christ was made manifest, the minds of the various contemporary peoples, their views, their emotional attitudes, whether they were Romans, Greeks, Syrians, Israelites, or others, were at variance with one another. But once His universal power was brought to bear, it gradually succeeded, after the lapse of three hundred years, in gathering together all those divergent minds under the protection, and within the governance, of one central Point 63–4

this is the reason why the universal Manifestations of God unveil Their countenances to man, and endure every calamity and sore affliction, and lay down Their lives as a ransom; it is to make these very people, the ready ones, the ones who have capacity, to become dawning points of light, and to bestow upon them the life that fadeth never. This is the true sacrifice: the offering of oneself, even as did Christ, as a ransom for the life of the world 64–5 consider the days of Christ, when none but a small band followed Him; then observe what a mighty tree that seed became, behold ye its fruitage 82

Transfiguration – re: meaning of 162

for this reason whoso looketh for Christ in His physical body hath looked in vain, and will be shut away from Him as by a veil. But whoso yearneth to find Him in the spirit will grow from day to day in joy and desire and burning love, in closeness to Him, and in beholding Him clear and plain. In this new and wondrous day, it behoveth thee to seek after the spirit of Christ. 167–8
Verily the heaven into which the Messiah rose up was not this unending sky, rather was His heaven the Kingdom of His beneficent Lord

they imagine that Christ was excluded from His heaven in the days when He walked the earth, that He fell from the heights of His sublimity, and afterwards mounted to those upper reaches of the sky, to the heaven which doth not exist at all, for it is but space. And they are waiting for Him to come down from there again, riding upon a cloud, . . . Rather, the cloud referred to in the Gospel is the human body, so called because the body is as a veil to man, which, even as a cloud, preventeth him from beholding the Sun of Truth that shineth from the horizon of Christ 168

for even as Christ said of them in the Gospel, the people are blind, they are deaf, they are dumb; and He said: 'I will heal them' 173

the diverse congregations have given up the ground of their belief, and adopted doctrines that are of no account in the sight of God. They are even as the Pharisees who both prayed and fasted, and then did sentence Jesus Christ to death. By the life of God! This thing is passing strange! 174

all the people of the world are buried in the graves of nature, or are slumbering, heedless and unaware. Just as Christ saith: 'I may come when you are not aware. The coming of the Son of Man is like the coming of a thief into a house, the owner of which is utterly unaware' 198–9

just as the New and Old Testaments propounded throughout all regions the Cause of Christ and were the pulsating power in the body of the human world – re: Covenant 223

Christ Jesus summoned all mankind to amity and peace. Unto Peter He said: 'Put up thy sword into the sheath.' Such was the bidding and counsel of the Lord Christ; and yet today the Christians one and all have drawn their swords from out the scabbard. How wide is the discrepancy between such acts and the clear Gospel text! 247–8

consider the day of Christ, which was the day of the renewal of the Kingdom of God. The people of the world attached no importance to it and did not realize its significance to such an extent that the sepulchre of Christ remained lost and unknown for three hundred years, until the maidservant of God, Helen, the mother of Constantine arrived and discovered the sacred spot 311

afterward Christ came, saying, 'I am born of the Holy Spirit.' Though it is now easy for the Christians to believe this assertion, at that time it was very difficult. According to the text of the Gospel the Pharisees said, 'Is not this the son of Joseph of Nazareth Whom we know? How can He say, therefore, I came down from heaven?' SAQ 16

Israel – re: morals of the whole world corrupt in the days of Christ 16

Abolish – re: Christ abolished a religion that had lasted fifteen hundred years 16

those who first strove to do away with Him were the Israelites, His own 17 kindred. To all outward appearances they overcame Him and brought Him into direst distress. At last they crowned Him with the crown of thorns and crucified Him. But Christ, while apparently in the deepest misery and affliction, proclaimed, 'This Sun will be resplendent, this Light will shine, My grace will surround the world, and all My enemies will be brought low.' And as He said, so it was; for all the kings of the earth have not been able to withstand Him. Nay, all their standards have been overthrown, while the banner of that Oppressed One has been raised to the zenith

Deny – re: Peter 35

also, most of the miracles of the Prophets which are mentioned have an inner significance. For instance, in the Gospel it is written that at the martyrdom of Christ darkness prevailed, and the earth quaked, and the veil of the Temple was rent in twain from the top to the bottom, and the dead came forth from their graves. If these events had happened, they would indeed have been awesome, and would certainly have been recorded in the history of the times. They would have become the cause of much troublings of heart. Either the soldiers would have taken down Christ from the cross, or they would have fled. These events are not related in any history; therefore, it is evident they ought not to be taken literally, but as having an inner significance 37–8

Daniel – re: rebuilding of Jerusalem; manifestation of Christ 40, 41–2

in Matthew, chapter 24, verse 3, Christ clearly says that what Daniel meant by this prophecy was the date of the manifestation, and this is the verse: 'As He sat upon the mount of Olives, the disciples came unto Him privately, saying, Tell us, when shall these things be? and what shall be the sign of Thy coming, and of the end of the world?' One of the explanations He gave them in reply was this (v. 15): 'When ye therefore shall see the abomination of desolation, spoken of by Daniel the Prophet, stand in the holy place, (whoso readeth, let him understand).' In this answer He referred them to the eighth chapter of the Book of Daniel, saying that everyone who reads will understand that it is this time that is spoken of. Consider how clearly the manifestation of the Báb is spoken of in the Old Testament and in the Gospel 42–3

but 'they shall not hurt nor destroy in all My holy mountain: for the earth shall be full of the knowledge of the Lord, as the waters cover the sea.' These conditions did not prevail in the time of the manifestation of Christ; for until today various and antagonistic nations exist in the world: very few acknowledge the God of Israel, and the greater number are without the knowledge of God. In the same way, universal peace did not come into existence in the time of Christ – that is to say, between the antagonistic and hostile nations there was neither peace nor concord, disputes and disagreements did not cease, and reconciliation and sincerity did not appear. So, even at this day, among the Christian sects and nations themselves, enmity, hatred and the most violent hostility are met with 63

denied with the greatest obstinacy the explanations of Christ and of His disciples *Pharisees* 71

Jew – re: Christ, Sun of Reality 77

Dove – re: 'which descended upon Christ' 85

Resurrection – re: meaning of Resurrection of Christ 104–5

in the same way there is a priority with regard to glory – that is to say, the most glorious precedes the glorious. Therefore, the Reality of Christ, Who is the Word of God, with regard to essence, attributes and glory, 116–17 certainly precedes the creatures. Before appearing in the human form, the Word of God was in the utmost sanctity and glory, existing in perfect beauty and splendour in the height of its magnificence. When through the wisdom of God the Most High it shone from the heights of glory in the world of the body, the Word of God, through this body, became oppressed, so that it fell into the hands of the Jews, and became the captive of the tyrannical and ignorant, and at last was crucified. That is why He addressed God, saying: 'Free Me from the bonds of the world of the body, and liberate Me from this cage, so that I may ascend to the heights of honour and glory, and attain unto the former grandeur and might which existed before the bodily world, that I may rejoice in the eternal world and may ascend to the original abode, the placeless world, the invisible kingdom

the Christ sacrificed Himself so that men might be freed from the imperfections of the physical nature and might become possessed of the virtues of the spiritual nature. This spiritual nature, which came into existence through the bounty of the Divine Reality, is the union of all perfections and appears through the breath of the Holy Spirit — 118

the Christ is the central point of the Holy Spirit: He is born of the Holy Spirit; He is raised up by the Holy Spirit; He is the descendant of the Holy Spirit – that is to say, that the Reality of Christ does not descend from Adam; no, it is born of the Holy Spirit — 118–19

therefore, this verse in Corinthians, 'As in Adam all die, even so in Christ shall all be made alive,' means, according to this terminology, that Adam is the father of man – that is to say, He is the cause of the physical life of mankind; His was the physical fatherhood. He is a living soul, but He is not the giver of spiritual life, whereas Christ is the cause of the spiritual life of man, and with regard to the spirit, His was the spiritual fatherhood. Adam is a living soul; Christ is a quickening spirit — 119

Sacrifice – re: Second Coming — 120–21

the position of Christ was that of absolute perfection; He made His divine perfections shine like the sun upon all believing souls, and the bounties of the light shone and radiated in the reality of men. That is why He says: 'I am the bread which descended from heaven; whosoever shall eat of this bread will not die' – that is to say, that whosoever shall partake of this divine food will attain unto eternal life: that is, every one who partakes of this bounty and receives these perfections will find eternal life, will obtain preexistent favours, will be freed from the darkness of error, and will be illuminated by the light of His guidance — 121

Serpent – re: attachment to world — 126

now, consider: Christ frequently repeated that the Ten Commandments in the Pentateuch were to be followed, and He insisted that they should be maintained. Among the Ten Commandments is one which says: 'Do not worship any picture or image.' At present in some of the Christian churches many pictures and images exist. It is, therefore, clear and evident that the Religion of God does not maintain its original principles among the people, but that it has gradually changed and altered until it has been entirely destroyed and annihilated. Because of this the manifestation is renewed, and a new religion established. But if religions did not change and alter, there would be no need of renewal — 165–6

again, consider how much the principles of the religion of Christ have been forgotten, and how many heresies have appeared. For example, Christ forbade revenge and transgression; furthermore, He commanded benevolence and mercy in return for injury and evil. Now reflect: among — 166 the Christian nations themselves how many sanguinary wars have taken place, and how much oppression, rapacity and bloodthirstiness have occurred! Many of these wars were carried on by command of the Popes. It is then clear and evident that in the passage of time religions become entirely changed and altered. Therefore, they are renewed

Gospel – re: called Good Master 170

Word – re: appeared in the Reality of Christ 206

Life – re: act in such a way 223

Wolf – re: turn the other cheek 269–70

Jesus Christ gave His life upon the cross for the unity of mankind. Those who believed in Him likewise sacrificed life, honour, possessions, family, everything, that this human world might be released from the hell of discord, enmity and strife. His foundation was the oneness of humanity PUP 5

with this small army Christ conquered the world of the East and the West. Kings and nations rose against Him. Philosophers and the greatest men of learning assailed and blasphemed His Cause. All were defeated and overcome, their tongues silenced, their lamps extinguished, their hatred quenched; no trace of them now remains. They have become as nonexistent, while His Kingdom is triumphant and eternal 5

the brilliant star of His Cause has ascended to the zenith, while night has enveloped and eclipsed His enemies. His name, beloved and adored by a few disciples, now commands the reverence of kings and nations of the world. His power is eternal; His sovereignty will continue forever, while those who opposed Him are sleeping in the dust, their very names unknown, forgotten. The little army of disciples has become a mighty cohort of millions. The Heavenly Host, the Supreme Concourse are His legions; the Word of God is His sword; the power of God is His victory 5

Jesus Christ knew this would come to pass and was content to suffer. His abasement was His glorification; His crown of thorns, a heavenly diadem. When they pressed it upon His blessed head and spat in His beautiful face, they laid the foundation of His everlasting Kingdom. He still reigns, while they and their names have become lost and unknown. He is eternal and glorious; they are nonexistent. They sought to destroy Him, but they destroyed themselves and increased the intensity of His flame by the winds of their opposition 5

the great nations of the world boast that their laws and civilization are based upon the religion of Christ. Why then do they make war upon each other? The Kingdom of Christ cannot be upheld by destroying and disobeying it. The banners of His armies cannot lead the forces of Satan 6

Christ was a divine Centre of unity and love. Whenever discord prevails instead of unity, wherever hatred and antagonism take the place of love and spiritual fellowship, Antichrist reigns instead of Christ 6

who is right in these controversies and hatreds between the sects? Did Christ command them to love or to hate each other? 6

when Christ appeared in this world, it was like the vernal bounty; the outpouring descended; the effulgences of the Merciful encircled all things; the human world found new life. Even the physical world partook of it. The divine perfections were upraised; souls were trained in the school of heaven so that all grades of human existence received life and light 10

Jesus Christ came to teach the people of the world this heavenly civilization and not material civilization. He breathed the breath of the Holy Spirit 11 into the body of the world and established an illumined civilization. Among the principles of divine civilization He came to proclaim is the Most Great Peace of mankind. Among His principles of spiritual civilization is the oneness of the kingdom of humanity. Among the principles of heavenly civilization He brought is the virtue of the human world. Among the principles of celestial civilization He announced is the improvement and betterment of human morals

Jesus Christ sought to create this love in the hearts. He suffered all difficulties and ordeals that perchance the human heart might become the fountain source of love 15

Christ appeared in this world nineteen hundred years ago to establish ties of unity and bonds of love between the various nations and different communities. He cemented together the sciences of Rome and the splendours of the civilization of Greece. He also accomplished affiliation between the Assyrian kingdom and the power of Egypt. The blending of these nations in unity, love and agreement had been impossible, but Christ through divine power established this condition among the children of men 18

Jesus Himself was poor. He did not belong to the rich. He passed His time in the desert, traveling among the poor, and lived upon the herbs of the field. He had no place to lay His head, no home. He was exposed in the open to heat, cold and frost – to inclement weather of all kinds – yet He chose this rather than riches. If riches were considered a glory, the Prophet Moses would have chosen them; Jesus would have been a rich man. When Jesus Christ appeared, it was the poor who first accepted Him, not the rich. Therefore, you are the disciples of Christ; you are His comrades, for He outwardly was poor, not rich 33

Jesus was a poor man. One night when He was out in the fields, the rain began to fall. He had no place to go for shelter so He lifted His eyes toward heaven, saying, 'O Father! For the birds of the air Thou hast created nests, for the sheep a fold, for the animals dens, for the fish places of refuge, but for Me Thou hast provided no shelter. There is no place where I may lay My head. My bed consists of the cold ground; My lamps at night are the stars, and My food is the grass of the field. Yet who upon earth is richer than I? For the greatest blessing Thou hast not given to the rich and mighty but unto Me, for Thou hast given Me the poor. To Me Thou hast granted this blessing. They are Mine. Therefore I am the richest man on earth 33–4

the second birth of which Jesus has spoken refers to the appearance of this heavenly nature in man. It is expressed in the baptism of the Holy Spirit, and he who is baptized by the Holy Spirit is a veritable manifestation of divine mercy to mankind. Then he becomes just and kind to all humanity; he entertains prejudice and ill will toward none; he shuns no nation or people 41

Jesus Christ declares that the sun rises upon the evil and the good, and the rain descends upon the just and the unjust – upon all humanity alike. Christ was a divine mercy which shone upon all mankind, the medium for the descent of the bounty of God, and the bounty of God is transcendent, unrestricted, universal 41

you must follow the example and footprints of Jesus Christ. Read the Gospels. Jesus Christ was mercy itself, was love itself. He even prayed in behalf of His executioners – for those who crucified Him – saying, 'Father, forgive them; for they know not what they do.' If they knew what they were doing, they would not have done it. Consider how kind 42

Jesus Christ was, that even upon the cross He prayed for His oppressors. We must follow His example. We must emulate the Prophets of God. We must follow Jesus Christ. We must free ourselves from all these imitations which are the source of darkness in the world

they are the children of the Kingdom. The Kingdom of heaven is for such 52–3
souls as these, for they are near to God. They have pure hearts. They have spiritual faces. The effect of the divine teachings is manifest in the perfect purity of their hearts. That is why Christ has addressed the world, saying, 'Except ye be converted, and become as little children, ye shall not enter into the kingdom of heaven' – that is, men must become pure in heart to know God

the appearance of Christ was a divine springtime. Therefore, it caused a 54–5
great commotion and vibrant movement in the world of humanity. The Sun of Reality dawned, the cloud of mercy poured down its rain, the breezes of providence moved, the world became a new world, mankind reflected an extraordinary radiance, souls were educated, minds were developed, intelligences became acute, and the human world attained a new freshness of life, like unto the advent of spring

during the days of Jesus Christ the Jews were expecting the appearance of 62
the Messiah, praying and beseeching God day and night that the Promised One might appear. Why did they reject Him when He did appear? They denied Him absolutely, refused to believe in Him. There was no abuse and persecution which they did not heap upon Him. They reviled Him with curses, placed a crown of thorns upon His head, led Him through the streets in scorn and derision and finally crucified Him. Why did they do this?

Jesus Christ was an Educator of humanity. His teachings were altruistic; 85
His bestowal, universal. He taught mankind by the power of the Holy Spirit and not through human agency, for the human power is limited, whereas the divine power is illimitable and infinite. The influence and accomplishment of Christ will attest this

if you reflect upon the essential teachings of Jesus, you will realize that they 86
are the light of the world. Nobody can question their truth. They are the very source of life and the cause of happiness to the human race. The forms and superstitions which appeared and obscured the light did not affect the reality of Christ. For example, Jesus Christ said, 'Put up thy sword into the sheath.' The meaning is that warfare is forbidden and abrogated

for Christ declared, 'Love your enemies, . . . and pray for them which . . . 86
persecute you; . . .' How can hatred, hostility and persecution be reconciled with Christ and His teachings?

the Sun of Reality, the Word of God, shone from the Messianic mirror 115
through the wonderful channel of Jesus Christ more fully and more wonderfully. Its effulgences were manifestly radiant, but even to this day the Jews are holding to the Mosaic mirror. Therefore, they are bereft of witnessing the lights of eternity in Jesus

when the Messianic star of Jesus Christ dawned, He declared He had come 117
to gather together the lost tribes or scattered sheep of Moses. He not only shepherded the flock of Israel but brought together people of Chaldea, Egypt, Syria, ancient Assyria and Phoenicia. These people were in a state of utmost hostility, thirsting for the blood of each other with the ferocity of animals; but Jesus Christ brought them together, cemented and united them in His Cause and established such a bond of love among them that enmity and warfare were abandoned. It is evident,

therefore, that the divine teachings are intended to create a bond of unity in the human world and establish the foundations of love and fellowship among mankind

Christ spoke a parable in which He said His words were like the seeds of the sower; some fall upon stony ground, some upon sterile soil, some are choked by thorns and thistles, but some fall upon the ready, receptive and fertile ground of human hearts. When seeds are cast upon sterile soil, no growth follows. Those cast upon stony ground will grow a short time, but lacking deep roots will wither away. Thorns and thistles destroy others completely, but the seed cast in good ground brings forth harvest and fruitage 149

the Jews were believers in Moses, awaiting the coming of the Messiah. The virtues and perfections of Moses became apparent in Jesus Christ most effulgently, but the Jews held to the name Moses, not adoring the virtues and perfections manifest in Him. Had they been adoring these virtues and seeking these perfections, they would assuredly have believed in Jesus Christ when the same virtues and perfections shone in Him 152

the essential teaching of Moses was the law of Sinai, the Ten Commandments. Christ renewed and again revealed the commands of the one God and precepts of human action 154

there is no intrinsic meaning in the leaves of a book, but the thought they convey leads you to reflect upon reality. The reality of Jesus was the perfect meaning, the Christhood in Him which in the Holy Books is symbolized as the Word 155

'the Word was with God.' The Christhood means not the body of Jesus but the perfection of divine virtues manifest in Him. Therefore, it is written, 'He is God.' This does not imply separation from God, even as it is not possible to separate the rays of the sun from the sun. The reality of Christ was the embodiment of divine virtues and attributes of God. For in Divinity there is no duality. All adjectives, nouns and pronouns in that court of sanctity are one; there is neither multiplicity nor division. The intention of this explanation is to show that the Words of God have innumerable significances and mysteries of meanings – each one a thousand and more 155

Christ ratified and proclaimed the foundation of the law of Moses. Muḥammad and all the Prophets have revoiced that same foundation of reality 366

when the law of God had seemingly passed from them and the foundation of the religion of God was apparently destroyed – Jesus Christ appeared. When He arose among the Jews, the first thing He did was to proclaim the validity of the Manifestation of Moses. He declared that the Torah, the Old Testament, was the Book of God and that all the prophets of Israel were valid and true 366

through Christianity the greatness of Moses became known among all nations. It is a fact that before the appearance of Christ, the name of Moses had not been heard of in Persia. In India they had no knowledge of Judaism, and it was only through the Christianizing of Europe that the teachings of the Old Testament became spread in that region . . . 366–7

Therefore, Christ really promulgated Judaism; for He was a Jew and not opposed to the Jews. He did not deny the Prophethood of Moses; on the contrary, He proclaimed and ratified it. He did not invalidate the Torah; He spread its teachings *Torah*

the Lord Christ said, 'He that hath seen Me hath seen the Father' – God manifested in man PT 26 may the world be for you no obstacle hiding the truth from your sight, as the human body of Christ hid His Divinity from the people of His day 45

Muḥammad 47

thus, all the spiritual prophecies concerning the coming of Christ were fulfilled, but the Jews shut their eyes that they should not see, and their ears that they should not hear, and the Divine Reality of Christ passed through their midst unheard, unloved and unrecognized 56

Disciple – re: Apostles of Christ 61

when in the Gospels, Christ speaks of 'water' *Gospel* 82

through the Love of God, Christ was sent into the world with His inspiring example of a perfect life of self-sacrifice and devotion, bringing to men the message of Eternal Life 83

the traces of the Spirit of Jesus Christ, the influence of His Divine Teaching, is present with us today, and is everlasting 91

Christ endured a life of sorrow, pain and grief, to bring a perfect example of love into the world – and in spite of this we continue to act in a contrary spirit one towards the other 121–2

in the day of Christ all nations were expecting that His Holiness Christ should come from the heaven, and He came from heaven, though outwardly He came from the womb of Mary BWF 387

in the day of the Manifestation of Christ, many souls became portionless and deprived because they were members of the Holy of Holies in Jerusalem. According to that membership, they became veiled from that brilliant Beauty. Therefore, turn thou thy face to the Church of God which consists in divine instructions and merciful exhortations. For what similarity is there between the church of stone and cement and the celestial Holy of Holies! 390

when Christ – glory be to Him! – appeared, a storm of trials arose . . . the winds of tests blew *Test* 395

the Cause of Bahá'u'lláh is the same as the Cause of Christ *Cause* 400

in the coming of Christ, the divine teachings were given in accordance with the infancy of the human race *Teachings* 400

Brother – re: Christ refused to associate with His brothers 437

in reality His Holiness Christ proclaimed and completed the law of Moses. He was the very helper and assister of Moses. He spread the book of Moses throughout the world and established anew the fundamentals of the law revealed by him. He abolished certain unimportant laws and forms which were no longer compatible with the exigencies of the time, such as divorce and plurality of wives FWU 75

if a Christian sets aside traditionary forms and blind imitation of ceremonials and investigates the reality of the gospels, he will discover that the foundation principles of the teachings of His Holiness Christ were mercy, love, fellowship, benevolence, altruism, the resplendence or radiance of divine bestowals, acquisition of the breaths of the Holy Spirit and oneness with God 105

know that the return of Christ for a second time doth not mean what the people believe, but, rather, signifieth the One promised to come after Him TAB 138

as to the resurrection of the body of Christ three days subsequent to His departure: This signifies the divine teachings and spiritual religion of His Holiness Christ, which constitute His spiritual body, which is living and perpetual forevermore 192 by the 'three days' of His death is meant that after the great martyrdom, the penetration of the divine teachings and the spread of the spiritual law became relaxed on account of the crucifixion of Christ. For the disciples were somewhat troubled by the violence of divine tests. But when they became firm, that divine spirit resurrected and that body – which signifies the divine word – arose 192

for the body of Christ was crucified and vanished, but the Spirit of Christ is always pouring upon the contingent world, and is manifest before the insight of the people of assurance 193–4

Pharisees – re: persecution of Christ 221, 230, 349

as to thy question concerning Christ: Know thou, He was perfect in respect of spirit as well as body. His material (body) was a perfect body in every respect; none of His material conditions were imperfect at all, . . . His heavenly condition was also a perfect one, comprising all the divine perfections. Reflect thou upon these words, so that the door of knowledge may be opened before thy face 228

Deny – re: denial of Christ by Peter 528

Atonement – re: the real atonement that His Holiness Christ made 543

as to the question that the holy and spiritual souls influence, help and guide the creatures after they have cast off this elemental mould – this is an established truth of the Bahá'ís. Nay even the Holy Manifestations of God extend a great Bounty and an evident Light after their ascent from this world. For His Holiness Christ there was more and greater promotion of the Word, manifestation of divine power, conversion of holy souls, and the giving of eternal life, after (His) martyrdom 543

the children who are born in the cradle of the love of God, who are nurtured by the breast of the knowledge of God, who are brought up in the bosom of the gift of God, and who are fostered in the lap of the training of God. Such children are those of whom it was said by Christ, 'Verily, they are the children of the Kingdom!' 606

Bahá'u'lláh has not abolished the teachings of Christ. He gave a fresh impulse to them and renewed them; explained and interpreted them; expanded and fulfilled them SW II 6, p8

thou hast asked about the statement in the Hidden Words, which reads: 'O Son of Spirit! Turn thy face so that thou mayest find Me within thee, Powerful, Mighty and Supreme.' This is the statement to which His Holiness, the Christ, referred His apostles in the Gospel, saying, 'The Father is in the Son, and the Son is in you.' II 7–8, pp11–12

This is evident that, when the hearts are purified and through divine education and heavenly teachings become the manifestors of infinite perfections, they are like clear mirrors, and the Sun of Truth will reflect with might, power and omnipotence in such a mirror, and to such an extent that whatever is brought before it is illumined and ignited

Qur'án – re: crucifixion of Christ II 7–8, p13

Paradise – re: explanation saying of Christ II 15, p16

His Holiness Christ was one person, without any worldly assistance and help, but through the effect of the Holy Spirit he was enabled to unite many nations and religions under the standard of Christianity – re: Holy Spirit VIII 8, p101

Holy Spirit – re: mention of Christ and Muḥammad VIII 8, p101

the life and morals of a spiritual man are in themselves an education to others. Let your thoughts, words and actions bring life to those around you. Do not think of your own limitations; dream only of the welfare of VIII 8, p102 the Kingdom of Abhá. See the influence of Jesus Christ among his apostles, then consider their influence on others. These simple men were helped by the power of the Holy Spirit. So may you receive the divine assistance. Our capabilities are limited, but the help of the Kingdom of Abhá is limitless

in this story (the 'miracle' of Jesus walking on the water) of our Lord Jesus, the Sea of Tiberius represents the ocean of creation, – the two shores represent earthly truth and spiritual truth. The boat or ark stands for arguments and reasons by which men acquire knowledge and in this boat Jesus' disciples were tossed on the waves of the ocean of creation. The shore which Jesus left in order to come to them, walking on the water, represents earthly knowledge. The haven or shore to which he guided them represents spiritual knowledge . . . VIII 9, pp114–15

The disciples of Jesus attempted to sail over the sea of creation in the ark of argument and reasoning, finding great difficulty and danger in proving the truth by so doing. But when Christ, the Light of the world, who knew all things by the light of inner spiritual illumination, came to them in their boat, walking by his knowledge over the ocean of existence, and having no need of the ark of argument, then immediately they were at their desired haven

Baptism – re: the baptism of Christians as practised today is not the teachings of Christ IX 9, p103

'Abdu'l-Bahá spoke to the pilgrims about the days of Christ and how he walked alone near the animals on the shore of Lake Tiberias (Sea of Galilee); and concerning the people, how they were prevented from seeing and knowing the Manifestation of God through their blindness, in these days. 'Abdu'l-Bahá said: 'The Supreme Báb was the promised one of the Qur'án, with regard to the question of the Seal of the Prophets. Muḥammad was known as the Seal of the Prophets. (The Muḥammadans think this title means that no prophet will appear after Muḥammad.) This belief is not only limited to the Moslems. The Jews believed that Moses was the Seal of the Prophets, that he sealed the prophethood of Laws. The Christians believe that after Christ, no prophet with Laws will come, but that Christ himself will descend from heaven. Yes, these creatures are not waiting for the manifestation of the Truth, they are waiting for the manifestation of their own superstitions. For example, the Moslems are waiting for the Dedjal (false Christ or anti-Christ) more than for the Qá'im (the Forerunner or Precursor of the Manifestation). They do not associate the appearance of the anti-Christ with the Forerunner. Nay, rather they associate the appearance of the Forerunner with the appearance of the anti-Christ. This (the anti-Christ) is known to them as unlimited or independent, the Forerunner as limited and dependent IX 10, p111

the mayor, the judge and other eminent officials of Tiberias were present, and all were exhilarated by his utterances. Then, as the lake reflected the wonder of the rising moon and the stars – the beauty of the creator – 'Abdu'l-Bahá spoke to the friends: 'His Holiness Christ, used to walk most of the nights when in the region of this lake. He was all alone, thinking of the illumination of the world of humanity. He did not rest for one moment. He was not at liberty for even one day. He spent His days as a wanderer, and was shelterless in these deserts and mountains. The place where He called the disciples to enter the Kingdom of God is in this region. They were engaged in fishing. His Holiness Christ, used to walk alone on the shore. When He saw the signs of acceptance in their faces, He said, "Come, so that I may make you the fishers of men," and they at IX 10, p112

once left everything and followed that Light personified!
'God be exalted! Always, in the beginning of the Cause, common souls, who in the estimation of the people , were of no importance whatever, have advanced to the divine Manifestation. For example, these fishermen believed in His Holiness Christ. In the Qur'án it is revealed that the ignorant of the people would say to His Holiness the Messenger (Muḥammad), "None have followed thee except the most degraded of the people; the learned sages, the nobles and the high class count thee as a fool." However, it cannot be said of this Cause, for everyone testifies that all of the learned philosophers and nobles of every nation were humble in the presence of the Blessed Beauty, and great numbers of these became believers'

Manna – re: disciples of Christ and spiritual food XI 16, p275

to Him Jesus Christ had referred as the 'Prince of this world,' as the 'Comforter' Who will 'reprove the world of sin, and of righteousness, and of judgment,' as the 'Spirit of Truth' Who 'will guide you into all truth,' Who 'shall not speak of Himself, but whatsoever He shall hear, that shall He speak,' as the 'Lord of the Vineyard,' and as the 'Son of Man' Who 'shall come in the glory of His Father' 'in the clouds of heaven with power and great glory,' with 'all the holy angels' about Him, and 'all nations' gathered before His throne – re: Bahá'u'lláh GPB 95

to His Day Jesus Christ Himself had referred as 'the regeneration when the Son of Man shall sit in the throne of His glory' – re: Bahá'u'lláh 96

the Lord of the Kingdom, Jesus Christ returned in the glory of the Father, was about to ascend His throne, and assume the sceptre of a world-embracing, indestructible sovereignty 151

the Gospels, in which the few sayings attributed to Jesus Christ afford no clear guidance regarding the future administration of the affairs of His Faith 213

not one of these did Christ conceive – re: sacraments *Church* WOB 20

consider the Faith proclaimed by Jesus. Though it first appeared in the East, yet not until its light had been shed upon the West did the full measure of its potentialities be manifest 75

the East hath ever been the dawning-place of the Sun of Truth. In the East all the Prophets of God have appeared . . . The West hath acquired illumination from the East but in some respects the reflection of the light hath been greater in the Occident. This is specially true of Christianity. Jesus Christ appeared in Palestine and His teachings were founded in that country. Although the doors of the Kingdom were first opened in that land and the bestowals of God were spread broadcast from its centre, the people of the West have embraced and promulgated Christianity more fully than the people of the East 75

Jerusalem – re: words of Christ addressed to 176

for the Faith of Bahá'u'lláh – if we would faithfully appraise it – can never, and in no aspect of its teachings, be at variance, much less in conflict, with the purpose animating, or the authority invested in, the Faith of Jesus Christ 185

the decline that had set in in the religious, the spiritual, the cultural, and the moral life of the Jewish people, at the time of the appearance of Jesus Christ ADJ 14

during the lifetime of Jesus Christ the believing, firm souls were few and numbered, but the heavenly blessings descended so plentifully that in a number of years countless souls entered beneath the shadow of the Gospel 47

Jesus Christ

'reflect upon the One Who was the Spirit of God (Jesus). Though He showed forth the utmost compassion and tenderness, yet they rose up against that Essence of Being and Lord of the seen and unseen, in such a manner that He could find no refuge wherein to rest. Each day He wandered unto a new place, and sought a new shelter' [words of Bahá'u'lláh] — PDC 80

Cavil – re: Jewish doctors — 101

a clergy that have interposed themselves between their flocks and the Christ returned in the glory of the Father *Church* — 106

Christianity – re: Sonship and Divinity of Jesus — 109

when Jesus spoke to those around Him, He addressed them primarily as individuals rather than as component parts of one universal, indivisible entity. The whole surface of the earth was as yet unexplored, and the organization of all its peoples and nations as one unit could, consequently, not be envisaged, how much less proclaimed or established — 119

our belief in Christ, as Bahá'ís, is so firm, so unshakeable and so exalted in nature that very few Christians are to be found now-a-days who love Him and reverence Him and have the faith in Him that we have. It is only from the dogmas and creeds of the churches that we dissociate ourselves; not from the Spirit of Christianity (Letter of Shoghi Effendi) — LG 121

concerning the Virgin Birth of Jesus; on this point, as on several others, the Bahá'í teachings are in full agreement with the doctrines of the Catholic Church. In the 'Kitáb-i-Íqán' p. 56, and in a few other Tablets still unpublished, Bahá'u'lláh confirms, however indirectly, the Catholic conception of the Virgin Birth. Also, 'Abdu'l-Bahá in the 'Some Answered Questions', Chap. XII, p. 73, explicitly states that 'Christ found existence through the Spirit of God' which statement necessarily implies, when reviewed in the light of the text, that Jesus was not the son of Joseph (Letter 14.10.35) — 366–7

in accepting Bahá'u'lláh you have accepted Christ in His appearance as the Father, as He Himself so clearly foretold. The Catholic Church does not believe this; on the contrary, it still awaits the return of Christ — BN 286, p1

Jews [see also *Israel, Jerusalem*]

'why is it then that this law is annulled and hath ceased to operate among the Jews?' He answered and said: 'When Nebuchadnezzar delivered Jerusalem to the flames, and put the Jews to death, only a few survived. The divines of that age, considering the extremely limited number of the Jews, and the multitude of the Amalekites, took counsel together, and came to the conclusion that were they to enforce the law of the Pentateuch, every survivor who had been delivered from the hand of Nebuchadnezzar would have to be put to death according to the verdict of the Book. Owing to such considerations, they totally repealed the penalty of death' — KI 85–6

alone the Jews believed in the divinity and oneness of God — SDC 44

then all the idolatrous nations as well as the Jews rose up in their might to kill the Divine fire that had been lit in the lamp of Jerusalem *Light* — 45

Affliction Nebuchadnezzar – re: Babylonian captivity — 79

and while those emblems of redemption were to outward seeming abandoned to the malevolence and persecution of their tormentors, in reality they had been delivered out of the hopeless darkness which encompassed the Jews and they shone forth in everlasting glory at the dawn of that new day — 82 that mighty Jewish nation toppled and crumbled away, but those few souls who sought shelter beneath the Messianic Tree transformed all human life — 82–3

only a small group of Jews professed belief in the Oneness of God and they were wretched outcasts — 83

another of the conditions is this, that in the days of the Messiah the Jews will prosper and triumph over all the peoples of the world, but now they are living in the utmost abasement and servitude in the empire of the Romans. Then how can this be the Messiah promised in the Torah?' — SAB 45–6

In this wise did they object to that Sun of Truth, although that Spirit of God was indeed the One promised in the Torah. But as they did not understand the meaning of these signs, they crucified the Word of God. Now the Bahá'ís hold that the recorded signs did come to pass in the Manifestation of Christ, although not in the sense which the Jews understood, the description in the Torah being allegorical. For instance, among the signs is that of sovereignty. For Bahá'ís say that the sovereignty of Christ was a heavenly, divine, everlasting sovereignty, not a Napoleonic sovereignty that vanisheth in a short time . . .

In like manner all the other signs have been made manifest, but the Jews did not understand. Although nearly twenty centuries have elapsed since Christ appeared with divine splendour, yet the Jews are still awaiting the coming of the Messiah and regard themselves as true and Christ as false

Histories – re: Josephus; many facts not included — 55

Messiah – re: ridicule by the Jews — 173

although a number of Jews sided with him *Judas Iscariot* — 212

all the peoples of the world are awaiting two Manifestations, Who must be contemporaneous; all wait for the fulfillment of this promise. In the Bible the Jews have the promise of the Lord of Hosts and the Messiah; in the Gospel the return of Christ and Elijah is promised — SAQ 39

thus among the Jews, at the end of the cycle of Moses, which coincides with the Christian manifestation, the Law of God disappeared, only a form without spirit remaining — 47

consider that if the Jews had not kept turning to the horizon of Moses, and had only regarded the Sun of Reality, without any doubt they would have recognized the Sun in the dawning-place of the reality of Christ, in the greatest divine splendour. But, alas! a thousand times alas! attaching themselves to the outward words of Moses, they were deprived of the divine bounties and the lordly splendours — 77

therefore, the Jews rejected Christ, and, God forbid! called the Messiah masíkh, considered Him to be the destroyer of the edifice of God — 111

now the question of the good or evil of things is determined by reason or by law. Some believe that it is determined by law; such are the Jews, who, believing all the commandments of the Pentateuch to be absolutely obligatory, regard them as matters of law, not of reason — 266

the Jews were expecting the appearance of the Messiah, looking forward to it with devotion of heart and soul, but because they were submerged in imitations, they did not believe in Jesus Christ when He appeared — PUP 180

but as to the Jewish doctors, Christian priests and monks who read those Books, verily, they know the letter only and they utter the words, as parrots, without understanding their inner meanings. They comprehend them not, because they are engrossed in worldly desires and lusts and their hearts are attached to mundane allurements. Verily, are they not — BWF 391 heedless of God and understand nothing and find not the right path?

when the disciples were calling in the name of Christ, the Jews scoffed, scorned and laughed at them *Disciple* 394

through failure to investigate reality the Jews rejected His Holiness Jesus Christ FWU 74

these statements and attitudes of the Jews were inherited from their fathers; blind allegiance to literal expectations which did not come to pass during the time of Jesus Christ 75

it was humbled to dust, and, in its ignominious collapse, suffered the same fate as the Jewish hierarchy, the chief persecutor of Jesus Christ, had suffered at the hands of its Roman masters, in the first century of the Christian Era, almost two thousand years before – re: the Caliphate GPB 407–8

addressing the Jewish people Bahá'u'lláh has written: 'The Most Great Law is come, and the Ancient Beauty ruleth upon the throne of David. Thus hath My Pen spoken that which the histories of bygone ages have related. At this time, however, David crieth aloud and saith: "O my loving Lord! Do Thou number me with such as have stood steadfast in Thy Cause, O Thou through Whom the faces have been illumined, and the footsteps have slipped!"' PDC 76–7

'the Jewish doctors' *Muḥammad* 80

'the Jewish and Christian divines' *Divines* 81

during the latter part of the first century of the Christian era – a disaster that razed to its foundations the Temple of Solomon, destroyed the Holy of Holies, laid waste the city of David, uprooted the Jewish hierarchy in Jerusalem, massacred thousands of the Jewish people – the persecutors of the religion of Jesus Christ – dispersed the remainder over the surface of the earth, and reared a pagan colony on Zion 96

cannot fail to observe the striking parallel between the cataclysmic visitation of Providence that has afflicted the most sacred institutions of the Jews in the Holy Land and the utter collapse in this, the first century of the Bahá'í era, of the Sultanate and the Caliphate, the highest institutions of orthodox Islám BA 170

fulfillment of prophecies uttered by the Founder of Faith and Centre of His Covenant culminating in establishment of Jewish State, signalizing birth after lapse of two thousand years of an independent nation in the Holy Land MBW 7

Job

as to the statement of Job, chapter 19, verses 25–27 *Redeemer* SAB 171

this did Job say after they had reproached him, and he himself had lamented the harms that his tribulations had wreaked upon him. And even when, from the terrible inroads of the sickness, his body was covered with worms, he sought to tell those about him that still he would be fully healed, and that in his very body, with his very eyes, he would gaze on his Redeemer 171–2

Job proved the fidelity of his love for God by being faithful through his great adversity, as well as during the prosperity of his life PT 50

reflect upon his holiness Job: What trials, calamities and perplexities did he not endure! But these tests were like unto the fire and his holiness Job was like unto pure gold. Assuredly gold is purified by being submitted to the fire and if it contain any alloy or imperfection, it will disappear. That is the reason why violent tests become the cause of the everlasting glory of the righteous and are conducive to the destruction and disappearance of the unrighteous TAB 655

Joel

Joel saith: 'For the Day of the Lord is great and very terrible; and who can abide it?' Firstly, in the sublime utterance set forth in the Gospel He saith that none is aware of the time of the Revelation, that none knoweth it except God, the All-Knowing, Who is cognizant of all. Secondly, He setteth forth the greatness of the Revelation — ESW 143

Announcement — 143–4

John

the Lord God Omnipotent hath been enthroned in His Kingdom and hath made all things new. This is the truth and what truth can be greater than that announced by the Revelation of St. John the Divine? *Alpha and Omega* — SAB 12–13

it is even as in the time of the Messiah, when the Pharisees and the pious were left without a portion, while Peter, John and Andrew, given neither to pious worship nor ascetic practice, won the day — 18

accordingly did Saint John the Divine tell of twelve gates in his vision, and twelve foundations. By 'that great city, the holy Jerusalem, descending out of heaven from God' is meant the holy Law of God, and this is set forth in many Tablets and still to be read in the Scriptures of the Prophets of the past: for instance, that Jerusalem was seen going out into the wilderness — 165

as to the woman in the Revelation of Saint John, chapter 12, who fled into the wilderness, and the great wonder appearing in the heavens – that woman clothed with the sun, with the moon under her feet: what is meant by the woman is the Law of God. For according to the terminology of the Holy Books, this reference is to the Law, the woman being its symbol here. And the two luminaries, the sun and the moon, are the two thrones, the Turkish and the Persian, these two being under the rule of the Law of God. The sun is the symbol of the Persian Empire, and the moon, that is, the crescent, of the Turkish. The twelve-fold crown is the twelve Imáms, who, even as the Apostles, supported the Faith of God. The newborn Child is the Beauty of the Adored One [the Báb] come forth out of the Law of God. He then saith that the woman fled into the wilderness, that is, the Law of God was carried out of Palestine to the desert of Hijaz, where it remained 1260 years – that is, until the advent of the promised Child. And as is well known, in the Holy Books, every day is accounted as one year — 172

the other kind resembles inspiration, and this is real – such are the revelations of Isaiah, of Jeremiah and of St. John, which are real – re: spiritual discoveries — SAQ 251

the 'Second Woe,' spoken of in the Apocalypse of St. John the Divine, had, at long last, appeared — GPB 58

the 'forty and two months,' during which the 'Holy City,' as predicted by St. John the Divine, would be trodden under foot, had elapsed – re: coming of the Báb — 58

which the writer of the Apocalypse had described as the 'new heaven' and the 'new earth,' as 'the Tabernacle of God,' as the 'Holy City,' as the 'Bride,' the 'New Jerusalem coming down from God' *Kitáb-i-Aqdas* — 213

the passage in the Gospel of St. John 14:26, is a reference to the Revelation of Bahá'u'lláh, through Whose coming this prophecy was fulfilled (Letter 21.4.39) — LG 419

John the Baptist

even as the companions of John (the Baptist) were prevented from acknowledging Him Who is the Spirit (Jesus) ESW 171

moreover, in the heavenly Scriptures it is written: 'John the Baptist was preaching in the wilderness of Judea, and saying, Repent ye: for the Kingdom of heaven is at hand.' By John is meant Yaḥyá KI 64–5

so, having regard to this state and station, Christ announced that John the Baptist was Elias, who was to come before Christ *Elias* BWF 371

Baptism – re: discourse on meaning SW IX 9, p103

He the 'Qá'im' (He Who ariseth) promised to the Shí'ahs, the 'Mihdí' (One Who is guided) awaited by the Sunnís, the 'Return of John the Baptist' expected by the Christians GPB 57–8

Joseph

and Joseph came to you aforetime with clear tokens, but ye ceased not to doubt of the message with which He came to you, until, when He died, ye said, 'God will by no means raise up a Messenger after Him.' Thus God misleadeth him who is the transgressor, the doubter KI 212–13

such in particular is the case with the divine reality of the Most Great Name, the Abhá Beauty. When once He standeth revealed unto the assembled peoples of the world and appeareth with such comeliness, such enchantments – alluring as a Joseph in the Egypt of the spirit – He enslaveth all the lovers on earth SAB 64

this exile became the cause of the progress of the descendants of Abraham, and the Holy Land was given to them. As a result the teachings of Abraham were spread abroad, a Jacob appeared among His posterity, and a Joseph who became ruler in Egypt *Abraham* SAQ 13

an envy as blind as that which had possessed the soul of Mírzá Yaḥyá, as deadly as that which the superior excellence of Joseph had kindled in the hearts of his brothers, as deep-seated as that which had blazed in the bosom of Cain and prompted him to slay his brother Abel GPB 246

also, 'Abdu'l-Bahá . . . explicitly states that Christ found existence through the spirit of God which statement necessarily implies, when reviewed in the light of the text, that Jesus was not the son of Joseph *Jesus Christ* (Letter 14.10.35) LG 366–7

Joshua

in Joshua's time there were thirty-one governments in the hands of the Israelites, and in every noble human attribute – learning, stability, determination, courage, honour, generosity – this people came to surpass all the nations of the earth *Israel* SDC 76–7

Judah

and Who 'shall assemble the outcasts of Israel, and gather together the dispersed of Judah from the four corners of the earth' – re: Bahá'u'lláh GPB 94–5

Judaism see *Israel, Jew*

Judas Iscariot

Judas Iscariot apostasized from his faith *Jesus Christ* SDC 45

Judas Iscariot was the greatest of the disciples, and he summoned the people to Christ. Then it seemed to him that Jesus was showing increasing regard to the Apostle Peter, and when Jesus said, 'Thou art Peter, and upon this rock I will build My church,' these words addressed to Peter, and this singling out of Peter for special honour, had a marked effect on the Apostle, and kindled envy within the heart of Judas SAB 163 the case of all of them resembleth the violation of the Covenant by Judas Iscariot and his followers. Consider: hath any result or trace remained after them? Not even a name hath been left by his followers and although a number of Jews sided with him it was as if he had no followers at all. This Judas Iscariot who was the leader of the apostles betrayed Christ for thirty pieces of silver. Take heed, O ye people of perception 212

Judge

'believe ye then part of the Book, and deny part?' How could ye judge that which ye understand not? *Qur'án* KI 169

thus the peoples of the world are judged by their countenance. By it, their misbelief, their faith, and their iniquity are all made manifest. Even as it is evident in this day how the people of error are, by their countenance, known and distinguished from the followers of divine Guidance [see also *Reckoning* 172–3] 173–4

at the time of the appearance of Him Whom God will make manifest the most distinguished among the learned and the lowliest of men shall both be judged alike. How often the most insignificant of men have acknowledged the truth, while the most learned have remained wrapt in veils. Thus in every Dispensation a number of souls enter the fire by reason of their following in the footsteps of others [see also *Truth*] SB 91

Judgment

this period of time is the Promised Age, the assembling of the human race to the 'Resurrection Day' and now is the great 'Day of Judgment.' Soon the whole world, as in springtime, will change its garb BWF 352

this judgment of God *Fire* PDC 4

I have, in the preceding pages, attempted to represent this world-afflicting ordeal that has laid its grip upon mankind as primarily a judgment of God pronounced against the peoples of the earth, who, for a century, have refused to recognize the One Whose advent had been promised to all religions, and in Whose Faith all nations can alone, and must eventually, seek their true salvation 115

Ka'bah

God, of a truth, revealed unto Me in the sacred house of the Ka'bah, 'Verily, I am God, no God is there but Me. I have singled Thee out for Myself and have chosen Thee as the Remembrance *Báb* SB 73

Apostle of God – re: debarred Him, for seven years 78–9

while He, through the potency of Whose Word the Ka'bah (the sanctuary of Mecca) hath become the object of adoration, is forsaken in this mountain *Mecca* 105

Káfí

even as it hath been recorded in the 'Káfí,' in the tradition of Jábir, in the 'Tablet of Fátimih,' concerning the character of the Qá'im: 'He shall manifest the perfection of Moses, the splendour of Jesus, and the patience of Job. His chosen ones shall be abased in His day. Their heads shall be offered as presents even as the heads of the Turks and the Daylamites. They shall be slain and burnt. Fear shall seize them; dismay and alarm shall strike terror in their hearts. The earth shall be dyed with their blood. Their womenfolk shall bewail and lament. These indeed are my friends!' Consider, not a single letter of this tradition hath remained unfulfilled. In most of the places their blessed blood hath been shed; in every city they have been made captives, have been paraded throughout KI 245 the provinces, and some have been burnt with fire – re: concerning the Qá'im [see also *Qá'im* 245–6]

Karím

I swear by God that not one breath, blowing from the meads of divine knowledge, hath ever been wafted upon his soul, nor hath he ever unravelled a single mystery of ancient wisdom. Nay, were the meaning of Knowledge ever to be expounded unto him, dismay would fill his heart, and his whole being would shake to its foundation. Notwithstanding his base and senseless statements, behold to what heights of extravagance his claims have reached! KI 188–9

Gracious God! How great is Our amazement at the way the people have gathered around him, and have borne allegiance to his person! Content with transient dust, these people have turned their face unto it, and cast behind their backs Him Who is the Lord of Lords. Satisfied with the croaking of the crow and enamoured with the visage of the raven, they have renounced the melody of the nightingale and the charm of the rose

and as to this man's attainments, his ignorance, understanding and belief, behold what the Book which embraceth all things hath revealed; 'Verily, the tree of Zaqqúm shall be the food of the Athím.' And then follow certain verses, until He saith: 'Taste this, for thou forsooth art the mighty Karím!' Consider how clearly and explicitly he hath been described in God's incorruptible Book! This man, moreover, feigning humility, hath in his own book referred to himself as the 'athím servant': 'Athím in the Book of God, mighty among the common herd, 'Karím' in name!* 190

powerful adversaries, among whom towered the figure of the inordinately ambitious and hypocritical Ḥájí Mírzá Karím Khán, who at the special request of the Sháh had in a treatise viciously attacked the new Faith and its doctrines, had now raised their heads, and, emboldened by the reverses it had sustained, were heaping abuse and calumnies upon it GPB 91

King

ye are but vassals, O kings of the earth! He Who is the King of Kings hath appeared, arrayed in His most wondrous glory G 210

thou art God's shadow on earth. Strive, therefore, to act in such a manner as befitteth so eminent, so august a station. If thou dost depart from following the things We have caused to descend upon thee and taught thee, thou wilt, assuredly, be derogating from that great and priceless honour 236

the one true God, exalted be His glory, hath bestowed the government of the earth upon the kings 240

and there beheld the vision of the King of glory from the 'Tree that belongeth neither to the East nor to the West.' There He heard the soul-stirring Voice of the Spirit speaking from out of the kindled Fire *Moses* KI 54

* Verily the fruit of the tree of Al Zakkum shall be the food of the impious: as the dregs of oil shall it boil in the bellies of the damned, like the boiling of the hottest water. And it shall be said to the tormentors, Take him, and drag him into the midst of hell: and pour on his head the torture of boiling water, saying, Taste this; for thou art that mighty and honourable person. Verily this is the punishment of which ye doubted. (*Qur'án*, 44:43–50. Translated by G. Sale.)

even those Kings of the earth who have refused to embrace His Faith and to put off the garment of unbelief, none the less confess and acknowledge the greatness and overpowering majesty of that Day-star of loving kindness – re: Muḥammad 110

Sovereignty – re: superiority of spiritual sovereignty to worldly dominions 123–4

He, the divine King, hath proclaimed the undisputed supremacy of the verses of His Book over all things that testify to His truth. For compared with all other proofs and tokens, the divinely-revealed verses shine as the sun, whilst all others are as stars 205

Gospel – re: advent of Muḥammad SB 117

in this Charter of the future world civilization its Author – at once the Judge, the Lawgiver, the Unifier and Redeemer of mankind – announces to the kings of the earth the promulgation of the 'Most Great Law'; pronounces them to be His vassals; proclaims Himself the 'King of Kings' – re: the Kitáb-i-Aqdas GPB 214

that same process which, swiftly and tragically, sealed the doom of kings and emperors, and extinguished their dynasties, has operated in the case of the ecclesiastical leaders of both Christianity and Islám, damaging their prestige, and, in some cases, overthrowing their highest institutions. 'Power hath been seized' indeed, from both 'kings and ecclesiastics.' The glory of the former has been eclipsed, the power of the latter irretrievably lost PDC 74

Kingdom

it is clear that this was a spiritual vision and a scene of the Kingdom *Transfiguration* SAB 162

know thou that the Kingdom is the real world, and this nether place is only its shadow stretching out. A shadow hath no life of its own; its existence is only a fantasy, and nothing more; it is but images reflected in water, and seeming as pictures to the eye 178

the outer expression used for the Kingdom is heaven; but this is a comparison and similitude, not a reality or fact, for the Kingdom is not a material place; it is sanctified from time and place. It is a spiritual world, a divine world, and the centre of the Sovereignty of God SAQ 241

the meaning is that the life of the Kingdom is the life of the spirit, the eternal life, and that it is purified from place, like the spirit of man which has no place 242

except ye . . . become as little children, ye shall not enter into the kingdom of heaven – that is, men must become pure in heart to know God PUP 52–3

this is the glorious time of which the Lord Jesus Christ spoke when He told us to pray 'Thy Kingdom come, Thy Will be done on earth as it is in Heaven' PT 88

consider! The Divine Gardener cuts off the dry or weak branch from the good tree and grafts to it, a branch from another tree. He both separates and unites. This is that which His Holiness Christ says: that from all the world they come and enter the Kingdom, and the children of the Kingdom shall be cast out. Noah's grandson, Canaan, was detested in the sight of Noah and others were accepted BWF 438

therefore in this world he must prepare himself for the life beyond. That which he needs in the world of the Kingdom must be obtained here FWU 63

what is he in need of in the Kingdom which transcends the life and limitation of this mortal sphere? That world beyond is a world of sanctity and radiance; therefore it is necessary that in this world he should 63

Kingdom

acquire these divine attributes. In that world there is need of spirituality, faith, assurance, the knowledge and love of God. These he must attain in this world so that after his ascension from the earthly to the heavenly Kingdom he shall find all that is needful in that life eternal

Jesus Christ – re: children of the Kingdom — TAB 605–6

the gathering of Israel at Jerusalem means, therefore, and prophesies, that Israel as a whole is gathering beneath the banner of God and will enter the Kingdom of the Ancient of Days *Prophecy* — LG 383

Kitáb-i-Aqdas

the Kitáb-i-Aqdas. Alluded to in the Kitáb-i-Íqán; the principal repository of that Law which the Prophet Isaiah had anticipated, and which the writer of the Apocalypse had described as the 'new heaven' and the 'new earth,' as 'the Tabernacle of God,' as the 'Holy City,' as the 'Bride,' the 'New Jerusalem coming down from God,' this 'Most Holy Book,' whose provisions must remain inviolate for no less than a thousand years, and whose system will embrace the entire planet, may well be regarded as the brightest emanation of the mind of Bahá'u'lláh, as the Mother Book of His Dispensation, and the Charter of His New World Order — GPB 213

in this Charter of the future world civilization its Author – at once the Judge, the Lawgiver, the Unifier and Redeemer of mankind – announces to the kings of the earth the promulgation of the 'Most Great Law'; pronounces them to be His vassals; proclaims Himself the 'King of Kings' — 214

Kitáb-i-Íqán

well may it be claimed that of all the books revealed by the Author of the Bahá'í Revelation, this Book alone, by sweeping away the age-long barriers that have so insurmountably separated the great religions of the world, has laid down a broad and unassailable foundation for the complete and permanent reconciliation of their followers — GPB 139

Knowledge

consider Moses! Armed with the rod of celestial dominion, adorned with the white hand of Divine knowledge — G 19

only those will attain to the knowledge of the Word of God that have turned unto Him, and repudiated the manifestations of Satan — KI 122–3

such a man hath attained the acme of knowledge *Learned* — 145–6

thou wouldst assuredly find unnumbered doors of knowledge set open before thee *Qur'án* — 147

their so-called learning, when compared with that Knowledge, is utter falsehood, and all their understanding naught but blatant error. Nay, whatsoever proceedeth from these Mines of divine Wisdom and these Treasuries of eternal knowledge is truth, and naught else but the truth. The saying: 'Knowledge is one point, which the foolish have multiplied' is a proof of Our argument, and the tradition: 'Knowledge is a light which God sheddeth into the heart of whomsoever He willeth' a confirmation of Our statement — 183–4

inasmuch as they have not apprehended the meaning of Knowledge, and have called by that name those images fashioned by their own fancy and which have sprung from the embodiments of ignorance, they therefore have inflicted upon the Source of Knowledge that which thou hast heard and witnessed — 184

methinks, he had forgotten the well-known tradition which sayeth: 'Knowledge is all that is knowable; and might and power, all creation' — 185

He Who is well-grounded in all knowledge, He Who is the Mother, the Soul, the Secret, and the Essence thereof *Qur'án* 213

although the outward meaning of 'Whom God causeth to err through a knowledge' is what hath been revealed, yet to Us it signifieth those divines of the age who have turned away from the Beauty of God, and who, clinging unto their own learning, as fashioned by their own fancies and desires, have denounced God's divine Message and Revelation. 'Say: it is a weighty Message, from which ye turn aside!' Likewise, He saith: 'And when Our clear verses are recited to them, they say, "This is merely a man who would fain pervert you from your father's worship." And they say, "This is none other than a forged falsehood"' 214–15

thus it is related in the 'Biháru'l-Anvár,' and the "Avalim,' and the 'Yanbú'' of Ṣádiq, son of Muḥammad, that he spoke these words: 'Knowledge is twenty and seven letters. All that the Prophets have revealed are two letters thereof. No man thus far hath known more than these two letters. But when the Qá'im shall arise, He will cause the remaining twenty and five letters to be made manifest.' Consider; He hath declared Knowledge to consist of twenty and seven letters, and regarded all the Prophets, from Adam even unto the 'Seal,' as Expounders of only two letters thereof and of having been sent down with these two letters. He also saith that the Qá'im will reveal all the remaining twenty and five letters. Behold from this utterance how great and lofty is His station 243–4

thus it is recorded: 'Every knowledge hath seventy meanings, of which one only is known amongst the people. And when the Qá'im shall arise, He shall reveal unto men all that which remaineth.' He also saith: 'We speak one word, and by it we intend one and seventy meanings; each one of these meanings we can explain' *Ṣádiq* 255

true knowledge, therefore, is the knowledge of God, and this is none other than the recognition of His Manifestation in each Dispensation. Nor is there any wealth save in poverty in all save God and sanctity from aught else but Him – a state that can be realized only when demonstrated towards Him Who is the Day-spring of His Revelation [see also *Station*] SB 89

Krishna

to the Hindus the reincarnation of Krishna – re: Bahá'u'lláh GPB 94

to Him the Bhagavad-Gita of the Hindus had referred as 'The Most Great Spirit,' the 'Tenth Avatar,' the 'Immaculate Manifestation of Krishna' – re: Bahá'u'lláh 95

Lament

Pharisees – re: were lamenting over their separation PDC 31

'when I came unto them, in My majesty, however, they turned aside from Me. They, verily, are of the fallen. That is what the Spirit (Jesus) prophesied when He came with the truth, and the Jewish doctors cavilled at Him, until they committed what made the Holy Spirit to lament, and the eyes of such as enjoy near access to God to weep' [words of Bahá'u'lláh] 101

Lamp

should the lamp of religion be obscured, chaos and confusion will ensue, and the lights of fairness and justice, of tranquillity and peace cease to shine TB 125

for in every age the light of God hath, to outward seeming, been quenched by the peoples of the earth, and the Lamps of God extinguished by them. KI 127

How then could the ascendancy of the sovereignty of these Lamps be explained? What could the potency of God's will to 'perfect His light' signify? As hath already been witnessed, so great was the enmity of the infidels, that none of these divine Luminaries ever found a place for shelter, or tasted the cup of tranquillity. So heavily were they oppressed, that the least of men inflicted upon these Essences of being whatsoever he listed . . . How, therefore, can such people be capable of understanding and expounding these words of God, these verses of everlasting glory?

Verse 127

'Lo: the Lamp of God is shining,' and summoning you to heed His Cause which, though hidden beneath the veils of ancient splendour, shineth in the land of 'Iráq above the day-spring of eternal holiness *Proof* 147

I am the Lamp which the Finger of God hath lit within its niche and caused to shine with deathless splendour SB 74

then it is said: 'These are the two olive trees, and the two candlesticks standing before the God of the earth.' These two souls are likened to olive trees because at that time all lamps were lighted by olive oil. The meaning is two persons from whom that spirit of the wisdom of God, which is the cause of the illumination of the world, appears. These lights of God were to radiate and shine; therefore, they are likened to two candlesticks: the candlestick is the abode of the light, and from it the light shines forth. In the same way the light of guidance would shine and radiate from these illumined souls – re: Muḥammad and 'Alí SAQ 49

Ascension – re: ascension of Holy Manifestation 155

Pharisees – re: persecution of Christ TAB 221

attachment to the lantern is not loving the light FWU 15

some souls were lovers of the name Abraham, loving the lantern instead of the light and when they saw this same light shining from another lantern they were so attached to the former lantern that they did not recognize its later appearance and illumination 16

if we are lovers of the light we adore it in whatever lamp it may become manifest but if we love the lamp itself and the light is transferred to another lamp we will neither accept nor sanction it 16

Language

the divers and widely-known languages now spoken by the peoples of the earth were originally unknown *Babel* G 173

the language He spoke while He crossed the Jordan became known as Hebrew ('Ibrání), which meaneth 'the language of the crossing'. The Books of God and the Sacred Scriptures were then revealed in that tongue 173

it is evident unto thee that the Birds of Heaven and Doves of Eternity speak a twofold language. One language, the outward language, is devoid of allusions, is unconcealed and unveiled; that it may be a guiding lamp and a beaconing light whereby wayfarers may attain the heights of holiness, and seekers may advance into the realm of eternal reunion. Such are the unveiled traditions and the evident verses already mentioned. The other language is veiled and concealed, so that whatever lieth hidden in the heart of the malevolent may be made manifest and their innermost being be disclosed [see also *Ṣádiq* 255] KI 254–5

Latter Days

'in the latter days a grievous calamity shall befall My people at the hands of WOB 179 their ruler, a calamity such as no man ever heard to surpass it. So fierce will it be that none can find a shelter. God will then send down One of My descendants, One sprung from My family, Who will fill the earth with equity and justice, even as it hath been filled with injustice and tyranny' – re: Tradition of Muḥammad

Law

O kings of the earth! The Most Great Law hath been revealed in this Spot, this scene of transcendent splendour G 210

be not forgetful of the law of God in whatever thou desirest to achieve, now or in the days to come 239

thus it is that the adherents of Jesus maintained that the law of the Gospel shall never be annulled *Gospel* KI 27

though they recognize in their hearts the Law of God to be one and the same, yet from every direction they issue a new command, and in every season proclaim a fresh decree. No two are found to agree on one and the same law, for they seek no God but their own desire, and tread no path but the path of error 30

in another sense, by the terms 'sun', 'moon', and 'stars' are meant such laws and teachings as have been established and proclaimed in every Dispensation, such as the laws of prayer and fasting. These have, according to the law of the Qur'án, been regarded, when the beauty of the Prophet Muḥammad had passed beyond the veil, as the most fundamental and binding laws of His dispensation. To this testify the texts of the traditions and chronicles 38

the law of prayer hath constituted a fundamental element of the Revelation of all the Prophets of God 39

Revealers – re: promulgated the Law of God 45

where is He Who is preserved to renew the ordinances and laws? – re: tradition *New* 240

behold, how, notwithstanding these and similar traditions, they idly contend that the laws formerly revealed, must in no wise be altered *Tradition* 240

out of Baní-Há<u>sh</u>im there shall come forth a Youth Who shall reveal new laws *Tradition* 242

Jesus Christ – re: the Law of Christ SDC 44–5

Purpose – re: in revealing the Divine Law 46

Israel – re: to forget the root-principles of the Mosaic Law and Faith 77

in brief, it was because they forgot the meaning of the Law of God that they became involved in ignorant fanaticism and blameworthy practices such as insurgence and sedition 78

Jesus Christ – re: founded the sacred law on a basis of moral character 82

and the laws of the great Evangel, the rock-foundation on which the civilization of the world was based, turned barren of results 86

love is the most great law that ruleth this mighty and heavenly cycle, the unique power that bindeth together the divers elements of this material world, the supreme magnetic force that directeth the movements of the spheres in the celestial realms SAB 27

the religion of God is one religion, but it must ever be renewed. Moses, for example, was sent forth to man and He established a Law, and the Children of Israel, through that Mosaic Law, were delivered out of their ignorance and came into the light; they were lifted up from their abjectness and attained to a glory that fadeth not 52 the descent of the New Jerusalem denoteth a heavenly Law, that Law which is the guarantor of human happiness and the effulgence of the world of God 59

by 'that great city, the holy Jerusalem, descending out of heaven from God' is meant the holy Law of God, and this is set forth in many Tablets and still to be read in the Scriptures of the Prophets of the past *John* 165

at one time the Teachings of God were as a staff, and by this means the Holy Scriptures were spread abroad, the Law of God was promulgated and His Faith established *Staff* 166

know, then, how much ground hath been gained by the Law of God and His Teachings in this dispensation, how they have reached such heights that they far transcend the dispensations gone before: truly this rod is purest gold, while those of other days were of iron and wood 167

John – re: the woman is the Law of God 172

Holy – re: the Law of God SAQ 47

thus among the Jews, at the end of the cycle of Moses, which coincides with the Christian manifestation, the Law of God disappeared, only a form without spirit remaining 47

and the Holy City means the material Law which may be abrogated *Holy of Holies* 48

for Muḥammad's spiritual Law corresponds to that of Christ in the Gospel, and most of His laws relating to material things correspond to those of the Pentateuch. This is the meaning of the old raiment 49

'and if any man would hurt them, fire proceedeth out of their mouth, and devoureth their enemies.' That is to say, that no one would be able to withstand them, that if a person wished to belittle their teachings and their law, he would be surrounded and exterminated by this same law which proceedeth out of their mouth; and everyone who attempted to injure, to antagonize and to hate them would be destroyed by a command which would come out of their mouth. And thus it happened: all their enemies were vanquished, put to flight and annihilated. In this most evident way God assisted them. 49–50

Afterwards it is said: 'These have power to shut heaven, that it rain not in the days of their prophecy,' meaning that in that cycle they would be like kings. The law and teachings of Muḥammad, and the explanations and commentaries of 'Alí, are a heavenly bounty; if they wish to give this bounty, they have power to do so. If they do not wish it, the rain will not fall: in this connection rain stands for bounty – re: Rev. 11

those 'kindreds, people and nations' signify those who are gathered under the shadow of the Qur'án, not permitting the Cause and Law of God to be, in outward appearance, entirely destroyed and annihilated – for there are prayer and fasting among them – but the fundamental principles of the Religion of God, which are morals and conduct, with the knowledge of divine mysteries, have disappeared; the light of the virtues of the world of humanity, which is the result of the love and knowledge of God, is extinguished; and the darkness of tyranny, oppression, satanic passions and desires has become victorious. The body of the Law of God, like a corpse, has been exposed to public view for twelve hundred and sixty days, each day being counted as a year, and this period is the cycle of Muḥammad 52–3

We have before explained that what is most frequently meant by the Holy City, the Jerusalem of God, which is mentioned in the Holy Book, is the Law of God. It is compared sometimes to a bride, and sometimes to Jerusalem, and again to the new heaven and earth 67

Tabernacle 67–8
the Law of God is also described as the Holy City, the New Jerusalem. It is evident that the New Jerusalem which descends from heaven is not a city of stone, mortar, bricks, earth and wood 68
Woman – re: clothed with the sun 68
Child 68–9, 70
Pentateuch – re: change and modification in the laws 96
and upon this belief the foundation of the church of God – which is the Law of God – shall be established *Peter* 135
the second classification or division comprises social laws and regulations applicable to human conduct. This is not the essential spiritual quality of religion. It is subject to change and transformation according to the exigencies and requirements of time and place. For instance, in the time of Noah certain requirements made it necessary that all seafood be allowable or lawful. During the time of the Abrahamic Prophethood it was considered allowable, because of a certain exigency, that a man should marry his aunt, even as Sarah was the sister of Abraham's mother. During the cycle of Adam it was lawful and expedient for a man to marry his own sister, even as Abel, Cain and Seth, the sons of Adam, married their sisters. But in the law of the Pentateuch revealed by Moses these marriages were forbidden and their custom and sanction abrogated PUP 365
but now, at last, the Holy City of the New Jerusalem has come again to the world, it has appeared anew under an Eastern sky PT 84
the laws of God may be likened unto the soul and material progress unto the body 108
all religious laws conform to reason, and are suited to the people for whom they are framed, and for the age in which they are to be obeyed 141–2
now, all questions of morality contained in the spiritual, immutable law of every religion are logically right 143
look how Abraham strove to bring faith and love among the people; how Moses tried to unite the people by sound laws 171
the principal repository of that Law which the Prophet Isaiah had anticipated *Kitáb-i-Aqdas* GPB 213
'the Most Great Law is come, and the Ancient Beauty ruleth upon the throne of David' [words of Bahá'u'lláh] PDC 76

Lazarus

as to the difference and distinction between Lazarus and that 'rich man': The first was spiritual, while the second was material. One was in the highest degree of knowledge and the other in the lowest depths of ignorance TAB 205

Leaders [see also *Church, Clerics, Divines, Priests*]

let others partake of its waters in My name, that the leaders of men in every land may fully recognize the purpose for which the Eternal Truth hath been revealed, and the reason for which they themselves have been created *Lord* G 214
leaders of religion, in every age, have hindered their people from attaining the shores of eternal salvation, inasmuch as they held the reins of authority in their mighty grasp. Some for the lust of leadership, others through want of knowledge and understanding, have been the cause of the deprivation of the people. By their sanction and authority, every Prophet of God hath drunk from the chalice of sacrifice, and winged His flight unto the heights of glory KI 15

Leaders

the denials and protestations of these leaders of religion have, in the main, been due to their lack of knowledge and understanding. Those words uttered by the Revealers of the beauty of the one true God, setting forth the signs that should herald the advent of the Manifestation to come, they never understood nor fathomed. Hence they raised the standard of revolt, and stirred up mischief and sedition 17

that the term 'sun' hath been applied to the leaders of religion is due to their lofty position, their fame, and renown. Such are the universally recognized divines of every age, who speak with authority, and whose fame is securely established. If they be in the likeness of the Sun of Truth, they will surely be accounted as the most exalted of all luminaries; otherwise, they are to be recognized as the focal centres of hellish fire 37

these leaders, owing to their immersion in selfish desires, and their pursuit of transitory and sordid things, have regarded these divine Luminaries as being opposed to the standards of their knowledge and understanding, and the opponents of their ways and judgments. As they have literally interpreted the Word of God, . . . they have therefore deprived themselves and all their people of the bountiful showers of the grace and mercies of God 82

these leaders of religion admit that none of these three specified conditions is applicable to them. The first two conditions are manifestly beyond their reach; as to the third, it is evident that at no time have they been proof against those tests that have been sent by God, and that when the divine Touchstone appeared, they have shown themselves to be naught but dross 82–3

notwithstanding the divinely-inspired admonitions of all the Prophets, the Saints, and Chosen ones of God, enjoining the people to see with their own eyes and hear with their own ears, they have disdainfully rejected their counsels and have blindly followed, and will continue to follow, the leaders of their Faith 164–5

such deeds and words have been solely instigated by leaders of religion, they that worship no God but their own desire, who bear allegiance to naught but gold, who are wrapt in the densest veils of learning, and who, enmeshed by its obscurities, are lost in the wilds of error. Even as the Lord of Being hath explicitly declared: 'What thinkest thou? He who hath made a God of his passions, and whom God causeth to err through a knowledge, and whose ears and whose heart He hath sealed up, and over whose sight He hath cast a veil – who, after his rejection by God, shall guide such a one? Will ye not then be warned? 214

let it be known, however, that none of these doctors and divines to whom we have referrred was invested with the rank and dignity of leadership. For well-known and influential leaders of religion, who occupy the seats of authority and exercise the functions of leadership, can in no wise bear allegiance to the Revealer of truth, except whomsoever thy Lord willeth. But for a few, such things have never come to pass. 'And few of My servants are the thankful' 228–9

to these leaders who 'esteem themselves the best of all creatures and have been regarded as the vilest by Him Who is the Truth,' who 'occupy the seats of knowledge and learning, and who have named ignorance knowledge, and called oppression justice,' and who, 'worship no God but their own desire, who bear allegiance to naught but gold, who are wrapt in the densest veils of learning, and who, enmeshed by its obscurities, are lost in the wilds of error,' – to these Bahá'u'lláh has chosen to address these words: 'O concourse of divines! Ye shall not PDC 81 henceforth behold yourselves possessed of any power, inasmuch as We have seized it from you, and destined it for such as have believed in God, the One, the All-Powerful, the Almighty, the Unconstrained'

'ye are lovers of names, and appear to have given yourselves up to them. For this reason make ye mention of the names of your leaders. And should any one like them, or superior to them, come unto you, ye would flee him. Through their names ye have exalted yourselves, and have secured your positions, and live and prosper. And were your leaders to reappear, ye would not renounce your leadership, nor would ye turn in their direction, nor set your faces towards them. We found you, as We found most men, worshiping names which they mention during the days of their life, and with which they occupy themselves. No sooner do the Bearers of these names appear, however, than they repudiate them, and turn upon their heels . . .Know ye that God will not, in this day, accept your thoughts, nor your remembrance of Him, nor your turning towards Him, nor your devotions, nor your vigilance, unless ye be made new in the estimation of this Servant, could ye but perceive it' – re: Súriy-i-Múlúk [words of Bahá'u'lláh] 89–90

Learned

consider, how can he that faileth in the day of God's Revelation to attain unto the grace of the 'Divine Presence' and to recognize His Manifestation, be justly called learned, though he may have spent aeons in the pursuit of knowledge, and acquired all the limited and material learning of men? It is surely evident that he can in no wise be regarded as possessed of true knowledge. Whereas, the most unlettered of all men, if he be honoured with this supreme distinction, he verily is accounted as one of those divinely-learned men whose knowledge is of God; for such a man hath attained the acme of knowledge, and hath reached the furthermost summit of learning KI 145–6

Christian – re: learned men of Christendom SB 123–4

an authoritative Tradition states: 'As for him who is one of the learned: he must guard himself, defend his faith, oppose his passions and obey the commandments of his Lord. It is then the duty of the people to pattern themselves after him.' Since these illustrious and holy words embody all the conditions of learning, a brief commentary on their meaning is appropriate. Whoever is lacking in these divine qualifications and does not demonstrate these inescapable requirements in his own life, should not be referred to as learned and is not worthy to serve as a model for the believers [see also *Guard* 34–5] SDC 34

Leper

through Him the leper recovered from the leprosy of perversity and ignorance G 85

leprosy may be interpreted as any veil that interveneth between man and the recognition of the Lord, his God. Whoso alloweth himself to be shut out from Him is indeed a leper, who shall not be remembered in the Kingdom of God, the Mighty, the All-Praised 85–6

Life

true life is not the life of the flesh but the life of the spirit *Death* KI 120–21

and for those who believed in Him He delineated a special way of life which constitutes the highest type of action on earth *Jesus Christ* SDC 82

that is why Christ said, 'Act in such a way that you may find eternal life, and that you may be born of water and the spirit, so that you may enter into the Kingdom' SAQ 223

Light

after the ascension of Jesus to the Realm of Glory, these few souls stood up with their spiritual qualities and with deeds that were pure and holy, and they arose by the power of God and the life-giving breaths of the Messiah to save all the peoples of the earth. Then all the idolatrous nations as well as the Jews rose up in their might to kill the Divine fire that had been lit in the lamp of Jerusalem. 'Fain would they put out God's light with their mouths: but God hath willed to perfect His light, albeit the infidels abhor it.' SDC 45

Likeness [see also *Idol*]

they made for them likenesses and pictures, decorated with jewels shining in the eyes; they placed these likenesses or pictures in the temples, churches and monasteries built on the tops of mountains, and worshipped them with respect, glory, majesty and reverence. This is the condition of the neglectful ones who are deprived of the Truth at the day of their existence among them [see also *Disciple*] BWF 394

Literal

Interpret – re: Word of God KI 82

in such utterances, the literal meaning . . . is not what hath been intended *Ṣádiq* 255

Interpret – re: Jews FWU 74–5

Lord

dedicate the precious days of your lives to the betterment of the world and the promotion of the Cause of Him Who is the Ancient and Sovereign Lord of all G 183

say: O friends! Drink your fill from this crystal stream that floweth through the heavenly grace of Him Who is the Lord of Names. Let others partake of its waters in My name, that the leaders of men in every land may fully recognize the purpose for which the Eternal Truth hath been revealed, and the reason for which they themselves have been created 214

arise to aid thy Lord at all times and in all circumstances, and be thou one of His helpers. Admonish, then, the people to lend a hearing ear to the words which the Spirit of God hath uttered in this irradiant and resplendent Tablet. Say: Sow not, O people, the seeds of dissension amongst men, and contend not with your neighbour. Be patient under all conditions, and place your whole trust and confidence in God. Aid ye your Lord with the sword of wisdom and of utterance. This indeed well becometh the station of man. To depart from it would be unworthy of God, the Sovereign Lord of all, the Glorified. The people, however, have been led astray, and are truly of the heedless 295

'O Moses, I truly am God, the Lord of the worlds' *Moses* ESW 118

'the Lord will roar from Zion, and utter His Voice from Jerusalem' *Amos* 145

O my brother! Take thou the step of the spirit, so that, swift as the twinkling of an eye, thou mayest flash through the wilds of remoteness and bereavement, attain the Riḍván of everlasting reunion, and in one breath commune with the heavenly Spirits. For with human feet thou canst never hope to traverse these immeasurable distances, nor attain thy goal. Peace be upon him whom the light of truth guideth unto all truth, and who, in the name of God, standeth in the path of His Cause, upon the shore of true understanding. KI 43

This is the meaning of the sacred verse: 'But nay! I swear by the Lord of the Easts and the Wests,' inasmuch as the 'Suns' referred to have each their own particular rising and setting place hath not that sovereignty, through the potency of one word, subdued, quickened, and revitalized the whole world? What! Can the lowly dust compare with Him Who is the Lord of Lords? What tongue dare utter the immensity of difference that lieth between them? Nay, all comparison falleth short in attaining the hallowed sanctuary of His sovereignty — 124

all men have proceeded from God and unto Him shall all return. All shall appear before Him for judgment. He is the Lord of the Day of Resurrection, of Regeneration and of Reckoning, and His revealed Word is the Balance — SB 157

the veil hath fallen away, the curtain is lifted, the clouds have parted, the Lord of Lords is in plain sight – yet all hath passed the sinners by — SAB 14

therefore, it is certain that the day woe is the day of the Lord; for in that day woe is for the neglectful, woe is for the sinners, woe is for the ignorant. That is why it is said, 'The second woe is past; behold the third woe cometh quickly!' This third woe is the day of the manifestation of Bahá'u'lláh, the day of God; and it is near to the day of the appearance of the Báb — SAQ 56

Book – re: the earth shall shine with the light of her Lord — GPB 96

the foundations of the long-awaited Kingdom of the 'Father' unassailably established *Father* — 110

the Promised One of all ages, unveiling His station in its plenitude, announced that 'He Who is the Lord of Lords is come overshadowed with clouds' — PDC 52

Lord of Hosts

say: O concourse of the rulers and of the learned and the wise! The Promised Day is come and the Lord of Hosts hath appeared. Rejoice ye with great joy by reason of this supreme felicity — TB 239

Amos – re: 'the Lord, the God of Hosts, is His name' — ESW 145–6

and still the people, even as the Messiah saith, slept on: for the day of the Manifestation, when the Lord of Hosts descended, found them wrapped in the slumber of unknowing. As He saith in the Gospel, My coming is even as when the thief is in the house, and the goodman of the house watcheth not — SAB 35

and now shall come to pass even greater things than these, for this is the summons of the Lord of Hosts, this is the trumpet-call of the living Lord, this is the anthem of world peace, this is the standard of righteousness and trust and understanding raised up among all the variegated peoples of the globe; this is the splendour of the Sun of Truth, this is the holiness of the spirit of God Himself — 82

Covenant – re: defender of the Covenant — 228

Manifestation – re: Lord of Hosts and the Messiah — SAQ 39

in the day of the manifestation of the Lord of Hosts, and at the epoch of the divine cycle of the Omnipotent which is promised and mentioned in all the books and writings of the Prophets – in that day of God, the Spiritual and Divine Kingdom will be established, and the world will be renewed — 56–7

the blessed Person of the Promised One is interpreted in the Holy Book as the Lord of Hosts, i.e., the heavenly armies — BWF 423

the Lord of Hosts became manifest to Moses and the children of Israel in a pillar of fire, and appeared to Christ in the fire of the love of God. This is that of which it is said in the Gospel: One must be baptized with fire and spirit — TAB 515

Lord of Hosts

Glad-Tidings – re: thou didst turn thy face toward the Lord of Hosts 639

indeed such a consummation, He assures us, had been actually prophesied 'through the tongue of the Prophets two or three thousand years before.' God, 'faithful to His promise,' had, 'to some of the Prophets' 'revealed and given the good news that the "Lord of Hosts should be manifested in the Holy Land"' [see also *Isaiah* 183; *David* 184] GPB 183

what is meant in the prophecies by the 'Lord of Hosts' and the 'Promised Christ' is the Blessed Perfection (Bahá'u'lláh) and His holiness the Exalted One (the Báb) WOB 139

Lord's Supper

whatsoever gathering is arranged with the utmost love, and where those who attend are turning their faces toward the Kingdom of God, and where the discourse is of the Teachings of God, and the effect of which is to cause those present to advance – that gathering is the Lord's, and that festive table hath come down from heaven SAB 89

the Supper of the Lord which His Highness the Spirit ate with the apostles was a heavenly supper and not one of material bread and water, for material objects have no connection with spiritual objects BWF 390

this heavenly food is knowledge, understanding, faith, assurance, love, affinity, kindness, purity of purpose, attraction of hearts and the union of souls. It was this manner of the Lord's Supper which descended from the heavenly kingdom in the day of Christ *Food* 408

Lot

the text makes it quite clear that Lot was not responsible for the action committed by his two daughters, as they gave him wine and made him drunk – re: Gen. 19:29–30 (Letter 29.10.38) DND 5

Luminaries

therefore, know thou of a certainty that these Luminaries of heavenly majesty, though their dwelling be in the dust, yet their true habitation is the seat of glory in the realms above. Though bereft of all earthly possessions, yet they soar in the realm of immeasurable riches. And whilst sore tried in the grip of the enemy, they are seated on the right hand of power and celestial dominion. Amidst the darkness of their abasement there shineth upon them the light of unfading glory, and upon their helplessness are showered the tokens of an invincible sovereignty KI 130

therefore, whosoever, and in whatever Dispensation, hath recognized and attained unto the presence of these glorious, these resplendent and most excellent Luminaries, hath verily attained unto the 'Presence of God' Himself, and entered the city of eternal and immortal life. Attainment unto such presence is possible only in the Day of Resurrection, which is the Day of the rise of God Himself through His all-embracing Revelation – re: SAB 107–8 143

Ma'ání

Bayán ESW 113

as to the Ma'ání, We are its meaning, and its side, and its hand, and its tongue, and its cause, and its command, and its knowledge, and its right. If We wish for something, it is God Who wisheth it, and He desireth that which We desire 113

Magi

in like manner, when the hour of the Revelation of Jesus drew nigh, a few of the Magi, aware that the star of Jesus had appeared in heaven, sought and followed it, till they came unto the city which was the seat of the KI 64

Kingdom of Herod. The sway of his sovereignty in those days embraced the whole of that land

these Magi said: 'Where is He that is born King of the Jews? for we have seen His star in the east and are come to worship Him!' When they had searched, they found out that in Bethlehem, in the land of Judea, the Child had been born. This was the sign that was manifested in the visible heaven 64

know thou, moreover, that We have addressed to the Magians Our Tablets, and adorned them with Our Law . . . We have revealed in them the essence of all the hints and allusions contained in their Books PDC 76

Malediction

'at that hour His malediction shall descend upon you, and your curse shall afflict you, and your religion shall remain an empty word on your tongues. And when these signs appear amongst you, anticipate the day when the red-hot wind will have swept over you, or the day when ye will have been disfigured, or when stones will have rained upon you' – re: Muḥammadan tradition PDC 99

Man

all men have been created to carry forward an ever-advancing civilization. The Almighty beareth Me witness: To act like the beasts of the field is unworthy of man. Those virtues that benefit his dignity are forbearance, mercy, compassion and loving-kindness towards all the peoples and kindreds of the earth [see *Lord*] G 214

then said the chiefs of His people who believed not, 'We see in Thee but a man like ourselves' *Cavil* KI 222

man's highest station, however, is attained through faith in God in every Dispensation and by acceptance of what hath been revealed by Him, and not through learning; inasmuch as in every nation there are learned men who are versed in divers sciences. Nor is it attainable through wealth; for it is similarly evident that among the various classes in every nation there are those possessed of riches. Likewise are other transitory things SB 89

a human being is distinguished from an animal in a number of ways. First of all, he is made in the image of God, in the likeness of the Supernal Light, even as the Torah saith, 'Let us make man in our image, after our likeness.' This divine image betokeneth all the qualities of perfection whose lights, emanating from the Sun of Truth, illumine the realities of men, and are among the perfect attributes that lie within wisdom and knowledge SAB 140

man is said to be the greatest representative of God, and he is the Book of Creation because all the mysteries of beings exist in him SAQ 236

there is no other being higher than a perfect man 237

man is, in reality, a spiritual being, and only when he lives in the spirit is he truly happy PT 72

man – the true man – is soul, not body; though physically man belongs to the animal kingdom, yet his soul lifts him above the rest of creation 85

man must cut himself free from all prejudice and from the result of his own imagination, so that he may be able to search for truth unhindered. Truth is one in all religions, and by means of it the unity of the world can be realized 129

all men are the leaves and fruit of one same tree, they are all branches of the tree of Adam, they all have the same origin. The same rain has fallen upon them all, the same warm sun makes them grow, they are all refreshed by the same breeze. The only differences that exist and that 129–30 keep them apart are these: there are the children who need guidance, the ignorant to be instructed, the sick to be tended and healed; thus, I say that the whole of humanity is enveloped by the Mercy and Grace of God. As the Holy Writings tell us: All men are equal before God. He is no respecter of persons

an humble man without learning, but filled with the Holy Spirit, is more powerful than the most nobly-born profound scholar without that inspiration — 165

consequently man must learn the lesson of kindness and beneficence from God Himself. Just as God is kind to all humanity, man also must be kind to his fellow creatures. If his attitude is just and loving toward his fellow men, toward all creation, then indeed is he worthy of being pronounced the image and likeness of God — FWU 79

man must seek to gain the acceptance of God and not that of the different classes of men. If one is praised and chosen by God, the accusation of all the creatures will cause no loss to him; and if the man is not accepted in the threshold of God, the praise and admiration of all men will be of no use to him — TAB 158

Man Child see *Child*

Manifestation [see also *Messenger*]

thus, viewed from the standpoint of their oneness and sublime detachment, the attributes of Godhead, Divinity, Supreme Singleness, and Inmost Essence, have been, and are applicable to those Essences of Being, inasmuch as they all abide on the throne of Divine Revelation, and are established upon the seat of Divine Concealment. Through their appearance the Revelation of God is made manifest, and by their countenance the Beauty of God is revealed. Thus it is that the accents of God Himself have been heard uttered by these Manifestations of the Divine Being — G 53

from the foregoing passages and allusions it hath been made indubitably clear that in the kingdoms of earth and heaven there must needs be manifested a Being, an Essence Who shall act as a Manifestation and Vehicle for the transmission of the grace of the Divinity Itself, the Sovereign Lord of all — 67

and of all men, the most accomplished, the most distinguished, and the most excellent are the Manifestations of the Sun of Truth. Nay, all else besides these Manifestations, live by the operation of their Will, and move and have their being through the outpourings of their grace — 178

they cavilled at those holy Manifestations, and protested saying: 'None hath followed you except the abject amongst us, those who are worthy of no attention — 179

he hath, indeed, partaken of this highest gift of God who hath recognized His Manifestation in this day — 195

their attack hath been more fierce than tongue or pen can describe. Not one single Manifestation of Holiness hath appeared but He was afflicted by the denials, the repudiation, and the vehement opposition of the people around Him. Thus it hath been revealed: 'O the misery of men! No Messenger cometh unto them but they laugh Him to scorn.' Again He saith: 'Each nation hath plotted darkly against their Messenger to lay violent hold on Him, and disputed with vain words to invalidate the truth' — KI 5

throughout all ages and centuries the Manifestations of power and glory have been subjected to such heinous cruelties that no pen dare describe them — 6 as He hath said: 'When the heaven shall be cloven asunder.' By 'heaven' is meant the heaven of divine Revelation, which is elevated with every Manifestation, and rent asunder with every subsequent one 44

behold how contrary are the ways of the Manifestations of God, as ordained by the King of creation, to the ways and desires of men 57

the sign of the invisible heaven must needs be revealed in the person of that perfect man who, before each Manifestation appeareth, educateth, and prepareth the souls of men for the advent of the divine Luminary, the Light of the unity of God amongst men [see also *Rúz-bih* 65] 66

such men, when acquainted with these circumstances, become so veiled that without the least question, they pronounce the Manifestation of God an infidel, and sentence Him to death. You must have heard of such things taking place all down the ages, and are now observing them in these days 74

likewise, it is clear, how in this day, the people of the Qur'án have perverted the text of God's holy Book, concerning the signs of the expected Manifestation, and interpreted it according to their inclination and desires 87

Gems of Holiness – re: discourse on Manifestations 99–100

that sovereignty which in every dispensation resideth within, and is exercised by, the person of the Manifestation, the Day-star of Truth 107–8

such is His earthly sovereignty, the evidences of which thou dost on every side behold. This sovereignty must needs be revealed and established either in the lifetime of every Manifestation of God or after His ascension unto His true habitation in the realms above 110–11

have clung to the ways of those abject manifestations of the Prince of Darkness 122

only those will attain to the knowledge of the Word of God who have turned unto Him, and repudiated the manifestations of Satan 122–3

in like manner, are the terms 'first' and 'last' applicable unto His Manifestations *First* 163

whenever the Manifestations of Holiness were revealed, the divines of their day have hindered the people from attaining unto the way of truth. To this testify the records of all the scriptures and heavenly books 165

were any of the all-embracing Manifestations of God to declare: 'I am God!' He verily speaketh the truth, and no doubt attacheth thereto. For it hath been repeatedly demonstrated that through their Revelation, their attributes and names, the Revelation of God, His name and His attributes, are made manifest in the world 178

thou wilt recognize the truth that no manifestation greater than the Prophets of God hath ever been revealed, and no testimony mightier than the testimony of their revealed verses hath ever appeared upon the earth 206

Cavil – re: they cavilled at those holy Manifestations 222

is not the object of every Revelation to effect a transformation in the whole character of mankind, a transformation that shall manifest itself both outwardly and inwardly, that shall affect both its inner life and external conditions? For if the character of mankind be not changed, the futility of God's universal Manifestations would be apparent 240–41

thy spirit is My place of revelation; cleanse it for My manifestation AHW 59

the holy Manifestations of God were sent down to make visible the oneness of humanity. For this did They endure unnumbered ills and tribulations, SAB 278

Manifestation

that a community from amongst mankind's divergent peoples could gather within the shadow of the Word of God and live as one, and could, with delight, and grace, demonstrate on earth the unity of humankind

all the peoples of the world are awaiting two Manifestations, Who must be contemporaneous; all wait for the fulfillment of this promise. In the Bible the Jews have the promise of the Lord of Hosts and the Messiah; in the Gospel the return of Christ and Elijah is promised — SAQ 39

Ascension – re: individual realities of the Divine Manifestations — 155

the Manifestations of universal Prophethood Who appeared independently are *Prophet* — 164–5

how often the Prophets of God and His supreme Manifestations in Their prayers confess Their sins and faults! This is only to teach other men, to encourage and incite them to humility and meekness, and to induce them to confess their sins and faults. For these Holy Souls are pure from every sin and sanctified from faults — 170

the supreme and most important happening in the human world is the Manifestation of God and the descent of the law of God — FWU 104

the holy Manifestations of God come into the world to dispel the darkness of the animal or physical nature of man, to purify him from his imperfections in order that his heavenly and spiritual nature may become quickened, his divine qualities awakened, his perfections visible, his potential powers revealed and all the virtues of the world of humanity latent within him may come to life. These holy Manifestations of God are the educators and trainers of the world of existence, the teachers of the world of humanity — 110

in accordance with the principle of progressive revelation every Manifestation of God must needs vouchsafe to the peoples of His day a measure of divine guidance ampler than any which a preceding and less receptive age could have received or appreciated — WOB 102

any variations in the splendour which each of these Manifestations of the Light of God has shed upon the world should be ascribed not to any inherent superiority involved in the essential character of any one of them, but rather to the progressive capacity, the ever-increasing spiritual receptiveness, which mankind, in its progress towards maturity, has invariably manifested — 166

Manna

the manna which came from heaven for the disciples, was neither cress, onion, lentil, garlic nor leek. It was bounty and knowledge; it was faith and assurance; it was love and attraction; it was attachment and enkindlement by the fire of the love of God *Food* — SW XI 16, p275

Mary [see also *Birth of Jesus*]

likewise, reflect upon the state and condition of Mary. So deep was the perplexity of that most beauteous countenance, so grievous her case, that she bitterly regretted she had ever been born. To this beareth witness the text of the sacred verse wherein it is mentioned that after Mary had given birth to Jesus, she bemoaned her plight and cried out: 'O would that I had died ere this, and been a thing forgotten, forgotten quite!' I swear by God! Such lamenting consumeth the heart and shaketh the being. Such consternation of soul, such despondency, could have been caused by no other than the censure of the enemy and the cavillings of the infidel and perverse. Reflect, what answer could Mary have given to the people around her? How could she claim that a Babe Whose father was unknown had been conceived of the Holy Ghost? Therefore did — KI 56–7

Mary, that veiled and immortal Countenance, take up her Child and return unto her home. No sooner had the eyes of the people fallen upon her than they raised their voice saying: 'O sister of Aaron! Thy father was not a man of wickedness, nor unchaste thy mother' [see *Spirit*]

Muḥammad – re: teachings of Muḥammad about Mary PT 47

and He came from heaven, though outwardly He came from the womb of Mary *Jesus Christ* BWF 387

Virgin – re: 'Mary the Magdalene and Mary the mother of Jacob' TAB 662

Mary Magdalene

Peter was a fisherman and Mary Magdalene a peasant, but as they were specially favoured with the blessings of Christ, the horizon of their faith became illumined, and down to the present day they are shining from the horizon of everlasting glory SAB 105

consider how many empresses have come and gone since the time of Christ. Each was the ruler of a country but now all trace and name of them is lost, while Mary Magdalene, who was only a peasant and a maidservant of God, still shineth from the horizon of everlasting glory 123

verily, Mary, the Magdalene, was a villager, but she kept firm in the Cause of Christ and confirmed the apostles at the time she declared to them (thus): 'Verily, Christ is alive and eternal and death did not overtake Him; and verily, the foundation of His religion is not shaken by His crucifixion at the hand of the oppressors!' By this her face is eternally shining from the horizon of guidance TAB 268

verily, Mary Magdalene was a villager, but on account of her keeping firm in the Cause of Christ after His death, she was rendered successful in such a matter, whereby her face is shining and beaming forth on the horizon of the universe forevermore! And she surpassed even men in defending the fortress of the Cause of God against the attack of the hosts of suspicions. This is indeed a glorious condition! This is indeed a great matter! This is indeed a manifest light! 601

Meaning

in such utterances, the literal meaning, as generally understood by the people, is not what hath been intended. Thus it is recorded: 'Every knowledge hath seventy meanings, of which one only is known amongst the people *Ṣádiq* KI 255

Mecca

thou beholdest how vast is the number of people who go to Mecca each year on pilgrimage and engage in circumambulation, while He, through the potency of Whose Word the Ka'bah (the sanctuary in Mecca) hath become the object of adoration, is forsaken in this mountain. He is none other but the Apostle of God Himself, inasmuch as the Revelation of God may be likened to the sun. No matter how innumerable its risings, there is but one sun, and upon it depends the life of all things SB 105

Medina

after the ascension of Muḥammad, and His passing to 'the seat of truth, in the presence of the potent King,' the tribes around Medina apostatized from their Faith, turning back to the idolatry of pagan times SDC 44

Message

'say: it is a weighty Message, from which ye turn aside' *Knowledge* KI 214

Messenger [see also *Manifestation*]

by the righteousness of God! These are the days in which God hath proved the hearts of the entire company of His Messengers and Prophets, and beyond them those that stand guard over His sacred and inviolable Sanctuary, the inmates of the celestial Pavilion and dwellers of the Tabernacle of Glory. How severe, therefore, the test to which they who join partners with God must needs be subjected! G 11–12

thou hast known how grievously the Prophets of God, His Messengers and Chosen Ones, have been afflicted. Meditate a while on the motive and reason which have been responsible for such a persecution. At no time, in no Dispensation, have the Prophets of God escaped the blasphemy of their enemies, the cruelty of their oppressors, the denunciation of the learned of their age, who appeared in the guise of uprightness and piety. Day and night they passed through such agonies as none can ever measure, except the knowledge of the one true God, exalted be His glory 57

unto the cities of all nations He hath sent His Messengers, Whom He hath commissioned to announce unto men tidings of the Paradise of His good pleasure, and to draw them nigh unto the Haven of abiding security, the Seat of eternal holiness and transcendent glory 145

this is not the day for any man to question his Lord. It behoveth whosoever hath hearkened to the Call of God, as voiced by Him Who is the Day Spring of Glory, to arise and cry out: 'Here am I, here am I, O Lord of all Names; here am I, here am I, O Maker of the heavens! I testify that, through Thy Revelation, the things hidden in the Books of God have been revealed, and that whatsoever hath been recorded by Thy Messengers in the sacred Scriptures hath been fulfilled' 163

this is the wilderness in which all the Messengers of God have wandered *Holy Land* 343

O the misery of men! No Messenger cometh unto them but they laugh Him to scorn *Manifestation* KI 5

these Manifestations of God have each a twofold station. One is the station of pure abstraction and essential unity. In this respect, if thou callest them all by one name, and dost ascribe to them the same attribute, thou hast not erred from the truth. Even as He hath revealed: 'No distinction do We make between any of His Messengers!' For they one and all summon the people of the earth to acknowledge the Unity of God, and herald unto them the Kawthar of an infinite grace and bounty. They are all invested with the robe of Prophethood, and honoured with the mantle of glory 152

should a poor and obscure person, destitute of the attire of the men of learning, address them saying: 'Follow ye, O people! the Messengers of God,' they would, greatly surprised at such a statement, reply: 'What! Meanest thou that all these divines, all these exponents of learning, with all their authority, their pomp and pageantry, have erred, and failed to distinguish truth from falsehood? Dost thou, and people like thyself, pretend to have comprehended that which they have not understood?' 165

and were any of them to voice the utterance: 'I am the Messenger of God,' He also speaketh the truth, the indubitable truth. Even as He saith: 'Muḥammad is not the father of any man among you, but He is the Messenger of God.' Viewed in this light, they are all but Messengers of that ideal King, that unchangeable Essence. And were they all to proclaim: 'I am the Seal of the Prophets,' they verily utter but the truth, beyond the faintest shadow of doubt. For they are all but one person, one soul, one spirit, one being, one revelation. They are all the 179 manifestation of the 'Beginning' and the 'End,' the 'First' and the 'Last,' the 'Seen' and 'Hidden' – all of which pertain to Him Who is the innermost Spirit of Spirits and eternal Essence of Essences. And were they to say: 'We are the servants of God,' this also is a manifest and indisputable fact. For they have been made manifest in the uttermost state of servitude, a servitude the like of which no man can possibly attain

by virtue of this station, they have claimed for themselves the Voice of Divinity and the like, whilst by virtue of their station of Messengership, they have declared themselves the Messengers of God. In every instance they have voiced an utterance that would conform to the requirements of the occasion, and have ascribed all these declarations to Themselves, declarations ranging from the realm of divine Revelation to the realm of creation, and from the domain of Divinity even unto the domain of earthly existence. Thus it is that whatsoever be their utterance, whether it pertain to the realm of Divinity, Lordship, Prophethood, Messengership, Guardianship, Apostleship or Servitude, all is true, beyond the shadow of a doubt 181

Christ ratified and proclaimed the foundation of the law of Moses. Muḥammad and all the Prophets have revoiced that same foundation of reality. Therefore, the purposes and accomplishments of the divine Messengers have been one and the same. They were the source of advancement of the body politic and the cause of the honour and divine civilization of humanity, the foundation of which is one and the same in every dispensation PUP 366

God hath sent down His Messengers to succeed to Moses and Jesus, and He will continue to do so till 'the end that hath no end' WOB 116

Messiah

all the people of Israel arose in protest against Him. They clamoured that He Whose advent the Bible had foretold must needs promulgate and fulfil the laws of Moses, whereas this youthful Nazarene, who laid claim to the station of the divine Messiah, had annulled the law of divorce and of the sabbath day – the most weighty of the laws of Moses KI 18

call thou to mind the day when the Jews, who had surrounded Jesus, Son of Mary, were pressing Him to confess His claim of being the Messiah and Prophet of God, so that they might declare Him an infidel and sentence Him to death *Jesus Christ* 132–3

that mighty Jewish nation toppled and crumbled away, but those few souls who sought shelter beneath the Messianic Tree transformed all human life SDC 82–3

it is even as in the time of the Messiah, when the Pharisees and the pious were left without a portion, while Peter, John and Andrew, given neither to pious worship nor ascetic practice, won the day SAB 18

then the whole world of being did quiver for joy, and still the people, even as the Messiah saith, slept on: for the day of the Manifestation, when the Lord of Hosts descended, found them wrapped in the slumber of unknowing. As He saith in the Gospel, My coming is even as when the thief is in the house, and the goodman of the house watcheth not 35

verily did the Pharisees rise up against Messiah, despite the bright beauty of His face and all His comeliness, and they cried out that He was not Messiah (Masíḥ) but a monster (Masíkh), because He had claimed to be Almighty God, the sovereign Lord of all, and told them, 'I am God's Son, and verily in the inmost being of His only Son, His mighty Ward, clearly revealed with all His attributes, all His perfections, standeth the Father' [see also *Pharisees*] 40

Messiah

Father – re: meaning of the Messiah's words, that the Father is in the Son 42

so long as these signs have not appeared, whoso layeth claim to be a Messiah is an imposter – re: saying of the Jews 44

another of the conditions is this, that in the days of the Messiah the Jews will prosper and triumph over all the peoples of the world, but now they are living in the utmost abasement and servitude in the empire of the Romans. Then how can this be the Messiah promised in the Torah? *Jews* 45–6

the exaltation of the Word, the revelation of the power of God, the conversion of God-fearing souls, the bestowal of everlasting life – it was following the Messiah's martyrdom that all these were increased and intensified 65

Heaven – re: meaning of Messiah coming from heaven and ascending to it 167–8

remember the Messiah, and His days on earth, and His abasement, and His tribulations, and how the people paid Him no mind. Remember how the Jews would hold Him up to ridicule, and mock at Him, and address Him with: 'Peace be upon thee, King of the Jews! Peace be upon thee, King of Kings!' How they would say that He was mad, and would ask how the Cause of that crucified One could ever spread out to the easts of the world and the wests thereof. None followed Him then, save only a few souls who were fishermen, carpenters, and other plain folk. Alas, alas, for such delusions 173

verily, upon Mount Sinai, Moses entered into a Covenant regarding the Messiah, with all those souls who would live in the day of the Messiah *Moses* 207

in the Bible the Jews have the promise of the Lord of Hosts and the Messiah *Jews* SAQ 39

therefore, the Jews rejected Christ, and, God forbid! called the Messiah masí<u>kh</u>, considered Him to be the destroyer of the edifice of God 111

the Jews were expecting the appearance of the Messiah, looking forward to it with devotion of heart and soul, but because they were submerged in imitations [see also *Pharisees* TAB 230] PUP 180

the real purport of these prophetic statements was that various peoples symbolized by the wolf and the lamb between whom love and fellowship were impossible would come together during the Messiah's reign, drink from the same fountain of life in his teachings and become his devoted followers. This was realized when . . . FWU 75

Mihdí

Abú-'Abdi'lláh, questioned concerning the character of the Mihdí, answered saying: 'He will perform that which Muḥammad, the Messenger of God, hath performed, and will demolish whatever hath been before Him even as the Messenger of God hath demolished the ways of those that preceded Him' KI 240

Qur'án – re: if all should be assured that this is that same Promised Mihdí SB 110

the divine Revelation associated with the advent of Him Who is your promised Mihdí hath proved far more wondrous than the Revelation wherewith Muḥammad, the Apostle of God, was invested. Would that ye might ponder. Verily, God raised up Muḥammad, the Apostle of God, from among the people of Arabia after he had reached forty years of age – a fact which every one of you affirmeth and upholdeth – while your Redeemer was raised up by God at the age of twenty-four amidst a people none of whom can speak or understand a single word of Arabic 146

Millennium

(Question: 'When is the time of the millennium? Will I see it?') concerning the one thousand years as recorded in the Book: It signifieth the beginning of this Manifestation until the end of its predominance throughout the contingent world; because this Cause is great, its powers are growing and its signs are dazzling. It shall continue in elevation, exaltation, growth, promulgation and promotion until it shall reach the apex of its glory in one thousand years . . . Thou shalt see its conquering power, its manifest dominion, its eternal might and its everlasting glory TAB 659–60

upon the consummation of this colossal, this unspeakably glorious enterprise – an enterprise that baffled the resources of Roman statesmanship and which Napoleon's desperate efforts failed to achieve – will depend the ultimate realization of that millennium of which poets of all ages have sung and seers have long dreamed. Upon it will depend the fulfillment of the prophecies uttered by the Prophets of old when swords shall be beaten into ploughshares and the lion and the lamb lie down together. It alone can usher in the Kingdom of the Heavenly Father as anticipated by the Faith of Jesus Christ. It alone can lay the foundation for the New World Order visualized by Bahá'u'lláh – a World Order that shall reflect, however dimly, upon this earthly plane, the ineffable splendours of the 'Abhá Kingdom WOB 46–7

the central, the underlying aim which animates it is the establishment of the New World Order as adumbrated by Bahá'u'lláh. The methods it employs, the standard it inculcates, incline it to neither East nor West, neither Jew nor Gentile, neither rich nor poor, neither white nor coloured. Its watchword is the unification of the human race; its standard the 'Most Great Peace'; its consummation the advent of that golden millennium – the Day when the kingdoms of this world shall have become the Kingdom of God Himself, the Kingdom of Bahá'u'lláh 157

Miracle

also, most of the miracles of the Prophets which are mentioned have an inner significance *Jesus Christ* SAQ 37

our purpose is not to deny such miracles; our only meaning is that they do not constitute decisive proofs, and that they have an inner significance 38

therefore, miracles are not a proof. For if they are proofs for those who are present, they fail as proofs to those who are absent 101

one thing, however, he wishes to bring to your attention, namely that miracles are always possible, even though they do not constitute a regular channel whereby God reveals His power to mankind. To reject miracles on the ground that they imply a breach of the laws of nature is a very shallow, well-nigh stupid argument, inasmuch as God Who is the Father of the Universe, can in His Wisdom and omnipotence bring about any change, no matter how temporary, in the operation of the laws which He himself created (Letter 27.2.38) LG 366

Mi'ráj

– re: dissertation on KI 185–6

Mirror

the greater the effort exerted for the refinement of this sublime and noble mirror, the more faithfully will it be made to reflect the glory of the names and attributes of God, and reveal the wonders of His signs and knowledge G 261

this mirror can be so cleansed from the dross of earthly defilements and 261

Mirror

purged from satanic fancies as to be able to draw nigh unto the meads of eternal holiness and attain the courts of everlasting fellowship

these sanctified Mirrors, these Day-springs of ancient glory *Gems of Holiness* KI 99

the most important thing is to polish the mirrors of hearts in order that they may become illumined and receptive of the divine light PUP 14

the meditative faculty is akin to the mirror . . . but if you turn the mirror of your spirits heavenwards, the heavenly constellations and the rays of the Sun of Reality will be reflected in your hearts, and the virtues of the Kingdom will be obtained PT 176

Mission

the mission of all the prophets, the relation of all the scriptures *Scripture* TAB 596

Union – re: Prophets, Scriptures 596

Mithras

the gradual infiltration into Christian doctrine of the principles of the Mithraic cult, of the Alexandrian school of thought, of the precepts of Zoroastrianism and of Grecian philosophy WOB 56–7

Monarch [see also *King*]

Gospel – re: advent of Muḥammad SB 117

Monk [see also *Seclusion*]

consider likewise, how numerous at this time are the monks who have secluded themselves in their churches, calling upon the Spirit, but when He appeared through the power of Truth, they failed to draw nigh unto Him and are numbered with those that have gone far astray. Happy are they that have abandoned them and set their faces towards Him Who is the Desire of all that are in the heavens and all that are on the earth TB 10

O Concourse of monks! If ye choose to follow Me, I will make you heirs of My Kingdom; and if ye transgress against Me, I will, in My long-suffering, endure it patiently 14

the pious deeds of the monks and priests among the followers of the Spirit . . . are remembered in His presence. In this Day, however, let them give up the life of seclusion and direct their steps towards the open world and busy themselves with that which will profit themselves and others. We have granted them leave to enter into wedlock that they may bring forth one who will make mention of God, the Lord of the seen and the unseen, the Lord of the Exalted Throne 24

say: O concourse of monks! Seclude not yourselves in your churches and cloisters. Come ye out of them by My leave, and busy, then, yourselves with what will profit you and others . . . Enter ye into wedlock, that after you another may arise in your stead. We, verily, have forbidden you lechery, and not that which is conducive to fidelity ESW 49

even as the pious deeds of the Christian monks profited them not – re: time of the manifestation of Muḥammad *Gospel* SB 102

the monks, referred to by European peoples as spiritual and religious leaders, had given up the abiding glory that comes from obedience to the sacred commandments and heavenly teachings of the Gospel, and had joined forces with the presumptuous and tyrannical rulers of the temporal governments of those times SDC 86

but as to the Jewish doctors, Christian priests and monks who read those Books, verily, they know the letter only and they utter the words, as parrots, without understanding their inner meanings *Book* BWF 391

Moon

'Islám is heaven; fasting is its sun, prayer, its moon' *Islám* KI 40

for instance, when Muḥammad, the Lord of being, was questioned concerning the new moons, He, as bidden by God, made reply: 'They are periods appointed unto men.' Thereupon, they that heard Him denounced Him as an ignorant man 182–3

John – re: symbolism of moon in Rev. 12 SAB 172

Moses

call thou to mind the days when He Who conversed with God tended, in the wilderness, the sheep of Jethro, His father-in-law. He hearkened unto the Voice of the Lord of mankind coming from the Burning Bush which had been raised above the Holy Land, exclaiming, 'O Moses! Verily I am God, thy Lord and the Lord of thy forefathers, Abraham, Isaac and Jacob' TB 265

consider Moses! Armed with the rod of celestial dominion, adorned with the white hand of Divine knowledge G 19

how do the divines of this age account for the effulgent glory which the Sadrah of Utterance hath shed upon the Son of 'Imrán (Moses) on the Sinai of Divine knowledge? He (Moses) hearkened unto the Word which the Burning Bush had uttered, and accepted it; and yet most men are bereft of the power of comprehending this, inasmuch as they have busied themselves with their own concerns, and are unaware of the things which belong unto God. Referring to this, the Siyyid of Findirisk hath well said: 'This theme no mortal mind can fathom; be it even that of Abú-Naṣr, or Abú-'Alí Síná (Avicenna)' ESW 41

present thyself before Me that thou mayest hear the mysteries which were heard by the Son of 'Imrán (Moses) upon the Sinai of Wisdom 86

and when Moses had fulfilled the term, and was journeying with His family, He perceived a fire on the mountain side. He said to His family: 'Wait ye, for I perceive a fire, haply I may bring you tidings from it, or a brand from the fire to warm you.' And when He came up to it, a Voice cried to Him out of the Bush from the right side of the Vale in the sacred Spot: 'O Moses, I truly am God, the Lord of the worlds!' 118

and when His day was ended, there came the turn of Moses. Armed with the rod of celestial dominion, adorned with the white hand of divine knowledge, and proceeding from the Párán of the love of God, and wielding the serpent of power and everlasting majesty, He shone forth from the Sinai of light upon the world. He summoned all the peoples and kindreds of the earth to the kingdom of eternity, and invited them to partake of the fruit of the tree of faithfulness [see also *Pharaoh* 11–12] KI 11

Israel – re: Manifestations since the time of Moses 18

consider Moses, son of 'Imrán, one of the exalted Prophets and Author of a divinely-revealed Book. Whilst passing, one day, through the market, in His early days, ere His ministry was proclaimed, He saw two men engaged in fighting. One of them asked the help of Moses against his opponent. Whereupon, Moses intervened and slew him. To this testifieth the record of the sacred Book 53–4

while returning, Moses entered the holy vale, situate in the wilderness of Sinai, and there beheld the vision of the King of glory from the 'Tree that belongeth neither to the East nor to the West.' There He heard the soul-stirring Voice of the Spirit speaking from out of the kindled Fire, bidding Him to shed upon Pharaohic souls the light of divine guidance; so that, liberating them from the shadows of the valley of self and desire, He might enable them to attain the meads of heavenly delight 54 when Moses came unto Pharaoh and delivered unto him, as bidden by God, the divine Message, Pharaoh spoke insultingly saying: 'Art thou not he that committed murder, and became an infidel?' 55

after Him came Moses, He Who held converse with God. The soothsayers of His time warned Pharaoh in these terms: 'A star hath risen in the heaven, and lo! it foreshadoweth the conception of a Child Who holdeth your fate and the fate of your people in His hand.' In like manner, there appeared a sage who, in the darkness of the night, brought tidings of joy unto the people of Israel, imparting consolation to their souls, and assurance to their hearts 63

even as the people of Israel, in the time of Moses, bartered away the bread of heaven for the sordid things of the earth, these people, likewise, sought to exchange the divinely-revealed verses for their foul, their vile, and idle desires *Israel* 208

indeed We conversed with Moses by the leave of God from the midst of the Burning Bush in the Sinai and revealed an infinitesimal glimmer of Thy Light upon the Mystic Mount and its dwellers, whereupon the Mount shook to its foundations and was crushed into dust SB 72

for example, from the inception of the mission of Jesus – may peace be upon Him – till the day of His ascension was the Resurrection of Moses. For during that period the Revelation of God shone forth through the appearance of that divine Reality, Who rewarded by His Word everyone who believed in Moses, and punished by His Word everyone who did not believe; inasmuch as God's Testimony for that Day was that which He had solemnly affirmed in the Gospel 107

and so in the day of Moses *Primal Will* 126

Hebrew – re: condition of, time coming of Moses SDC 75–6

He [Moses] gathered Israel's scattered tribes into the shelter of the unifying and universal word of God 76

Law – re: Mosaic Law and Children of Israel SAB 52

the meaning is that certain personages guided the people with a staff grown out of the earth, and shepherded them with a rod, like unto the rod of Moses *Rod* 166

consider Moses, He Who conversed with God. Verily, upon Mount Sinai, Moses entered into a Covenant regarding the Messiah, with all those souls who would live in the day of the Messiah. And those souls, although they appeared many centuries after Moses, were nevertheless – so far as the Covenant, which is outside time, was concerned – present there with Moses. The Jews, however, were heedless of this and remembered it not, and thus they suffered a great and clear loss – re: PHW 19, 71 *Covenant* 207 207

the flight of Moses, the Prophet of Sinai, revealed the Flame of the Lord's burning Fire 281

Moses suddenly appeared among them . . . This unique Personage, single and alone, rescued the Children of Israel from bondage through the power of religious training and discipline PUP 362

Christ ratified and proclaimed the foundation of the law of Moses. Muḥammad and all the Prophets have revoiced that same foundation of reality 366

you may not know that the first address of Muḥammad to His tribe was the statement, 'Verily, Moses was a Prophet of God, and the Torah is a Book of God. Verily, O ye people, ye must believe in the Torah, in Moses and the prophets. Ye must accept all the prophets of Israel as 367 valid.' In the Qur'án, the Muslim Bible, there are seven statements or repetitions of the Mosaic narrative, and in all the historic accounts Moses is praised

Muḥammad – re: words concerning Moses PT 47

in the work of the Kingdom of God one should not consider capacity or ability; the confirmation of the Spirit will descend, because the weakest souls through the confirmation of the Holy Spirit become the most powerful. Some souls who are outwardly ignorant through this gift become learned men. The weakest souls become the strongest. Many times a woman has surpassed a thousand men, or, rather, through this help can withstand all the people of the world. SW VIII 8, p104

His Holiness Moses was apparently a shepherd but through the divine power he overcame Pharaoh and his armies. Likewise the disciples were the weakest souls but through the breath of the Holy Spirit and the assistance of the Kingdom of God they became the strongest ones

the circumstances in which the Vehicle of this newborn Revelation, following with such swiftness that of the Báb, received the first intimations of His sublime mission recall, and indeed surpass in poignancy the soul-shaking experience of Moses when confronted by the Burning Bush in the wilderness of Sinai; of Zoroaster when awakened to His mission by a succession of seven visions; of Jesus when coming out of the waters of the Jordan He saw the heavens opened and the Holy Ghost descend like a dove and light upon Him; of Muḥammad when in the Cave of Hira, outside of the holy city of Mecca, the voice of Gabriel bade Him 'cry in the name of Thy Lord'; and of the Báb when in a dream He approached the bleeding head of the Imám Ḥusayn, and, quaffing the blood that dripped from his lacerated throat, awoke to find Himself the chosen recipient of the outpouring grace of the Almighty GPB 93

an experience vividly recalling the vision of God that caused Moses to fall in a swoon, and the voice of Gabriel which plunged Muḥammad into such consternation that, hurrying to the shelter of His home, He bade His wife, Khadíjih, envelop Him in His mantle 101

this enforced and hurried departure of Bahá'u'lláh from His native land, accompanied by some of His relatives, recalls in some of its aspects, the precipitate flight of the Holy Family into Egypt; the sudden migration of Muḥammad, soon after His assumption of the prophetic office, from Mecca to Medina; the exodus* of Moses, His brother and His followers from the land of their birth, in response to the Divine summons, and above all the banishment of Abraham from Ur of the Chaldees to the Promised Land 107

the Holy Land – the Land promised by God to Abraham, sanctified by the Revelation of Moses, honored by the lives and labors of the Hebrew patriarchs, judges, kings and prophets, revered as the cradle of Christianity, and as the place where Zoroaster, according to 'Abdu'l-Bahá's testimony, had 'held converse with some of the Prophets of Israel' 183

* It was both physical and spiritual. They journeyed to the Promised Land, and geography and history both prove that this was a physical journey.

Moses viewed the Promised Land, but died before it was reached, having given over his charge to Joshua.

The crossing of the Red Sea has a spiritual meaning. It was a spiritual journey, through and above the sea of corruption and iniquity of Pharaoh and his people, or army. By the help of God, through Moses, the Israelites were able to cross this sea safely and reach the Promised Land (spiritual state), while Pharaoh and his people were drowned in their own corruption.

The Egyptian history recorded even trifling events. Had such a wonderful thing happened as the parting of the physical sea, it would also have been recorded . . . ('Abdu'l-Bahá, quoted by H. S. Goodall and E. G. Cooper, *Daily Lessons Received at 'Akká: January 1908*, Wilmette, Bahá'í Publishing Trust, RP 1979, p. 45.)

Most Great Remembrance

Gate SB 46

O ye kinsmen of the Most Great Remembrance! This Tree of Holiness, dyed crimson with the oil of servitude, hath verily sprung forth out of your own soil in the midst of the Burning Bush, yet ye comprehend nothing whatever thereof, neither of His true, heavenly attributes, nor of the actual circumstances of His earthly life, nor of the evidences of His powerful and unblemished behaviour. Actuated by your own fancies, you consider Him to be alien to the sovereign Truth, while in the estimation of God He is none other than the Promised One Himself, invested with the power of the sovereign Truth, and verily He is, as decreed in the Mother Book, held answerable in the midst of the Burning Bush 52

Call – re: from the Burning Bush 69

Most Great Spirit

at so critical an hour and under such appalling circumstances the 'Most Great Spirit,' as designated by Himself, and symbolized in the Zoroastrian, the Mosaic, the Christian, the Muḥammadan Dispensations by the Sacred Fire, the Burning Bush, the Dove and the Angel Gabriel respectively, descended upon, and revealed itself, personated by a 'Maiden,' to the agonized soul of Bahá'u'lláh GPB 101

Mother

O Thou Mother of the Remembrance! May the peace and salutation of God rest upon thee. Indeed thou hast endured patiently in Him Who is the sublime Self of God. Recognize then the station of thy Son Who is none other than the mighty Word of God. He hath verily pledged Himself to be answerable for thee both in thy grave and on the Judgement Day, while thou hast, in the Preserved Tablet of God, been immortalized as the 'Mother of the Faithful' by the Pen of His Remembrance SB 52–3

the Founder of the Christian Faith is designated by Bahá'u'lláh as the 'Spirit of God,' is proclaimed as the One Who 'appeared out of the breath of the Holy Ghost,' and is even extolled as the 'Essence of the Spirit.' His mother is described as 'that veiled and immortal, that most beauteous, countenance,' and the station of her Son eulogized as a 'station which hath been exalted above the imaginings of all that dwell on earth' PDC 109–10

Mountain [see also *Carmel*]

Burning Bush – re: Mystic Mount SB 72

but 'they shall not hurt nor destroy in all My holy mountain: for the earth shall be full of the knowledge of the Lord, as the waters cover the sea' . . . but these verses apply word for word to Bahá'u'lláh. Likewise in this marvellous cycle the earth will be transformed, and the world of humanity arrayed in tranquillity and beauty. Disputes, quarrels and murders will be replaced by peace, truth and concord; among the nations, peoples, races and countries, love and amity will appear *Jesus Christ* SAQ 63

Muḥammad [see also *Apostle of God*]

every discerning observer will recognize that in the Dispensation of the Qur'án both the Book and the Cause of Jesus were confirmed. As to the matter of names, Muḥammad, Himself, declared: 'I am Jesus.' He recognized the truth of the signs, prophecies, and words of Jesus, and G 21–2 testified that they were all of God. In this sense, neither the person of Jesus nor His writings hath differed from that of Muḥammad and of His holy Book, inasmuch as both have championed the Cause of God, uttered His praise, and revealed His commandments. Thus it is that Jesus, Himself, declared: 'I go away and come again unto you'

to this testifieth the tradition: 'Manifold and mysterious is My relationship with God. I am He, Himself, and He is I, Myself, except that I am that I am, and He is that He is.' And in like manner, the words: 'Arise, O Muḥammad, for lo, the Lover and the Beloved are joined together and made one in Thee.' He similarly saith: 'There is no distinction whatsoever between Thee and Them, except that They are Thy Servants' 66

behold, O Muḥammad, how the sayings and doings of the followers of Shí'ih Islám have dulled the joy and fervour of its early days, and tarnished the pristine brilliancy of its light. In its primitive days, whilst they still adhered to the precepts associated with the name of their Prophet, the Lord of mankind, their career was marked by an unbroken chain of victories and triumphs *Islám* 68–9

consider that which hath been sent down unto Muḥammad, the Apostle of God. The measure of the Revelation of which He was the bearer had been clearly foreordained by Him Who is the Almighty, the All-Powerful. They that heard him, however, could apprehend His purpose only to the extent of their station and spiritual capacity. He, in like manner, uncovered the face of Wisdom in proportion to their ability to sustain the burden of His Message 76–7

in like manner, when Muḥammad, the Prophet of God – may all men be a sacrifice unto Him – appeared, the learned men of Mecca and Medina arose, in the early days of His Revelation, against Him and rejected His Message, while they who were destitute of all learning recognized and embraced His Faith 83

what explanation can they give concerning that which the Seal of the Prophets (Muḥammad) – may the souls of all else but Him be offered up for His sake – hath said?: 'Ye, verily, shall behold your Lord as ye behold the full moon on its fourteenth night' – re: the divines ESW 41–2

Interpret – re: Christian divines KI 26

inasmuch as those signs which were to accompany the dawn of the Muḥammadan Dispensation did not actually come to pass *Christianity* 26

Islám – re: fasting and prayer 40

Qiblih – re: changing of, to Mecca 50

addressed Rúz-bih saying: 'O Rúz-bih! when thou hast taken up my body and buried it, go to Ḥijáz for there the Day-star of Muḥammad will arise. Happy art thou, for thou shalt behold His face!' *Rúz-bih* 65

Sign – re: which must herald the Revelation of Muḥammad 83–4

yea, in the writings and utterances of the Mirrors reflecting the sun of the Muḥammadan Dispensation mention hath been made of 'Modification by the exalted beings' and 'alteration by the disdainful.' Such passages, however, refer only to particular cases. Among them is the story of Ibn-i-Ṣúríyá 84

Ibn-i-Ṣúríyá – re: people of Khaybar and penalty of adultery 84–5

even as the sovereignty of Muḥammad, the Messenger of God, is today apparent and manifest amongst the people. You are well aware of what befell His Faith in the early days of His dispensation. What woeful sufferings did the hand of the infidel and erring, the divines of that age and their associates, inflict upon that spiritual Essence, that most pure 108 and holy Being! How abundant the thorns and briars which they have strewn over His path [see also *Divines*]

for this reason did Muḥammad cry out: 'No Prophet of God hath suffered such harm as I have suffered.' And in the Qur'án are recorded all the calumnies and reproaches uttered against Him, as well as all the afflictions which He suffered. Refer ye thereunto, that haply ye may be informed of that which hath befallen His Revelation. So grievous was His plight, that for a time all ceased to hold intercourse with Him and His companions. Whoever associated with Him fell a victim to the relentless cruelty of His enemies 109

We shall cite in this connection only one verse of that Book. Shouldst thou observe it with a discerning eye, thou wilt, all the remaining days of thy life, lament and bewail the injury of Muḥammad, that wronged and oppressed Messenger of God. That verse was revealed at a time when Muḥammad languished weary and sorrowful beneath the weight of the opposition of the people, and of their unceasing torture. In the midst of His agony, the Voice of Gabriel, calling from the Sadratu'l-Muntahá, was heard saying: 'But if their opposition be grievous to Thee – if Thou canst, seek out an opening into the earth or a ladder into heaven.' The implication of this utterance is that His case had no remedy, that they would not withhold their hands from Him unless He should hide Himself beneath the depths of the earth, or take His flight unto heaven 109–10

the following is an evidence of the sovereignty exercised by Muḥammad, the Day-star of Truth. Hast thou not heard how with one single verse He hath sundered light from darkness, the righteous from the ungodly, and the believing from the infidel? All the signs and allusions concerning the Day of Judgment, which thou hast heard, such as the raising of the dead, the Day of Reckoning, the Last Judgment, and others have been made manifest through the revelation of that verse. These revealed words were a blessing to the righteous who on hearing them exclaimed: 'O God our Lord, We have heard, and obeyed.' They were a curse to the people of iniquity who, on hearing them affirmed: 'We have heard and rebelled.' Those words, sharp as the sword of God, have separated the faithful from the infidel, and severed father from son 111–12

they refuse to recognize the trumpet-blast which so explicitly in this text was sounded through the revelation of Muḥammad. They deprive themselves of the regenerating Spirit of God that breathed into it, and foolishly expect to hear the trumpet-sound of the Seraph of God who is but one of His servants! Hath not the Seraph himself, the angel of the Judgment Day, and his like been ordained by Muḥammad's own utterance? 116

furthermore, it is already evident and known unto thee that those things to which the Jews and Christians have clung, and the cavillings which they heaped upon the Beauty of Muḥammad, the same have in this day been upheld by the people of the Qur'án, and been witnessed in their denunciations of the 'Point of the Bayán' – may the souls of all that dwell within the kingdom of divine Revelations be a sacrifice unto Him! Behold their folly: they utter the self-same words, uttered by the Jews of old, and know it not! How well and true are His words concerning them: 'Leave them to entertain themselves with their cavillings!' 'As Thou livest, O Muḥammad! they are seized by the frenzy of their vain fancies' 135

when the Unseen, the Eternal, the divine Essence, caused the Day-star of Muḥammad to rise above the horizon of knowledge, among the cavils which the Jewish divines raised against Him was that after Moses no 135–6

Prophet should be sent of God. Yea, mention hath been made in the scriptures* of a Soul Who must needs be made manifest and Who will advance the Faith, and promote the interests of the people of Moses, so that the Law of the Mosaic Dispensation may encompass the whole earth. Thus hath the King of eternal glory referred in His Book to the words uttered by those wanderers in the vale of remoteness and error: '"The hand of God," say the Jews, "is chained up." Chained up be their own hands! And for that which they have said, they were accursed. Nay, outstretched are both His hands!' 'The hand of God is above their hands'

thou wouldst certainly recognize that all these things which have in this day hindered this people from attaining the shores of the ocean of eternal grace, the same things in the Muḥammadan Dispensation prevented the people of that age from recognizing that divine Luminary, and from testifying to His truth. Thou wilt also apprehend the mysteries of 'return' and 'revelation,' and wilt securely abide within the loftiest chambers of certitude and assurance 147–8

Sacrifice – re: miracle of Abel and Cain 148

likewise, Muḥammad, in another verse, uttereth His protest against the people of that age. He saith: 'Although they had before prayed for victory over those who believed not, yet when there came unto them, He of Whom they had knowledge, they disbelieved in Him. The curse of God on the infidels!' Reflect how this verse also implieth that the people living in the days of Muḥammad were the same people who in the days of the Prophets of old contended and fought in order to promote the Faith, and teach the Cause, of God. And yet, how could the generations living at the time of Jesus and Moses, and those who lived in the days of Muḥammad, be regarded as being actually one and the same people? [see also *Return* 151, 154–5] 150

thus hath Muḥammad, the Point of the Qur'án, revealed: 'I am all the Prophets.' Likewise, He saith: 'I am the first Adam, Noah, Moses, and Jesus.' Similar statements have been made by 'Alí. Sayings such as this, which indicate the essential unity of those Exponents of Oneness, have also emanated from the Channels of God's immortal utterance, and the Treasuries of the gems of divine knowledge, and have been recorded in the scriptures [see also *Imám* 153] 152–3

reflect for a while upon the behaviour of the companions of the Muḥammadan Dispensation. Consider how, through the reviving breath of Muḥammad, they were cleansed from the defilements of earthly vanities, were delivered from selfish desires, and were detached from all 159–60

* There are many references to the coming of Muḥammad, in both the Old and New Testament. Deuteronomy, Chapter 33, verse 2: 'And He said, the Lord came from Sinai, and rose up from Seir unto them; He shined forth from Mount Paran, and He came with ten thousands of Saints: from His right hand went a fiery law for them.' 'The Lord coming from Sinai' refers to the Mosaic dispensation. 'Rose up from Seir unto them,' refers to a mountain in Galilee and means the Christian dispensation; 'and He came with ten thousands of Saints' is the Bahá'í dispensation. All references to Mount Paran refer to Muḥammad. Paran is a mountain in Arabia. The word 'Paraclete' also refers to Muḥammad. Paraclete means 'the Praiser' in Greek, and Muḥammad means 'the Praiser' in Arabic. Further references to Muḥammad in the 'Answered Questions' . . . Genesis, Chapter 21, verse 21: 'And He dwelt in the Wilderness of Paran' refers to Muḥammad. The Arabs are the descendants of Ishmael. Numbers, Chapter 12, verse 3: the word Paran occurs. The wilderness of Paran is in Trans-Jordan. David could easily get to it. The reference in Deuteronomy is the most important reference (Chapter 33, verse 2). Genesis, Chapter 17, verse 20: 'And as for Ishmael . . . and will make him fruitful, and will multiply him exceedingly; twelve princes shall he beget', etc. The twelve princes are the twelve Imams. Also in Deuteronomy, Chapter 18, verse 18: 'I will raise them up a prophet from among their brethren.' This refers to their cousins, the Arabs, brethren meaning cousin here in relationship, and the prophet is Muḥammad. If it had meant Christ it would have said 'seed' and not 'brethren'. (Shoghi Effendi, quoted by May Maxwell and Mary Maxwell, *Haifa Notes of Shoghi Effendi's Words*, 1937. Approved by Shoghi Effendi.)

else but Him. Behold how they preceded all the peoples of the earth in attaining unto His holy Presence – the Presence of God Himself – how they renounced the world and all that is therein, and sacrificed freely and joyously their lives at the feet of that Manifestation of the All-Glorious. And now, observe the 'return' of the self-same determination, the self-same constancy and renunciation, manifested by the companions of the Point of the Bayán

yet how many are those who, through failure to understand its meaning, have allowed the term 'Seal of the Prophets' to obscure their understanding, and deprive them of the grace of His manifold bounties! Hath not Muḥammad, Himself, declared: 'I am all the Prophets?' Hath He not said as We have already mentioned: 'I am Adam, Noah, Moses, and Jesus?' Why should Muḥammad, that immortal Beauty, Who hath said: 'I am the first Adam' be incapable of saying also: 'I am the last Adam'? For even as He regarded Himself to be the 'First of the Prophets' – that is Adam – in like manner, the 'Seal of the Prophets' is also applicable unto that Divine Beauty. It is admittedly obvious that being the 'First of the Prophets,' He likewise is their 'Seal' 162

even as the Lord of being hath in His unerring Book, after speaking of the 'Seal' in His exalted utterance: 'Muḥammad is the Apostle of God and the Seal of the Prophets,' hath revealed unto all people the promise of 'attainment unto the divine Presence' 169

Messenger 179

for instance, when Muḥammad, the Lord of being, was questioned concerning the new moons, He, as bidden by God, made reply: 'They are periods appointed unto men.' Thereupon, they that heard Him denounced Him as an ignorant man. 182–3

Likewise, in the verse concerning the 'Spirit,' He saith: 'And they will ask Thee of the Spirit. Say, "the Spirit proceedeth at My Lord's command."' As soon as Muḥammad's answer was given, they all clamorously protested, saying: 'Lo! an ignorant man who knoweth not what the Spirit is, calleth Himself the Revealer of divine Knowledge!' And now behold the divines of the age who, because of their being honoured by His name, and finding that their fathers have acknowledged His Revelation, have blindly submitted to His truth [see also *Word* 181–2]

We accidently came upon the story of the 'Mi'ráj' of Muḥammad, of Whom was spoken: 'But for Thee, I would not have created the spheres' 185–6

whilst the Lord of the 'Mi'ráj' Himself was never burdened with a single letter of these limited and obscure learnings, and never defiled His radiant heart with any of these fanciful illusions? How truly hath he said: 'All human attainment moveth upon a lame ass, whilst Truth, riding upon the wind, darteth across space' 187

in the days of Muḥammad the Messenger of God the Qur'án *Word* 199

for instance, the Qur'án was an impregnable stronghold unto the people of Muḥammad 200

all the things that people required in connection with the Revelation of Muḥammad and His laws were to be found revealed and manifest in that Riḍván of resplendent glory *Book* 200–1

Muḥammad, Himself, as the end of His mission drew nigh, spoke these words: 'Verily, I leave amongst you My twin weighty testimonies: The Book of God and My Family' *Book* 201

inasmuch as Muḥammad hath confined His testimonies to His Book and to His Family, and whereas the latter hath passed away, there remaineth His Book only as His one testimony amongst the people *Book* 202

Word – re: tales of the Ancients 211–12
Calumny – re: denunciations of Muḥammad 215
'ye oppress and persecute us, and yet, what else have we done except that we have believed in God and in the verses sent down unto us through the tongue of Muḥammad, and in those which descended upon the Prophets of old?' *Companions* 218
this generation still awaiteth in expectation of beholding the promised One who should uphold the Law of the Muḥammadan Dispensation *Truth* 239–40
Mihdí – re: He will perform that which Muḥammad, the Messenger of God, hath performed 240
Biḥár – re: Qá'im – signs 254
the belief that divine revelation ended with the coming of Muḥammad *'Abdu'ṣ-Ṣáḥib Primal Point* SB 31
thou contendest, 'How can we recognize Him when we have heard naught but words which fall short of irrefutable proofs?' Yet since thou hast acknowledged and recognized Muḥammad, the Apostle of God, through the Qur'án, how canst thou withhold recognition from Him Who sent thee the Book, despite thy calling thyself 'His servant'? Verily He doth exercise undisputed authority over His revelations unto all mankind – re: address to 'Abdu'ṣ-Ṣáḥib 33
if ye are truly faithful to Muḥammad, the Apostle of God *Qur'án* 46
the conclusive Proof of God in favour of His Remembrance is similar to the one wherewith Muḥammad, the Seal of the Prophets, was invested 71
this Religion is indeed, in the sight of God, the essence of the Faith of Muḥammad *Religion* 71
when the Apostle of God (Muḥammad) appeared, He did not announce unto the unbelievers that the Resurrection had come, for they could not bear the news 78
it is clear and evident that the object of all preceding Dispensations hath been to pave the way for the advent of Muḥammad, the Apostle of God 105
if all those who were expecting the fulfilment of the promise of Jesus had been assured of the manifestation of Muḥammad, the Apostle of God, not one would have turned aside from the sayings of Jesus 110
– re: Tree of divine Truth *Tree* 112
this is what happened to the monarchs that held fast unto the Gospel. They awaited the coming of the Prophet of God (Muḥammad), and when He did appear, they failed to recognize Him *Islám* 117
Primal Will – re: appearance in the Prophets 126
how numerous the people who engaged in contests with Muḥammad, the Apostle of God, and were eventually reduced to naught, inasmuch as they were powerless to bring forth proofs similar to that which God had sent down unto Him. Had they been abashed and modest, and had they realized the nature of the proofs wherewith He was invested, they would never have challenged Him 132
they shut themselves out as by a veil from God and failed to observe that which He had desired for them to perform as true believers. They pondered not upon such people as lived in the days of Muḥammad, who believed likewise that they were seeking the good-pleasure of God, while they had actually cut themselves off therefrom, once they had failed to secure the good-pleasure of Muḥammad. Nevertheless they comprehended not 136
then when God manifested Muḥammad as His Messenger and as the 137

Repository of His good-pleasure, they neglected to quicken their souls *Gospel*

Gospel – re: guides of error 143

Mihdí – re: divine Revelation associated with 146

when God sent forth His Prophet Muḥammad, on that day the termination of the prophetic cycle was foreordained in the knowledge of God. Yea, that promise hath indeed come true *Day* 161

the military expeditions of Muḥammad, on the contrary, were always defensive actions: a proof of this is that during thirteen years, in Mecca, He and His followers endured the most violent persecutions. At this period they were the target for the arrows of hatred: some of His companions were killed and their property confiscated; others fled to foreign lands. Muḥammad Himself, after the most extreme persecutions by the Qurayshites, who finally resolved to kill Him, fled to Medina in the middle of the night. Yet even then His enemies did not cease their persecutions, but pursued Him to Medina, and His disciples even to Abyssinia SAQ 18–19

Muḥammad never fought against the Christians; on the contrary, He treated them kindly and gave them perfect freedom. A community of Christian people lived at Najrán and were under His care and protection. Muḥammad said, 'If anyone infringes their rights, I Myself will be his enemy, and in the presence of God I will bring a charge against him.' In the edicts which He promulgated it is clearly stated that the lives, properties and honour of the Christians and Jews are under the protection of God 21

these details indicate the condition of the people to whom Muḥammad was sent. The first question which He put to them was, 'Why do you not accept the Pentateuch and the Gospel, and why do you not believe in Christ and in Moses?' This saying presented difficulties to them, and they argued, 'Our forefathers did not believe in the Pentateuch and the Gospel; tell us, why was this?' He answered, 'They were misled; you ought to reject those who do not believe in the Pentateuch and the Gospel, even though they are your fathers and your ancestors' 22

now, Muḥammad was the root, and 'Alí the branch, like Moses and Joshua. It is said they 'are clothed in sackcloth,' meaning that they, apparently, were to be clothed in old raiment, not in new raiment; in other words, in the beginning they would possess no splendour in the eyes of the people, nor would their Cause appear new: for Muḥammad's spiritual Law corresponds to that of Christ in the Gospel, and most of His laws relating to material things correspond to those of the Pentateuch. This is the meaning of the old raiment [see also *Witness Law*] 48–9

Lamp – re: two olive trees, two candlesticks 49

Servant – re: standing in the service of God 49

for to these two witnesses God granted both outward and inward power, that they might educate and correct the ferocious, bloodthirsty, tyrannical nomad Arabs – re: Muḥammad and 'Alí *Power* 50

Testimony – re: and when they shall have finished their testimony 51

this beast means the Umayyads who attacked them from the pit of error, and who rose against the religion of Muḥammad *Beast* 51

Body – re: Law of God 52–3

this woman is that bride, the Law of God that descended upon Muḥammad *Woman* 68

in the same way in the Qur'án it is said to Muḥammad: 'We have granted 169–70

Thee a manifest victory, so that God may forgive Thee Thy preceding and subsequent sin.' This address, although apparently directed to Muḥammad, was in reality for all the people. This mode of address, as before said, was used by the perfect wisdom of God, so that the hearts of the people might not be troubled, anxious and tormented

Christ ratified and proclaimed the foundation of the law of Moses. Muḥammad and all the Prophets have revoiced that same foundation of reality — PUP 366

you may not know that the first address of Muḥammad to His tribe was the statement, 'Verily, Moses was a Prophet of God, and the Torah is a Book of God. Verily, O ye people, ye must believe in the Torah, in Moses and the prophets. Ye must accept all the prophets of Israel as valid' — 367

consider that Muḥammad was born among the savage and barbarous tribes of Arabia, lived among them and was outwardly illiterate and uninformed of the Holy Books of God. The Arabian people were in the utmost ignorance and barbarism. They buried their infant daughters alive, considering this to be an evidence of a valorous and lofty nature. They lived in bondage and serfdom under the Persian and Roman governments and were scattered throughout the desert, engaged in continual strife and bloodshed. When the light of Muḥammad dawned, the darkness of ignorance was dispelled from the deserts of Arabia. In a short period of time those barbarous peoples attained a superlative degree of civilization which, with Baghdád as its center, extended as far westward as Spain and afterward influenced the greater part of Europe — 367–8

in the Qur'án we read that Muḥammad spoke to his followers, saying: 'Why do you not believe in Christ, and in the Gospel? Why will you not accept Moses and the Prophets, for surely the Bible is the Book of God? In truth, Moses was a sublime Prophet, and Jesus was filled with the Holy Spirit. He came to the world through the Power of God, born of the Holy Spirit and of the blessed Virgin Mary. Mary, His mother, was a saint from Heaven. She passed her days in the Temple at prayer and food was sent to her from above. Her father, Zacharias, came to her and asked her from whence the food came, and Mary made answer, "From on high." Surely God made Mary to be exalted above all other women' — PT 47

this is what Muḥammad taught His people concerning Jesus and Moses, and He reproached them for their lack of faith in these great Teachers, and taught them the lessons of truth and tolerance. Muḥammad was sent from God to work among a people as savage and uncivilized as the wild beasts. They were quite devoid of understanding, nor had they any feelings of love, sympathy and pity. Women were so degraded and despised that a man could bury his daughter alive, and he had as many wives to be his slaves as he chose. — 47–8

Among these half animal people Muḥammad was sent with His divine Message. He taught the people that idol worship was wrong, but that they should reverence Christ, Moses and the Prophets. Under His influence they became a more enlightened and civilized people and arose from the degraded state in which He found them. Was not this a good work, and worthy of all praise, respect and love?

His Holiness the Prophet Muḥammad made a covenant concerning His Holiness the Báb and the Báb was the One promised by Muḥammad, for Muḥammad gave the tidings of His coming — BWF 358

whatever the European and American historians have written regarding His Highness Muḥammad, the Messenger of God, most of it is falsehood. — SW II 15, pp7,16

Consider ye, is it possible for a person afflicted with epilepsy to establish a great nation?

Therefore, this statement of the European historians, regarding that Holy Personage, is unqualified falsehood.

Reflect ye, that that illustrious Personage was born in the Sahara of Arabia among the ignorant tent dwellers, affiliating and associating with them until he grew to manhood and maturity, never studying the sciences and arts; nay, even he was apparently illiterate and uninstructed. Notwithstanding all this, he brought forth such a nation, established such a religion and uttered such explanations regarding scientific questions with great perspicuity, and raised such a community from the nadir of ignorance and barbarism to the zenith of civilization and prosperity! Through his influence, science, literature, philosophy, crafts and trades made wonderful progress during the medieval ages in Andalusia and Ba<u>gh</u>dád.

Now is it possible that such an illustrious Personage be afflicted with epilepsy?

likewise Muḥammad unified the wild, savage tribes of Arabs and made them the conquerors of Asia. Consequently there must needs be divine power for the accomplishment of this universal aim. Human power fails in this undertaking *Holy Spirit* — VIII 8, P101

the people among whom He appeared were the most decadent race in the civilized world, grossly ignorant, savage, cruel, steeped in prejudice, servile in their submission to an almost deified hierarchy, recalling in their abjectness the Israelites of Egypt in the days of Moses, in their fanaticism the Jews in the days of Jesus, and in their perversity the idolators of Arabia in the days of Muḥammad – re: Persian people – time of the Báb — GPB 4

the audacity of Mullá Ḥusayn who, at the command of the Báb, had attired his head with the green turban worn and sent to him by his Master, who had hoisted the Black Standard, the unfurling of which would, according to the Prophet Muḥammad, herald the advent of the vicegerent of God on earth — 38

Brother – re: words of Muḥammad quoted by Quddús at <u>Sh</u>ay<u>kh</u> Ṭabarsí — 80

'you must attach great importance,' writes 'Abdu'l-Bahá in the Tablets of the Divine Plan, 'to the Indians, the original inhabitants of America. For these souls may be likened unto the ancient inhabitants of the Arabian Peninsula, who, prior to the Revelation of Muḥammad, were like savages. When the Muḥammadan Light shone forth in their midst, they became so enkindled that they shed illumination upon the world. Likewise, should these Indians be educated and properly guided, there can be no doubt that through the Divine teachings they will become so enlightened that the whole earth will be illumined' — ADJ 46

'consider the Seal of the Prophets (Muḥammad) – may the souls of all else except Him be His sacrifice! – How grievous the things which befell that Lord of all being at the hands of the priests of idolatry, and of the Jewish doctors, after He had uttered the blessed words proclaiming the unity of God! By My life! My pen groaneth, and all created things cry out by reason of the things that have touched Him, at the hands of such as have broken the Covenant of God and His Testament, and denied His Testimony, and gainsaid His signs' [words of Bahá'u'lláh] — PDC 80–81

as to Muḥammad, the Apostle of God, let none among His followers who read these pages, think for a moment that either Islám, or its Prophet, or His Book, or His appointed Successors, or any of His authentic — 108 teachings, have been, or are to be in any way, or to however slight a degree, disparaged

the conception of nationality, the attainment to the state of nationhood, may, therefore, be said to be the distinguishing characteristics of the Muḥammadan Dispensation, in the course of which the nations and races of the world, and particularly in Europe and America, were unified and achieved political independence 120

Names

He was formally designated Bahá'u'lláh, an appellation specifically recorded in the Persian Bayán, signifying at once the glory, the light and the splendour of God, and was styled the 'Lord of Lords,' the 'Most Great Name,' the 'Ancient Beauty,' the 'Pen of the Most High,' the 'Hidden Name,' the 'Preserved Treasure,' 'He Whom God will make manifest,' the 'Most Great Light,' the 'All-Highest Horizon,' the 'Most Great Ocean,' the 'Supreme Heaven,' the 'Pre-Existent Root,' the 'Self-Subsistent,' the 'Day-Star of the Universe,' the 'Great Announcement,' the 'Speaker on Sinai,' the 'Sifter of Men,' the 'Wronged One of the World,' the 'Desire of the Nations,' the 'Lord of the Covenant,' the 'Tree beyond which there is no passing' GPB 94

'ye are lovers of names, and appear to have given yourselves up to them' [words of Bahá'u'lláh] *Leaders* PDC 89

'a day shall be witnessed by My people,' their own traditions condemn them, 'whereon there will have remained naught of Islám but a name, and of the Qur'án naught but a mere appearance. The doctors of that age shall be the most evil the world hath ever seen. Mischief hath proceeded from them, and on them it will recoil' – re: Muḥammadan tradition 99

Nation

'the wolf also shall dwell with the lamb, and the leopard shall lie down with the kid; and the calf and the young lion and the fatling together; and a little child shall lead them' . . . the leopard and the lamb, the lion and the calf, the child and the asp, are metaphors and symbols for various nations, peoples, antagonistic sects and hostile races, who are as opposite and inimical as the wolf and lamb. We say that by the breath of the spirit of Christ they found concord and harmony, they were vivified, and they associated together SAQ 62–3

the nationalistic philosophy, the parent of an unbridled and obsolete nationalism, which, having dethroned Islám, has indirectly assaulted the front-line of the Christian church in non-Christian lands, and is dealing such heavy blows to Catholic, Anglican, and Presbyterian Missions in Persia, Turkey, and the Far East PDC 105

Evolution – re: successive stages of unification 118

nowhere in the Gospels do we find any reference to the unity of nations 119

the Faith of Islám, the succeeding link in the chain of Divine Revelation, introduced, as Bahá'u'lláh Himself testifies, the conception of the nation as a unit and a vital stage in the organization of human society, and embodied it in its teaching. This indeed is what is meant by this brief yet highly significant and illuminating pronouncement of Bahá'u'lláh: 'Of old (Islamic Dispensation) it hath been revealed: "Love of one's country is an element of the Faith of God."' This principle was established and stressed by the Apostle of God, inasmuch as the evolution of human society required it at that time. Nor could any stage above and beyond it have been envisaged, as world conditions preliminary to the establishment of a superior form of organization were as yet unobtainable. 120

Nation

The conception of nationality, the attainment to the state of nationhood, may, therefore, be said to be the distinguishing characteristics of the Muḥammadan Dispensation, in the course of which the nations and races of the world, and particularly in Europe and America, were unified and achieved political independence

Nazarene

Messiah – re: this youthful Nazarene [Jesus Christ] KI 18

the so-called Nazarenes, who persevered, above a century, in the practice of the Mosaic Law WOB 57

Near Ones

the good deeds of the righteous are the sins of the Near Ones *Sin* SAQ 126

Nebuchadnezzar*

Jews – re: survivors of massacre of Jerusalem and enforcement of the Pentateuch KI 85–6

the banners of their sovereignty were reversed; the ignorance, foolishness, abasement and self-love of their religious leaders and their scholars were brought to light in the coming of Nebuchadnezzar, King of Babylon, who destroyed them. After a general massacre, and the sacking and razing of their houses and even the uprooting of their trees, he took captive whatever remnants his sword had spared and carried them off to Babylon. Seventy years later the descendants of these captives were released and went back to Jerusalem SDC 78

Affliction – re: by Nebuchadnezzar and Titus 79

Torah – re: Nebuchadnezzar came and conquered the Holy Land PUP 363

Neglect

nevertheless some have remained neglectful of and separated from these SDC 54

* The book of Daniel is based on an historical point of view, especially the second chapter concerning the dream of Nebuchadnezzar and the interpretation made by Daniel which clearly indicates the coming of the Lord in the latter days . . .

Then [Daniel] said: 'O king, thou hast seen in the dream a grand looking image. The head of that image was gold, his breast was silver, his belly and thighs were of brass, his legs of iron and his feet part of iron and part of clay. And when thou wert looking at the image, a large stone was cut out of heaven without hands, and came right on the image and destroyed it. Then all the parts of the body of the image were broken in pieces and scattered. It was utterly broken and destroyed.' He said, 'This dream is true and this will happen. God has explained to the king, in this dream, the events which will happen in the latter days. Know thou, O king, that that golden head is thine, that is to say, the Chaldean kingdom, and then after thy kingdom will come another kingdom which is inferior to thine, but it will also be a great kingdom, and that represents the breast which is of silver. Then will follow another kingdom which will be still smaller than the two, and it is represented by the brass of which the belly and thighs were made. The fourth kingdom shall be as strong as iron, etc. But the fourth kingdom will be divided into two parts, one part will continue to be strong and firm like iron, while the other will be weakened, like clay. At the time of this fourth kingdom, God, himself, will come and will break all the fourth kingdom into pieces and then he will build up; and that stone, which was cut out of heaven, without hands, and came down, is no other than the kingdom of God itself, which will fill all the earth. And it is written here that that stone grew so large that it filled all the earth.' This was the dream of the king, and the king, hearing Daniel, fell down and worshipped him. Then, after he had explained to him the dream, he said, 'I will give you the interpretation of the dream.'

In all the writings and prophecies both in Revelation and in Daniel by 'kingdom' is meant the appearance of a religion of God . . . (Mírzá Abu'l Faḍl, 'Explanation of Daniel's Interpretation of Nebuchadnezzar's Dream', SW VII, 13, pp. 18, 19, 22. Mírzá Abu'l Faḍl identifies the four religions as Sabeanism, Christianity, Zoroastrianism and Islám in that geographical region, and the stone as the Bahá'í Revelation.)

qualities of extraordinary sympathy and loving-kindness, and have been prevented from attaining to the inner significances of the Holy Books. Not only do they scrupulously shun the adherents of religions other than their own, they do not even permit themselves to show them common courtesy

for in that day woe is for the neglectful, woe is for the sinners, woe is for the ignorant *Lord* SAQ 56

New

and, on the other, spread out a new and highly exalted earth in the hearts of men *Resurrection* KI 48

Creation – re: 'shall we be restored in a new creation?' 114–15

notwithstanding all the verses of the Qur'án, and the recognized traditions, which are all indicative of a new Faith, a new Law, and a new Revelation, this generation still waiteth in expectation of beholding the promised One who should uphold the Law of the Muḥammadan Dispensation. The Jews and the Christians in like manner uphold the same contention *Truth* 239–40

among the utterances that foreshadow a new Law and a new Revelation are the passages in the 'Prayer of Nudbih': "Where is He Who is preserved to renew the ordinances and laws? Where is He Who hath the authority to transform the Faith and the followers thereof?" He hath, likewise, revealed in the Zíyárat: "Peace be upon the Truth made new." Abú-'Abdi'lláh, questioned concerning the character of the Mihdí, answered saying: "He will perform that which Muḥammad, the Messenger of God, hath performed, and will demolish whatever hath been before Him even as the Messenger of God hath demolished the ways of those that preceded Him" 240

out of Baní-Háshim there shall come forth a Youth Who shall reveal new laws. He shall summon the people unto Him, but none will heed His call *Tradition* 242

the Lord God Omnipotent hath been enthroned in His Kingdom and hath made all things knew *Alpha and Omega* SAB 12

we are told in the Holy Scripture that the New Jerusalem shall appear on earth. Now it is evident that this celestial city is not built of material stones and mortar, but that it is a city not made with hands, eternal in the Heavens PT 84

which the writer of the Apocalypse had described as the 'new heaven' and the 'new earth' *Kitáb-i-Aqdas* GPB 213

Night

once the mind and heart have grasped the fact that God guides men through a Mouthpiece, a human being, a Prophet, infallible and unerring, it is only a logical projection of this acceptance to also accept the station of 'Abdu'l-Bahá and the Guardians. The Guardians are the evidence of the maturity of mankind in the sense that at long last men have progressed to the point of having one world, and of needing one world management for human affairs. In the spiritual realm they have also reached the point where God could leave, in human hands, guided directly by the Báb and Bahá'u'lláh, as the Master states in His Will, the affairs of His Faith for this Dispensation. This is what is meant by 'this is the day which will not be followed by night'. In this Dispensation, divine guidance flows on to us in this world after the Prophet's ascension, through first the Master, and then the Guardians. If a person can accept Bahá'u'lláh's function, it should not present any difficulty to them to also LG 231–2 accept what He has ordained in a divinely guided individual in matters pertaining to the Faith (Letter 25.11.48)

Nimrod

at one time Thou didst deliver Me into the hands of Nimrod; at another Thou hast allowed Pharaoh's rod to persecute Me G 88

ere He manifested Himself, Nimrod dreamed a dream. Thereupon, he summoned the soothsayers, who informed him of the rise of a star in the heaven *Abraham* KI 62

how numerous the occasions when the Nimrods kindled fires wherewith to burn Me, but Thou didst make them balm for Me SB 185

Abraham – re: Abraham's triumph over Nimrod GPB 8

recalls the 'arrogance' of the Persian Emperor in the days of Muḥammad, the 'transgression' of Pharaoh in the days of Moses, and of the 'impiety' of Nimrod in the days of Abraham – re: to 'Alí Pás͟há in Súriy-i-Ra'ís 174

Noah

among the Prophets was Noah. For nine hundred and fifty years He prayerfully exhorted His people and summoned them to the haven of security and peace. None, however, heeded His call. Each day they inflicted on His blessed person such pain and suffering that no one believed He could survive. How frequently they denied Him, how malevolently they hinted their suspicion against Him KI 7

for instance, consider that among the Prophets was Noah. When He was invested with the robe of Prophethood, and was moved by the Spirit of God to arise and proclaim His Cause, whoever believed in Him and acknowledged His Faith, was endowed with the grace of a new life. Of him it could be truly said that he was reborn and revived 154

Primal Will – re: appearance in the Prophets SB 126

Law – re: use of seafood PUP 365

Noah's grandson, Canaan, was detested in the sight of Noah and others were accepted *Kingdom* BWF 438

Obey

these revealed words were a blessing to the righteous who on hearing them exclaimed: 'O God our Lord, We have heard, and obeyed' *Muḥammad* KI 111

O people of the earth! Whoso obeyeth the Remembrance of God and His Book hath in truth obeyed God and His chosen ones and he will, in the life to come, be reckoned in the presence of God among the inmates of the Paradise of His good-pleasure SB 43

Old

'two verses have made Me old' [words of Muḥammad] *Steadfastness* KI 233

Old Testament

the Old Testament and the Holy Books which preceded it, in which the actual precepts uttered by the Prophet Himself are non-existent GPB 213

Who in the Old Testament hath been named Jehovah, Who in the Gospel hath been designated as the Spirit of Truth, and in the Qur'án acclaimed as the Great Announcement – re: Bahá'u'lláh WOB 104

One

for they are all but one person, one soul, one spirit, one being, one revelation. They are all the manifestation of the 'Beginning' and the 'End,' the 'First' and the 'Last,' the 'Seen' and 'Hidden' *Messenger* KI 179

Oppression

what 'oppression' is greater than that which hath been recounted? What 'oppression' is more grievous than that a soul seeking the truth, and wishing to attain unto the knowledge of God, should know not where to go for it and from whom to seek it? For opinions have sorely differed, and the ways unto the attainment of God have multiplied. This 'oppression' is the essential feature of every Revelation. Unless it cometh to pass, the Sun of Truth will not be made manifest. For the break of the morn of divine guidance must needs follow the darkness of the night of error [see also *Tradition*] KI 31

Orchard

you are like unto the man who layeth out an orchard and planteth all kinds of fruit trees therein. When the time is at hand for him, the lord, to come, ye will have taken possession of the orchard in his name, and when he doth come in person, ye will shut him out from it. SB 135

Verily We planted the Tree of the Qur'án and provided its Orchard with all kinds of fruit, whereof ye all have been partaking. Then when We came to take over that which We had planted, ye pretended not to know Him Who is the Lord thereof

Pagan

compare the evidences of Divine visitation which befell the persecutors of Jesus Christ with these historic retributions which, in the latter part of the first century of the Bahá'í Era, have hurled to dust the chief adversary of the religion of Bahá'u'lláh. Had not the Roman Emperor, in the second half of the first century of the Christian Era, after a distressful siege of Jerusalem, laid waste the Holy City, destroyed the Temple, desecrated and robbed the Holy of Holies of its treasures, and transported them to Rome, reared a pagan colony on the mount of Zion, massacred the Jews, and exiled and dispersed the survivors? WOB 176

the pagan worshipers who constituted, at that time, the bulk of the population of the Western Roman Empire, found themselves surrounded, and in certain instances menaced, by the prevailing sect of the Neo-Platonists, by the followers of nature religions, by Gnostic philosophers, by Philonism, Mithraism, the adherents of the Alexandrian cult, and a multitude of kindred sects and beliefs, in much the same way as the defenders of the Christian Faith, the preponderating religion of the western world, are realizing, in the first century of the Bahá'í Era, how their influence is being undermined by a flood of conflicting beliefs, practices and tendencies which their own bankruptcy had helped to create. It was, however, this same Christian Religion, which has now fallen into such a state of impotence, that eventually proved itself capable of sweeping away the institutions of paganism and of swamping and suppressing the cults that had flourished in that age 184–5

Divines – re: the pagan priests PDC 81

and finally the gospel of modern paganism, unconcealed, aggressive, and unrelenting, which, in the years preceding the present turmoil, and increasingly since its outbreak, has swept over the continent of Europe, invading the citadels, and sowing confusion in the hearts of the supporters, of the Catholic, the Greek Orthodox, and the Lutheran churches, in Austria, Poland, the Baltic and Scandinavian states, and more recently in Western Europe, the home and center of the most powerful hierarchies of Christendom 105

Paraclete*

His Holiness Christ made a covenant concerning the Paraclete and gave the tidings of His coming – re: Muḥammad BWF 358

Paradise

there they will meet the believers in Paradise, who will address them with the words 'Peace, Peace' lingering on their lips *Faith* SB 63

since that Day is a great Day it would be sorely trying for thee to identify thyself with the believers. For the believers of that Day are the inmates of Paradise, while the unbelievers are the inmates of the fire. And know thou of a certainty that by Paradise is meant recognition of and submission unto Him Whom God shall make manifest, and by the fire the company of such souls as would fail to submit unto Him or to be resigned to His good-pleasure 82–3

all the rest were accounted as inmates of the fire, though they considered themselves as dwellers in Paradise – re: non-acceptance of Muḥammad by Arabs *'Alí* 83

then when God made Paradise known unto them, they would not enter therein – re: Christians *Gospel* 143

Qur'án – re: declined to enter 143

relative to the Paradise explained by Muḥammad in the Qur'án, such utterances are spiritual and are cast into the mould of words and figures of speech, for at that time people did not possess the capacity of comprehending spiritual significances. It is similar to that reference to His Highness Christ who, addressing His disciples said, 'I shall not partake of the fruit of the vine any more until I reach the Kingdom of My Father.' Now it is evident His Highness Christ did not mean material grapes, but it was a spiritual condition and a heavenly state which He interpreted as this fruit. SW II 15, p16

Now whatever is revealed in the Qur'án has the same import

Path

they have strayed far from the fresh and thirst-subduing waters, and gathered round the salt that burneth bitterly. Concerning them, the Dove of Eternity hath spoken: 'And if they see the path of righteousness, they will not take it for their path; but if they see the path of error, for their path will they take it. This, because they treated Our signs as lies, and were heedless of them' KI 105

O concourse of the faithful! Incline your ears to My Voice, proclaimed by this Remembrance of God. Verily God hath revealed unto Me that the Path of the Remembrance which is set forth by Me is, in very truth, the straight Path of God, and that whoever professeth any religion other than this upright Faith, will, when called to account on the Day of Judgement, discover that as recorded in the Book no benefit hath he reaped out of God's Religion SB 63

* The word 'Paraclete' also refers to Muḥammad. Paraclete means 'the Praiser' in Greek, and Muḥammad means 'the Praiser' in Arabic. (Shoghi Effendi, quoted by May Maxwell and Mary Maxwell, *Haifa Notes of Shoghi Effendi's Words*, 1937, p. 26.)

Paul*

in the Epistle to the Romans Saint Paul hath written: 'Let every soul be subject unto the higher powers. For there there is no power but of God; the powers that be are ordained of God. Whosoever therefore resisteth the power, resisteth the ordinance of God' ESW 91

one's conduct must be like the conduct of Paul, and one's faith similar to that of Peter *Peter* SAB 223–4

think of Judas Iscariot; he began well, but remember his end! On the other hand, Paul, the Apostle, was in his early life an enemy of Christ, whilst later he became His most faithful servant PT 147

to the hour of His advent St. Paul had alluded as the hour of the 'last trump,' the 'trump of God' – re: Bahá'u'lláh GPB 96

Peace

universal peace will raise its tent in the center of the earth, and the blessed Tree of Life will grow and spread to such an extent that it will overshadow the East and the West. Strong and weak, rich and poor, antagonistic sects and hostile nations – which are like the wolf and the lamb, the leopard and kid, the lion and the calf – will act toward each other with the most complete love, friendship, justice and equity. The world will be filled with science, with the knowledge of the reality of the mysteries of beings, and with the knowledge of God SAQ 64

universal peace and concord will be realized between all the nations, and that Incomparable Branch will gather together all Israel, signifying that in this cycle Israel will be gathered in the Holy Land, and that the Jewish people who are scattered to the East and West, South and North, will be assembled together 65

Pentateuch

that City is none other than the Word of God revealed in every age and dispensation. In the days of Moses it was the Pentateuch; in the days of Jesus, the Gospel G 268–9

and came to the conclusion that were they to enforce the law of the Pentateuch, every survivor who had been delivered from the hand of Nebuchadnezzar would have to be put to death according to the verdict of the Book. Owing to such considerations, they totally repealed the penalty of death [see also *Divines* 87–8] *Jews* KI 85–6

these details indicate the condition of the people to whom Muḥammad was sent. The first question which He put to them was, 'Why do you not accept the Pentateuch and the Gospel, and why do you not believe in Christ and in Moses?' *Muḥammad* SAQ 22

for example, there is in the Pentateuch a law that if anyone break the Sabbath, he shall be put to death. Moreover, there are ten sentences of 96

* It may interest the student of the Bible to note that, according to Shoghi Effendi, the Guardian of the Bahá'í Faith, the rise and fall of Mírzá Yaḥyá was clearly foretold by St. Paul in the following passages:

> Let no man deceive you by any means; for that day shall not come, except there come a falling away first, and that man of sin be revealed, the son of perdition; who opposeth and exalteth himself above all that is called God, or that is worshipped; so that he as God sitteth in the temple of God, showing himself that he is God . . .
>
> And then shall that Wicked be revealed, whom the Lord shall consume with the spirit of His mouth, and shall destroy with the brightness of His coming . . .

(II Thess. 2:3,4,8; stated by Shoghi Effendi in a letter to Isfandíyár-i-Majzúb, 17.11. 35. Adib Taherzadeh, *The Revelation of Bahá'u'lláh*, Vol. II, Oxford, George Ronald, 1977, p. 298.)

Pentateuch

death in the Pentateuch. Would it be possible to keep these laws in our time? It is clear that it would be absolutely impossible. Consequently, there are changes and modifications in the laws, and these are a sufficient proof of the supreme wisdom of God

now, consider: Christ frequently repeated that the Ten Commandments in 165
the Pentateuch were to be followed, and He insisted that they should be maintained *Religion*

now the question of the good or evil of things is determined by reason or by 266
law. Some believe that it is determined by law; such are the Jews, who, believing all the commandments of the Pentateuch to be absolutely obligatory, regard them as matters of law, not of reason. Thus they say that one of the commandments of the Pentateuch is that it is unlawful to partake of meat and butter together because it is *taref*, and *taref* in Hebrew means unclean, as *kosher* means clean. This, they say, is a question of law and not of reason

but in the law of the Pentateuch revealed by Moses these marriages were PUP 365
forbidden and their custom and sanction abrogated *Law*

Pentecost

at the feast of Pentecost they gathered together and detached themselves SAQ 106
from the things of this world . . . and the power of the Holy Spirit became manifested – re: meaning of *Disciple*

all that hath since been effected along the line of diffusing the holy TAB 301
fragrances of Christ, uplifting the Word of God, spreading the Gospel, training souls and guiding the people, hath been wholly from the result of the effects produced by that assemblage of the disciples *Assemblage*

People

there can be no doubt whatever that the peoples of the world, of whatever G 216
race or religion, derive their inspiration from one heavenly Source, and are the subjects of one God. The difference between the ordinances under which they abide should be attributed to the varying requirements and exigencies of the age in which they were revealed

they who are the people of God have no ambition except to revive the 269–70
world, to ennoble its life, and regenerate its peoples. Truthfulness and good-will have, at all times, marked their relations with all men. Their outward conduct is but a reflection of their inward life, and their inward life a mirror of their outward conduct

these revealed words were a blessing to the righteous who on hearing them KI 111
exclaimed: 'O God our Lord, We have heard, and obeyed.' They were a curse to the people of iniquity who, on hearing them affirmed: 'We have heard and rebelled' *Muḥammad*

and now, be fair; How could those people living in the days of Muḥammad 149
have existed, thousands of years before, in the age of Adam or other Prophets? Why should Muḥammad, that Essence of truthfulness, have charged the people of His day with the murder of Abel or other Prophets? Thou hast none other alternative except to regard Muḥammad as an impostor or a fool – which God forbid! – or to maintain that these people of wickedness were the self-same people who in every age opposed and cavilled at the Prophets and Messengers of God, till they finally caused them all to suffer martyrdom [see also *Sacrifice* 148]

likewise, Muḥammad, in another verse, uttereth His protest against the 150
people of that age. He saith: 'Although they had before prayed for victory over those who believed not, yet when there came unto them, He of Whom they had knowledge, they disbelieved in Him. The curse of God on the infidels!' *Muḥammad*

and the people also, utterly ignoring God and taking them for their masters, have placed themselves unreservedly under the authority of these pompous and hypocritical leaders, for they have no sight, no hearing, no heart, of their own to distinguish truth from falsehood – re: divines – 'veils of glory' 164

be fair: Were these people to acknowledge the truth of these luminous words and holy allusions, and recognize God as 'Him that doeth whatsoever He pleaseth,' how could they continue to cleave unto these glaring absurdities? Nay, with all their soul, they would accept and submit to whatsoever He saith. I swear by God! But for the divine Decree, and the inscrutable dispensations of Providence, the earth itself would have utterly destroyed all this people! 'He will, however, respite them until the appointed time of a known day' 171–2

people of error *Countenance* 173

consider the way of the people. They ignore these well-founded traditions, all of which have been fulfilled, and cling unto those of doubtful validity, and ask why these have not been fulfilled. And yet, those things which to them were inconceivable have been made manifest [see also *Tradition* 238, 239; *Truth* 239–40] 239

according to the Divine Law of Muḥammad, it is not permissible to compel the People of the Book to acknowledge and accept the Faith [see also *Tradition* – re: spreading the Faith by the sword] SDC 43

they indeed are 'the people of the right,' whose 'noble habitation' is fixed on the foundations of the World Order of Bahá'u'lláh – the Ark of everlasting salvation in this most grievous Day. Of all the kindreds of the earth they alone can recognize, amidst the welter of a tempestuous age, the Hand of the Divine Redeemer that traces its course and controls its destinies. They alone are aware of the silent growth of that orderly world polity whose fabric they themselves are weaving WOB 194

Persecution

thou hast known how grievously the Prophets of God, His Messengers and Chosen Ones, have been afflicted. Meditate a while on the motive and reason which have been responsible for such a persecution. At no time, in no Dispensation, have the Prophets of God escaped the blasphemy of their enemies, the cruelty of their oppressors, the denunciation of the learned of their age, who appeared in the guise of uprightness and piety. Day and night they passed through such agonies as none can ever measure, except the knowledge of the one true God, exalted be His glory G 57

Israel – re: persecution of the apostles TAB 361

a series of degradations recalling the fate which, in the first century of the Christian Era, befell the Jewish people, the city of Jerusalem, the Temple of Solomon, the Holy of Holies, and an ecclesiastical hierarchy, whose members were the avowed persecutors of the religion of Jesus Christ GPB 228

compare, moreover, these words which the persecuted Christ, as witnessed by the Gospel, addressed to Jerusalem, with Bahá'u'lláh's apostrophe to Constantinople, revealed while He lay in His far-off prison *Jerusalem* WOB 176

a witness and a warning unto all nations of what must, sooner or later, befall those wielders of earthly dominion, be it royal or ecclesiastic, who might dare to challenge or persecute the appointed Channels and Embodiments of Divine authority and power PDC 99

we need only recall the nineteen hundred years of abject misery and dispersion which they who, only for the short space of three years, persecuted the Son of God have had to endure, and are still enduring 99

Person

'the Báb, the Exalted One,' 'Abdu'l-Bahá more specifically affirms in another Tablet, 'is the Morn of Truth, the splendor of Whose light shineth throughout all regions. He is also the Harbinger of the Most Great Light, the Abhá Luminary. The Blessed Beauty is the One promised by the sacred books of the past, the revelation of the Source of light that shone upon Mount Sinai, Whose fire glowed in the midst of the Burning Bush. We are, one and all, servants of their threshold, and stand each as a lowly keeper at their door.' 'Every proof and prophecy,' is His still more emphatic warning, 'every manner of evidence, whether based on reason or on the text of the scriptures and traditions, are to be regarded as centered in the persons of Bahá'u'lláh and the Báb. In them is to be found their complete fulfillment' — WOB 127–8

Personal

what is meant by a personal God *God* — LG 419

Peter

even as in the time of the Messiah, when the Pharisees and the pious were left without a portion, while Peter, John and Andrew, given neither to pious worship nor ascetic practice, won the day — SAB 18

Peter was a fisherman and Mary Magdalene a peasant, but as they were specially favoured with the blessings of Christ, the horizon of their faith became illumined, and down to the present day they are shining from the horizon of everlasting glory — 105

when Jesus said, 'Thou art Peter, and upon this rock I will build My church,' these words addressed to Peter, and this singling out of Peter for special honour, had a marked effect on the Apostle, and kindled envy in the heart of Judas *Judas Iscariot* — 163

one's conduct must be like the conduct of Paul, and one's faith similar to that of Peter. This musk-scented breeze shall perfume the nostrils of the people of the world, and this spirit shall resuscitate the dead — 223–4

Sword – re: 'Put up thy sword into the sheath' — 247–8

Deny – re: denied Christ three times — SAQ 35

Disciple – re: use of animal food — 93

in the Gospel of St. Matthew it is said: 'Thou art Peter, and upon this rock I will build My church.' — 135

This utterance of Christ is a confirmation of the statement of Peter, when Christ asked: Whom do you believe Me to be? and Peter answered: I believe that 'Thou art the Son of the living God.' Then Christ said to him: 'Thou art Peter' – for Cephas in Aramaic means rock – 'and upon this rock I will build My church.' For the others in answer to Christ said that He was Elias, and some said John the Baptist, and some others Jeremias or one of the Prophets.

Christ wished by suggestion, or an allusion, to confirm the words of Peter; so on account of the suitability of his name, Peter, He said: 'and upon this rock I will build My church,' meaning, thy belief that Christ is the Son of the living God will be the foundation of the Religion of God, and upon this belief the foundation of the church of God – which is the Law of God – shall be established

Caiaphas lived a comfortable and happy life while Peter's life was full of sorrow and trial; which of these two is the more enviable? Assuredly we should choose the present state of Peter, for he possesses immortal life whilst Caiaphas has won eternal shame. The trials of Peter tested his fidelity — PT 50 but Peter was a catcher of fish; as he turned his face toward the Word of God, the fame of his imperishable, deathless and immortal glory encircled East and West; and he found in the sovereignty of the Kingdom, eternal and everlasting majesty *Caiaphas* TAB 223

and the great one among them was Peter the disciple, who, through the burning of the fire of test and persecution, was in great fear and denied Christ three times 528

Primacy – re: no written and explicit affirmations from Christ WOB 145

whilst St. Peter had spoken of it as the 'Day of God, wherein the heavens being on fire shall be dissolved, and the elements shall melt with fervent heat.' His Day he, furthermore, had described as 'the times of refreshing,' 'the times of restitution of all things, which God hath spoken by the mouth of all His holy Prophets since the world began' – re: Bahá'u'lláh GPB 96

'Peter,' 'Abdu'l-Bahá has testified, 'according to the history of the Church, was also incapable of keeping count of the days of the week. Whenever he decided to go fishing, he would tie up his weekly food into seven parcels, and every day he would eat one of them, and when he had reached the seventh, he would know that the Sabbath had arrived, and thereupon would observe it.' If the Son of Man was capable of infusing into apparently so crude and helpless an instrument such potency as to cause, in the words of Bahá'u'lláh, 'the mysteries of wisdom and of utterance to flow out of his mouth,' and to exalt him above the rest of His disciples, and render him fit to become His successor and the founder of His Church, how much more can the Father, Who is Bahá'u'lláh, empower the most puny and insignificant among His followers to achieve, for the execution of His purpose, such wonders as would dwarf the mightiest achievements of even the first apostle of Jesus Christ ADJ 38

this is the day whereon the Rock (Peter) crieth out and shouteth, and celebrateth the praise of its Lord, the All-Possessing, the Most High, saying: 'Lo! The Father is come, and that which ye were promised in the Kingdom is fulfilled [words of Bahá'u'lláh] PDC 32

as to the position of Christianity, let it be stated without any hesitation or equivocation that . . . the primacy of Peter, the Prince of the Apostles, is upheld and defended – re: by Bahá'ís *Christianity* 109

Admittance – re: acceptance of primacy of Peter an essential prerequisite of admittance into the Bahá'í Faith 110

Pharaoh

surely you are aware of the fierce opposition of Pharaoh and his people, and of the stones of idle fancy which the hands of the infidels cast upon that blessed Tree. So much so that Pharaoh and his people finally arose and exerted their utmost endeavour to extinguish with the waters of falsehood and denial the fire of that sacred Tree G 19

there He heard the soul-stirring Voice of the Spirit speaking from out of the kindled Fire, bidding Him to shed upon Pharaohic souls the light of divine guidance *Moses* KI 54

when Moses came unto Pharaoh and delivered unto him, as bidden by God, the divine Message, Pharaoh spoke insultingly saying: 'Art thou not he that committed murder, and became an infidel?' 55

after Him came Moses, He Who held converse with God. The soothsayers of His time warned Pharaoh in these terms: 'A star hath risen in the heaven, and lo! it foreshadoweth the conception of a Child Who holdeth your fate and the fate of your people in His hand' *Moses* 63

Pharaoh

Asíyih – re: daughter of Pharaoh TAB 218

He was so carried away by the captivating accent of the Voice that He detached Himself from the world and set out in the direction of Pharaoh and his people, invested with the power of thy Lord Who exerciseth sovereignty over all that hath been and shall be. The people of the world are now hearing that which Moses did hear, but they understand not 265

if we say that according to the text of the Bible, 'God hardened Pharaoh's heart' that he might not believe in Moses, this signifies that, verily, He did not soften his heart. And when we wish to say that God hath not guided a certain one of His servants, this would be interpreted (by people) that God led him astray 610

the 'transgression' of Pharaoh in the days of Moses, and of the 'impiety' of Nimrod in the days of Abraham GPB 174

the appalling misery and wretchedness to which the Israelites had sunk, under the debasing and tyrannical rule of the Pharaohs ADJ 14

Pharisees

Spirit – re: they failed to attain His presence TB 9–10

Messiah – re: they cried out that He was not Messiah (Masíḥ) but a monster (Masíkh) SAB 40

never would the Pharisees have been emboldened to calumniate Him and charge Him with that grievous sin, but for their ignorance of the inner core of mysteries and the fact that they paid no heed to His splendours and regarded not His proofs 40–41

even as the Pharisees who both prayed and fasted, and then did sentence Jesus Christ to death *Congregations* 174

every day of their lives they were the targets for the Pharisees' darts of mockery, vilification and abuse *Apostles of Christ* 238

but failing justice, the people attack, dispute and openly deny the evidence, like the Pharisees who, at the manifestation of Christ, denied with the greatest obstinacy the explanations of Christ and of His disciples SAQ 71

observe that the Pharisees called His Holiness, the sweet and divine Christ, Beelzebub or the head of evil spirits. This people (the people of the world) are in the depths of ignorance and their reproach and detraction are like praise and congratulation TAB 132

reflect thou how the Pharisees persecuted and looked down in contempt upon His Holiness the Christ. The result was that His lamp became ignited, His light began to shine and His followers sparkled like unto the stars from the horizon of existence; and the consequence to the Pharisees was the pangs of remorse and regrets 221

how many men and women awaited the manifestation of the Messiah after Moses? Yet when His beauty shone forth and His face appeared, they (the people) did not recognize Him, but continued to follow the superstitions of the Pharisees, who used to say: 'Where is the authority of the Messiah? Where is the throne of David, the Glorious? Where is his iron rod? Where are his innumerable hosts? Where are his attacking armies? Where are the angels of heaven? 230

remember what the Pharisees published concerning Jesus, attributed to Him and said about Him and how they oppressed Him until they paraded Him in Jerusalem in such a form as made the angels of sanctity to weep in the Sublime Kingdom 349

of the same class are the Pharisees and priests in this manifest day. 'Leave them to amuse themselves with their vain discourses.' They are as people 349 deluded by their temptations and are isolated from the gifts of your Lord, the Clement, the Merciful. 'They are deaf, dumb and blind; therefore, they will not understand'

'how many the Pharisees who were waiting to behold Him, and were lamenting over their separation from Him! And yet . . . they turned aside from Him and disputed with Him' [words of Bahá'u'lláh] PDC 31

Philosophy

it is furthermore a matter of record in numerous historical works that the philosophers of Greece such as Pythagoras, acquired the major part of their philosophy, both divine and material, from the disciples of Solomon. And Socrates after having eagerly journeyed to meet with some of Israel's most illustrious scholars and divines, on his return to Greece established the concept of the oneness of God and the continuing life of the human soul after it has put off its elemental dust. Ultimately, the ignorant among the Greeks denounced this man who had fathomed the inmost mysteries of wisdom, and rose up to take his life [see also TB 144–8] SDC 77

Piety

– re: all things have their consummation in belief in Him KI 92–3

Poet

also, 'And they say, "Shall we then abandon our gods for a crazed poet?"' The implication of this verse is manifest. Behold what they observed after the verses were revealed. They called Him a poet, scoffed at the verses of God, and exclaimed saying: 'These words of his are but tales of the Ancients!' By this they meant that those words which were spoken by the peoples of old Muḥammad had compiled and called them the Word of God KI 211–12

Point

compare His manifestation with that of the Point of the Qur'án – re: Him Whom God shall make manifest *'Alí* SB 83

Point of the Bayán *Deed* 95

Apostle of God – re: behold the Point of the Bayán 96

Pope

among the Popes there are also some blessed souls who followed in the footsteps of Christ, particularly in the first centuries of the Christian era when temporal things were lacking and the tests of God were severe. But when they came into possession of governmental power SAQ 136

Christ – re: wars sanctioned by Popes 166

Poverty

this poverty and these riches, this abasement and glory, this dominion, power, and the like, upon which the eyes and hearts of these vain and foolish souls are set, – all these things fade into nothingness in that Court! Even as He hath said: 'O men! Ye are but paupers in need of God; but God is the Rich, the Self-Sufficing.' By 'riches' therefore is meant independence of all else but God, and by 'poverty' the lack of things that are of God [see also *Value* PHW 51] KI 132

Power

then it is said: 'And smite the earth with all plagues, as often as they will,' meaning that they also would have the power and the material force necessary to educate the wicked and those who are oppressors and SAQ 50

Power

tyrants, for to these two witnesses God granted both outward and inward power, that they might educate and correct the ferocious, bloodthirsty, tyrannical nomad Arabs, who were like beasts of prey – re: Muḥammad and ‘Alí [see *Witness* 48–50]

Prayer

nay rather, in every Dispensation the law concerning prayer hath been emphasized and universally enforced. To this testify the recorded traditions ascribed to the lights that have emanated from the Day-star of Truth, the essence of the Prophet Muḥammad — KI 39

in all Dispensations the law of prayer hath constituted a fundamental element of the Revelation of all the Prophets of God – a law the form and manner of which hath been adapted to the varying requirements of every age. Inasmuch as every subsequent Revelation hath abolished the manners, habits, and teachings that have been clearly, specifically, and firmly established by the former Dispensation, these have accordingly been symbolically expressed in terms of ‘sun’ and ‘moon’. ‘That He might prove you, which of you excel in deeds’ — 39

Prayer of Nudbih – re: new Law, new Revelation *New* — 240

Prelates

the beturbaned prelates of the Islámic church who, in the words of Bahá’u’lláh, ‘decked their heads with green and white, and committed what made the Faithful Spirit to groan,’ were ruthlessly swept away, except for a handful who, in order to safeguard themselves against the fury of an impious populace, are now compelled to submit to the humiliation of producing, whenever the occasion demands it, the license granted them by the civil authorities to wear this vanishing emblem of a vanished authority – re: Shí‘ih clergy — PDC 92

‘the dark blue and white domes,’ – an allusion by ‘Abdu’l-Bahá to the rotund and massive head-gears of the priests of Persia – had indeed been ‘inverted.’ Those whose heads had borne them, the arrogant, fanatical, perfidious, and retrograde clericals, ‘in the grasp of whose authority,’ as testified by Bahá’u’lláh, ‘were held the reins of the people,’ whose ‘words are the pride of the world,’ and whose ‘deeds are the shame of the nations,’ recognizing the wretchedness of their state, betook themselves, crestfallen and destitute of hope, to their homes, there to drag out a miserable existence. Impotent and sullen, they are watching the operations of a process which, having reversed their policy and ruined their handiwork, is irresistibly moving towards a climax — 92–3

Presence

ponder a while upon the verses concerning the Divine Presence, which have been sent down in the Qur’án by Him Who is the Lord of the kingdom of names, perchance thou mayest discover the Straight Path, and be made an instrument for the guidance of His creatures – re: discourse on Presence 115–19 — ESW 115

in all the Divine Books the promise of the Divine Presence hath been explicitly recorded. By this Presence is meant the Presence of Him Who is the Day-spring of the signs, and the Dawning-Place of the clear tokens, and the Manifestation of the Excellent Names, and the Source of the attributes, of the true God, exalted be His glory. God in His Essence and in His own Self hath ever been unseen, inaccessible, and unknowable. By Presence, therefore, is meant the Presence of the One Who is His Viceregent amongst men — 118 whosoever, and in whatever Dispensation, hath recognized and attained unto the presence of these glorious, these resplendent and most excellent Luminaries, hath verily attained unto the 'Presence of God' Himself, and entered the city of eternal and immortal life. Attainment unto such presence is possible only in the Day of Resurrection, which is the Day of the rise of God Himself through His all-embracing Revelation *Essence* — KI 142–3

consider, how can he that faileth in the day of God's Revelation to attain unto the grace of the 'Divine Presence' and to recognize His Manifestation, be justly called learned, though he may . . . *Learned* — 145–6

nothing more exalted or more explicit than 'attainment unto the divine Presence' hath been revealed in the Qur'án *Qur'án* — 169

hath revealed unto all people the promise of 'attainment unto the divine Presence' *Muḥammad* — 169

Priests [see also *Divines, Leaders*]

O concourse of priests! Leave the bells, and come forth, then, from your churches. It behoveth you, in this day, to proclaim aloud the Most Great Name among the nations. Prefer ye to be silent, whilst every stone and every tree shouteth aloud: 'The Lord is come in His great glory!' — TB 13

when, however, the time approached for the effulgent beauty of Muḥammad to dawn upon the world, the control of Christian affairs passed into the hands of ignorant priests. Those heavenly breezes, soft-flowing from the regions of Divine grace, died away, and the laws of the great Evangel, the rock-foundation on which the civilization of the world was based, turned barren of results, this out of misuse and because of the conduct of persons who, seemingly fair, were yet inwardly foul — SDC 85–6

alas, of what avail is it. When the weapons are in cowards' hands, no man's life and property are safe, and thieves only grow the stronger. When, in the same way, a far-from-perfect priesthood acquire control of affairs, they come down like a massive curtain between the people and the light of Faith — 96

Book – re: they know the letter only — BWF 391

High Priest – re: Zoroastrian — PDC 77

Divines – re: the pagan priests — 81

not one Prophet of God was made manifest Who did not fall a victim to the relentless hate, to the denunciation, denial and execration of the clerics of His day! Woe unto them — 82

– re: discourse on Shí'ih priests and their institutions — 92–5

Names – re: naught of Islám but a name — 99

this horde of degraded priests, stigmatized by Bahá'u'lláh as 'doctors of doubt,' as the 'abject manifestations of the Prince of Darkness,' as 'wolves' and 'pharaohs,' as 'focal centres of hellish fire,' as 'voracious beasts preying upon the carrion of the souls of men,' and, as testified by their own traditions, as both the sources and victims of mischief – re: Shí'ih clergy — 99

Primacy

could Peter, the admitted chief of the Apostles, or the Imám 'Alí, the cousin and legitimate successor of the Prophet, produce in support of the primacy with which both had been invested written and explicit affirmations from Christ and Muḥammad that could have silenced those who either among their contemporaries or in a later age have repudiated their authority and, by their action, precipitated the schisms that persist until the present day? — WOB 145

Primacy

and of the primacy of St. Peter, the Prince of the Apostles – re: essential prerequisites of admittance into the Bahá'í Faith *Admittance* PDC 110

Primal Point

I am the Primal Point from which have been generated all created things. I am the Countenance of God Whose splendour can never be obscured, the Light of God Whose radiance can never fade. Whoso recognizeth Me, assurance and all good are in store for him, and whoso faileth to recognize Me, infernal fire and all evil await him SB 12

since thou hast acknowledged the revelation of Muḥammad, the Apostle of God, then there is no other way open before thee but to testify that whatever is revealed by the Primal Point hath also proceeded from God, the Help in Peril, the Self-Subsisting. Is it not true that the Qur'án hath been sent down from God and that all men are powerless before its revelation? Likewise these words have also been revealed by God, if thou dost but perceive – re: address to 'Abdu'-ṣ-Ṣáḥib 31

and hadst thou attained the presence of thy Lord in this land, and been of them that truly believe that the Face of God is beheld in the person of the Primal Point, it would have been far more advantageous than prostrating thyself in adoration from the beginning that hath no beginning until the present time – re: address to Sulaymán, divine of Masqaṭ 36

Primal Tree

at the present time, however, only adverse effects have resulted; for although He hath appeared in the midmost heart of Islám, and all people profess it by reason of their relationship to Him (the Qá'im), yet unjustly have they consigned Him to the Mountain of Mákú, and this notwithstanding that in the Qur'án the advent of the Day of Resurrection hath been promised unto all by God. For on that Day all men will be brought before God and will attain His Presence; which meaneth appearance before Him Who is the Tree of divine Reality and attainment unto His presence; inasmuch as it is not possible to appear before the Most Holy Essence of God, nor is it conceivable to seek reunion with Him. That which is feasible in the matter of appearance before Him and of meeting Him is attainment unto the Primal Tree SB 108

Primal Will

know thou that the First Remembrance, which is the Primal Will of God, may be likened unto the sun *Remembrance* SB 126

it is this Primal Will which appeareth resplendent in every Prophet and speaketh forth in every revealed Book. It knoweth no beginning, inasmuch as the First deriveth its firstness from It; and knoweth no end, for the Last oweth its lastness unto It 126

in the time of the First Manifestation the Primal Will appeared in Adam; in the day of Noah It became known in Noah; in the day of Abraham in Him; and so in the day of Moses; the day of Jesus; the day of Muḥammad, the Apostle of God 126

Primal Word

I am one of the sustaining pillars of the Primal Word of God. Whosoever hath recognized Me, hath known all that is true and right, and hath attained all that is good and seemly; and whosoever hath failed to recognize Me, hath turned away from all that is true and right and hath succumbed to everything evil and unseemly – re: extract from Epistle to Muḥammad S͟háh SB 11

Prince

Gospel – re: Prince of this world SAB 170

Principle

the principles of the Divine religions can hardly be evaluated by the acts of those who only claim to follow them. For every excellent thing, peerless though it may be, can still be diverted to the wrong ends SDC 72

Baptism – re: the principle of baptism is purification by repentance SAQ 91

Progressive Revelation [see also *Manifestation, Messenger, Religion, Revelation*]

its teachings revolve around the fundamental principle that religious truth is not absolute but relative, that Divine Revelation is progressive, not final. Unequivocally and without the least reservation it proclaims all established religions to be divine in origin, identical in their aims, complementary in their functions, continuous in their purpose, indispensable in their value to mankind WOB 58

– re: Zoroastrian prophecy 101–2

this same prophecy, we must furthermore recognize, attests the independent character of the Bábí Dispensation and corroborates indirectly the truth that in accordance with the principle of progressive revelation every Manifestation of God must needs vouchsafe to the people of His day a measure of divine guidance ampler than any which a preceding and less receptive age could have received or appreciated. For this reason, and not for any superior merit which the Bahá'í Faith may be said to inherently possess, does this prophecy bear witness to the unrivalled power and glory with which the Dispensation of Bahá'u'lláh has been invested – a Dispensation the potentialities of which we are but beginning to perceive and the full range of which we can never determine 102–3

the Faith of Bahá'u'lláh should indeed be regarded, if we wish to be faithful to the tremendous implications of its message, as the culmination of a cycle, the final stage in a series of successive, of preliminary and progressive revelations. These, beginning with Adam and ending with the Báb, have paved the way and anticipated with an ever-increasing emphasis the advent of that Day of Days in which He Who is the Promise of All Ages should be made manifest 103

'It is evident that every age in which a Manifestation of God hath lived is divinely ordained and may, in a sense, be characterized as God's appointed Day. This Day, however, is unique and is to be distinguished from those that have preceded it. The designation "Seal of the Prophets" fully reveals and demonstrates its high station' [words of Bahá'u'lláh] 107

'Concerning the Manifestations that will come down in the future "in the shadows of the clouds," know verily that in so far as their relation to the source of their inspiration is concerned they are under the shadow of the Ancient Beauty. In their relation, however, to the age in which they appear, each and every one of them "doeth whatsoever He willeth"' [words of 'Abdu'l-Bahá] 111

'God hath sent down His Messengers to succeed to Moses and Jesus, and He will continue to do so till "the end that hath no end"; so that His grace may, from the heaven of Divine bounty, be continually vouchsafed to mankind' [words of Bahá'u'lláh] 116

'Know of a certainty', Bahá'u'lláh explains in this connection, 'that in every Dispensation the light of Divine Revelation has been vouchsafed to men in direct proportion to their spiritual capacity' 117

Progressive Revelation

just as the organic evolution of mankind has been slow and gradual, and involved successively the unification of the family, the tribe, the city-state, and the nation, so has the light vouchsafed by the Revelation of God, at various stages in the evolution of religion, and reflected in the successive Dispensations of the past, been slow and progressive. Indeed the measure of Divine Revelation, in every age, has been adapted to, and commensurate with, the degree of social progress achieved in that age by a constantly-evolving humanity PDC 118

Promise

the promises of God, as recorded in the holy Scriptures, have all been fulfilled G 13

bestir yourselves, O people, in anticipation of the days of Divine justice, for the promised hour is now come 17

say: O people! The Day, promised unto you in all the Scriptures, is now come 313

as to the Manifestation of the Greatest Name (Bahá'u'lláh): This was the Divine Manifestation which appeared upon the earthly world. This is He whom God promised in all His Books and Scriptures, such as the Bible, the Gospels and the Qur'án. All of these Books indicate this fact, and the least doubt cannot possibly occur to the minds concerning this clear fact, as is recorded in every detail in the heavenly Books, especially in the brilliant and holy Tablets. But notwithstanding this fact, if there is anyone who hesitates therein, do not dispute with him, nay rather prove this to him with all joy and fragrance, lest he be obstinately compelled to rebellion TAB 613–14

Promised Land

this is the promised Land in which He Who is the Revelation of God was destined to be made manifest *Holy Land* G 343

Moses n.

Promised One

behold, how the divers peoples and kindreds of the earth have been waiting for the coming of the Promised One G 9

verily I say, this is the Day in which mankind can behold the Face, and hear the Voice, of the Promised One 10

Most Great Remembrance – re: in the estimation of God He is none other SB 52

now the Ever-Living Lord hath made manifest and invested with supreme testimony this long-awaited Promised One from a place no one could imagine and from a person whose knowledge was deemed of no account. His age is no more than twenty-five years, yet His glory is such as none of the learned among the people of Islám can rival; inasmuch as man's glory lieth in his knowledge. Behold the learned who are honoured by virtue of their ability to understand the Holy Writings, and God hath exalted them to such a degree that in referring to them He saith: 'None knoweth the meaning thereof except God and them that are well-grounded in knowledge.' How strange then that this twenty-five-year-old untutored one should be singled out to reveal His verses in so astounding a manner [see also *Writings* 118–9] 118

consider the manifold favours vouchsafed by the Promised One, and the effusions of His bounty which have pervaded the concourse of the followers of Islám to enable them to attain unto salvation. Indeed observe how He Who representeth the origin of creation, He Who is the Exponent of the verse, 'I, in very truth, am God', identified Himself as 119 the Gate (Báb) for the advent of the promised Qá'im, a descendant of Muḥammad, and in His first Book enjoined the observance of the laws of the Qur'án, so that the people might not be seized with perturbation by reason of a new Book and a new Revelation and might regard His Faith as similar to their own, perchance they would not turn away from the Truth and ignore the thing for which they had been called into being

His celebrated answer to the question put to Him by the President of that assembly. 'I am,' He exclaimed, 'I am, I am the Promised One! I am the One Whose name you have for a thousand years invoked, at Whose mention you have risen, Whose advent you have longed to witness, and the hour of Whose Revelation you have prayed God to hasten. Verily, I say, it is incumbent upon the peoples of both the East and the West to obey My word, and to pledge allegiance to My person' – re: interrogation of the Báb at Tabríz GPB 21

the Kitáb-i-Íqán (Book of Certitude), revealed within the space of two days and two nights, in the closing years of that period (1278 A.H. – 1862 A.D.). It was written in fulfillment of the prophecy of the Báb, Who had specifically stated that the Promised One would complete the text of the unfinished Persian Bayán, and in reply to the questions addressed to Bahá'u'lláh by the as yet unconverted maternal uncle of the Báb 138

'followers of the Gospel,' Bahá'u'lláh addressing the whole of Christendom exclaims, 'behold the gates of heaven are flung open. He that had ascended unto it is now come. Give ear to His voice calling aloud over land and sea, announcing to all mankind the advent of this Revelation – a Revelation through the agency of which the Tongue of Grandeur is now proclaiming: "Lo, the sacred Pledge hath been fulfilled, for He, the Promised One, is come!"' 'The voice of the Son of Man is calling aloud from the sacred vale: "Here am I, here am I, O God my God!" . . . whilst from the Burning Bush breaketh forth the cry: "Lo, the Desire of the world is made manifest in His transcendent glory!" The Father hath come. That which ye were promised in the Kingdom of God is fulfilled. This is the Word which the Son veiled when He said to those around Him that at that time they could not bear it . . . Verily the Spirit of Truth is come to guide you unto all truth . . . He is the One Who glorified the Son and exalted His Cause . . . ' 'The Comforter Whose advent all the scriptures have promised is now come that He may reveal unto you all knowledge and wisdom. Seek Him over the entire surface of the earth, haply ye may find Him' WOB 104–5

it was to him who styling himself 'the servant of the servants of God' that the Promised One of all ages, unveiling His station in its plenitude, announced that 'He Who is the Lord of Lords is come overshadowed with clouds.' It was he, who, claiming to be the successor of St. Peter, was reminded by Bahá'u'lláh that 'this is the day whereon the Rock (Peter) crieth out and shouteth . . . saying: "Lo, the Father is come, and that which ye were promised in the Kingdom is fulfilled."' – re: Tablet to the Pope PDC 52

Proof

therefore, it hath been said: 'To seek evidence, when the Proof hath been established is but an unseemly act, and to be busied with the pursuit of knowledge when the Object of all learning hath been attained is truly blameworthy.' Say O people of the earth! Behold this flamelike-Youth that speedeth across the limitless profound of the Spirit, heralding unto you the tidings: 'Lo: the Lamp of God is shining,' and summoning you to heed His Cause which, though hidden beneath the veils of ancient splendour, shineth in the land of 'Iráq KI 147

Proof

since thou dost adduce proofs from the Qur'án, God shall, with proofs from that self-same Book, vindicate Himself in the Bayán. This is none other than a decree of God; He is truly the All-Knowing, the All-Powerful SB 35

the conclusive Proof of God in favour of His Remembrance is similar to the one wherewith Muḥammad, the Seal of the Prophets, was invested *Book* 71

the evidence set forth by God can never be compared with the evidences produced by any one of the peoples and kindreds of the earth; and beyond a shadow of doubt no evidence is set forth by God save through the One Who is appointed as His supreme Testimony. Moreover, the proof of revealed verses doth, alone and of itself, conclusively demonstrate the utter impotence of all created things on earth, for this is a proof which hath proceeded from God and shall endure until the Day of Resurrection 109

it is incumbent upon a lowly servant to acquiesce to whatever proof God hath appointed, and not to follow his own idle fancy. If the wishes of the people were to be gratified not a single disbeliever would remain on earth. For once the Apostle of God had fulfilled the wishes of the people they would unhesitatingly have embraced His Faith. May God save thee, shouldst thou seek any evidence according to thy selfish desire; rather it behooveth thee to uphold the unfailing proof which God hath appointed. The object of thy belief in God is but to secure His good-pleasure. How then dost thou seek as a proof of thy faith a thing which hath been and is contrary to His good-pleasure? 122

in every nation thou beholdest unnumbered spiritual leaders who are bereft of true discernment, and among every people thou dost encounter myriads of adherents who are devoid of the same characteristic. Ponder for a while in thy heart, have pity on thyself and turn not aside thine attention from proofs and evidences. However, seek not proofs and evidences after thine idle fancy; but rather base thy proofs upon what God hath appointed 124

had they realized the nature of the proofs wherewith He was invested, they would never have challenged Him *Muḥammad* 132

Bayán – re: is Our conclusive proof 159

Prophecy

– re: discourse on fulfillment of Muslim prophecies ESW 132–3

'Akká – re: Biblical prophecies 144, 145, 178–9

were the signs of the Manifestation of God in every age to appear in the visible realm in accordance with the text of established traditions, none could possibly deny or turn away, nor would the blessed be distinguished from the miserable, and the transgressor from the God-fearing. Judge fairly: Were the prophecies recorded in the Gospel to be literally fulfilled; were Jesus, Son of Mary, accompanied by angels, to descend from the visible heaven upon the clouds; who would dare to disbelieve, who would dare to reject the truth, and wax disdainful? Nay, such consternation would immediately seize all the dwellers of the earth that no soul would feel able to utter a word, much less to reject or accept the truth KI 80–81

A<u>dh</u>irbáyján – re: Imám Báqir SB 16–17

consider how the prophecies correspond to one another. In the Apocalypse, the appearance of the Promised One is appointed after forty-two months, and Daniel expresses it as three times and a half, SAQ 71 which is also forty-two months, which are twelve hundred and sixty days. In another passage of John's Revelation it is clearly spoken of as twelve hundred and sixty days, and in the Holy Book it is said that each day signifies one year. Nothing could be clearer than this agreement of the prophecies with one another

interpreting in a masterly fashion the obscure, the designedly allegorical and abstruse traditions, verses and prophecies in the Islamic holy Writ, and adducing, in support of their contention, the meekness and apparent helplessness of the Imám Ḥusayn who, despite his defeat, his discomfiture and ignominious martyrdom, had been hailed by their antagonists as the very embodiment and the matchless symbol of God's all-conquering sovereignty and power – re: early followers of Báb GPB 37

– re: prophecies fulfilled by the Báb 58

and finally carried Him as far as the shores of the Holy Land, thereby fulfilling the prophecies recorded in both the Old and the New Testaments, redeeming the pledge enshrined in various traditions attributed to the Apostle of God and the Imáms who succeeded Him, and ushering in the long-awaited restoration of Israel to the ancient cradle of its Faith – re: exile of Bahá'u'lláh 107

– re: prophecies regarding the 'Lord of Hosts' and 'Akká 183–4

what is meant in the prophecies by the 'Lord of Hosts' and the 'Promised Christ' is the Blessed Perfection (Bahá'u'lláh) and His Holiness the Exalted One (the Báb) WOB 139

Jerusalem – re: prophetic words of Christ 176

concerning the passage in the 'Dispensation of Bahá'u'lláh' in which the Guardian quotes 'Abdu'l-Bahá's interpretation of the prophecy referring to the times when the sun would stand still in the heavens, he wishes me to explain that the days referred to in this prophecy have to be reckoned differently. In the Sacred Scriptures of various religions there are to be found frequent references to days, but these have to be considered as indicating different periods of time, as for instance in the Qur'án a day is reckoned as one thousand years. The first ten days in the above-mentioned prophecy represent each a century, making thus a total of one thousand lunar years. As to the twenty days referring to the Bábí Dispensation, each of them represents only one lunar year, the total of twenty years marking the duration of the Revelation of the Báb. The thirty days in the last Dispensation should not be reckoned numerically, but should be considered as symbolizing the incomparable greatness of the Bahá'í Revelation which, though not final, is none-the-less thus far the fullest revelation of God to man. From a physical point of view, the thirty days represent the maximum time taken by the sun to pass through a sign of the zodiac. They thus represent a culminating point in the evolution of this star. So also from a spiritual standpoint these thirty days should be viewed as indicating the highest, though not the final, stage in the spiritual evolution of mankind – re: Zoroastrian prophecy [*see* WOB 101–2] (Letter 7.8.34) LG 353–4

you have asked Me a question with regard to the gathering of the children of Israel in Jerusalem in accordance with the prophecy. 383–4

Jerusalem, the Holy of Holies, is a revered Temple, a sublime name, for it is the City of God . . . The gathering of Israel at Jerusalem means, therefore, and prophesies, that Israel as a whole is gathering beneath the banner of God and will enter the Kingdom of the Ancient of Days. For the celestial Jerusalem, which has as its centre the Holy of Holies, is a City of the Kingdom, a Divine City. The East and West are but a small corner of that City.

Prophecy

Moreover, materially as well (as spiritually), the Israelites will gather in the Holy Land. This is irrefutable prophecy, for the ignominy which Israel has suffered for well-nigh twenty-five hundred years will now be changed into eternal glory, and in the eyes of all, the Jewish people will become glorified to such an extent as to draw the jealousy of its enemies and the envy of its friends (Tablet of the Master, 1897)

sometimes people strive all their lives to render outstanding service. Here is the time and opportunity to render historic services; in fact the most unique in history, aiding in the fulfilment of Daniel's prophecies of the Last Day, and the 1335 days, when men are to be blessed by the Glory of the Lord, covering the entire globe – which is the real goal of the Ten Year Crusade. BN 313, p7

In other words, when we fulfil the Ten Year Crusade we will have brought into fulfilment Daniel's great prophecy of 'Blessed is he who waits and comes to the 1335 days.' What could be more wonderful than taking part in the fulfilment of religious prophecy of over 3,000 years

see also *'Akká, Banquet-Hall of God, Daniel, Muḥammad* n., *Nebuchadnezzar* n., *Year, Zawrá'*

Prophet

the soul of every Prophet of God, of every Divine Messenger, hath thirsted for this wondrous Day G 11

nay, all the Prophets of God, His well-favoured, His holy and chosen Messengers are, without exception, the bearers of His names, and the embodiments of His attributes 48

it is clear and evident to thee that all the Prophets are the Temples of the Cause of God, Who have appeared clothed in divers attire 51

thou hast known how grievously the Prophets of God, His Messengers and Chosen Ones, have been afflicted. Meditate a while on the motive and reason which have been responsible for such a persecution. At no time, in no Dispensation, have the Prophets of God escaped the blasphemy of their enemies, the cruelty of their oppressors, the denunciation of the learned of their age, who appeared in the guise of uprightness and piety. Day and night they passed through such agonies as none can ever measure, except the knowledge of the one true God, exalted be His glory 57

in thine esteemed letter thou hadst inquired which of the Prophets of God should be regarded as superior to others. Know thou assuredly that the essence of all the Prophets of God is one and the same. Their unity is absolute 78

the Prophets of God should be regarded as physicians whose task is to foster the well-being of the world and its peoples, that, through the spirit of oneness, they may heal the sickness of a divided humanity. To none is given the right to question their words or disparage their conduct, for they are the only ones who can claim to have understood the patient and to have correctly diagnosed its ailments 79

Divine Physician – re: treatment in this day not identical with that which he prescribed before 80

in it have appeared the Prophets of God and His chosen Ones *Holy Land* 343

examine the wondrous behaviour of the Prophets, and recall the defamations and denials uttered by the children of negation and falsehood KI 5–6

were men to meditate upon the lives of the Prophets of old, so easily would they come to know and understand the ways of these Prophets that they would cease to be veiled by such deeds and words as are contrary to their 53 own worldly desires, and thus consume every intervening veil with the fire burning in the Bush of divine knowledge, and abide secure upon the throne of peace and certitude

from Him is derived their sovereignty *Gems of Holiness* 99–100

moreover, the Prophets of old, each and every one, whenever announcing to the people of their day the advent of the coming Revelation, have invariably and specifically referred to that sovereignty with which the promised Manifestation must needs be invested. This is attested by the records of the scriptures of the past. This sovereignty hath not been solely and exclusively attributed to the Qá'im. Nay rather, the attribute of sovereignty and all other names and attributes of God have been and will ever be vouchsafed unto all the Manifestations of God, before and after Him [see also *Companions*, various items] 106–7

in every age and century, the purpose of the Prophets of God and their chosen ones hath been no other but to affirm the spiritual significance of the terms 'life,' 'resurrection,' and 'judgment' 120

Seal of the Prophets *Muḥammad* 162

denial and execration of the clerics of His day *Clerics* 165–6

they protested saying: 'No independent Prophet, according to our Scriptures, should arise after Moses and Jesus to abolish the Law of divine Revelation. Nay, he that is to be made manifest must needs fulfil the Law.' Thereupon this verse, indicative of all the divine themes, and testifying to the truth that the flow of the grace of the All-Merciful can never cease, was revealed: 'And Joseph came to you aforetime with clear tokens, but ye ceased not to doubt of the message with which He came to you, until, when He died, ye said, "God will by no means raise up a Messenger after Him." Thus God misleadeth him who is the transgressor, the doubter' 212–13

it is this Primal Will which appeareth resplendent in every Prophet and speaketh forth in every revealed Book *Primal Will* SB 126

no one hath been or will ever be invested with prophethood other than Thee, nor hath any sacred Book been or will be revealed unto any one except Thee. Such is the decree ordained by Him Who is the All-Encompassing, the Best Beloved 159

the events that transpired at the advent of the Prophets of the past, and Their ways and works and circumstances, are not adequately set down in authoritative histories, and are referred to only in condensed form in the verses of the Qur'án, the Holy Traditions and the Torah. Since, however, all events from the days of Moses until the present time are contained in the mighty Qur'án, the authoritative Traditions, the Torah and other reliable sources SDC 74–5

and it is a basic principle of the Law of God that in every Prophetic Mission, He entereth into a Covenant with all believers – a Covenant that endureth until the end of that Mission, until the promised day when the Personage stipulated at the outset of the Mission is made manifest [see also *Covenant* *Messiah*] SAB 207

the independent Prophets are the lawgivers and the founders of a new cycle. Through Their appearance the world puts on a new garment, the foundations of religion are established, and a new book is revealed. Without an intermediary they receive bounty from the Reality of Divinity, and their illumination is an essential illumination SAQ 164

the other Prophets are followers and promoters, for they are branches and not independent; they receive the bounty of the independent Prophets, 164 and they profit by the light of the Guidance of the universal Prophets. They are like the moon, which is not luminous and radiant in itself, but receives its light from the sun

the Manifestations of universal Prophethood Who appeared independently are, for example, Abraham, Moses, Christ, Muḥammad, the Báb and Bahá'u'lláh. But the others who are followers and promoters are like Solomon, David, Isaiah, Jeremiah and Ezekiel. For the independent Prophets are founders; They establish a new religion and make new creatures of men; They change the general morals, promote new customs and rules, renew the cycle and the Law 164–5

Question. – In the Holy Books there are some addresses of reproach and rebuke directed to the Prophets. Who is addressed, and for whom is the rebuke? 167

Answer. – All the divine discourses containing reproof, though apparently addressed to the Prophets, in reality are directed to the people, through a wisdom which is absolute mercy, in order that the people may not be discouraged and disheartened. They, therefore, appear to be addressed to the Prophets; but though outwardly for the Prophets, they are in truth for the people and not for the Prophets

for example, when the children of Israel rebelled and said to Moses: 'We cannot fight with the Amalekites, for they are powerful, mighty and courageous.' God then rebuked Moses and Aaron, though Moses was in complete obedience and not in rebellion 167–8

Jacob – re: apparent rebuke to the Prophet 168–9

furthermore, in Numbers, chapter 20, verse 23: 'And the Lord spake unto Moses and Aaron in mount Hor, by the coast of the land of Edom, saying, Aaron shall be gathered unto his people: for he shall not enter into the land which I have given unto the children of Israel, because ye rebelled against My word at the water of Meribah'; and in verse 13: 'This is the water of Meribah; because the children of Israel strove with the Lord, and He was sanctified in them.' 169

Observe: the people of Israel rebelled, but apparently the reproach was for Moses and Aaron. As it is said in the Book of Deuteronomy, chapter 3, verse 26: 'But the Lord was wroth with Me for your sakes, and would not hear Me: and the Lord said unto Me, Let it suffice Thee; speak no more unto Me of this matter.'

Now this discourse and reproach really refer to the children of Israel, who, for having rebelled against the command of God, were held captive a long time in the arid desert, on the other side of Jordan, until the time of Joshua – upon him be salutations. This address and reproach appeared to be for Moses and Aaron, but in reality they were for the people of Israel [see also *Sin Gospel* 170]

it is evident, then, that the proofs of the validity and inspiration of a Prophet of God are the deeds of beneficent accomplishment and greatness emanating from Him. If He proves to be instrumental in the elevation and betterment of mankind, He is undoubtedly a valid and heavenly Messenger [see also *Foundation* 363] PUP 366

it is self-evident that the prophets are the educators of men and the teachers of the human race. They come to bestow universal education upon humanity, to give humanity training, to uplift the human race from the abyss of despair and desolation and enable man to attain the apogee of advancement and glory FWU 94

then the Master asked Esmael: 'How old was Moses?' SW XIII 6, p152

'One hundred and twenty years,' he replied. 'But the patriarchs, such as Noah and others lived many hundreds of years.'

The Master said: 'The age of those ancient prophets as recorded in the Old Testament is symbolic. It has a spiritual interpretation. Wert thou informed of the science of anatomy thou wouldst realize that this human mechanism and these material organs cannot last more than one hundred and twenty years'

'with each and every Prophet, Whom We have sent down in the past,' He further adds, 'We have established a separate Covenant concerning the "Remembrance of God" and His Day' WOB 126

how often have the Prophets of God, not excepting Bahá'u'lláh Himself, chosen to appear, and deliver their Message in countries and amidst peoples and races, at a time when they were either fast declining, or had already touched the lowest depths of moral and spiritual degradation ADJ 14

and having responded to the call which these Prophets have raised, to unreservedly recognize and courageously testify to this indubitable truth, that not by reason of any racial superiority, political capacity, or spiritual virtue which a race or nation might possess, but rather as a direct consequence of its crying needs, its lamentable degeneracy, and irremediable perversity, has the Prophet of God chosen to appear in its midst, and with it as a lever has lifted the entire human race to a higher and nobler plane of life and conduct. For it is precisely under such circumstances, and by such means that the Prophets have, from time immemorial, chosen and were able to demonstrate their redemptive power to raise from the depths of abasement and of misery, the people of their own race and nation, empowering them to transmit in turn to other races and nations the saving grace and the energizing influence of their Revelation 14–15

'Abdu'l-Bahá used often to say that the difference between a prophet and an ordinary person is that the latter looks only to the present. He does not try to imagine the future victories and thereby forget the present trivial obstructions. The prophet, however, having a deep insight in the future condition of things sees his ultimate victory and does not get disheartened even though he sees a whole-sale massacre of his followers. DND 13

As Bahá'ís we should follow the prophet's method. We know that the Cause will ultimately conquer and its ranks be fully united

after Bahá'u'lláh many Prophets will, no doubt, appear but they will be all under His shadow. Although they may abrogate the laws of the Dispensation, in accordance with the needs and requirements of the age in which they appear, they nevertheless draw their spiritual force from this mighty Revelation. The Faith of Bahá'u'lláh constitutes, indeed, the stage of maturity in the development of mankind. His appearance has released such spiritual forces which will continue to animate, for many long years to come, the world in its development. Whatever progress may be achieved in later ages – after the unification of the whole human race is achieved – will be but improvements in the machinery of the world. For the machinery itself has been already created by Bahá'u'lláh. The task of continually improving and perfecting this machinery is one which later Prophets will be called upon to achieve. They will thus move and work within the orbit of the Bahá'í cycle (Letter 14.11.35) LG 354–5

just as in the past the Prophets have been persecuted and their Mission ridiculed, so has the message of Bahá'u'lláh been scoffed at as a mere impracticable idealism. From His earliest youth He was put in chains, expatriated and persecuted. But what do we observe in this day? Less than forty years after His death, the principles He advocated are the only solution for the practical political politics, the spiritual truths He voiced 355 are the crying needs of man and the very thing he requires for his moral and spiritual development (Letter 26.2.33)

the Prophets 'regarded as one and the same person' include the Lesser Prophets as well, and not merely those who bring a 'Book'. The station is different, but They are Prophets and Their nature thus different from that of ours (Letter 8.2.49) 368–9

the Prophets are pre-existent. The soul or spirit of the individual comes into being with the conception of the physical body. The Prophets, unlike us, are pre-existent. The soul of Christ existed in the spiritual world before His birth in this world. We cannot imagine what that world is like, so words are inadequate to picture His state of being. We cannot know God directly only through His prophets. We see perfection of God through His Prophets. Time and space are physical things: God, the Creator, is not in a 'place' as we conceive of place in physical terms. God is Infinite Essence, the Creator. We cannot picture Him or His state: If we did, we would be His equals, not His creatures. God is never flesh, but mirrored in the attributes of His Prophets. We see His divine characteristics and perfections (Letter 9.10.47) 375

the atoms of the Prophets are just atoms, like all others, but the association of this great spiritual power with them leaves in the place They are laid to rest, a spiritual atmosphere, if one can use this expression. They are, no doubt, endowed with a tremendous spiritual influence and far-reaching power. But the physical character of Their atoms are not different from other people's, any more than Their bodies and physical functions are different (Letter 28.10.49) [see also *Ascendancy* – re: blood of Ḥusayn KI 127–8] 377

Prophetic Cycle

when God sent forth His Prophet Muḥammad, on that day the termination of the prophetic cycle was foreordained in the knowledge of God *Day* SB 161

Holy of Holies – re: spiritual Law does not change and is established in all the prophetic cycles SAQ 47

Whose advent at once signalized the termination of the 'Prophetic Cycle' and the inception of the 'Cycle of Fulfilment' – re: the Báb GPB 57

a Revelation, hailed as the promise and crowning glory of past ages and centuries, as the consummation of all the Dispensations within the Adamic Cycle, inaugurating an era of at least a thousand years' duration, and a cycle destined to last no less than five thousand centuries, signalizing the end of the Prophetic Era and the beginning of the Era of Fulfilment 100

Providence

praise and thanksgiving be unto Providence that out of all the realities in existence He has chosen the reality of man and has honoured it with intellect and wisdom, the two most luminous lights in either world. Through the agency of this great endowment, He has in every epoch cast on the mirror of creation new and wonderful configurations. If we look objectively upon the world of being, it will become apparent that from age to age, the temple of existence has continually been embellished with a fresh grace, and distinguished with an ever-varying splendour, deriving from wisdom and the power of thought SDC 1

Purpose

in every age and century, the purpose of the Prophets of God and their chosen ones hath been no other but to affirm the spiritual significance of the terms 'life,' 'resurrection' and 'judgment' KI 120 in this way the primary purpose of revealing the Divine Law – which is to bring about happiness in the after life and civilization and the refinement of character in this – will be realized *Soul* SDC 46

God's purpose is none other than to usher in, in ways He alone can bring about, and the full significance of which He alone can fathom, the Great, the Golden Age of a long-divided, a long-afflicted humanity. Its present state, indeed even its immediate future, is dark, distressingly dark. Its distant future, however, is radiant, gloriously radiant – so radiant that no eye can visualize it PDC 116

Qá'im

Ḥusayn – re: return of G 12

the Imám Ṣádiq hath said: 'When our Qá'im will arise, the earth will shine with the light of her Lord.' Likewise, a lengthy tradition is attributed to Abí-'Abdi'lláh – peace be upon him – in which these sublime words are found: 'Thereupon will He Who is the All-Compelling – exalted and glorified be He – descend from the clouds with the angels.' And in the mighty Qur'án: 'What can such expect but that God should come down to them overshadowed with clouds?' [see also *Tradition* *Shí'ih* 119–20] ESW 112

the blind fanaticism of former times hath withheld the hapless creatures from the Straight Path. Meditate on the Shí'ih sect. For twelve hundred years they have cried 'O Qá'im!', until in the end all pronounced the sentence of His death, and caused Him to suffer martyrdom, notwithstanding their belief in, and their acceptance and acknowledgment of, the True One – exalted be His glory – and of the Seal of the Prophets, and of the Chosen Ones 163

they confidently assert that such traditions as indicate the advent of the expected Qá'im have not yet been fulfilled, whilst they themselves have failed to inhale the fragrance of the meaning of these traditions, and are still oblivious of the fact that all the signs foretold have come to pass, that the way of God's holy Cause hath been revealed, and the concourse of the faithful, swift as lightning, are, even now, passing upon that way, whilst these foolish divines wait expecting to witness the signs foretold. Say, O ye foolish ones! Wait ye even as those before you are waiting KI 83

why is it that the sovereignty of the Qá'im . . . hath not in the least been made manifest? *Sovereignty* 106

this sovereignty hath not been solely and exclusively attributed to the Qá'im *Prophet* 106–7

furthermore, by sovereignty is meant the all-encompassing, all-pervading power which is inherently exercised by the Qá'im whether or not He appear to the world clothed in the majesty of earthly dominion. This is solely dependent upon the will and pleasure of the Qá'im Himself 107

have they not heard the well-known tradition: 'When the Qá'im riseth, that day is the Day of Resurrection?' In like manner, the Imáms, those unquenchable lights of divine guidance, have interpreted the verse: 'What can such expect but that God should come down to them overshadowed with clouds,' – a sign which they have unquestionably regarded as one of the features of the Day of Resurrection – as referring to Qá'im and His manifestation 144

Knowledge – re: twenty-seven letters 243–4

Káfí – re: tradition concerning character and sufferings of the Qá'im 245

and yet no one hath paused to reflect that if the promised Qá'im should reveal the laws and ordinances of a former Dispensation, why then should such traditions have been recorded, and why should there arise 245–6 such a degree of strife and conflict that the people should regard the slaying of these companions as an obligation imposed upon them, and deem the persecution of these holy souls as a means of attaining unto the highest favour

Biḥár – re: 'in our Qá'im there shall be four signs' 254

Knowledge – re: seventy meanings 255

it is clear and evident that the object of all preceding Dispensations hath been to pave the way for the advent of Muḥammad, the Apostle of God. These, including the Muḥammadan Dispensation, have had, in their turn, as their objective the Revelation proclaimed by the Qá'im SB 105–6

Primal Tree – re: He hath appeared in the midmost heart of Islám 108

even as the Revelation of the Qá'im (He Who ariseth), a descendant of Muḥammad – may the blessings of God rest upon Him – is exactly like unto the Revelation of the Apostle of God Himself (Muḥammad). He appeareth not, save for the purpose of gathering the fruits of Islám from the Qur'ánic verses which He (Muḥammad) hath sown in the hearts of men. The fruits of Islám cannot be gathered except through allegiance unto Him (the Qá'im) and by believing in Him 108

ponder likewise the Dispensation of the Apostle of God which lasted twelve hundred and seventy years till the dawn of the manifestation of the Bayán. He directed everyone to await the advent of the Promised Qá'im. All deeds which in the Islamic Dispensation began with Muḥammad should find their consummation through the appearance of the Qá'im. God hath made Him manifest invested with the proof wherewith the Apostle of God was invested, so that none of the believers in the Qur'án might entertain doubts about the validity of His Cause, for it is set down in the Qur'án that none but God is capable of revealing verses 118

Him Who is your Qá'im, your Guide, your Mihdí, your Lord *Bayán* 139

the promised Qá'im (He who ariseth), the Ṣáḥibu'z-Zamán (the Lord of the Age), Who assumed the exclusive right of annulling the whole Qur'ánic Dispensation, Who styled Himself 'the Primal Point from which have been generated all created things . . . the Light of God Whose radiance can never fade' GPB 4

Mírzá Aḥmad-i-Azghandí, the most learned, the wisest and the most outstanding among the 'ulamás of Khurásán, who, in anticipation of the advent of the promised Qá'im, had compiled above twelve thousand traditions and prophecies concerning the time and character of the expected Revelation, had circulated them among His fellow-disciples, and had encouraged them to quote them extensively to all congregations and in all meetings 12–13

requested the Báb to expound and demonstrate the truth of Muḥammad's specific mission. To this request, which those present had felt compelled to decline, the Báb readily responded. In less than two hours, and in the space of fifty pages, He had not only revealed a minute, a vigorous and original dissertation on this noble theme, but had also linked it with both the coming of the Qá'im and the return of the Imám Ḥusayn – an exposition that prompted Manúchihr Khán to declare before that gathering his faith in the Prophet of Islám, as well as his recognition of the supernatural gifts with which the Author of so convincing a treatise was endowed 14–15

'I am the Word which the Qá'im is to utter, the Word which shall put to flight the chiefs and nobles of the earth!' *Ṭáhirih* [see also *Bugle* 33] – re: Ṭáhirih at Badasht 32–3 as those same 'Seven Goats' who, according to Islamic tradition, should, on the Day of Judgment, 'walk in front' of the promised Qá'im, and whose death was to precede the impending martyrdom of their true Shepherd – re: Seven Martyrs of Ṭihrán 48

Siyyid Káẓim-i-Rashtí, Shaykh Aḥmad's disciple and successor, had likewise written: 'The Qá'im must needs be put to death. After He has been slain the world will have attained the age of eighteen.' In his Sharḥ-i-Qaṣídiy-i-Lámíyyih he had even alluded to the name 'Bahá.' Furthermore, to his disciples, as his days drew to a close, he had significantly declared: 'Verily, I say, after the Qá'im the Qayyúm will be made manifest. For when the star of the former has set the sun of the beauty of Ḥusayn will rise and illuminate the whole world. Then will be unfolded in all its glory the "Mystery" and the "Secret" spoken of by Shaykh Aḥmad . . . To have attained unto that Day of Days is to have attained unto the crowning glory of past generations, and one goodly deed performed in that age is equal to the pious worship of countless centuries' 97

all of them (the companions of the Qá'im) shall be slain except One Who shall reach the plain of 'Akká, the Banquet-Hall of God' – re: Bahá'u'lláh *Banquet-Hall of God* 184

He Whom Bahá'u'lláh has acclaimed in the Kitáb-i-Íqán as that promised Qá'im Who has manifested no less than twenty-five out of the twenty-seven letters which all the Prophets were destined to reveal – so great a Revealer has Himself testified to the preeminence of that superior Revelation that was soon to supersede His own WOB 100

Qiblih

He continued to turn His face, while praying, unto Jerusalem, the holy city, until the time when the Jews began to utter unseemly words against Him – words which if mentioned would ill befit these pages and would weary the reader. Muḥammad strongly resented these words. Whilst, wrapt in meditation and wonder, He was gazing toward heaven, He heard the kindly Voice of Gabriel, saying: 'We behold Thee from above, turning Thy face to heaven; but We will have Thee turn to a Qiblih which shall please Thee.' On a subsequent day, when the Prophet, together with His companions, was offering the noontide prayer, and had already performed two of the prescribed Rik'ats, the Voice of Gabriel was heard again: 'Turn Thou Thy face towards the sacred Mosque.' In the midst of that same prayer, Muḥammad suddenly turned His face away from Jerusalem and faced the Ka'bih [see also *Test* 50–51] KI 50

none of the many Prophets sent down, since Moses was made manifest, as Messengers of the Word of God, such as David, Jesus, and others among the more exalted Manifestations who have appeared during the intervening period between the Revelations of Moses and Muḥammad, ever altered the law of the Qiblih 51

why should the Qiblih have been changed, thus casting such dismay amongst the people, causing the companions of the Prophet to waver, and throwing so great a confusion into their midst? Yea, such things as throw consternation into the hearts of all men come to pass only that each soul may be tested by the touchstone of God, that the true may be known and distinguished from the false. Thus hath He revealed after the breach amongst the people: 'We did not appoint that which Thou wouldst have to be the Qiblih, but that We might know him who followeth the Apostle from him who turneth on his heels.' 'Affrighted asses fleeing from a lion' 52

Qur'án

say: Perused ye not the Qur'án? Read it, that haply ye may find the Truth, for this Book is verily the Straight Path. This is the Way of God unto all who are in the heavens and all who are on the earth. If ye have been careless of the Qur'án, the Bayán cannot be regarded to be remote from you. Behold it open before your eyes. Read ye its verses, that perchance ye desist from committing that which will cause the Messengers of God to mourn and lament — G 44

drink with healthy relish, O people of Bahá. Ye are indeed they with whom it shall be well. This is what they who have near access to God have attained. This is the flowing water ye were promised in the Qur'án, and later in the Bayán, as a recompense from your Lord, the God of Mercy. Blessed are they that quaff it — 45–6

likewise, in the Qur'án He saith: 'Of what ask they of one another? Of the Great Announcement' *Announcement* — ESW 143

in another sense, by the terms 'sun', 'moon', and 'stars' are meant such laws and teachings as have been established and proclaimed in every Dispensation, such as the laws of prayer and fasting. These have, according to the law of the Qur'án, been regarded, when the beauty of the Prophet Muḥammad had passed beyond the veil, as the most fundamental and binding laws of His dispensation — KI 38

Muḥammad, the Seal of the Prophets, and the most distinguished of God's chosen Ones, hath likened the Dispensation of the Qur'án unto heaven *Islám* — 40

gracious God! Notwithstanding the warning which, in marvelously symbolic language and subtle allusions, hath been uttered in days past, and which was intended to awaken the peoples of the world and to prevent them from being deprived of their share of the billowing ocean of God's grace, yet such things as have already been witnessed have come to pass! Reference to these things hath also been made in the Qur'án, as witnessed by this verse: 'What can such expect but that God should come down to them overshadowed with clouds?' A number of the divines, who hold firmly to the letter of the Word of God, have come to regard this verse as one of the signs of that expected resurrection which is born of their idle fancy — 75–6

Sign – re: corrupting the text — 84

likewise, it is clear, how in this day, the people of the Qur'án have perverted the text of God's holy Book, concerning the signs of the expected Manifestation, and interpreted it according to their inclination and desires — 87

let them, at all times, fix their gaze upon the essentials of His Cause, lest when He, Who is the Quintessence of truth, the inmost Reality of all things, the Source of all light, is made manifest, they cling unto certain passages of the Book, and inflict upon Him that which was inflicted in the Dispensation of the Qur'án — 92

when the light of Qur'ánic Revelation was kindled within the chamber of Muḥammad's holy heart, He passed upon the people the verdict of the Last Day, the verdict of resurrection, of judgment, of life, and of death. Thereupon the standards of revolt were hoisted, and the doors of derision opened [see also *Creation* 114–15] — 114

furthermore, it is already evident and known unto thee that those things to which the Jews and the Christians have clung, and the cavillings which they heaped upon the Beauty of Muḥammad, the same have in this day — 135 been upheld by the people of the Qur'án, and been witnessed in their denunciations of the 'Point of the Bayán'

although the commentators of the Qur'án have related in divers manners 136–7
the circumstances attending the revelation of this verse, yet thou shouldst endeavour to apprehend the purpose thereof. He saith: How false is that which the Jews have imagined! How can the hand of him Who is the King in truth, Who caused the countenance of Moses to be made manifest, and conferred upon Him the robe of Prophethood – how can the hand of such a One be chained and fettered? How can He be conceived as powerless to raise up yet another Messenger after Moses? Behold the absurdity of their saying; how far it hath strayed from the path of knowledge and understanding! Observe how in this day also, all these people have occupied themselves with such foolish absurdities. For over a thousand years they have been reciting this verse, and unwittingly pronouncing their censure against the Jews, utterly unaware that they themselves, openly and privily, are voicing the sentiments and belief of the Jewish people

most of the verses of the Qur'án indicate, and bear witness to, this spiritual 140–41
theme. The verse: 'Neither is there aught which doth not celebrate His praise' is eloquent testimony thereto; and 'We noted all things and wrote them down,' a faithful witness thereof. Now, if by 'attainment unto the Presence of God' is meant attainment unto the knowledge of such revelation, it is evident that all men have already attained unto the presence of the unchangeable Countenance of that peerless King. Why, then, restrict such revelation to the Day of Resurrection?

and likewise, He hath revealed in the Qur'án *Abase* 146

O my friend, were the bird of thy mind to explore the heavens of the 147–8
Revelation of the Qur'án, were it to contemplate the realm of divine knowledge unfolded therein, thou wouldst assuredly find unnumbered doors of knowledge set open before thee. Thou wouldst certainly recognize that all these things which have in this day hindered this people from attaining the shores of the ocean of eternal grace, the same things in the Muḥammadan Dispensation prevented the people of that age from recognizing that divine Luminary, and from testifying to His truth

strive therefore to comprehend the meaning of 'return' which hath been so 151
explicitly revealed in the Qur'án itself *Return*

Testimony 151–2

how strange! These people with one hand cling to those verses of the 168–9
Qur'án and those traditions of the people of certitude which they have found to accord with their inclinations and interests, and with the other reject those which are contrary to their selfish desires. 'Believe ye then part of the Book, and deny part? How could ye judge that which ye understand not?

to this attainment to the presence of the immortal King testify the verses of 169
the Book, some of which We have already mentioned. The one true God is My witness! Nothing more exalted or more explicit than 'attainment unto the divine Presence' hath been revealed in the Qur'án. Well is it with him that hath attained thereunto, in the day wherein most of the people, even as ye witness, have turned away therefrom

twelve hundred and eighty years have passed since the dawn of the 172
Muḥammadan Dispensation, and with every break of day, these blind and ignoble people have recited their Qur'án, and yet have failed to grasp one letter of that Book! Again and again they read those verses which clearly testify to the reality of these holy themes, and bear witness

to the truth of the Manifestations of eternal Glory, and still apprehend not their purpose. They have even failed to realize, all this time, that, in every age, the reading of the scriptures and holy books is for no other purpose except to enable the reader to apprehend their meaning and unravel their innermost mysteries. Otherwise reading, without understanding, is of no abiding profit unto man

We then asked him saying: 'Hast thou not read the Qur'án, and art thou not 173
aware of this blessed verse: "On that day shall neither man nor spirit be asked of his Sin?"' Dost thou not realize that by 'asking is not meant asking by tongue or speech, even as the verse itself doth indicate and prove it?' For afterward it is said: 'By their countenance shall the sinners be known, and they shall be seized by their forelocks and their feet' [see also *Judge*] *Reckoning*

for instance, the Qur'án was an impregnable stronghold unto the people of 200
Muḥammad. In His days, whosoever entered therein, was shielded from the devilish assaults, the menacing darts, the soul-devouring doubts, and blasphemous whisperings of the enemy. Upon him was also bestowed a portion of the everlasting and goodly fruits – the fruits of wisdom, from the divine Tree. To him was given to drink the incorruptible waters of the river of knowledge, and to taste the wine of the mysteries of divine Unity

its guidance can never err, its testimony no other testimony can excel 201
Tradition

in the disconnected letters of the Qur'án the mysteries of the divine 202–3
Essence are enshrined, and within their shells the pearls of His Unity are treasured. For lack of space We do not dwell upon them at this moment. Outwardly they signify Muḥammad Himself, Whom God addresseth saying: 'O Muḥammad, there is no doubt nor uncertainty about this Book which hath been sent down from the heaven of divine Unity. In it is guidance unto them that fear God.' Consider, how He hath appointed and decreed this self-same Book, the Qur'án, as a guidance unto all that are in heaven and on earth. He, the divine Being, and unknowable Essence, hath, Himself, testified that this Book is, beyond all doubt and uncertainty, the guide of all mankind until the Day of Resurrection – re: Alif Lám Mím [Qur'án 2:1]

for it is evident that whoso hath failed to acknowledge the truth of the 204
Qur'án hath in reality failed to acknowledge the truth of the preceding Scriptures *Scripture*

yea, the blind can perceive naught from the sun except its heat, and the arid 209
soil hath no share of the showers of mercy. 'Marvel not if in the Qur'án the unbeliever perceiveth naught but the trace of letters, for in the sun, the blind findeth naught but heat'

and yet, the unfailing testimony of God to both the East and the West is 210
none other than the Qur'án *Testimony*

even as thou dost witness how the people of the Qur'án, like unto the 213
people of old, have allowed the words 'Seal of the Prophets' to veil their eyes. And yet, they themselves testify to this verse: 'None knoweth the interpretation thereof but God and they that are well-grounded in knowledge.' And when He Who is well-grounded in all knowledge, He Who is the Mother, the Soul, the Secret, and the Essence thereof, revealeth that which is the least contrary to their desire, they bitterly oppose Him and shamelessly deny Him

most of the verses of the Qur'án are indicative of this theme *Book* 219

notwithstanding all the verses of the Qur'án, and the recognized traditions 239
Truth

why dost thou burden thy soul with that which is far more abject than the deeds of Pharaoh, and still callest thyself one of the faithful? How dost thou peruse the verses of the Qur'án, while thou art of the unjust? Never would the Jews, nor the Christians nor any such people as have rejected the truth consent to inflict wrongs upon the son of their Prophet's daughter – re: verses addressed to Muḥammad Sháh SB 26

is it not true that the Qur'án hath been sent down from God and that all men are powerless before its revelation? Likewise these words have also been revealed by God, if thou dost but perceive – re: 'Abdu'ṣ-Ṣáḥib *Primal Point* 31

yet since thou hast acknowledged and recognized Muḥammad, the Apostle of God, through the Qur'án, how canst thou withhold recognition from Him Who sent thee the Book, despite thou calling thyself 'His servant'? *'Abdu'ṣ-Ṣáḥib* 33

since thou dost adduce proofs from the Qur'án – re: to Sulaymán – divine in land of Masqaṭ *Proof* 35

O people of the city! Ye have disbelieved your Lord. If ye are truly faithful to Muḥammad, the Apostle of God and the Seal of the Prophets, and if ye follow His Book, the Qur'án, which is free from error, then here is the like of it – this Book, which We have, in truth and by the leave of God, sent down unto Our Servant. If ye fail to believe in Him, then your faith in Muḥammad and His Book which was revealed in the past will indeed be treated as false in the estimation of God. If ye deny Him, the fact of your having denied Muḥammad and His Book will, in very truth and with absolute certainty, become evident unto yourselves 46

O people of the Qur'án! Ye are as nothing unless ye submit unto the Remembrance of God and unto this Book. If ye follow the Cause of God, We will forgive you your sins, and if ye turn aside from Our command, We will, in truth, condemn your souls in Our Book, unto the Most Great Fire. We, verily, do not deal unjustly with men, even to the extent of a speck on a date-stone 61

when the verses of this Book are recited to the infidels they say: 'Give us a book like the Qur'án and make changes in the verses.' Say: 'God hath not given Me that I should change them at My pleasure.' I follow only what is revealed unto Me. Verily, I shall fear My Lord on the Day of Separation, whose advent He hath, in very truth, irrevocably ordained 66

O ye concourse of the believers! Utter not words of denial against Me once the Truth is made manifest, for indeed the mandate of the Báb hath befittingly been proclaimed unto you in the Qur'án aforetime. I swear by your Lord, this Book is verily the same Qur'án which was sent down in the past 67

compare His manifestation with that of the Point of the Qur'án – re: Him Whom God shall make manifest *'Alí* 83

the Commentary on the Súrih of Joseph had, in the first year of this Revelation, been widely distributed. Nevertheless, when the people realized that fellow supporters were not forthcoming they hesitated to accept it; while it never occurred to them that the very Qur'án whereunto unnumbered souls bear fealty today, was revealed in the midmost heart of the Arab world, yet to outward seeming for no less than seven years no one acknowledged its truth except the Commander of the Faithful (Imám 'Alí) – may the peace of God rest upon Him – who, in response to the conclusive proofs advanced by God's supreme Testimony, recognized the Truth and did not fix his eyes on others 90

before the revelation of the Qur'án everyone bore witness to His piety and 96 noble virtues. Behold Him then after the revelation of the Qur'án. What outrageous insults were levelled against Him, as indeed the pen is ashamed to recount

this truth hath likewise been laid bare in the Qur'án where in numerous instances God hath set down that whoever should pass judgement contrary to the bounds fixed by Him, would be deemed an infidel *Bayán* 102

in these days how few are those who abide by the standard laid down in the Qur'án. Nay, nowhere are they to be found, except such as God hath willed. Should there be, however, such a person, his righteous deeds would prove of no avail unto him, if he hath failed to follow the standard revealed in the Bayán; even as the pious deeds of the Christian monks profited them not, inasmuch as at the time of the manifestation of the Apostle of God – may the blessings of God rest upon Him – they contented themselves with the standard set forth in the Gospel 102

had the divine standard laid down in the Qur'án been truly observed, adverse judgements would not have been pronounced against Him Who is the Tree of divine Truth. As it hath been revealed: 'Almost might the heavens be rent and the earth be cleft asunder and the mountains fall down in fragments.' And yet how much harder than these mountains their hearts must be to have remained unmoved! Indeed no paradise is more glorious in the sight of God than attainment unto His good-pleasure 102–3

had human beings been able to accomplish this deed surely someone would have brought forth at least one verse during the period of twelve hundred and seventy years which hath elapsed since the revelation of the Qur'án until that of the Bayán *Verse* 105

and from the moment when the Tree of the Bayán appeared until it disappeareth is the Resurrection of the Apostle of God, as is divinely foretold in the Qur'án; the beginning of which was when two hours and eleven minutes had passed on the eve of the fifth of Jamádíyu'l-Avval, 1260 A.H., which is the year 1270 of the Declaration of the Mission of Muḥammad. This was the beginning of the Day of Resurrection of the Qur'án, and until the disappearance of the Tree of divine Reality is the Resurrection of the Qur'án 107

He appeareth not, save for the purpose of gathering the fruits of Islám from the Qur'ánic verses which He (Muḥammad) hath sown in the hearts of men. The fruits of Islám cannot be gathered except through allegiance unto Him (the Qá'im) and by believing in Him *Qá'im* 108

notwithstanding that in the Qur'án the advent of the Day of Resurrection hath been promised unto all by God *Primal Tree* 108

so likewise in the Revelation of the Point of the Bayán, if all should be assured that this is that same Promised Mihdí (One Who is guided) whom the Apostle of God foretold, not one of the believers in the Qur'án would turn aside from the sayings of the Apostle of God [see also *Jesus Christ*] 110

at the time of the revelation of the Qur'án He asserted His transcendent power through the advent of Muḥammad *Tree* 112

so that none of the believers in the Qur'án might entertain doubts about the validity of His Cause, for it is set down in the Qur'án that none but God is capable of revealing verses *Qá'im* 118

He could, within the space of five days and nights, reveal the equivalent of the Qur'án – re: the Báb *Writings* 118–19

but if thou hast embraced the Faith [of Islám] by recognizing the Qur'án as 120 the testimony, because thou hast heard the learned and the faithful express their powerlessness before it, or if thou hast, upon hearing the divine verses and by virtue of thy spontaneous love for the True Word of God, responded in a spirit of utter humility and lowliness – a spirit which is one of the mightiest signs of true love and understanding – then such proofs have been and will ever be regarded as sound *Testimony*

verily We planted the Tree of the Qur'án and provided its Orchard with all kinds of fruit, whereof ye all have been partaking. Then when We came to take over that which We had planted, ye pretended not to know Him Who is the Lord thereof *Orchard* 135

they behaved as the people unto whom the Qur'án was given are now behaving *Gospel* 137

He Who hath revealed the Qur'án unto Muḥammad, the Apostle of God, ordaining in the Faith of Islám that which was pleasing unto Him, hath likewise revealed the Bayán, in the manner ye have been promised *Bayán* 139

as to those who have debarred themselves from the Revelation of God, they have indeed failed to understand the significance of a single letter of the Qur'án, nor have they obtained the slightest notion of the Faith of Islám, otherwise they would not have turned away from God, Who hath brought them into being, Who hath nurtured them, hath caused them to die and hath proffered life unto them, by clinging to parts of their religion, thinking that they are doing righteous works for the sake of God 140

ye will go astray far beyond the peoples unto whom the Gospel, or the Qur'án or any other Scripture was given – re: in the time of Him Whom God shall make manifest *Astray* 141

those unto whom the Qur'án is given have wrought likewise. They performed their acts of devotion for the sake of God, hoping that He might enable them to join the righteous in Paradise. However, when the gates of Paradise were flung open to their faces, they declined to enter. They suffered themselves to enter into the fire, though they had been seeking refuge therefrom in God [see also *Gospel*] 143

if we ponder a while over the Qur'ánic verses and proofs, and the traditional accounts which have come down to us from those stars of the heaven of Divine Unity, the Holy Imáms, we shall be convinced of the fact that if a soul is endowed with the attributes of true faith and characterized with spiritual qualities he will become to all mankind an emblem of the outstretched mercies of God SDC 55

Prophet – re: in condensed form in the verses of the Qur'án 74–5

Affliction – re: children of Israel 79

can they claim that what went on under the previous government was in conformity with the Qur'án? For example, in the days when Ḥájí Mírzá Áqásí was Prime Minister, it was heard from many sources that the governor of Gulpáygán seized thirteen defenseless bailiffs of that region, all of them of holy lineage, all of them guiltless, and without a trial, and without obtaining any higher sanction, beheaded them in a single hour 100

as it was before explained, in the terminology of the Holy Books three days and a half signify three years and a half, and three years and a half are forty and two months, and forty and two months twelve hundred and sixty days; and as each day by the text of the Holy Book signifies one year, the meaning is that for twelve hundred and sixty years, which is the cycle of the Qur'án, the nations, tribes and peoples would look at their bodies – that is to say, that they would make a spectacle of the Religion of God: though they would not act in accordance with it, still, they would SAQ 52 not suffer their bodies – meaning the Religion of God – to be put in the grave. That is to say, that in appearance they would cling to the Religion of God and not allow it to completely disappear from their midst, nor the body of it to be entirely destroyed and annihilated. Nay, in reality they would leave it, while outwardly preserving its name and remembrance

Moses – re: references to, in the Qur'án PUP 367

in regard to the verse, which is revealed in the Qur'án, that His Highness, Christ, was not killed and was not crucified, by this is meant the Reality of Christ. Although they crucified this elemental body, yet the merciful reality and the heavenly existence remain eternal and undying, and it was protected from the oppression and persecution of the enemies, for Christ is Eternal and Everlasting. How can He die? This death and crucifixion were imposed on the physical body of Christ, and not upon the Spirit of Christ – re: Qur'án 4:157 SW II 7–8, p13

whom He identifies, in still another Tablet, with one of the 'Messengers charged with imposture' mentioned in the Qur'án – re: Bahá'u'lláh, referring to Quddús GPB 49

He alone was the Object of that prodigious eulogy, that masterly interpretation of the Ṣád of Ṣamad, penned in part, in that same Fort by that same youthful hero, under the most distressing circumstances, and equivalent in dimensions to six times the volume of the Qur'án – re: Quddús at Shaykh Ṭabarsí; ode to Bahá'u'lláh 69

His advent He, in that Book, in a súrih said to have been termed by Him 'the heart of the Qur'án,' had foreshadowed as that of the 'third' Messenger, sent down to 'strengthen' the two who preceded Him – re: Muḥammad on Bahá'u'lláh 96

Abode – re: Baghdád 109–10

the Qur'án which, though explicit in the laws and ordinances formulated by the Apostle of God, is silent on the all-important subject of the succession 213

'O people of the Qur'án,' Bahá'u'lláh, addressing the combined forces of Sunní and Shí'ih Islám, significantly affirms, 'Verily, the Prophet of God, Muḥammad, sheddeth tears at the sight of your cruelty. Ye have assuredly followed your evil and corrupt desires, and turned away your face from the light of guidance. Erelong will ye witness the result of your deeds; for the Lord, My God, lieth in wait and is watchful of your behaviour WOB 179

Day – re: tradition on decline of Islám 179

they must strive to obtain, from sources that are authoritative and unbiased, a sound knowledge of the history and tenets of Islám – the source and background of their Faith – and approach reverently and with a mind purged from pre-conceived ideas the study of the Qur'án which, apart from the sacred scriptures of the Bábí and Bahá'í Revelations, constitutes the only Book which can be regarded as an absolutely authenticated Repository of the Word of God ADJ 41

'at still another, We address the people of the Qur'án saying: "Fear the All-Merciful, and cavil not at Him through Whom all religions were founded"' [words of Bahá'u'lláh] PDC 76

in the Sacred Scriptures of various religions there are to be found frequent references to days . . . as for instance in the Qur'án a day is reckoned as one thousand years (Letter 7.8.34) LG 353

[an explanation of the passage on p. 231 of G, beginning with the words: 'From it (earth) have We created you'] 357

Bahá'u'lláh in quoting this passage seeks to refute the argument of the Muslims, who attach a purely literal interpretation to this verse of the Qur'án, and therefore consider it as implying bodily resurrection. To these Muslims, He says, that you who literally believe that the human body will return to dust and will be raised from it again, and therefore attach so much importance to this mortal world, how then can you wax so proud, and boast over things which are but perishable and consequently void of any true and lasting value (Letter 7.2.39)

when the Qur'án denies Christ is the Son of God it is not refuting His words but the false interpretation of them by the Christians who read into them a relationship of an almost corporeal nature, whereas Almighty God has no parents or offspring. What is meant by Christ, is His spirit's relation to the Infinite Spirit, and this the Qur'án does not deny. It is in a sense attributable – this kind of Sonship – to all the Prophets (Letter 19.5.45) 372–3

the Guardian would certainly advise, and even urge the friends to make a thorough study of the Qur'án as the knowledge of this Sacred Scripture is absolutely indispensable for every believer who wishes to adequately understand and intelligently read the writings of Bahá'u'lláh (Letter 2.12.35) 430

Rebirth

incline your ears to the sweet melody of this Prisoner. Arise, and lift up your voices, that haply they that are fast asleep may be awakened. Say: O ye who are as dead! The Hand of Divine bounty proffereth unto you the Water of Life. Hasten and drink your fill. Whoso hath been re-born in this Day, shall never die; whoso remaineth dead, shall never live G 212–13

even as Jesus said: 'Ye must be born again.' Again He saith: 'Except a man be born of water and of the Spirit, he cannot enter into the Kingdom of God. That which is born of the flesh is flesh; and that which is born of the Spirit is spirit.' The purport of these words is that whosoever in every dispensation is born of the Spirit and is quickened by the breath of the Manifestation of Holiness, he verily is of those who have attained unto 'life' and 'resurrection' and have entered into the 'paradise' of the love of God – re: *Baptism* KI 118

have not this people exemplified the mysteries of 'rebirth' and 'return'? *Transform* 155–6

material development may be likened to the glass of a lamp whereas divine virtues and spiritual susceptibilities are the light within the glass. The lamp chimney is worthless without the light; likewise man in his material condition requires the radiance and vivification of the divine graces and merciful attributes. Without the presence of the Holy Spirit he is lifeless . . . His Holiness Christ announced, 'That which is born of flesh is flesh and that which is born of spirit is spirit,' meaning that man must be born again. As the babe is born into the light of this physical world so must the physical and intellectual man be born into the light of the world of divinity FWU 58–9

Reckoning

mention was made concerning the signs of the Day of Judgment, Resurrection, Revival, and Reckoning. He urged Us to explain how, in this wondrous Dispensation, the peoples of the world were brought to a reckoning, when none were made aware of it. Thereupon, We imparted unto him, according to the measure of his capacity and understanding, certain truths of Science and ancient Wisdom. We then asked him saying: 'Hast thou not read the Qur'án, and art thou not aware of this KI 173 blessed verse: "On that day shall neither man nor spirit be asked of his Sin?" Dost thou not realize that by 'asking is not meant asking by tongue or speech, even as the verse itself doth indicate and prove it?' For afterward it is said: 'By their countenance shall the sinners be known, and they shall be seized by their forelocks and their feet' [see also *Judge*]

Redeemer

while your Redeemer was raised up by God at the age of twenty-four amidst people none of whom can speak or understand a single word of Arabic *Mihdí* — SB 146

as to the statement of Job, chapter 19, verses 25–27, 'I know that my Redeemer liveth, and that He shall stand at the latter day upon the earth,' the meaning here is: I shall not be abased, I have a Sustainer and a Guardian, and my Helper, my Defender will in the end be made manifest. And although now my flesh be weak and clothed with worms, yet shall I be healed, and with these mine own eyes, that is, mine inner sight, I shall behold Him [see also *Job*] — SAB 171

Reformation

what contribution the Reformation did really make was to seriously challenge, and partly undermine, the edifice which the Fathers of the Church had themselves reared, and to discard and demonstrate the purely human origin of the elaborate doctrines, ceremonies and institutions which they had devised. The Reformation was a right challenge to the man-made organization of the Church, and as such was a step in advance. In its origins, it was a reflection of the new spirit which Islám had released, and a God-sent punishment to those who had refused to embrace its truth (Letter 28.12.36) — LG 373

Rehoboam

Idol – re: Jeroboam and worship of idols — SDC 77

Religion

and now concerning thy question regarding the nature of religion. Know thou that they who are truly wise have likened the world unto the human temple. As the body of man needeth a garment to clothe it, so the body of mankind must needs be adorned with the mantle of justice and wisdom. Its robe is the Revelation vouchsafed unto it by God. Whenever this robe hath fulfilled its purpose, the Almighty will assuredly renew it. For every age requireth a fresh measure of the light of God. Every Divine Revelation hath been sent down in a manner that befitted the circumstances of the age in which it hath appeared — G 80–81

this Religion is indeed, in the sight of God, the essence of the Faith of Muḥammad; haste ye then to attain the celestial Paradise and the all-highest Garden of His good-pleasure in the presence of the One True God, could ye but be patient and thankful before the evidences of the signs of God — SB 71

the perfection of the religion of Islám was consummated at the beginning of this Revelation *Islám* — 107

not only do they scrupulously shun the adherents of religions other than their own, they do not even permit themselves to show them common courtesy *Neglect* — SDC 54

the principles of the Divine religions can hardly be evaluated by the acts of those who only claim to follow them *Principle* — 72

nothing can be effected in the world, not even conceivably, without unity and agreement, and the perfect means for engendering fellowship and union is true religion — 73 true religion promotes the civilization and honour, the prosperity and prestige, the learning and advancement of a people once abject, enslaved and ignorant, and how, when it falls into the hands of religious leaders who are foolish and fanatical, it is diverted to the wrong ends, until this greatest of splendours turns into blackest night 80

the purpose of these references is to establish the fact that the religions of God are the true source of the spiritual and material perfections of man, and the fountainhead for all mankind of enlightenment and beneficial knowledge 94

the purpose of these statements is to make it abundantly clear that the Divine religions, the holy precepts, the heavenly teachings, are the unassailable basis of human happiness, and that the peoples of the world can hope for no real relief or deliverance without this one great remedy. This panacea must, however, be administered by a wise and skilled physician 99

Holy of Holies – re: foundation of the religion of Muḥammad SAQ 47–8

these foundations of the Religion of God, which are spiritual and which are the virtues of humanity, cannot be abrogated; they are irremovable and eternal, and are renewed in the cycle of every Prophet.
The second part of the Religion of God, which refers to the material world, and which comprises fasting, prayer, forms of worship, marriage and divorce, the abolition of slavery, legal processes, transactions, indemnities for murder, violence, theft and injuries – this part of the Law of God, which refers to material things, is modified and altered in each prophetic cycle in accordance with the necessities of the times 48

'their bodies' means the Religion of God, and 'the street' means in public view *Dead* 52

Qur'án – re: dead in streets; 1260 years 52

but as the clergy have neither understood the meaning of the Gospels nor comprehended the symbols, therefore, it has been said that religion is in contradiction to science, and science in opposition to religion *Symbol* 104–5

Buddha also established a new religion *Buddha* [see also TAB 565 – re: Buddhist prophecies] 165

but if religions did not change and alter, there would be no need of renewal *Jesus Christ* 165

in the passage of time religions become entirely changed and altered. Therefore, they are renewed *Jesus Christ* 166

religion is the outer expression of the divine reality PUP 140

inasmuch as human interpretations and blind imitations differ widely, religious strife and disagreement have arisen among mankind, the light of true religion has been extinguished and the unity of the world of humanity destroyed 141

it is evident, therefore, that this condition will not be remedied without a reformation in the world of religion. In other words, the fundamental reality of the divine religions must be renewed, reformed, revoiced to mankind 141

it is evident, therefore, that counterfeit and spurious religious teaching, antiquated forms of belief and ancestral imitations which are at variance with the foundations of divine reality must also pass away and be reformed 144

briefly, the old conditions of animosity, bigotry and hatred between religious systems must be dispelled and the new conditions of love, agreement and spiritual brotherhood be established among them 181 but when we speak of religion, we mean the essential foundation or reality of religion, not the dogmas and blind imitations which have gradually encrusted it and which are the cause of the decline and effacement of a nation. These are inevitably destructive and a menace and hindrance to a nation's life – even as it is recorded in the Torah and confirmed in history that when the Jews became fettered by empty forms and imitations, the wrath of God became manifest. When they forsook the foundations of the law of God, Nebuchadnezzar came and conquered the Holy Land 363

we should earnestly seek and thoroughly investigate realities, recognizing that the purpose of the religion of God is the education of humanity and the unity and fellowship of mankind. Furthermore, we will establish the point that the foundations of the religions of God are one foundation 364

such a Covenant had invariably been the feature of every previous religion. It had existed, under various forms, with varying degrees of emphasis, had always been couched in veiled language, and had been alluded to in cryptic prophecies, in abstruse allegories, in unauthenticated traditions, and in the fragmentary and obscure passages of the sacred Scriptures. In the Bábí Dispensation, however, it was destined to be established in clear and unequivocal language, though not embodied in a separate document. Unlike the Prophets gone before Him, Whose Covenants were shrouded in mystery, unlike Bahá'u'lláh, Whose clearly defined Covenant was incorporated in a specially written Testament, and designated by Him as 'the Book of My Covenant,' the Báb chose to intersperse His Book of Laws, the Persian Bayán, with unnumbered passages, some designedly obscure, mostly indubitably clear and conclusive, in which He fixes the date of the promised Revelation, extols its virtues, asserts its pre-eminent character, assigns to it unlimited powers and prerogatives, and tears down every barrier that might be an obstacle to its recognition GPB 27–8

its teachings revolve around the fundamental principle that religious truth is not absolute but relative, that Divine Revelation is progressive, not final. Unequivocally and without the least reservation it proclaims all established religions to be divine in origin, identical in their aims, complementary in their functions, continuous in their purpose, indispensable in their value to mankind WOB 58

to contend that any particular religion is final, that 'all Revelation is ended, that the portals of Divine mercy are closed, that from the daysprings of eternal holiness no sun shall rise again, that the ocean of everlasting bounty is forever stilled, and that out of the Tabernacle of ancient glory the Messengers of God have ceased to be made manifest' would indeed be nothing less than sheer blasphemy 58

far from aiming at the overthrow of the spiritual foundation of the world's religious systems, its avowed, its unalterable purpose is to widen their basis, to restate their fundamentals, to reconcile their aims, to reinvigorate their life, to demonstrate their oneness, to restore the pristine purity of their teachings, to coordinate their functions and to assist in the realization of their highest aspirations. These divinely-revealed religions, as a close observer has graphically expressed it, 'are doomed not to die, but to be reborn . . . "Does not the child succumb in the youth and the youth in the man; yet neither child nor youth perishes?"' 114

there can be no doubt that the decline of religion as a social force, of which the deterioration of religious institutions is but an external phenomenon, is chiefly responsible for so grave, so conspicuous an evil – re: signs of moral downfall 186 'religion,' writes Bahá'u'lláh, 'is the greatest of all means for the establishment of order in the world and for the peaceful contentment of all that dwell therein. The weakening of the pillars of religion hath strengthened the hands of the ignorant and made them bold and arrogant. Verily I say, whatsoever hath lowered the lofty station of religion hath increased the waywardness of the wicked, and the result cannot be but anarchy 186

no wonder, therefore, that when, as a result of human perversity, the light of religion is quenched in men's hearts, and the divinely appointed Robe, designed to adorn the human temple, is deliberately discarded, a deplorable decline in the fortunes of humanity immediately sets in, bringing in its wake all the evils which a wayward soul is capable of revealing. The perversion of human nature, the degradation of human conduct, the corruption and dissolution of human institutions, reveal themselves, under such circumstances, in their worst and most revolting aspects. Human character is debased, confidence is shaken, the nerves of discipline are relaxed, the voice of human conscience is stilled, the sense of decency and shame is obscured, conceptions of duty, of solidarity, of reciprocity and loyalty are distorted, and the very feeling of peacefulness, of joy and of hope is gradually extinguished 187

Malediction – re: Muslim tradition PDC 99

'the way of God and the religion of God have ceased to be of any worth in the eyes of men' [words of Bahá'u'lláh] *God* 112–13

the inestimable value of religion is that when a man is vitally connected with it, through a real and living belief in it and in the Prophet who brought it, he receives a strength greater than his own which helps him to develop his good characteristics and overcome his bad ones. The whole purpose of religion is to change not only our thoughts but our acts; when we believe in God and His Prophets and His teachings, we find we are growing, even though we perhaps thought ourselves incapable of growth and change! (Letter 3.10.43) LG 419

he quite agrees . . . that the dangers facing the modern youth are becoming increasingly grave, and call for immediate solution. But, as experience clearly shows, the remedy to this truly sad and perplexing situation is not to be found in traditional and ecclesiastical religion. The dogmatism of the church has been discarded once for all. What can control youth and save it from the pitfalls of the crass materialism of the age is the power of a genuine, constructive and living Faith such as the one revealed to the world by Bahá'u'lláh. Religion, as in the past, is still the world's sole hope, but not that form of religion which our ecclesiastical leaders strive vainly to preach. Divorced from true religion, morals lose their effectiveness and cease to guide and control men's individual and social life. But when true religion is combined with true ethics, then moral progress becomes a possibility and not a mere ideal. 511–12

The need of our modern youth is for such a type of ethics founded on pure religious faith. Not until these two are rightly combined and brought into full action can there be any hope for the future of the race (Letter 17.4.26)

Remembrance

whoso obeyeth the Remembrance of God and His Book hath in truth obeyed God and His chosen ones *Obey* SB 43

fear ye God and breathe not a word concerning His Most Great Remembrance other than what hath been ordained by God, inasmuch as We have established a separate covenant regarding Him with every 46

Remembrance

Prophet and His followers . . . ere long the veil shall be lifted from your eyes at the appointed time. Ye shall then behold the sublime Remembrance of God, unclouded and vivid

O Thou Mother of the Remembrance! May the peace and salutation of God rest upon thee. Indeed thou hast endured patiently in Him Who is the sublime Self of God. Recognize then the station of thy Son Who is none other than the mighty Word of God *Mother* 52–3

Path – re: Path of the Remembrance is the straight path of God 63

Call – re: from the Burning Bush 69

know thou that the First Remembrance, which is the Primal Will of God, may be likened unto the sun. God hath created Him through the potency of His might, and He hath, from the beginning that hath no beginning, caused Him to be manifested in every Dispensation through the compelling power of His behest, and God will, to the end that knoweth no end, continue to manifest Him according to the good-pleasure of His invincible Purpose 126

Repentance

John, son of Zacharias, said what My Forerunner hath said: 'Saying, repent ye, for the Kingdom of heaven is at hand. I indeed baptize you with water unto repentance, but He that cometh after Me is mightier than I, Whose shoes I am not worthy to bear' ESW 158

repentance is the return from disobedience to obedience. Man, after remoteness and deprivation from God, repents and undergoes purification: and this is a symbol signifying 'O God! make my heart good and pure, freed and sanctified from all save Thy love' SAQ 91

although the ablution of repentance was the institution of John, it was in reality formerly practiced in the religion of God 91–2

Resurrection

the meaning of the 'cleaving of the heavens' – one of the signs that must needs herald the coming of the last Hour, the Day of Resurrection *Cleaving of the Heaven* KI 44

and now, comprehend the meaning of this verse: 'The whole earth shall on the Resurrection Day be but His handful, and in His right hand shall the heavens be folded together. Praise be to Him! and high be He uplifted above the partners they join with him!' 47

by the term 'earth' is meant the earth of understanding and knowledge, and by 'heavens' the heavens of divine Revelation. Reflect thou, how, in one hand, He hath, by His mighty grasp, turned the earth of knowledge and understanding, previously unfolded, into a mere handful, and, on the other, spread out a new and highly exalted earth in the hearts of men, thus causing the freshest and loveliest blossoms, and the mightiest and loftiest trees to spring forth from the illumined bosom of man 48

'what can such expect but that God should come down to them overshadowed with clouds?' A number of the divines, who hold firmly to the letter of the Word of God, have come to regard this verse as one of the signs of that expected resurrection which is born of their idle fancy. This, notwithstanding the fact that similar references have been made in most of the heavenly Books, and have been recorded in all the passages connected with the signs of the coming Manifestation 75–6

as most of the divines have failed to apprehend the meaning of these verses, and have not grasped the significance of the Day of Resurrection, they therefore have foolishly interpreted these verses according to their idle and faulty conception 78 such is their low estate in this, the Day of Resurrection! They have even failed to perceive that were the signs of the Manifestation of God in every age to appear in the visible realm in accordance with the text of established traditions, none could possibly deny or turn away, nor would the blessed be distinguished from the miserable, and the transgressor from the God-fearing 80

you will readily recognize that the terms sovereignty, wealth, life, death, judgment and resurrection, spoken of by the scriptures of old, are not what this generation hath conceived and vainly imagined *Sovereignty* 107

He passed upon the people the verdict of the Last Day, the verdict of resurrection, of judgment, of life, and of death *Qur'án* 114

some have contended that by 'attainment unto the Divine Presence' is meant the 'Revelation' of God in the Day of Resurrection. Should they assert that the 'Revelation' of God signifieth a 'Universal Revelation,' it is clear and evident that such revelation already existeth in all things 139

now, if by 'attainment unto the Presence of God' is meant attainment unto the knowledge of such a revelation, it is evident that all men have already attained unto the presence of the unchangeable Countenance of that peerless King. Why, then, restrict such revelation to the Day of Resurrection? 140–41

attainment unto such presence is possible only in the Day of Resurrection, which is the Day of the rise of God Himself through His all-embracing Revelation *Essence* 143

it hath been demonstrated and definitely established, through clear evidences, that by 'Resurrection' is meant the rise of the Manifestation of God to proclaim His Cause, and by 'attainment unto the divine Presence' is meant attainment unto the presence of His Beauty in the person of His Manifestation 170

the Day of Resurrection is a day on which the sun riseth and setteth like unto any other day. How oft hath the Day of Resurrection dawned, and the people of the land where it occurred did not learn of the event. Had they heard, they would not have believed, and thus they were not told SB 78

when the Apostle of God (Muḥammad) appeared, He did not announce unto the unbelievers that the Resurrection had come, for they could not bear the news *Apostle of God* 78

their hearts are deprived of the power of true insight, and thus they cannot see, while those endowed with the eyes of the spirit circle like moths round the Light of Truth until they are consumed. It is for this reason that the Day of Resurrection is said to be the greatest of all days, yet it is like unto any other day *Bayán* 79

thus on the Day of Resurrection God will ask everyone of his understanding and not of his following in the footsteps of others *Truth* 90

what is intended by the Day of Resurrection is the Day of the appearance of the Tree of divine Reality, but it is not seen that any one of the followers of Shí'ih Islám hath understood the meaning of the Day of Resurrection; rather have they fancifully imagined a thing which with God hath no reality. In the estimation of God and according to the usage of such as are initiated into divine mysteries, what is meant by the Day of Resurrection is this, that from the time of the appearance of Him Who is the Tree of divine Reality, at whatever period and under whatever name, until the moment of His disappearance, is the Day of Resurrection 106–7

and from the inception of the Revelation of the Apostle of God – may the blessing of God be upon Him – till the day of His ascension was the 107

Resurrection of Jesus – peace be upon Him – wherein the Tree of divine Reality appeared in the person of Muḥammad, rewarding by His Word everyone who was a believer in Jesus, and punishing by His Word everyone who was not a believer in Him

and from the moment when the Tree of the Bayán appeared until it disappeareth is the Resurrection of the Apostle of God, as is divinely foretold in the Qur'án; the beginning of which was when two hours and eleven minutes had passed on the eve of the fifth of Jamádíyu'l-Avval, 1260 A.H., which is the year 1270 of the Declaration of the Mission of Muḥammad. This was the beginning of the Day of Resurrection of the Qur'án, and until the disappearance of the Tree of divine Reality is the Resurrection of the Qur'án 107

notwithstanding that in the Qur'án the advent of the Day of Resurrection hath been promised unto all by God *Primal Tree* 108

how vast the number of people who will, on the Day of Resurrection, regard themselves to be in the right, while they shall be accounted as false through the Dispensation of Providence, inasmuch as they will shut themselves out as by a veil from Him Whom God shall make manifest and refuse to bow down in adoration before Him Who, as divinely ordained in the Book, is the Object of their creation 143

say, verily, the criterion by which truth is distinguished from error shall not appear until the Day of Resurrection *Truth* 143

the resurrections of the Divine Manifestations are not of the body. All Their states, Their conditions . . . and Their instructions have a spiritual and divine signification, and have no connection with material things SAQ 103

therefore, we say that the meaning of Christ's resurrection is as follows: the disciples were troubled and agitated after the martyrdom of Christ. The Reality of Christ, which signifies His teachings, His bounties, His perfections and His spiritual power, was hidden and concealed for two or three days after His martyrdom, and was not resplendent and manifest. No, rather it was lost, for the believers were few in number and were troubled and agitated. The Cause of Christ was like a lifeless body; and when after three days the disciples became assured and steadfast, and began to serve the Cause of Christ, and resolved to spread the divine teachings, putting His counsels into practice, and arising to serve Him, the Reality of Christ became resplendent and His bounty appeared; His religion found life; His teachings and His admonitions became evident and visible. In other words, the Cause of Christ was like a lifeless body until the life and the bounty of the Holy Spirit surrounded it. 104–5

Such is the meaning of the resurrection of Christ, and this was a true resurrection. But as the clergy have neither understood the meaning of the Gospels nor comprehended the symbols *Science*

Retribution

this great retributive calamity, for which the world's supreme leaders, both secular and religious, are to be regarded as primarily answerable, as testified by Bahá'u'lláh, should not, if we would correctly appraise it, be regarded solely as a punishment meted out by God to a world that has, for a hundred years, persisted in its refusal to embrace the truth of the redemptive Message proffered to it by the supreme Messenger of God in this day. It should be viewed also, though to a lesser degree, in the light of a divine retribution for the perversity of the human race in general, in casting itself adrift from those elementary principles which must, at all times, govern, and can alone safeguard, the life and progress of mankind. Humanity has, alas, with increasing insistence, preferred, instead of acknowledging and adoring the Spirit of God as embodied in PDC 112

His religion in this day, to worship those false idols, untruths and half-truths, which are obscuring its religions, corrupting its spiritual life, convulsing its political institutions, corroding its social fabric, and shattering its economic structure

Return

strive therefore to comprehend the meaning of 'return' which hath been so explicitly revealed in the Qur'án itself, and which none hath as yet understood. What sayest thou? If thou sayest that Muḥammad was the 'return' of the Prophets of old, as is witnessed by this verse, His Companions must likewise be the 'return' of the bygone Companions, even as the 'return' of the former people is clearly attested by the text of the above-mentioned verses [see also *Testimony* 151–2] KI 151

wherefore, should one of these Manifestations of Holiness proclaim saying: 'I am the return of all the Prophets,' He verily speaketh the truth. In like manner, in every subsequent Revelation, the return of the former Revelation is a fact, the truth of which is firmly established 154

inasmuch as the return of the Prophets of God, as attested by verses and traditions, hath been conclusively demonstrated, the return of their chosen ones also is therefore definitely proven. This return is too manifest in itself to require any evidence or proof. For instance, consider that among the Prophets was Noah. When He was invested with the robe of Prophethood, and was moved by the Spirit of God to arise and proclaim His cause, whoever believed in Him and acknowledged His Faith, was endowed with the grace of a new life. Of him it could be truly said that he was reborn and revived, inasmuch as previous to his belief in God and his acceptance of His Manifestation, he had set his affections on the things of the world, such as attachment to earthly goods, to wife, children, food, drink, and the like, so much so that in the daytime and in the night season his own concern had been to amass riches and procure for himself the means of enjoyment and pleasure [see also *Tradition Transform* 155–6] 154–5

therefore, those who in every subsequent Dispensation preceded the rest of mankind in embracing the Faith of God, who quaffed the clear waters of knowledge at the hand of the divine Beauty, and attained the loftiest summits of faith and certitude, these can be regarded in name, in reality, in deeds, in words, and in rank, as the 'return' of those who in a former Dispensation had achieved similar distinctions 158–9

a return is indeed referred to in the Holy Scriptures, but by this is meant the return of the qualities, conditions, effects, perfections, and inner realities of the lights which recur in every dispensation. The reference is not to specific, individual souls and identities SAB 183

in the same way, if we regard the return of the individual, it is another individual; but if we regard the qualities and perfections, the same have returned. Therefore, when Christ said, 'This is Elias,' He meant: this person is a manifestation of the bounty, the perfections, the character, the qualities and the virtues of Elias. John the Baptist said, 'I am not Elias.' Christ considered the qualities, the perfections, the character and the virtues of both, and John regarded his substance and individuality [see also *Elias* BWF 371] SAQ 134

for what the divine Prophets meant by 'return' is not the return of the essence, but that of the qualities 288

know that the return of Christ for a second time doth not mean what the people believe, but, rather, signifieth the One promised to come after Him TAB 138

the 'Return of John the Baptist' expected by the Christians – re: Báb GPB 58

Revealer

their hearts seem not to be inclined to knowledge and the door thereof, neither think they of its manifestations, inasmuch as in idle fancy they have found the door that leadeth unto earthly riches, whereas in the manifestation of the Revealer of knowledge they find naught but the call to self-sacrifice – re: foolish leaders KI 30

moreover, consider the hardships and bitterness of the lives of these Revealers of the divine Beauty. Reflect, how single-handed and alone they faced the world and all its peoples, and promulgated the Law of God! No matter how severe the persecutions inflicted upon those holy, those precious, and tender Souls, they still remained, in the plenitude of their power, patient, and, despite their ascendancy, they suffered and endured 45

Revelation

the Revelation which, from time immemorial, hath been acclaimed as the Purpose and Promise of all the Prophets of God, and the most cherished Desire of His Messengers, hath now, by virtue of the pervasive Will of the Almighty and at His irresistible bidding, been revealed unto men. The advent of such a Revelation hath been heralded in all the sacred Scriptures G 5

contemplate with thine inward eye the chain of successive Revelations that hath linked the Manifestation of Adam with that of the Báb. I testify before God that each one of these Manifestations hath been sent down through the operation of the Divine Will and Purpose 74

every true Prophet hath regarded His Message as fundamentally the same as the Revelation of every other Prophet gone before Him 78

the measure of the revelation of the Prophets of God in this world, however, must differ. Each and every one of them hath been the Bearer of a distinct Message, and hath been commissioned to reveal Himself through specific acts 78

every Divine Revelation hath been sent down in a manner that befitted the circumstances of the age in which it hath appeared 81

know of a certainty that in every Dispensation the light of Divine Revelation hath been vouchsafed unto men in direct proportion to their spiritual capacity 87

every discerning eye can, in this Day, perceive the dawning light of God's Revelation, and every attentive ear can recognize the Voice that was heard from the Burning Bush 270

anticipate ye the Revelation of Him Who conversed with Moses from the Burning Bush on Sinai *'Alí* ESW 42

Ḥusayn – re: a Revelation Whose Revealer will be He Who revealed Thee 42

this 'oppression' is the essential feature of every Revelation. Unless it cometh to pass, the Sun of Truth will not be made manifest. For the break of the morn of divine guidance must needs follow the darkness of the night of error KI 31

Oppression 31

inasmuch as every subsequent Revelation hath abolished the manners, habits, and teachings that have been clearly, specifically, and firmly established by the former Dispensation, these have accordingly been symbolically expressed in terms of 'sun' and 'moon'. 'That He might prove you, which of you excel in deeds' 39

the 'cleaving of the heaven' – one of the signs that must needs herald the 44 coming of the last Hour, the Day of Resurrection. As He hath said: 'When the heaven shall be cloven asunder.' By 'heaven' is meant the heaven of divine Revelation, which is elevated with every Manifestation, and rent asunder with every subsequent one. By 'cloven asunder' is meant that the former Dispensation is superseded and annulled. I swear by God! That this heaven being cloven asunder is, to the discerning, an act mightier than the cleaving of the skies

that a divine Revelation which for years hath been securely established; beneath whose shadow all who have embraced it have been reared and nurtured; by the light of whose law generations of men have been disciplined; the excellency of whose word men have heard recounted by their fathers; in such wise that human eye hath beheld naught but the pervading influence of its grace, and mortal ear hath heard naught but the resounding majesty of its command – what act is mightier than that such a Revelation should, by the power of God, be 'cloven asunder' and be abolished at the appearance of one soul? Reflect, is this a mightier act than that which these abject and foolish men have imagined the 'cleaving of the heaven' to mean? 44–5

so potent and universal is this revelation, that it hath encompassed all things, visible and invisible. Thus hath He revealed: 'Hath aught else save Thee a power of revelation which is not possessed by Thee, that it could have manifested Thee? Blind is the eye which doth not perceive Thee.' Likewise, hath the eternal King spoken: 'No thing have I perceived, except that I perceived God within it, God before it, or God after it.' Also in the tradition of Kumayl it is written: 'Behold, a light hath shone forth out of the Morn of eternity, and lo! its waves have penetrated the inmost reality of all men' 102

the sentiments and belief of the Jewish people! Thou art surely aware of their idle contention, that all Revelation is ended, that the portals of Divine mercy are closed, that from the day-springs of eternal holiness no sun shall rise again, that the Ocean of everlasting bounty is forever stilled, and that out of the Tabernacle of ancient glory the Messengers of God have ceased to be made manifest. Such is the measure of the understanding of these small-minded, contemptible people [see also *Qur'án*] 137

but in what revelation will they believe, if they reject God and His verses *Verse* 206

His rank excelleth that of all the Prophets, and His Revelation transcendeth the comprehension and understanding of all their chosen ones. A Revelation, of which the Prophets of God, His saints and chosen ones, have either not been informed, or which, in pursuance of God's inscrutable Decree, they have not disclosed, – such a Revelation these mean and depraved people have sought to measure with their own deficient minds, their own deficient learning and understanding. Should it fail to conform to their standards, they straightway reject it. 'Thinkest thou that the greater part of them hear or understand? They are even like unto the brutes! yea, they stray even further from the path!' 244

Covenant – re: next Revelation, next Book SB 87

this doth not mean, however, that one ought not to yield praise unto former Revelations. On no account is this acceptable, inasmuch as it behooveth man, upon reaching the age of nineteen, to render thanksgiving for the day of his conception as an embryo. For had the embryo not existed, how could he have reached his present state 89

that which is intended by 'Revelation of God' is the Tree of divine Truth 112 that betokeneth none but Him, and it is this divine Tree that hath raised and will raise up Messengers, and hath revealed and will ever reveal Scriptures. From eternity unto eternity this Tree of divine Truth hath served and will ever serve as the throne of the revelation and concealment of God among His creatures, and in every age is made manifest through whomsoever he pleaseth. At the time of the revelation of the Qur'án He asserted His transcendent power through the advent of Muḥammad

Revelation, Book of see *John, Beast, Bride, Child, Daniel, Dead, Dragon, Elders, Ḥusayn, Rod, Servant, Sword, Witness, Woe, Woman*

Ridicule

in yet another passage He saith: 'And when he becometh acquainted with any of Our verses he turneth them to ridicule. There is a shameful punishment for them!' The people derisively observed saying: 'Work thou another miracle, and give us another sign!' One would say: 'Make now a part of the heaven to fall down upon us'; and another: 'If this be the very truth from before Thee, rain down stones upon us from heaven.' Even as the people of Israel, in the time of Moses, bartered away the bread of heaven for the sordid things of the earth, these people, likewise, sought to exchange the divinely-revealed verses for their foul, their vile, and idle desires — KI 207–8

Right

how vast the number of people who will, on the Day of Resurrection, regard themselves to be in the right, while they shall be accounted as false through the dispensation of Providence, inasmuch as they will shut themselves out as by a veil from Him Whom God shall make manifest and refuse to bow down in adoration before Him Who, as divinely ordained in the Book, is the Object of their creation — SB 143

Rod [see also *Jesse*]

in brief, the Scripture saith: 'And he that talked with me had a rod made out of gold, that is, a measure, wherewith he measured the city and the gates thereof and the towers thereof.' The meaning is that certain personages guided the people with a staff grown out of the earth, and shepherded them with a rod, like unto the rod of Moses. Others trained and shepherded the people with a rod of iron, as in the dispensation of Muḥammad. And in this present cycle, because it is the mightiest of dispensations, that rod grown out of the vegetable kingdom and that rod of iron will be transformed into a rod of purest gold, taken from out the endless treasure houses in the Kingdom of the Lord. By this rod will the people be trained — SAB 166

at one time the Teachings of God were as a staff, and by this means the Holy Scriptures were spread abroad, the Law of God was promulgated and His Faith established. Then followed a time when the staff of the true Shepherd was as iron. And today, in this new and splendid age, the rod is even as pure gold — 166–7

the 'Man Child,' mentioned in the Book of Revelation, destined to 'rule all nations with a rod of iron' *Man Child* — GPB 58

Rúz-bih

likewise, ere the beauty of Muḥammad was unveiled, the signs of the visible heaven were made manifest. As to the signs of the invisible heaven, there appeared four men who successively announced unto the people the joyful tidings of the rise of that divine Luminary. Rúz-bih, — KI 65 later named Salmán, was honoured by being in their service. As the end of one of these approached, he would send Rúz-bih unto the other, until the fourth who, feeling his death to be nigh, addressed Rúz-bih saying: 'O Rúz-bih! when thou hast taken up my body and buried it, go to Ḥijáz for there the Day-star of Muḥammad will arise. Happy art thou, for thou shalt behold His face!'

Sabbath

whereas this youthful Nazarene, who laid claim to the station of the divine Messiah, had annulled the law of divorce and of the sabbath day – the most weighty of all the laws of Moses *Annul* — KI 18

for example, there is in the Pentateuch a law that if anyone break the Sabbath, he shall be put to death [see also *Torah* SAB 45] *Pentateuch* — SAQ 96

Sackcloth

Witness — SAQ 48

now, Muḥammad was the root, and 'Alí the branch, like Moses and Joshua. It is said they 'are clothed in sackcloth,' meaning that they, apparently, were to be clothed in old raiment, not in new raiment; in other words, in the beginning they would possess no splendor in the eyes of the people, nor would their Cause appear new; for Muḥammad's spiritual Law corresponds to that of Christ in the Gospel, and most of His laws relating to material things correspond to those of the Pentateuch. This is the meaning of the old raiment — 48–9

Sacraments

not one of the sacraments of the Church; not one of the rites and ceremonies which the Christian Fathers have elaborately devised and ostentatiously observed . . . Not one of these did Christ conceive, none did He specifically invest with sufficient authority to either interpret His Word, or to add to what He had not specifically enjoined — WOB 20

Sacrifice

Abraham – re: Ishmael — G 75

know thou that when the Son of Man yielded up His breath to God, the whole creation wept with a great weeping. By sacrificing Himself, however, a fresh capacity was infused into all created things — 85

whereas in the manifestation of the Revealer of knowledge they find naught but the call to self-sacrifice – re: foolish leaders *Revealer* — KI 30

scornfully spoke these words unto Muḥammad: 'Verily, God hath entered into a covenant with us that we are not to credit an apostle until he present us a sacrifice which fire out of heaven shall devour.' The purport of this verse is that God hath covenanted with them that they should not believe in any messenger unless he work the miracle of Abel and Cain, that is, offer a sacrifice, and the fire from heaven consume it; even as they had heard it recounted in the story of Abel, which story is recorded in the scriptures. To this, Muḥammad, answering, said: 'Already have Apostles before me come to you with sure testimonies, and with that of which ye speak. Wherefore slew ye them? Tell me, if ye are men of truth' — 148–9

the Christ sacrificed Himself so that men might be freed from the imperfections of the physical nature *Jesus Christ* — SAQ 118

but Christ, Who is the Word of God, sacrificed Himself. This has two meanings, an apparent and an esoteric meaning. The outward meaning is this: Christ's intention was to represent and promote a Cause which was to educate the human world, to quicken the children of Adam, and — 120–21 to enlighten all mankind; and since to represent such a great Cause – a Cause which was antagonistic to all the people of the world and all the nations and kingdoms – meant that He would be killed and crucified, so Christ in proclaiming His mission sacrificed His life. He regarded the cross as a throne, the wound as a balm, the poison as honey and sugar. He arose to teach and educate men, and so He sacrificed Himself to give the spirit of life. He perished in body so as to quicken others by the spirit

those who declare a wish to suffer much for Christ's sake must prove their sincerity; those who proclaim their longing to make great sacrifices can only prove their truth by their deeds — PT 50

Jesus Christ – re: perfect life of self-sacrifice and devotion — 83

the mystery of sacrifice is that man should sacrifice all his conditions for the divine station of God — TAB 65

Atonement – re: He sacrificed Himself for the life of the world — 543

Abraham – re: martyrdom of Purest Branch — GPB 188

Ṣádiq

the Imám Ṣádiq hath said: 'Servitude is a substance, the essence of which is Divinity' *Divinity* — ESW 111

the Imám Ṣádiq hath said: 'When our Qá'im will arise, the earth will shine with the light of her Lord' *Qá'im* — 112

in another passage, it is related of Ṣádiq, son of Muḥammad, that he spoke the following: 'There shall appear a Youth from Baní-Há<u>sh</u>im, Who will bid the people to plight fealty unto Him. His Book will be a new Book, unto which He shall summon the people to pledge their faith. Stern is His Revelation unto the Arab. If ye hear about Him, hasten unto Him' — KI 241

Knowledge – re: twenty-seven letters — 243–4

such things are to be attributed to naught but the faithlessness of the divines and doctors of the age. Of these, Ṣádiq, son of Muḥammad, hath said: 'The religious doctors of that age shall be the most wicked of the divines beneath the shadow of heaven. Out of them hath mischief proceeded, and unto them it shall return' — 247–8

thus hath Ṣádiq, son of Muḥammad, spoken: 'God verily will test them and sift them.' This is the divine standard, this is the Touchstone of God, wherewith He proveth His servants. None apprehendeth the meaning of these utterances except them whose hearts are assured, whose souls have found favour with God, and whose minds are detached from all else but Him. In such utterances, the literal meaning, as generally understood by the people, is not what hath been intended. Thus it is recorded: 'Every knowledge hath seventy meanings, of which one only is known amongst the people. And when the Qá'im shall arise, He shall reveal unto men all that which remaineth.' He also saith: 'We speak one word, and by it we intend one and seventy meanings; each one of these meanings we can explain' — 255

Saint

saints are men who have freed themselves from the world of matter and who have overcome sin. They live in the world but are not of it, their thoughts being continually in the world of the spirit. Their lives are spent in holiness, and their deeds show forth love, justice and godliness. They are illumined from on high; they are bright and shining lamps in the dark places of the earth. These are the saints of God — PT 60–61

they had been children of darkness, they became sons of God, they became saints! Strive therefore to follow in their steps, leaving all worldly things behind, and striving to attain to the Spiritual Kingdom *Disciple* — 61

Salmán

Rúz-bih – re: Rúz-bih, later named Salmán KI 65

Confederates – re: then Salmán came into the presence of the Prophet and said SDC 26–7

Salvation

We, verily, have come for your sakes, and have borne the misfortunes of the world for your salvation *Evangel* TB 10

leaders of religion, in every age, have hindered their people from attaining the shores of eternal salvation, inasmuch as they held the reins of authority in their mighty grasp *Leader* KI 15

Alpha and Omega – re: the remedy of true salvation SAB 13

Teachings – re: ark of salvation 61

thou didst ask whether, at the advent of the Kingdom of God, every soul was saved. The Sun of Truth hath shone forth in splendour all over the world, and its luminous rising is man's salvation and his eternal life – but only he is of the saved who hath opened wide the eye of his discernment and beheld that glory 191

it is said in the Kitáb-i-Aqdas '. . . whoso is deprived thereof, hath gone astray, though he be the author of every righteous deed.' What is the meaning of this verse? . . . SAQ 238

This blessed verse means that the foundation of success and salvation is the knowledge of God, and that the result of the knowledge of God are the good actions which are the fruits of faith. . .

Therefore, the blessed verse means that good actions alone, without the knowledge of God, cannot be the cause of eternal salvation, everlasting success, and prosperity, and entrance into the Kingdom of God

out of it went forth the earliest tidings of the Message of Salvation – re: Baghdád *Lord of Hosts* GPB 110

Sanctuary

the 'cleansing of the Sanctuary,' prophesied by Daniel and confirmed by Jesus Christ in His reference to 'the abomination of desolation,' had been accomplished – re: declaration of the Báb GPB 58

Satan

and repudiated the manifestations of Satan *Knowledge* KI 123

and whoso shall withdraw from the remembrance of the Merciful, We will chain a Satan unto him, and he shall be his fast companion 257

remember how Adam and the others once dwelt together in Eden. No sooner, however, did a quarrel break out between Adam and Satan than they were, one and all, banished from the Garden, and this was meant as a warning to the human race, a means of telling humankind that dissension – even with the Devil – is the way to bitter loss. This is why, in our illumined age, God teacheth that conflicts and disputes are not allowable, not even with Satan himself SAB 275

the greatest of degradation is to leave the Shadow of God and enter under the shadow of Satan BWF 434

the evil spirit, Satan or whatever is interpreted as evil, refers to the lower nature in man. This baser nature is symbolized in various ways . . . God has never created an evil spirit; all such ideas and nomenclature are symbols expressing the mere human or earthly nature of man. It is an essential condition of the soil of earth that thorns, weeds and fruitless FWU 77

Satan

trees may grow from it. Relatively speaking, this is evil; it is simply the lower state and baser product of nature.

It is evident therefore that man is in need of divine education and inspiration; that the spirit and bounties of God are essential to his development. That is to say, the teachings of Christ and the prophets are necessary for his education and guidance

Science

well versed in every science, yet it is their adherence to the holy Word of God which will determine their faith *Word* — SB 88

but as the clergy have neither understood the meaning of the Gospels nor comprehended the symbols, therefore, it has been said that religion is in contradiction to science, and science in opposition to religion . . . but . . . when the symbol is explained, science in no way contradicts it; but, on the contrary, science and the intelligence affirm it *Symbol* — SAQ 104–5

Scripture

if any man were to meditate on that which the Scriptures, sent down from the heaven of God's holy Will, have revealed, he would readily recognize that their purpose is that all men shall be regarded as one soul, so that the seal bearing the words 'The Kingdom shall be God's' may be stamped on every heart — TB 162

every good thing is of God, and every evil thing is from yourselves. Will ye not comprehend? This same truth hath been revealed in all the Scriptures, if ye be of them that understand — G 149

I testify that, through Thy Revelation, the things hidden in the Books of God have been revealed, and that whatsoever hath been recorded by Thy Messengers in the sacred Scriptures hath been fulfilled — 163

whoso, while reading the Sacred Scriptures, is tempted to choose therefrom whatever may suit him with which to challenge the authority of the Representative of God among men, is, indeed, as one dead — 175

that which can ensure the victory of Him Who is the Eternal Truth, His hosts and helpers on earth, have been set down in the sacred Books and Scriptures, and are as clear and manifest as the sun. These hosts are such righteous deeds, such conduct and character, as are acceptable in His sight — 286

the Day, promised unto you in all the Scriptures, is now come. Fear ye God, and withhold not yourselves from recognizing the One Who is the Object of your creation. Hasten ye unto Him. Better is this for you than the world and all that is therein — 313

Holy Land – re: promises for Holy Land in the Scriptures — 343

Sovereignty – re: of the Manifestation — KI 106–7

they have even failed to realize, all this time, that, in every age, the reading of the scriptures and holy books is for no other purpose except to enable the reader to apprehend their meaning and unravel their innermost mysteries. Otherwise reading, without understanding, is of no abiding profit unto man *Qur'án* — 172

thus will these mysteries be unravelled, not by the aid of acquired learning, but solely through the assistance of God and the outpourings of His grace. 'Ask ye, therefore, of them that have the custody of the Scriptures, if ye know it not' — 192

it is incumbent upon us not to depart from God's irresistible injunction and fixed decree, as revealed in the above-mentioned verse. We should acknowledge the holy and wondrous Scriptures, for failing to do this we — 204 have failed to acknowledge the truth of this blessed verse. For it is evident that whoso hath failed to acknowledge the truth of the Qur'án hath in reality failed to acknowledge the truth of the preceding Scriptures [see also *Book* 202; *Qur'án* 202–3]

what thing of value to mankind has ever come into being which was not first set forth either directly or by implication in the Holy Scriptures? SDC 96

it is easy to read the Holy Scriptures, but it is only with a clean heart and a pure mind that one may understand their true meaning. Let us ask God's help to enable us to understand the Holy Books PT 56–7

the Spirit breathing through the Holy Scriptures is food for all who hunger. God Who has given the revelation to His Prophets will surely give of His abundance daily bread to all those who ask Him faithfully 57

New – re: Jerusalem 84

verily, the mission of all the prophets, the revelation of all the scriptures, the diffusion of the instructions of God and the descent of His law, were all in order to establish agreement and union and to strengthen love and harmony among nations of different customs and thoughts, of diverse beliefs, doctrines, rites and habits; of various classes, tribes and races TAB 596

all the Divine Books and Scriptures have predicted and announced unto men the advent of the Most Great Revelation. None can adequately recount the verses recorded in the Books of former ages which forecast this supreme Bounty, this most mighty Bestowal GPB 100

the Scriptures of past Dispensations celebrate the great jubilee that must needs greet this most great Day of God. Well is it with him that hath lived to see this Day and hath recognized its station WOB 106

all the signs have been revealed; every prophetic allusion hath been manifested. Whatever hath been enshrined in all the Scriptures of the past hath been made evident. To doubt or hesitate is no more possible . . . Time is pressing. The Divine Charger is impatient, and can tarry no longer. Ours is the duty to rush forward and, ere it is too late, win the victory 111–12

'the time foreordained unto the peoples and kindreds of the earth,' affirms Bahá'u'lláh, 'is now come. The promises of God, as recorded in the Holy Scriptures, have all been fulfilled . . . This is the Day which the Pen of the Most High hath glorified in all the Holy Scriptures. There is no verse in them that doth not declare the glory of His holy Name, and no Book that doth not testify unto the loftiness of this most exalted theme PDC 76

Sea

'for the first heaven and the first earth were passed away; and there was no more sea' *Tabernacle* SAQ 67

Seal

on this day the blessed words 'But He is the Apostle of God, and the Seal of the Prophets' have found their consummation in the verse 'The day when mankind shall stand before the Lord of the worlds.' Render thou thanksgiving unto God, for so great a bounty ESW 114

Seal of the Prophets *Muḥammad* KI 162, 169

for verily, 'No vision taketh in Him, but He taketh in all vision.' Notwithstanding all these indubitable facts and lucid statements, they have foolishly clung to the term 'seal,' and remained utterly deprived of the recognition of Him Who is the Revealer of both the Seal and the Beginning, in the day of His presence. 'If God should chastise men for their perverse doings, He would not leave upon the earth a moving thing! But to an appointed time doth He respite them' 170

Seal

were they all to proclaim: 'I am the Seal of the Prophets,' they verily utter the truth *Messenger* 179

even as thou dost witness how the people of the Qur'án, like unto the people of old, have allowed the words 'Seal of the Prophets' to veil their eyes *Qur'án* 213

Seclusion [see also *Monk*]

O people of the earth! Living in seclusion or practising asceticism is not acceptable in the presence of God. It behoveth them that are endued with insight and understanding to observe that which will cause joy and radiance. Such practices as are sprung from the loins of idle fancy or are begotten of the womb of superstition ill beseem men of knowledge. In former times and more recently some people have been taking up their abodes in the caves of the mountains while others have repaired to graveyards at night. Say, give ear unto the counsels of this Wronged One. Abandon the things current amongst you and adopt that which the faithful Counsellor biddeth you. Deprive not yourselves of the bounties which have been created for your sake TB 71

Second Coming

it is clear to all that Christ came from heaven, although apparently He came from the womb of Mary. At the first coming He came from heaven, though apparently from the womb; in the same way, also, at His second coming He will come from heaven, though apparently from the womb. The conditions that are indicated in the Gospel for the second coming of Christ are the same as those that were mentioned for the first coming, as we said before SAQ 110–11

Isaiah – re: prophecies about second coming 111

the second coming of Christ also will be in like manner: the signs and conditions which have been spoken of all have meanings, and are not to be taken literally [see also *Star* 111–12] 111

Seed

He Who, both on His father's and mother's side, was of the seed of the illustrious Fáṭimih, and Who was a descendant of the Imám Ḥusayn, the most eminent among the lawful successors of the Prophet of Islám, proceeded, in fulfillment of Islamic traditions, to visit the Kaaba GPB 9

Seek

what 'oppression' is more grievous than that a soul seeking the truth, and wishing to attain unto the knowledge of God, should know not where to go for it and from whom to seek it? *Oppression* KI 31

whensoever he hath fulfilled the conditions implied in the verse: 'Whoso maketh efforts for Us,' he shall enjoy the blessing conferred by the words: 'In Our ways shall We assuredly guide him' 195

Seir*

thou didst write as to Seir. Seir is a locality near Nazareth in Galilee SAB 171

Self

so fierce is this fire of self burning within them, that at every moment they seem to be afflicted with fresh torments *Smoke* KI 77

Jesus Christ – re: self-sacrifice PT 83

* 'Rose up from Seir unto them' refers to a mountain in Galilee and means the Christian Dispensation – re: Deut. 33:2 *Muḥammad* n.

Seraph

and foolishly expect to hear the trumpet-sound of the Seraph of God who is but one of His servants! Hath not the Seraph himself, the angel of the Judgment Day, and his like been ordained by Muḥammad's own utterance? *Muḥammad* KI 116

Serpent

the meaning of the serpent is attachment to the human world. This attachment of the spirit to the human world led the soul and spirit of Adam from the world of freedom to the world of bondage and caused Him to turn from the Kingdom of Unity to the human world. When the soul and spirit of Adam entered the human world, He came out from the paradise of freedom and fell into the world of bondage. From the height of purity and absolute goodness, He entered into the world of good and evil SAQ 123–4

no, it means what has already been said: Adam is the spirit of Adam, and Eve is His soul; the tree is the human world, and the serpent is that attachment to this world which constitutes sin, and which has infected the descendants of Adam. Christ by His holy breezes saved men from this attachment and freed them from this sin 126

Servant

'servitude is a substance, the essence of which is Divinity' – re: words of Ṣádiq *Divinity* ESW 111

and were they to say: 'We are the servants of God,' this also is a manifest and indisputable fact. For they have been made manifest in the uttermost state of servitude, a servitude the like of which no man can possibly attain *Messenger* KI 179

Apostleship or Servitude *Voice* 181

and few of My servants are the thankful *Leaders* 229

then it is said: 'They are standing before God,' meaning that they are standing in the service of God, and educating the creatures of God, such as the barbarous nomad Arab tribes of the Arabian peninsula, whom they educated in such a way that in those days they reached the highest degree of civilization, and their fame and renown became worldwide – re: Muḥammad and 'Alí – Rev. 11 SAQ 49

Seven Martyrs of Ṭihrán

– re: martyrdom GPB 47

Seven Goats *Qá'im* 48

Seven Valleys

a treatise that may well be regarded as His greatest mystical composition, designated as the 'Seven Valleys,' which He wrote in answer to the questions of Shaykh Muḥyi'd-Dín, the Qáḍí of Khániqayn, in which He describes the seven stages which the soul of the seeker must needs traverse ere it can attain the object of its existence GPB 140

Sháh-Bahrám

to the Zoroastrians the promised Sháh-Bahrám – re: Bahá'u'lláh GPB 94

a period of three thousand years of conflict and contention must needs precede the advent of the World-Savior Sháh-Bahrám, Who would triumph over Ahriman and usher in an era of blessedness and peace *Zoroaster* 95

that same Voice, identifying itself with the voice of the promised Sháh-Bahrám, has declared: 'O high priests!' *High Priest* PDC 77

Sharí‘ah Law

the annulment of the Sharí‘ah Law and the promulgation of a universal Civil Code – re: following the abolition of the Sultanate and fall of the Caliphate WOB 175

Shí‘ih

reflect, O Shaykh, upon the Shí‘ih sect. How many the edifices which they reared with the hands of idle fancies and vain imaginings, and how numerous the cities which they built! At length those vain imaginings were converted into bullets and aimed at Him Who is the Prince of the world. Not one single soul among the leaders of that sect acknowledged Him in the Day of His Revelation! Whenever His blessed name was mentioned, all would say: ‘May God hasten the joy His coming will bring!’ On the day of the Revelation of that Sun of Truth, however, all, as hath been observed, have exclaimed, saying: ‘May God hasten His chastisement!’ He Who was the Essence of being and the Lord of the seen and unseen they suspended, and committed what made the Tablet to weep, and the Pen to groan, and the cries of the sincere to break forth, and the tears of the favoured ones to flow ESW 119–20

meditate on the Shí‘ih sect. For twelve hundred years they have cried ‘O Qá’im!’ *Qá’im* 163

– re: description of Shí‘ih priesthood at the time of the appearance of the Báb GPB 4

deliberately refused to purchase life by that mere lip-denial which, under the name of taqíyyih, Shí‘ih Islám had for centuries recognized as a wholly justifiable and indeed commendable subterfuge in the hour of peril – re: Seven Martyrs of Ṭihrán [*see* Qur’án 16:106] 47

to Shí‘ih Islám the return of the Imám Ḥusayn – re: Bahá’u’lláh 94

Shimr

and had he seen Mullá Ḥusayn of Bushrúyih, he would have been convinced that the Chief of Martyrs (Imám Ḥusayn) had returned to earth; and had he witnessed my deeds, he would assuredly have said: ‘This is Shimr come back with sword and lance . . .’ In truth, I know not what had been shown to these people, or what they had seen, that they came forth to battle with such alacrity and joy . . . The imagination of man cannot conceive the vehemence of their courage and valor – re: companions at Shaykh Ṭabarsí GPB 81

Sign

the meaning of the ‘cleaving of the heaven’ – one of the signs that must needs herald the coming of the last Hour, the Day of Resurrection *Cleave* KI 44

and now, concerning His words: ‘And then shall appear the sign of the Son of man in heaven.’ By these words it is meant that when the sun of the heavenly teachings hath been eclipsed, the stars of the divinely-established laws have fallen, and the moon of true knowledge – the educator of mankind – hath been obscured; when the standards of guidance and felicity have been reversed, and the morn of truth and righteousness hath sunk in night, then shall the sign of the Son of man appear in heaven. By ‘heaven’ is meant the visible heaven [see also *Star*] 61–2

before the revelation of each of the Mirrors reflecting the divine Essence, the signs heralding their advent must needs be revealed in the visible heaven as well as in the invisible, wherein is the seat of the sun of knowledge, of the moon of wisdom, and of the stars of understanding 66 and utterance. The sign of the invisible heaven must needs be revealed in the person of that perfect man who, before each Manifestation appeareth, educateth, and prepareth the souls of men for the advent of the divine Luminary, the Light of the unity of God amongst men

and are still oblivious of the fact that all the signs foretold have come to pass, that the way of God's holy Cause hath been revealed, and the concourse of the faithful, swift as lightning, are, even now, passing upon that way, whilst these foolish divines wait expecting to witness the signs foretold *Qá'im* 83

were they to be questioned concerning those signs that must needs herald the revelation and rise of the sun of the Muḥammadan Dispensation, to which We have already referred, none of which have been literally fulfilled, and were it to be said to them: 'Wherefore have ye rejected the claims advanced by Christians and the peoples of other faiths and regard them as infidels,' knowing not what answer to give, they will reply: 'These Books have been corrupted and are not, and never have been, of God.' Reflect: the words of the verses themselves eloquently testify to the truth that they are of God. A similar verse hath been also revealed in the Qur'án, were ye of them that comprehend. Verily I say, throughout all this period they have utterly failed to comprehend what is meant by corrupting the text 83–4

this, because they treated Our signs as lies, and were heedless of them – re: stray – in error *Path* 105

in our Qá'im there shall be four signs from four Prophets, Moses, Jesus, Joseph, and Muḥammad *Biḥár* 254

Significance

furthermore, how numerous are those peoples of divers beliefs, of conflicting creeds, and opposing temperaments, who, through the reviving fragrance of the Divine springtime, breathing from the Riḍván of God, have been arrayed with the new robe of divine Unity, and have drunk from the cup of His singleness! KI 112–13
This is the significance of the well-known words: 'The wolf and the lamb shall feed together.' Behold the ignorance and folly of those who, like the nations of old, are still expecting to witness the time when these beasts will feed together in one pasture

Testimony – re: significance of 'return' 151–2

Sin

confession of sins and transgressions before human beings is not permissible TB 24

so long as one's nature yieldeth unto evil passions, crime and transgression will prevail 70

if ye become aware of a sin committed by another, conceal it, that God may conceal your own sin ESW 55

'arise from thy bed; thy sins are forgiven thee' *Jesus Christ* KI 133–4

'on that day shall neither man nor spirit be asked of his Sin?' Dost thou not realize that by 'asking is not meant asking by tongue or speech, even as the verse itself doth indicate and prove it?' For afterward it is said: 'By their countenance shall the sinners be known, and they shall be seized by their forelocks and their feet' *Qur'án* 173

'woe to every lying sinner, who heareth the verses of God recited to him, and then, as though he heard them not, persisteth in proud disdain! Apprise him of a painful punishment' *Verse* 206–7

Sin

baptism is a symbol of repentance from all sin [discourse on] *Baptism* SAQ 91

all sin comes from the demands of nature, and these demands, which arise from the physical qualities, are not sins with respect to the animals, while for man they are sin 119

this attachment of the soul and spirit to the human world, which is sin, was inherited by the descendants of Adam *Adam* 124

Serpent – re: Adam is the spirit of Adam, and Eve is His soul 126

the sin in Adam is relative to His position. Although from this attachment there proceed results, nevertheless, attachment to the earthly world, in relation to attachment to the spiritual world, is considered as a sin. The good deeds of the righteous are the sins of the Near Ones. This is established. So bodily power is not only defective in relation to spiritual power; it is weakness in comparison 126

how often the Prophets of God and His supreme Manifestations in Their prayers confess Their sins and faults! This is only to teach other men, to encourage and incite them to humility and meekness, and to induce them to confess their sins and faults. For these Holy Souls are pure from every sin and sanctified from faults [see also *Gospel*] 170

Sinai

Mount Sinai is astir with the joy of beholding Our countenance. She hath lifted her enthralling voice in glorification of her Lord, saying: 'O Lord! I sense the fragrance of Thy garment. Methinks Thou art near, invested with the signs of God TB 15

present thyself before Me that thou mayest hear the mysteries which were heard by the Son of 'Imrán (Moses) upon the Sinai of Wisdom ESW 86

hast thou ears, O world, wherewith to hear the voice of the True One, and to judge equitably this Revelation Which, as soon as it appeared, Sinai exclaimed: 'He that discoursed upon Me is come with evident signs and resplendent tokens 173

Moses – re: revelation to Moses in Sinai KI 54

and when the appointed hour hath struck, do Thou, by the leave of God, the All-Wise, reveal from the heights of the Most Lofty and Mystic Mount a faint, an infinitesimal glimmer of Thy impenetrable Mystery, that they who have recognized the radiance of the Sinaic Splendour may faint away and die as they catch a lightning glimpse of the fierce and crimson Light that envelops Thy Revelation. And God is, in very truth, Thine unfailing Protector SB 53

hearken unto the Voice of Thy Lord calling from Mount Sinai, 'Verily there is no God but Him, and I am the Most Exalted One Who hath been veiled in the Mother Book according to the dispensations of Providence' 70

indeed We conversed with Moses by the leave of God from the midst of the Burning Bush in the Sinai and revealed an infinitesimal glimmer of Thy Light upon the Mystic Mount and its dwellers, whereupon the Mount shook to its foundations and was crushed into dust 72

I am the Flame of that supernal Light that glowed upon Sinai in the gladsome Spot, and lay concealed in the midst of the Burning Bush *Burning Bush* 74

the light hath shone forth, and radiance floodeth Mount Sinai, and a gentle wind bloweth from over the gardens of the Ever-Forgiving Lord; the sweet breaths of the spirit are passing by, and those who lay buried in the grave are rising up – and still do the heedless slumber on in their tombs SAB 14

upon Mount Sinai, Moses entered into a Covenant regarding the Messiah *Moses* 207

Smoke

likewise, He saith: 'On the day when the heaven shall give out a palpable smoke, which shall enshroud mankind: this will be an afflictive torment.' The All-Glorious hath decreed these very things, that are contrary to the desires of wicked men, to be the touchstone and standard whereby He proveth His servants, that the just may be known from the wicked, and the faithful distinguished from the infidel. The symbolic term 'smoke' denotes grave dissensions, the abrogation and demolition of recognized standards, and the utter destruction of their narrow-minded exponents. What smoke more dense and overpowering than the one which hath now enshrouded all the peoples of the world, which hath become a torment unto them, and from which they hopelessly fail to deliver themselves, however much they strive KI 76–7

Socrates

Philosophy SDC 77

among these philosophers was the famous Socrates. He visited the Holy Land and studied with the prophets of Israel, acquiring principles of their philosophical teaching and a knowledge of their advanced arts and sciences FWU 95

Sodom

the great city, which spiritually is called Sodom and Egypt *Dead* SAQ 51–2

Solomon

it is furthermore a matter of record in numerous historical works that the philosophers of Greece such as Pythagoras, acquired the major part of their philosophy, both divine and material, from the disciples of Solomon *Philosophy* SDC 77

a disaster that razed to its foundations the Temple of Solomon PDC 96

Son

Father – re: Word which the Son concealed TB 11

know thou that when the Son of Man yielded up His breath to God *Jesus Christ* G 85–6

these are the melodies, sung by Jesus, Son of Mary, in accents of majestic power in the Riḍván of the Gospel *Gospel* KI 24

and they shall see the Son of man coming in the clouds of heaven *Jesus Christ* 25

Sign – re: 'and then shall appear the sign of the Son of man in heaven' 61–2

and then shall all the tribes of the earth mourn, and they shall see the Son of man coming in the clouds of heaven with power and great glory.' These words signify that in those days men will lament the loss of the Sun of the divine beauty, of the Moon of knowledge, and of the Stars of divine wisdom. Thereupon, they will behold the countenance of the promised One, the adored Beauty, descending from heaven and riding upon the clouds. By this is meant that the divine Beauty will be made manifest from the heaven of the will of God, and will appear in the form of the human temple 66–7

Jesus Christ – re: Son of Man; statements of Jesus 132–3, 134

[Jesus] told them, 'I am God's Son, and verily in the inmost being of His only Son, His mighty Ward, clearly revealed with all His attributes, all His perfections, standeth the Father' *Messiah* SAB 40

Father – re: the meaning of the words that the Father is in the Son 42

wherefore did the Messiah bid them to keep this hidden, 'till the Son of Man were risen from the dead' *Transfiguration* 162

Son

as He Himself hath said, . . . 'The Son of Man is in heaven' *Heaven* 168

all the people of the world are buried in the graves of nature, or are slumbering, heedless and unaware. Just as Christ saith: 'I may come when you are not aware. The coming of the Son of Man is like the coming of a thief into a house, the owner of which is utterly unaware' 198–9

as Christ found existence through the Spirit of God, He called Himself the Son of God *Jesse* SAQ 62–3

Disciple – re: they became sons of God PT 61

His Holiness Christ, addressing the believers, uttereth the following in the Gospel: 'Be awake lest the Son of Man come and find ye asleep!' TAB 631

Sorcery

and likewise, He saith: 'And had We sent down unto Thee a Book written on parchment, and they had touched it with their hands, the infidels would surely have said 'This is naught but palpable sorcery' *Book* KI 219

Soul

He hath endowed every soul with the capacity to recognize the signs of God. How could He, otherwise, have fulfilled His testimony unto men G 105

how could such Souls have consented to surrender themselves unto their enemies if they believed all the worlds of God to have been reduced to this earthly life 158

know, verily, that the soul is a sign of God, a heavenly gem whose reality the most learned of men have failed to grasp, and whose mystery no mind, however acute, can ever hope to unravel 158

he is indeed a captive who hath not recognized the Supreme Redeemer, but hath suffered his soul to be bound, distressed and helpless, in the fetters of his desires 168

if a soul of his own accord advances toward God he will be accepted at the Threshold of Oneness, for such a one is free of personal considerations, of greed and selfish interests, and he has taken refuge within the sheltering protection of his Lord. He will become known among men as trustworthy and truthful, temperate and scrupulous, high-minded and loyal, incorruptible and God-fearing. In this way the primary purpose in revealing the Divine Law – which is to bring about happiness in the after life and civilization and the refinement of character in this – will be realized SDC 46

Salvation – re: whether every soul was saved SAB 191

Serpent – re: Eve, the soul of Adam SAQ 126

regarding the 'two wings' of the soul: These signify wings of ascent. One is the wing of knowledge, the other of faith, as this is the means of the ascent of the human soul to the lofty station of divine perfections BWF 382

Sovereignty

and now, to resume Our argument concerning the question: Why is it that the sovereignty of the Qá'im, affirmed in the text of recorded traditions, and handed down by the shining stars of the Muḥammadan Dispensation, hath not in the least been made manifest? Nay, the contrary hath come to pass. Have not His disciples and companions been afflicted of men? Are they not still the victims of the fierce opposition of their enemies? Are they not today leading the life of abased and impotent mortals? Yea, the sovereignty attributed to the Qá'im and spoken of in the scriptures, is a reality, the truth of which none can doubt. This sovereignty, however, is not the sovereignty which the minds of men have falsely imagined [see also *Prophet* 106–7; *Qá'im* 107] KI 106 you will readily recognize that the terms sovereignty, wealth, life, death, judgment and resurrection, spoken of by the scriptures of old, are not what this generation hath conceived and vainly imagined. Nay, by sovereignty is meant that sovereignty which in every dispensation resideth within, and is exercised by, the person of the Manifestation, the Day-star of Truth. That sovereignty is the spiritual ascendancy which He exerciseth to the fullest degree over all that is in heaven and on earth, and which in due time revealeth itself to the world in direct proportion to its capacity and spiritual receptiveness [see also *Muḥammad* 108] 107–8

such is His earthly sovereignty, the evidences of which thou dost on every side behold. This sovereignty must needs be revealed and established either in the lifetime of every Manifestation of God or after His ascension unto His true habitation in the realms above 110–11

the following is an evidence of the sovereignty exercised by Muḥammad, the Day-star of Truth *Muḥammad* 111–12

Our purpose in setting forth these truths hath been to demonstrate the sovereignty of Him Who is the King of kings. Be fair: Is this sovereignty which, through the utterance of one Word, hath manifested such pervading influence, ascendancy, and awful majesty, is this sovereignty superior, or is the worldly dominion of these kings of the earth who, despite their solicitude for their subjects and their help of the poor, are assured only of an outward and fleeting allegiance, while in the hearts of men they inspire neither affection nor respect 123–4

Lord – re: all comparison falleth short 124

know, therefore, O questioning seeker, that earthly sovereignty is of no worth, nor will it ever be, in the eyes of God and His chosen Ones. Moreover, if ascendancy and dominion be interpreted to mean earthly supremacy and temporal power, how impossible will it be for thee to explain these verses: 'And verily Our host shall conquer.' 'Fain would they put out God's light with their mouths: But God hath willed to perfect His light, albeit the infidels abhor it.' 'He is the Dominant, above all things.' Similarly, most of the Qur'án testifieth to this truth 125–6

Spirit [see also *Jesus Christ*]

consider those who rejected the Spirit when He came unto them with manifest dominion. How numerous the Pharisees who had secluded themselves in synagogues in His name, lamenting over their separation from Him, and yet when the portals of reunion were flung open and the divine Luminary shone resplendent from the Dayspring of Beauty, they disbelieved in God, the Exalted, the Mighty. They failed to attain His presence, notwithstanding that His advent had been promised them in the Book of Isaiah as well as in the Books of the Prophets and the Messengers TB 9–10

and now, meditate upon this most great convulsion, this grievous test. Notwithstanding all these things, God conferred upon that essence of the Spirit, Who was known amongst the people as fatherless, the glory of Prophethood, and made Him His testimony unto all that are in heaven and on earth – re: Christ *Mary* KI 57

likewise, in the verse concerning the 'Spirit,' He saith: 'And they will ask Thee of the Spirit. Say, "The Spirit proceedeth at My Lord's command."' *Muḥammad* 182–3

in this wise did they object to that Sun of Truth, although that Spirit of God was indeed the One promised in the Torah. But as they did not understand the meaning of these signs, they crucified the Word of God SAB 45

Father – re: Comforting Spirit 59

Spirit

it would destroy the spiritual life *Beast* SAQ 51

Adam is the cause of man's physical life; but the Reality of Christ – that is to say, the Word of God – is the cause of spiritual life. It is 'a quickening spirit,' meaning that all the imperfections which come from the requirements of the physical life of man are transformed into human perfections by the teachings and education of that spirit. Therefore, Christ was a quickening spirit, and the cause of life in all mankind 119–20

Life – re: words of Christ 223–4

likewise, the human spirit has its limitations. It cannot comprehend the phenomena of the Kingdom transcending the human station, for it is a captive of powers and life forces which have their operation upon its own plane of existence, and it cannot go beyond that boundary. PUP 58

There is, however, another Spirit which may be termed the Divine, to which Jesus Christ refers when He declares that man must be born of its quickening and baptized with its living fire. Souls deprived of that Spirit are accounted as dead, though they are possessed of the human spirit. Jesus Christ has pronounced them dead inasmuch as they have no portion of the Divine Spirit

for the body of Christ was crucified and vanished, but the Spirit of Christ is always pouring upon the contingent world, and is manifest before the insight of the people of assurance TAB 193–4

this is that of which it is said in the Gospel: One must be baptized with fire and spirit *Lord of Hosts* 515

the indwelling Spirit of God which, in the Apostolic Age of the Church, animated its members, the pristine purity of its teachings, the primitive brilliancy of its light, will, no doubt, be reborn and revived as the inevitable consequence of this redefinition of its fundamental verities, and the clarification of its original purpose WOB 185

the Founder of the Christian Faith is designated by Bahá'u'lláh as the 'Spirit of God,' is proclaimed as the One Who 'appeared out of the breath of the Holy Ghost,' and is even extolled as the 'Essence of the Spirit' PDC 109

Spiritual

it is a spiritual world, a divine world, and the centre of the Sovereignty of God *Kingdom* SAQ 241

spiritual discoveries are of two kinds: one kind is of the imagination and is only the assertion of a few people; the other kind resembles inspiration, and this is real – such are the revelations of Isaiah, of Jeremiah and of St. John, which are real 251

the visions of the Prophets are not dreams; no, they are spiritual discoveries and have reality 251

the comprehension of that other life depends on our spiritual birth PT 94

all the Manifestations of God and His Prophets have taught the same truths and given the same spiritual law . . . It is therefore evident that whilst the spiritual law never alters, the practical rules must change their application with the necessities of the time. The spiritual aspect of religion is the greater, the more important of the two, and this is the same for all time, it never changes 142

Staff see *Rod*

Standard

one of the great events which is to occur in the Day of the manifestation of that Incomparable Branch (Bahá'u'lláh) is the hoisting of the Standard SAQ 65 of God among all nations. By this is meant that all nations and kindreds will be gathered together under the shadow of this Divine Banner, which is no other than the Lordly Branch itself,* and will become a single nation. Religious and sectarian antagonism, the hostility of races and peoples, and differences among nations, will be eliminated. All men will adhere to one religion, will have one common faith, will be blended into one race, and become a single people. All will dwell in one common fatherland, which is the planet itself

hoisted the Black Standard – re: Mullá Ḥusayn *Muḥammad* GPB 38

Star

a star will appear in the heaven, heralding unto its people the advent of that most great light. In like manner, in the invisible heaven a star shall be made manifest who, unto the peoples of the earth, shall act as a harbinger of the break of that true and exalted Morn. These twofold signs, in the visible and the invisible heaven, have announced the Revelation of each of the Prophets of God, as is commonly believed KI 62

Magi – re: story of the Nativity 64

among other things it is said that the stars will fall upon the earth. The stars are endless and innumerable, and modern mathematicians have established and proved scientifically that the globe of the sun is estimated to be about one million and a half times greater than the earth, and each of the fixed stars to be a thousand times greater than the sun. If these stars were to fall upon the surface of the earth, how could they find place there? It would be as though a thousand million of Himalaya mountains were to fall upon a grain of mustard seed . . . SAQ 111–12

It is clear and evident that these signs have symbolic signification, and that they are not literal. They are fully explained in the Kitáb-i-Íqán. Refer to it

Station

man's highest station, however, is attained through faith in God in every Dispensation and by acceptance of what hath been revealed by Him, and not through learning *Man* SB 89

Steadfastness

steadfastness in the Faith is a sure testimony, and a glorious evidence of the truth. Even as the 'Seal of the Prophets' hath said: 'Two verses have made Me old.' Both these verses are indicative of constancy in the Cause of God. Even as He saith: 'Be thou steadfast as thou hast been bidden' KI 233

Storm

the Covenant of Bahá'u'lláh had, by such acts as these, and others too numerous to recount, been manifestly violated. Another blow, stunning in its first effects, had been administered to the Faith and had caused its structure momentarily to tremble. The storm foreshadowed by the writer of the Apocalypse had broken. The 'lightnings,' the 'thunders,' the 'earthquake' which must needs accompany the revelation of the 'Ark of His Testament,' had all come to pass – re: perfidy of Mírzá Muḥammad-'Alí GPB 249

Succession

the Old Testament and the Holy Books which preceded it, in which the actual precepts uttered by the Prophet Himself are non-existent; unlike the Gospels, in which the few sayings attributed to Jesus Christ afford no GPB 213–14

* see *Jesse* n.

clear guidance regarding the future administration of the affairs of His Faith; unlike even the Qur'án which, though explicit in the laws and ordinances formulated by the Apostle of God, is silent on the all-important subject of the succession, the Kitáb-i-Aqdas, revealed from first to last by the Author of the Dispensation Himself, not only preserves for posterity the basic laws and ordinances on which the fabric of His future World Order must rest, but ordains, in addition, to the function of interpretation which it confers upon His Successor, the necessary institutions through which the integrity and unity of His Faith can alone be safeguarded

in the Muḥammadan Revelation, however, although His Faith as compared with that of Christ was, so far as the administration of His Dispensation is concerned, more complete and more specific in its provisions, yet in the matter of succession, it gave no written, no binding and conclusive instructions to those whose mission was to propagate His Cause. For the text of the Qur'án, the ordinances of which regarding prayer, fasting, marriage, divorce, inheritance, pilgrimage, and the like, have after the revolution of thirteen hundred years remained intact and operative, gives no definite guidance regarding the Law of Succession, the source of all the dissensions, the controversies, and schisms which have dismembered and discredited Islám WOB 21

can any passage of the Qur'án, which in respect to its legal code, its administrative and devotional ordinances marks already a notable advance over previous and more corrupted Revelations, be construed as placing upon an unassailable basis the undoubted authority with which Muḥammad had, verbally and on several occasions, invested His successor? 145

there is certainly an element of truth at the basis of the organization of the Christian Church. For instance, the primacy of Peter and his right to succession after Jesus have been established by the latter, though only orally and not in an explicit and definite language. The real reason why Christ did not make some explicit statement regarding His succession is not known, and cannot be known. For how can we, poor humans, claim to unravel the mysteries of God's mind and purpose, and to grasp the inscrutable dispensations of His providence. The utmost we can do is to give some explanations, but these must necessarily fail to give the fundamental reason to the problem we seek to solve (Letter 28.12.36) LG 373

Suffer

those who declare a wish to suffer much for Christ's sake must prove their sincerity; those who proclaim their longing to make great sacrifices can only prove their truth by their deeds. Job proved the fidelity of his love for God by being faithful through his great adversity, as well as during the prosperity of his life. The apostles of Christ who steadfastly bore all their trials and sufferings – did they not prove their faithfulness? Was not their endurance the best proof? PT 50

through suffering he will attain to an eternal happiness which nothing can take from him. The apostles of Christ suffered: they attained eternal happiness 178

Summon

this exalted tradition is attested and substantiated by these words which He hath revealed: 'The day when the Summoner shall summon to a stern business' [see also *Tradition*] KI 238–9

the divine call of the celestial Herald from beyond the Veil of Glory, 239 summoning mankind to renounce utterly all the things to which they cleave, is repugnant to their desire; and this is the cause of the bitter trials and violent commotions which have occurred [see also *People Truth*]

Sun

'Islám is heaven; fasting is its sun, prayer, its moon' *Islám* KI 40

'sun' and 'moon' *Symbol* 41–2

a woman clothed with the sun, and the moon under her feet, and upon her head a crown of twelve stars *Woman* SAQ 68

Sunní

the 'Mihdí' (One Who is guided) awaited by the Sunnís – re: the Báb GPB 58

to the entire company of the ecclesiastical leaders of Sunní Islám in Constantinople He addresses a specific message in the Súriy-i-Múlúk in which He denounces them as heedless and spiritually dead; reproaches them for their pride and for failing to seek His presence; unveils to them the full glory and significance of His Mission; affirms that their leaders, had they been alive, would have 'circled around Him'; condemns them as 'worshippers of names' and lovers of leadership; and avows that God will find naught acceptable from them unless they 'be made new' in His estimation 175

a formal, a complete and permanent separation of the Turkish state from the Sunní faith was proclaimed; the Sharí'ah canonical Law was annulled; ecclesiastical institutions were disendowed; a civil code was promulgated; religious orders were suppressed; the Sunní hierarchy was dissolved; the Arabic tongue, the language of the Prophet of Islám, fell into disuse, and its script was superseded by the Latin alphabet; the Qur'án itself was translated into Turkish 228

Superstition [see also *Dogma*]

Jesus Christ – re: the forms and superstitions which appeared PUP 86

Súrih

in another passage He likewise saith: 'And if ye be in doubt as to that which We have sent down to Our Servant, then produce a Súrih like it, and summon your witnesses, beside God, if ye are men of truth.' Behold, how lofty is the station, and how consummate the virtue, of these verses which He hath declared to be His surest testimony, His infallible proof KI 204–5

Sword

those words, sharp as the sword of God, have separated the faithful from the infidel, and severed father from son *Muḥammad* KI 111–12

'I am a Prophet by the sword' *Tradition* SDC 44

Christ Jesus summoned all mankind to amity and peace. Unto Peter He said: 'Put up thy sword into the sheath.' Such was the bidding and counsel of the Lord Christ; and yet today the Christians one and all have drawn their swords from out the scabbard. How wide is the discrepancy between such acts and how clear the Gospel text SAB 247–8

Jesus Christ said, 'Put up thy sword into the sheath.' The meaning is that warfare is forbidden and abrogated; but consider the Christian wars which took place afterward *Christianity* PUP 86

Symbol

Annul – re: in symbolic language KI 41

it is unquestionable that in every succeeding Revelation the 'sun' and 'moon' of the teachings, laws, commandments, and prohibitions which 41–2 have been established in the preceding Dispensation, and which have overshadowed the people of that age, become darkened, that is, are exhausted, and cease to exert their influence. Consider now, had the people of the Gospel recognized the meaning of the symbolic terms 'sun' and 'moon,' had they sought, unlike the froward and perverse, enlightenment from Him Who is the Revealer of divine knowledge, they would have surely comprehended the purpose of these terms, and would not have become afflicted and oppressed by the darkness of their selfish desires

the symbolic term 'smoke' denotes grave dissensions, the abrogation and demolition of recognized standards, and the utter destruction of their narrow-minded exponents *Smoke* 76

man cannot free himself from the rage of the carnal passions except by the help of the Holy Spirit. That is why He says baptism with the spirit, with water and with fire is necessary, and that it is essential – that is to say, the spirit of divine bounty, the water of knowledge and life, and the fire of the love of God. Man must be baptized with this spirit, this water and this fire so as to become filled with the eternal bounty. Otherwise, what is the use of baptizing with material water? No, this baptism with water was a symbol of repentance, and of seeking forgiveness of sins. SAQ 92

But in the cycle of Bahá'u'lláh there is no longer need of this symbol; for its reality, which is to be baptized with the spirit and love of God, is understood and established

Bread – re: meaning of the Last Supper 99

in the same way, His resurrection from the interior of the earth is also symbolical; it is a spiritual and divine fact, and not material; and likewise His ascension to heaven is a spiritual and not material ascension *Resurrection* 104

such is the meaning of the resurrection of Christ, and this was a true resurrection. But as the clergy have neither understood the meaning of the Gospels nor comprehended the symbols, therefore, it has been said that religion is in contradiction to science, and science in opposition to religion, as, for example, this subject of the ascension of Christ with an elemental body to the visible heaven is contrary to the science of mathematics. But when the truth of this subject becomes clear, and the symbol is explained, science in no way contradicts it; but, on the contrary, science and the intelligence affirm it 104–5

therefore, this story of Adam and Eve who ate from the tree, and their expulsion from Paradise, must be thought of simply as a symbol 123

water is the cause of life, and when Christ speaks of water, He is symbolizing that which is the cause of Everlasting Life. PT 82

This life-giving water of which He speaks is like unto fire, for it is none other than the Love of God, and this Love means life to our souls.

By the fire of the Love of God the veil is burnt which separates us from the Heavenly Realities, and with clear vision we are enabled to struggle onward and upward, ever progressing in the paths of virtue and holiness, and becoming the means of light to the world

this is a prophetic symbol, meaning the coming again of the Divine Teaching to enlighten the hearts of men – re: New Jerusalem 84

Ark – re: Ark and Flood LG 378

Tabernacle

Zion ESW 145

so in chapter 21, verses 1, 2 and 3 of the Revelation of St. John, it is said: SAQ 67–8

'And I saw a new heaven and a new earth: for the first heaven and the first earth were passed away; and there was no more sea. And I John saw the holy city, new Jerusalem, coming down from God out of heaven, prepared as a bride adorned for her husband. And I heard a great voice out of heaven saying, Behold, the tabernacle of God is with men, and He will dwell with them, and they shall be His people, and God Himself shall be with them, and be their God.'

Notice how clear and evident it is that the first heaven and earth signify the former Law. For it is said that the first heaven and earth have passed away and there is no more sea – that is to say, that the earth is the place of judgment, and on this earth of judgment there is no sea, meaning that the teachings and the Law of God will entirely spread over the earth, and all men will enter the Cause of God, and the earth will be completely inhabited by believers; therefore, there will be no more sea, for the dwelling place and abode of man is the dry land. In other words, at that epoch the field of that Law will become the pleasure-ground of man. Such earth is solid; the feet do not slip upon it

in it the Tabernacle of the promised 'Lord of Hosts' was first erected – re: Ba<u>gh</u>dád: the 'Abode of Peace' *Father* GPB 110

in that same year Bahá'u'lláh's tent, the 'Tabernacle of Glory,' was raised on Mt. Carmel, 'the Hill of God and His Vineyard,' the home of Elijah, extolled by Isaiah as the 'mountain of the Lord,' to which 'all nations shall flow' 194

Tale

'these words of his are but tales of the Ancients' – re: Muḥammad *Poet* KI 212

Ṭáhirih

still others must have recalled with throbbing hearts the Islamic tradition foreshadowing the appearance of Fáṭimih herself unveiled while crossing the Bridge (Ṣirát) on the promised Day of Judgment – re: Ṭáhirih's announcement at Bada<u>sh</u>t GPB 32

undeterred, unruffled, exultant with joy, Ṭáhirih arose, and, without the least premeditation and in a language strikingly resembling that of the Qur'án, delivered a fervid and eloquent appeal to the remnant of the assembly, ending it with this bold assertion: 'I am the Word which the Qá'im is to utter, the Word which shall put to flight the chiefs and nobles of the earth!' Thereupon, she invited them to embrace each other and celebrate so great an occasion. 32–3

On that memorable day the 'Bugle' mentioned in the Qur'án was sounded, the 'stunning trumpet-blast' was loudly raised, and the 'Catastrophe' came to pass – re: Bada<u>sh</u>t

Teachings

then wilt thou see that today these heavenly Teachings are the remedy for a sick and suffering world, and a healing balm for the sores on the body of mankind. They are the spirit of life, the ark of salvation, the magnet to draw down eternal glory, the dynamic power to motivate the inner self of man SAB 61

in the coming of Christ, the divine teachings were given in accordance with the infancy of the human race. The teachings of Bahá'u'lláh have the same basic principles, but are according to the stage of the maturity of the world and the requirements of this illumined age BWF 400

Temple

it is clear and evident to thee that all the Prophets are the Temples of the Cause of God, Who have appeared clothed in divers attire G 51

Temple

'and the temple of God was opened in heaven' means that the divine Jerusalem is found, and the Holy of Holies has become visible *Holy* SAQ 59

'and the temple of God was opened in heaven' means also that by the diffusion of the divine teachings, the appearance of these heavenly mysteries, and the rising of the Sun of Reality, the doors of success and prosperity will be opened in all directions, and the signs of goodness and heavenly benedictions will be made plain 60

'and there was seen in His temple the ark of His Testament' *Testament* 60

consider how the first institute of His Holiness Moses, after His exodus from Egypt, was the 'Tent of Martyrdom' which He raised and which was the traveling Temple. It was a tent which they pitched in the desert, wherever they abode, and worshipped in it. Likewise, after His Holiness Christ – may the spirit of the world be a sacrifice to Him! – the first institute by the disciples was a Temple. They planned a church in every country BWF 418

Ten Commandments

now, consider: Christ frequently repeated that the Ten Commandments in the Pentateuch were to be followed, and He insisted that they should be maintained *Jesus Christ* SAQ 165

Test

whereupon, a profound dismay seized suddenly the companions of the Prophet. Their faith was shaken severely. So great was their alarm, that many of them, discontinuing their prayers, apostatized their faith. Verily, God caused not this turmoil, but to test and prove His servants. Otherwise, He, the ideal King, could easily have left the Qiblih unchanged, and could have caused Jerusalem to remain the Point of Adoration unto His Dispensation, thereby withholding not from that holy city the distinction of acceptance which had been conferred upon it [see also *Qiblih*] KI 50–51

yea, such things as throw consternation into the hearts of all men come to pass only that each soul may be tested by the touchstone of God, that the true may be known and distinguished from the false *Qiblih* 52

but inasmuch as the divine Purpose hath decreed that the true should be known from the false, and the sun from the shadow, He hath, therefore, in every season sent down upon mankind the showers of tests from His realm of glory 53

it is evident that at no time have they been proof against those tests that have been sent by God *Leaders* 82–3

the trials of Peter tested his fidelity. Tests are benefits from God, for which we should thank Him PT 50

as ye have heard of the former times, when Christ – glory be to Him! – appeared, . . . the winds of tests blew, the thunder of temptation descended and hosts of people surrounded the houses of the friends; then the weak ones were shaken and were misled after once being guided BWF 395

but these tests were like unto the fire and his holiness Job was like unto pure gold *Job* TAB 655

Testament

'and there was seen in His temple the ark of His Testament' – that is to say, the Book of His Testament will appear in His Jerusalem, the Epistle of the Covenant will be established, and the meaning of the Testament and of the Covenant will become evident. The renown of God will overspread the East and West, and the proclamation of the Cause of SAQ 60–61

God will fill the world. The violators of the Covenant will be degraded and dispersed, and the faithful cherished and glorified, for they cling to the Book of the Testament and are firm and steadfast in the Covenant.
'And there were lightnings, and voices, and thunderings, and an earthquake, and great hail,' meaning that after the appearance of the Book of the Testament there will be a great storm, and the lightnings of the anger and the wrath of God will flash, the noise of the thunder of the violation of the Covenant will resound, the earthquake of doubts will take place, the hail of torments will beat upon the violators of the Covenant, and even those who profess belief will fall into trials and temptations

in short, from these Holy Utterances and those of His Holiness Christ, it becomes clear, evident and proved, that man should associate with people who are firm in the Covenant and Testament, and befriend the pure ones; because bad associates bring about infection of bad qualities BWF 437

Testimony

but having weighed the testimony of God by the standard of their own knowledge, gleaned from the teachings of the leaders of their faith, and found it at variance with their limited understanding, they arose to perpetrate such unseemly acts KI 15

and made Him His testimony unto all that are in heaven and on earth – re: Christ *Spirit* 57

and if thou dwellest in the land of testimony, content thyself with that which He, Himself, hath revealed: 'Is it not enough for them that We have sent down unto Thee the Book?' This is the testimony which He, Himself, hath ordained; greater proof than this there is none, nor ever will be: 'This proof is His Word; His own Self, the testimony of His truth 91–2

and if thou deniest this, thou hast surely repudiated the truth of the Qur'án, the surest testimony of God unto men. In like manner, endeavour to grasp the significance of 'return,' 'revelation,' and 'resurrection,' as witnessed in the days of the Manifestations of the divine Essence, that thou mayest behold with thine own eyes the 'return' of the holy souls into sanctified and illumined bodies, and mayest wash away the dust of ignorance, and cleanse the darkened self with the waters of mercy flowing from the Source of divine Knowledge; that perchance thou mayest, through the power of God and the light of divine guidance, distinguish the Morn of everlasting splendour from the darksome night of error 151–2

that Book constitutes an abiding testimony to its people after Muḥammad *Book* 201

Muḥammad, Himself, as the end of His mission drew nigh, spoke these words: 'Verily, I leave amongst you My twin weighty testimonies: The Book of God and My Family' *Book* 201–2

no testimony mightier than the testimony of their revealed verses hath ever appeared upon the earth *Verse* 206

and yet, the unfailing testimony of God to both the East and the West is none other than the Qur'án. Were it beyond the comprehension of men, how could it have been declared as a universal testimony unto all people? 210

and beyond a shadow of doubt no evidence is set forth by God save through the One Who is appointed as His supreme Testimony *Proof* SB 109

should a Christian contend, 'How can I deem the Qur'án a testimony while I am unable to understand it?' such a contention would not be acceptable. Likewise the people of the Qur'án disdainfully observe, 'We 120 are unable to comprehend the eloquence of the verses in the Bayán, how can we regard it as a testimony?' Whoever uttereth such words, say unto him, 'O thou untutored one! By what proof hast thou embraced the Religion of Islám? Is it the Prophet on whom thou hast never set eyes? Is it the miracles which thou hast never witnessed? If thou hast accepted Islám unwittingly, wherefore hast thou done so? But if thou hast embraced the Faith by recognizing the Qur'án as the testimony, because thou hast heard the learned and the faithful express their powerlessness before it, or if thou hast, upon hearing the divine verses and by virtue of thy spontaneous love for the True Word of God, responded in a spirit of utter humility and lowliness – a spirit which is one of the mightiest signs of true love and understanding – then such proofs have been and will ever be regarded as sound

that which God testifieth is none other than what His supreme Testimony testifieth. Were all the peoples of the world to testify unto a thing and were He to testify unto another, His testimony will be regarded as God's testimony, while aught else but Him hath been and will ever be as naught; for it is through His might that a thing assumeth existence 121

'and when they shall have finished their testimony' means when they should have performed that which they are commanded, and should have delivered the divine message, promoting the Law of God and propagating the heavenly teachings, to the intent that the signs of spiritual life might be manifest in souls, and the light of the virtues of the world of humanity might shine forth, until complete development should be brought about among the nomad tribes – re: Muḥammad and 'Alí SAQ 51

Text see *Corruption of the Text*

Theosophy

a Bahá'í cannot at the same time be a Theosophist; many theosophists have become believers and very enlightened ones, but as we do not believe in reincarnation we obviously cannot be active as Theosophists and Bahá'ís at the same time DND 140

Times

His Day he, furthermore, had described as 'the times of refreshing,' 'the times of restitution of all things, which God hath spoken by the mouth of all His holy Prophets since the world began' *Peter* GPB 96

Torah

Text KI 86–7

they will then, of course, insist that the Torah has been tampered with, and in proof will quote the Qur'ánic verse: 'They pervert the text of the Word of God.' It is, however, known where such distortion has occurred, and is a matter of record in critical texts and commentaries *Abraham* SDC 29–30

Prophet – re: events at the advent of 74–5

the Revelation of Christ, according to the clear text of the Torah, will be attested by certain signs, and so long as these signs have not appeared, whoso layeth claim to be a Messiah is an imposter – re: saying of the Jews SAB 44

another of the conditions is this: the promulgation of all the laws of the Torah; yet this man has abrogated these laws, and has even broken the sabbath day, although it is the clear text of the Torah that whosoever layeth claim to prophethood and revealeth miracles and breaketh the sabbath day, must be put to death 45

Jews – re: [Jesus] was indeed the One promised in the Torah 45 the description in the Torah being allegorical *Jesus Christ* 45

but there are some teachings of the past, such as those of the Torah, which cannot be carried out at the present day. It is the same with the other religions and the tenets of the various sects and the different parties 306

even as it is recorded in the Torah and confirmed in history that when the Jews became fettered by empty forms and imitations, the wrath of God became manifest. When they forsook the foundations of the law of God, Nebuchadnezzar came and conquered the Holy Land. He killed and made captive the people of Israel, laid waste the country and populous cities and burned the villages PUP 363

he destroyed Jerusalem, despoiled the great Temple, desecrated the Holy of Holies and burned the Torah, the heavenly book of Scriptures – re: Nebuchadnezzar 363

in the Torah there are many commands concerning the punishment of a murderer. It would not be allowable or possible to carry out these ordinances today 365

Jesus Christ – re: He declared that the Torah, the Old Testament, was the Book of God 366

through the instrumentality of Christ, through the translation of the New Testament, the little volume of the Gospel, the Old Testament, the Torah, has been translated into six hundred languages and spread everywhere in the world. The names of the Hebrew prophets became household words among the nations, who believed that the children of Israel were, verily, the chosen people of God 366–7

therefore, Christ really promulgated Judaism; for He was a Jew and not opposed to the Jews. He did not deny the Prophethood of Moses; on the contrary, He proclaimed and ratified it. He did not invalidate the Torah; He spread its teachings. That portion of the ordinances of Moses which concerned transactions and unimportant conditions underwent transformation, but the essential teachings of Moses were revoiced and confirmed by Christ without change. He left nothing unfinished or incomplete 367

you may not know that the first address of Muḥammad to His tribe was the statement, 'Verily, Moses was a Prophet of God, and the Torah is a Book of God. Verily, O ye people, ye must believe in the Torah, in Moses and the prophets. Ye must accept all the prophets of Israel as valid 367

'at one time,' writes Bahá'u'lláh, 'We address the people of the Torah and summon them unto Him Who is the Revealer of verses, Who hath come from Him Who layeth low the necks of men PDC 76

Torment

'Alí – re: those who have put the kindred of 'Alí to death SB 5

erelong We will, in very truth, torment such as waged war against Ḥusayn (Imám Ḥusayn), in the Land of the Euphrates *Ḥusayn* 70

Touchstone

furthermore, the sign of truth and falsehood is designated and appointed in the Book. By this divinely-appointed touchstone, the claims and pretensions of all men must needs be assayed, so that the truthful may be known and distinguished from the imposter. This touchstone is no other than this verse: 'Wish for death, if ye are men of truth' KI 227

behold how the divine Touchstone hath, according to the explicit text of the Book, separated and distinguished the true from the false. Notwithstanding, they are still oblivious of this truth, and in the sleep of 228 heedlessness, are pursuing the vanities of the world, and are occupied with thoughts of vain and earthly leadership

'God verily will test them and sift them.' This is the divine standard, this is the Touchstone of God, wherewith He proveth His servants *Ṣádiq* 255

Tradition

likewise, a lengthy tradition is attributed to Abí-'Abdi'lláh *Qá'im* ESW 112

and in the tradition of Mufaḍḍal it is said: 'The Qá'im will lean His back against the Sanctuary, and will stretch forth His hand, and lo, it shall be snow-white but unhurt. And He shall say: "This is the hand of God, the right hand of God, that cometh from God, at the command of God!"' In whichever manner these traditions are interpreted, in that same manner let them also interpret that which the Most Sublime Pen hath set down [see also *'Alí Abí-'Abdi'lláh*] 112

this heedless one hath now clung to the practice of Rawḍih-khání (traditional lamentation for the Imám Ḥusayn). He – I swear by God – is in evident error. For it is the belief of this people that during the Revelation of the Qá'im, the Imáms – may the peace of God be upon them – have arisen from their sepulchres. This verily is the truth, and no doubt is there about it – re: opens with reference to Mírzá Yaḥyá 121–2

whensoever the light of Manifestation of the King of Oneness settleth upon the throne of the heart and soul, His shining becometh visible in every limb and member. At that time the mystery of the famed tradition gleameth out of the darkness: 'A servant is drawn unto Me in prayer until I answer him; and when I have answered him, I become the ear wherewith he heareth . . .' For thus the Master of the house hath appeared within His home, and all the pillars of the dwelling are ashine with His light SV 22

Divines – re: identified with 'people of the Book' who have repelled their fellow-men from the straight path of God KI 16

for this reason, in all chronicles and traditions reference hath been made unto these things, namely that iniquity shall cover the surface of the earth and darkness shall envelop mankind. As the traditions referred to are well known, and as the purpose of this servant is to be brief, He will refrain from quoting the text of these traditions [see also *Oppression*] 31–2

Law – re: traditions testify to the laws of prayer and fasting as most fundamental and binding [see also *Prayer* 39] 38

they have even failed to perceive that were the signs of the Manifestation of God in every age to appear in the visible realm in accordance with the text of the established traditions, none could possibly deny or turn away, nor would the blessed be distinguished from the miserable, and the transgressor from the God-fearing – re: Jesus [see also *Prophecy*] 80

as they have literally interpreted the Word of God, and the sayings and traditions of the Letters of Unity, and expounded them according to their own deficient understanding, they have therefore deprived themselves and all their people of the bountiful showers of the grace and mercies of God. And yet they bear witness to this well-known tradition: 'Verily Our Word is abstruse, bewilderingly abstruse' 82

they confidently assert that such traditions as indicate the advent of the expected Qa'ím have not yet been fulfilled, whilst they themselves have failed to inhale the fragrance of the meaning of these traditions *Qa'ím* 83

They are the Treasuries of divine knowledge, and the Repositories of celestial wisdom. Through them is transmitted a grace that is infinite, and by them is revealed the light that can never fade. Even as He hath 100 said: 'There is no distinction whatsoever between Thee and Them; except that they are Thy servants, and are created of Thee.' This is the significance of the tradition: 'I am He, Himself, and He is I, myself'

also in the tradition of Kumayl it is written: 'Behold, a light hath shone forth out of the Morn of eternity, and lo! its waves have penetrated into the inmost reality of all men' *Revelation* 102

have they not heard the well-known tradition: 'When the Qa'ím ariseth, that day is the Day of Resurrection?' *Qa'ím* 144

Return – re: Prophets and chosen ones 154

aside from these things, before his partaking of the reviving waters of faith, he had been so wedded to the traditions of his forefathers, and so passionately devoted to the observance of their customs and laws, that he would have preferred to suffer death rather than violate one letter of those superstitious forms and manners current amongst his people. Even as the people have cried: 'Verily we found our fathers with a faith, and verily, in their footsteps we follow' 155

Ḥusayn – re: 'end', 'return' and 'creation without beginning or end' 167–8

how strange! These people with one hand cling to those verses of the Qur'án and those traditions of the people of certitude which they have found to accord with their inclinations and interests, and with the other reject those which are contrary to their selfish desires. 'Believe ye then part of the Book, and deny part? How could ye judge that which ye understand not?' 168–9

Knowledge – re: 'Knowledge is a light which God sheddeth into the heart of whomsoever He willeth 183–4

methinks, he had forgotten the well-known tradition which sayeth: 'Knowledge is all that is knowable; and might and power, all creation' 185

its guidance can never err, its testimony no other testimony can excel. All other traditions, all other books and records, are bereft of such distinction, inasmuch as both the traditions and they that have spoken them are confirmed and proven solely by the text of that Book. Moreover, the traditions themselves grievously differ, and their obscurities are manifold – re: Qur'án 201

although many traditions have been revealed by that Source of Prophethood and Mine of divine Guidance – re: Qur'án *Book* 201–2

could they seek to justify themselves by saying: 'We have clung to a certain tradition, and not having beheld the literal fulfillment thereof, we have therefore raised such cavils against the Embodiments of divine Revelation, and kept remote from the law of God?' 220

among them is the tradition, 'And when the Standard of Truth is made manifest, the people of both the East and the West curse it.' . . . those people who, despite the love and yearning for truth which they profess, curse the followers of Truth when once He hath been made manifest. To this truth the above-mentioned tradition beareth witness. It is evident that the reason for such behaviour is none other than the annulment of those rules, customs, habits, and ceremonials to which they have been subjected. Otherwise, were the Beauty of the Merciful to comply with those same rules and customs, which are current amongst the people, and were He to sanction their observances, such conflict and mischief would in no wise be made manifest in the world 238

this exalted tradition is attested and substantiated by these words which He hath revealed: 'The day when the Summoner shall summon to a stern business' 238–9 consider the way of the people. They ignore these well-founded traditions all of which have been fulfilled, and cling unto those of doubtful validity, and ask why these have not been fulfilled 239

notwithstanding all the verses of the Qur'án, and the recognized traditions, which are all indicative of a new Faith, a new Law, and a new Revelation, this generation still awaiteth in expectation of beholding the promised One who should uphold the Law of the Muḥammadan Dispensation. The Jews and the Christians in like manner uphold the same contention 239–40

among the utterances that foreshadow a new Law and a new Revelation *New* 240

behold, how, notwithstanding these and similar traditions, they idly contend that the laws formerly revealed, must in no wise be altered. And yet, is not the object of every Revelation to effect a transformation . . . that shall manifest itself both outwardly and inwardly, that shall affect both its inner life and external conditions? For if the character of mankind be not changed, the futility of God's universal Manifestation would be apparent 240–41

Ṣádiq – re: traditions of the Imám Ṣádiq about 'a Youth from Baní-Há<u>sh</u>im' [see also *Aválim*] 241

notwithstanding all these evident and significant traditions, all these unmistakable and undisputed allusions, the people have rejected the immaculate Essence of knowledge and of holy utterance, and have turned unto the exponents of rebellion and error. Despite these recorded traditions and revealed utterances, they speak only that which is prompted by their own selfish desires *Contrary* 242

and now, consider this other tradition, and observe how all these things have been foretold. In 'Arba'in' it is recorded: "Out of Baní-Há<u>sh</u>im there shall come forth a Youth Who shall reveal new laws. He shall summon the people unto Him, but none will heed His call. Most of His enemies will be the divines. His bidding they will not obey, but will protest saying: 'This is contrary to that which hath been handed down unto us by the Imáms of the Faith."' In this day, all are repeating these very same words, utterly unaware that He is established upon the throne of 'He doeth whatsoever He willeth,' and abideth upon the seat of 'He ordaineth whatsoever He pleaseth' 242–3

how, We wonder, do they explain the aforementioned tradition, a tradition which, in unmistakable terms, foreshadoweth the revelation of things inscrutable, and the occurrence of new and wondrous events in His Day? Such marvellous happenings kindle so great a strife amongst the people, that all the divines and doctors sentence Him and His companions to death, and all the peoples of the earth arise to oppose Him – re: Letters of Knowledge 244–5

Káfí 245

and yet no one hath paused to reflect that if the promised Qá'im should reveal the laws and ordinances of a former Dispensation, why then should such traditions have been recorded *Qá'im* 245–6

Zawrá' – re: martyrdoms at Rayy 246–7

and now observe how, according to this tradition, Zawrá' is no other but the land of Rayy. In that place His companions have been with great suffering put to death, and all these holy beings have suffered martyrdom at the hands of the Persians, as recorded in the tradition 247

wherefore, then, do not these grovelling, worm-like men pause to meditate upon these traditions, all of which are manifest as the sun in its noon-tide 247 glory? For what reason do they refuse to embrace the Truth, and allow certain traditions, the significance of which they have failed to grasp, to withhold them from the recognition of the Revelation of God and His Beauty, and to cause them to dwell in the infernal abyss [see also *Ṣádiq* 247–8]

notwithstanding all these consummate verses, these unmistakable allusions, which have been revealed in the 'Most weighty Revelation,' the Trust of God amongst men, and despite these evident traditions, each more manifest than the most explicit utterance, the people have ignored and repudiated their truth, and have held fast to the letter of certain traditions which, according to their understanding, they have found inconsistent with their expectations, and the meaning of which they have failed to grasp. They have thus shattered every hope, and deprived themselves of the pure wine of the All-Glorious, and the clear and incorruptible waters of the immortal Beauty 253

according to the tradition, Mufaḍḍal asked Ṣádiq saying: 'What of the sign of His manifestation, O my master?' He made reply: 'In the year sixty, His Cause shall be made manifest, and His Name shall be proclaimed' 253–4

mention of the sorrows, the imprisonment and afflictions inflicted upon that Essence of divine virtue hath been made in the former traditions *Biḥár* 254

have they forgotten the celebrated ḥadí̱th (Holy Tradition): 'Seek after knowledge, even unto China'? It is certain that the people of China are, in the sight of God, among the most rejected of men, because they worship idols and are unmindful of the omniscient Lord *Christianity* SDC 26

Abraham – re: contents of traditional and written history 29–30

an authoritative Tradition states: 'As for him who is one of the learned: he must guard himself, defend his faith, oppose his passions and obey the commandments of his Lord. It is then the duty of the people to pattern themselves after him *Learned* 34

the Traditions 'I am a Prophet by the sword' and 'I am commanded to threaten the lives of the people until they say, "There is none other God but God"' referred to the idolaters of the Days of Ignorance, who in their blindness and bestiality had sunk below the level of human beings. A faith born of sword thrusts could hardly be relied upon, and would for any trifling cause revert to error and unbelief. After the ascension of Muḥammad, and His passing to 'the seat of truth, in the presence of the potent King,' the tribes around Medina apostatized from their Faith, turning back to the idolatry of pagan times 44

traditional accounts *Imám* 55

Prophet – re: histories of 74–5

the third method of understanding is by tradition – that is, through the text of the Holy Scriptures – for people say, 'In the Old and New Testaments, God spoke thus.' This method equally is not perfect, because the traditions are understood by the reason. As the reason itself is liable to err, how can it be said that in interpreting the meaning of the traditions it will not err, for it is possible for it to make mistakes, and certainty cannot be attained. This is the method of the religious leaders; whatever they understand and comprehend from the text of the books is that which their reason understands from the text, and not necessarily the real truth; for the reason is like a balance, and the meanings contained in the text of the Holy Books are like the thing which is weighed. If the balance is untrue, how can the weight be ascertained? SAQ 298

Tradition

if a man would succeed in his search after truth, he must, in the first place, shut his eyes to all the traditional superstitions of the past. PT 135

The Jews have traditional superstitions, the Buddhists and the Zoroastrians are not free from them, neither are the Christians! All religions have gradually become bound by tradition and dogma

we should, therefore, detach ourselves from the external forms and practices of religion. We must realize that these forms and practices, however beautiful, are but garments clothing the warm heart and the living limbs of Divine truth. We must abandon the prejudices of tradition if we would succeed in finding the truth at the core of all religions 136

a man who had committed to memory no less than thirty thousand traditions – re: Vaḥíd GPB 11

little did he imagine that by this very act he would be instrumental in fulfilling the authentic tradition ascribed to the Prophet of Islám regarding the inevitability of that which should come to pass in Á<u>dh</u>irbáyján – re: Grand Vizir exiling Báb to Máh-kú 18

still others must have recalled with throbbing hearts the Islamic tradition foreshadowing the appearance of Fáṭimih herself unveiled while crossing the Bridge (Ṣirát) – re: Ṭáhirih appearing unveiled at the conference of Bada<u>sh</u>t 32

who else could be meant by this tradition, called Ḥadí<u>th</u>-i-Jábir, recorded in the Káfí, and authenticated by Bahá'u'lláh in the Kitáb-i-Íqán, which, in indubitable language, sets forth the signs of the appearance of the promised Qá'im? 'His saints shall be abased in His time, and their heads shall be exchanged as presents, even as the heads of the Turk and the Daylamite are exchanged as presents; they shall be slain and burned, and shall be afraid, fearful and dismayed; the earth shall be dyed with their blood, and lamentation and wailing shall prevail amongst their women; these are My saints indeed' [see *Brother*] 80

not only have the peoples of the earth ignored, and some of them even assailed, a Faith which is at once the essence, the promise, the reconciler, and the unifier of all religions, but they have drifted away from their own religions, and set up on their subverted altars other gods wholly alien not only to the spirit but to the traditional forms of their ancient faiths PDC 112

Traditor

those who, in the first two centuries of the Christian era, 'purchased an ignominious life by betraying the holy Scriptures into the hands of the infidels,' the scandalous conduct of those bishops who were thereby branded as traditors WOB 56

Transfiguration

thou didst ask as to the transfiguration of Jesus, with Moses and Elias and the Heavenly Father on Mount Tabor, as referred to in the Bible. This occurrence was perceived by the disciples with their inner eye, wherefore it was a secret hidden away, and was a spiritual discovery of theirs. Otherwise, if the intent be that they witnessed physical forms, that is, witnessed that transfiguration with their outward eyes, then there were many others at hand on that plain and mountain, and why did they fail to behold it? And why did the Lord charge them that they should tell no man? It is clear that this was a spiritual vision and a scene of the Kingdom. Wherefore did the Messiah bid them to keep this hidden, 'till the Son of Man were risen from the dead,' – that is, until the Cause of God should be exalted, and the Word of God prevail, and the reality of Christ rise up SAB 162

Transform

these same people, though wrapt in all these veils of limitation, and despite the restraint of such observances, as soon as they drank the immortal draught of faith, from the cup of certitude, at the hand of the Manifestation of the All-Glorious, were so transformed that they would renounce for His sake their kindred, their substance, their lives, their beliefs, yea, all else save God! So overpowering was their yearning for God, so uplifting their transports of ecstatic delight, that the world and all that is therein faded before their eyes into nothingness. Have not this people exemplified the mysteries of 'rebirth' and 'return'? KI 155–6

Tree

so much so that Pharaoh and his people finally arose and exerted their utmost endeavour to extinguish with the waters of falsehood and denial the fire of that sacred Tree *Pharaoh* G 19

the 'Tree that belongeth neither to the East nor to the West' *Moses* KI 54

had the divine standard laid down in the Qur'án been truly observed, adverse judgements would not have been pronounced against Him Who is the Tree of divine Truth *Qur'án* SB 102

from eternity unto eternity this Tree of divine Truth hath served and will ever serve as the throne of the revelation and concealment of God among His creatures, and in every age is made manifest through whomsoever He pleaseth. At the time of the revelation of the Qur'án He asserted His transcendent power through the advent of Muḥammad 112

the Tree of Life, of which mention is made in the Bible, is Bahá'u'lláh SAB 57

the tree of good and evil signifies the human world *Adam* [see also *Serpent* 126] SAQ 123

the tree of life is the highest degree of the world of existence: the position of the Word of God, and the supreme Manifestation. Therefore, that position has been preserved; and, at the appearance of the most noble supreme Manifestation, it became apparent and clear. For the position of Adam, with regard to the appearance and manifestation of the divine perfections, was in the embryonic condition; the position of Christ was the condition of maturity and the age of reason; and the rising of the Greatest Luminary was the condition of the perfection of the essence and of the qualities. This is why in the supreme Paradise the tree of life is the expression for the center of absolutely pure sanctity – that is to say, of the divine supreme Manifestation 124

this tree of life was the position of the Reality of Christ; through His manifestation it was planted and adorned with everlasting fruits 124

from the seed of reality religion has grown into a tree which has put forth leaves and branches, blossoms and fruit. After a time this tree has fallen into a condition of decay. The leaves and blossoms have withered and perished; the tree has become stricken and fruitless. It is not reasonable that man should hold to the old tree, claiming that its life forces are undiminished, its fruit unequaled, its existence eternal. The seed of reality must be sown again in human hearts in order that a new tree may grow therefrom and new divine fruits refresh the world PUP 141–2

Trial

it is clear, then, that tests and trials are, for sanctified souls, but God's bounty and grace, while to the weak, they are a calamity, unexpected and sudden SAB 182

even those who profess belief will fall into trials and temptations *Testament* SAQ 60–61

Trial

Test – re: the trials of Peter PT 50

sometimes at the height of the crisis itself, more often when the crisis was past, the significance of these trials has manifested itself to men's eyes, and the necessity of such experiences has been demonstrated, far and wide and beyond the shadow of a doubt, to both friend and foe. Seldom, if indeed at any time, has the mystery underlying these portentous, God-sent upheavals remained undisclosed, or the profound purpose and meaning of their occurrence been left hidden from the minds of men GPB 61–2

Tribes

the barbarous cruelty, the gross idolatry and immorality, which had for so long been the most distressing features of the tribes of Arabia and brought such shame upon them when Muḥammad arose to proclaim His Message in their midst – re: of Arabia ADJ 14

Trinity

verily, Christ is Our Word which We communicated unto Mary; and let no one say what the Christians term as 'the third of three', inasmuch as it would amount to slandering the Remembrance Who, as decreed in the Mother Book, is invested with supreme authority. Indeed God is but one God, and far be it from His glory that there should be aught else besides Him SB 60–61

– re: discourse on Trinity SAQ 113–15

but as to the question of the Trinity, know . . . there are necessarily three things: The Giver of the Grace, and the Grace, and the Recipient of the Grace; the Source of the Effulgence, and the Effulgence, and the Recipient of the Effulgence TAB 117

the question of the Trinity, since the time of His Holiness Christ until now, is the belief of the Christians, and to the present time all the learned among them are perplexed and confounded. All have confessed that the question is beyond the grasp of reason, for three cannot become one, nor one three 512

but there are, in the Gospels, clear expressions indicative of Trinity; among them: 'The Father is in the Son and the Son is in the Father.' As Christians did not understand the meaning of this expression, their thoughts were scattered 513

the reality of this question is as follows: Divine Oneness is proven and He revealeth Himself in the Holy Essences. The sun is one sun but manifesteth itself in different mirrors. If thou lookest into the mirror and seest the manifestation of the sun, thou wilt say, the sun is in the mirror and this sun manifest in the mirror is the same sun of the heavens; although two suns, yet in reality they are one. The sun hath not descended from its high and lofty station, it hath not taken up its abode in the mirror, but hath manifested itself therein 513–14

the Christ reality was like unto a pure mirror and the Sun of Reality shone upon it from the Holy Horizon. Therefore, it became evident that the sun is one with regard to reality but manifesting itself in all mirrors 514

Trumpet

and likewise, He saith: 'Say to them that are of a fearful heart: be strong, fear not, behold your God.' This blessed verse is a proof of . . . the greatness of the Cause, inasmuch as the blast of the trumpet must needs spread confusion . . . amongst all men. Well is it with him who hath been illumined with the light of trust and detachment. The tribulations of that Day will not hinder or alarm him [see also *Isaiah* 146] ESW 147 they refuse to recognize the trumpet-blast which so explicitly in this text was sounded through the revelation of Muḥammad *Muḥammad* KI 116

Ṭáhirih – re: Badasht GPB 32–3

Truth

'all human attainment moveth upon a lame ass, whilst Truth, riding upon the wind, darteth across space' *Muḥammad* KI 187

'wish for death, if ye are men of truth' *Touchstone* 227

'and when the Standard of Truth is made manifest, the people of both the East and the West curse it' *Tradition* 238

the signs and tokens of the Truth shine even as the midday sun, and yet the people are wandering, aimlessly and perplexedly, in the wilderness of ignorance and folly. Notwithstanding all the verses of the Qur'án, and the recognized traditions, which are all indicative of a new Faith, a new Law, and a new Revelation, this generation still awaiteth in expectation of beholding the promised One who should uphold the Law of the Muḥammadan Dispensation. The Jews and the Christians in like manner uphold the same contention 239–40

this is indeed the eternal Truth which God, the Ancient of Days, hath revealed unto His omnipotent Word – He Who hath been raised up from the midst of the Burning Bush. This is the Mystery which hath been hidden from all that are in heaven and on earth, and in this wondrous Revelation it hath, in very truth, been set forth in the Mother Book by the hand of God, the Exalted SB 41

Qur'án – re: for seven years no one acknowledged its truth except 'Alí 90

thus on the Day of Resurrection God will ask everyone of his understanding and not of his following in the footsteps of others. How often a person, having inclined his ears to the holy verses, would bow down in humility and would embrace the Truth, while his leader would not do so. Thus every individual must bear his own responsibility, rather than someone else bearing it for him [see also *Judge*] 90–91

if ye wish to distinguish truth from error, consider those who believe in Him Whom God shall make manifest and those who disbelieve in Him at the time of His appearance *Essence* 142

say, verily, the criterion by which truth is distinguished from error shall not appear until the Day of Resurrection. This ye will know, if ye be of them that love the Truth. And ere the advent of the Day of Resurrection ye shall distinguish truth from aught else besides it according to that which hath been revealed in the Bayán 143

Ascendancy – re: of any one of the followers of the Truth 153

the Day is approaching when God will render the hosts of Truth victorious *God* 153–4

Turn

if these people shun and reject such a divine Soul, such holy Breath, to whom, We wonder, could they cling, to whose face besides His Face could they turn? Yea – 'All have a quarter of the Heavens to which they turn.' We have shown thee these two ways; walk thou the way thou choosest. This verily is the truth, and after truth there remaineth naught but error KI 221

'Umar

he it was who had the impudence and temerity to tell 'Abdu'l-Bahá to His face that just as 'Umar had succeeded in usurping the successorship of GPB 249 the Prophet Muḥammad, he, too, felt himself able to do the same – re: Mírzá Muḥammad-'Alí

Umayyads

Beast – re: in Book of Revelation, means the Umayyads SAQ 51

Dead – re: Jerusalem, where the Umayyads then had their dominions 51–2

the Umayyads were always waiting to get possession of the Promised One 70

Woman

Union

verily, the mission of all the prophets, the relation of all the scriptures, the diffusion of the instructions of God and the descent of His law, were all in order to establish agreement and union and to strengthen love and harmony among nations of different customs and thoughts, of diverse beliefs, doctrines, rites and habits; of various classes, tribes and races TAB 596

Unity

know thou assuredly that the essence of all the Prophets of God is one and the same. Their unity is absolute G 78

regard thou the one true God as One Who is apart from, and immeasurably exalted above, all created things. The whole universe reflecteth His glory, while He is Himself independent of, and transcendeth His creatures. This is the true meaning of Divine unity. He Who is the Eternal Truth is the one Power Who exerciseth undisputed sovereignty over the world of being, Whose image is reflected in the mirror of the entire creation. All existence is dependent upon Him, and from Him is derived the source of the sustenance of all things. This is what is meant by Divine unity; this is its fundamental principle 165

Unjust

and they who act unjustly shall soon know what lot awaiteth them KI 227

'Urvatu'l-Vuthqa

they constitute the indissoluble Bond, the firm Cord, the 'Urvatu'l-Vuthqa, the inextinguishable Light. Through them floweth the river of divine knowledge, and gloweth the fire of His ancient and consummate wisdom – re: verses of the Qur'án KI 205

Utterance

thus it is that whatsoever be their utterance, whether it pertain to the realm of Divinity, Lordship, Prophethood, Messengership, Guardianship, Apostleship or Servitude, all is true, beyond the shadow of a doubt KI 181

Voice

Value

be not troubled in poverty nor confident in riches, for poverty is followed by riches, and riches are followed by poverty. Yet to be poor in all save God is a wondrous gift, belittle not the value thereof, for in the end it will make thee rich in God, and thus thou shalt know the meaning of the utterance, 'In truth ye are the poor,' and the holy words, 'God is the all-possessing,' shall even as the true morn break forth gloriously resplendent upon the horizon of the lover's heart, and abide secure on the throne of wealth PHW 51

what thing of value to mankind has ever come into being which was not first set forth either directly or by implication in the Holy Scriptures? SDC 96

Vanity

is it not sufficient witness against the faithlessness of those who for a trifle betrayed their faith, who bartered away immortality for that which perisheth, who gave up the Kawthar of the divine Presence for salty springs, and whose one aim in life is to usurp the property of others? Even as thou dost witness how all of them have busied themselves with the vanities of the world, and have strayed far from Him Who is the Lord, the Most High KI 224

Veil

veils of glory *Divines* KI 164

not one Prophet of God was made manifest Who did not fall a victim to the relentless hate, to the denunciation, denial, and execration of the clerics of His day! Woe unto them for the iniquities their hands have formerly wrought! Woe unto them for that which they are now doing! What veils of glory more grievous than these embodiments of error! By the righteousness of God! to pierce such veils is the mightiest of all acts, and to rend them asunder the most meritorious of all deeds 165–6

furthermore, among the 'veils of glory' are such terms as the 'Seal of the Prophets' and the like, the removal of which is a supreme achievement in the sight of these base-born and erring souls. All, by reason of these mysterious sayings, these grievous 'veils of glory,' have been hindered from beholding the light of truth [see also *'Alí*] 166

We have consumed this densest of all veils, with the fire of the love of the Beloved – the veil referred to in the saying: 'The most grievous of all veils is the veil of knowledge.' Upon its ashes, We have reared the tabernacle of divine knowledge. We have, praise be to God, burned the 'veils of glory' with the fire of the beauty of the Best-Beloved 187–8

Leaders – re: who are wrapt in the densest veils of learning; 'over whose sight He hath cast a veil' 214

Verse

myriads of holy verses have descended from the heaven of might and grace, yet no one hath turned thereunto, nor ceased to cling to those words of men, not one letter of which they that have spoken them comprehend. For this reason the people have doubted incontestable truths, such as these, and caused themselves to be deprived of the Riḍván of divine knowledge, and the eternal meads of celestial wisdom KI 105–6

similarly, the sacred verse 'Fain would they put out God's light with their mouths: But God hath willed to perfect His light, albeit the infidels abhor it.' Were it to be literally interpreted it would never correspond with the truth. For in every age the light of God hath, to outward seeming, been quenched by the peoples of the earth, and the Lamps of God extinguished by them *Lamp* 126–7

how numerous are those revealed verses which explicitly bear witness unto this most weighty truth and exalted Theme! And yet they have rejected it, and, after their own desire, misconstrued its meaning. Even as He hath revealed: 'As for those who believe not in the signs of God, or that they shall ever meet Him, these of My mercy shall despair, and for them doth a grievous chastisement await [see also *Attain*] 138

this people have repudiated all these verses, that unmistakably testify to the reality of 'attainment unto the divine Presence.' No theme hath been more emphatically asserted in the holy scriptures 139

to ponder the verses of the Book in their heart *Book* 174

Verse

Súrih – re: produce a Súrah like it 204–5
hath proclaimed the undisputed supremacy of the verses of His Book over all things that testify to His truth *King* 205
likewise, He saith: 'Such are the verses of God: with truth do We recite them to Thee. But in what revelation will they believe, if they reject God and His verses?' If thou wilt grasp the implication of this verse, thou wilt recognize the truth that no manifestation greater than the Prophets of God hath ever been revealed, and no testimony mightier than the testimony of their revealed verses hath ever appeared upon the earth. Nay, this testimony no other testimony can ever excel, except that which thy Lord thy God willeth 206
in another passage He saith: 'Woe to every lying sinner, who heareth the verses of God recited to him, and then, as though he heard them not, persisteth in proud disdain! Apprise him of a painful punishment.' The implications of this verse, alone, suffice all that is in heaven and on earth, were the people to ponder the verses of their Lord. For thou hearest how in this day the people disdainfully ignore the divinely-revealed verses, as though they were the meanest of all things. And yet, nothing greater than these verses hath ever appeared, nor will ever be made manifest in the world 206–7
Ridicule – re: 'And when he becometh acquainted with any of our verses he turneth them to ridicule' 207–8
in another passage He saith: 'And when Our clear verses are recited to them, their only argument is to say, "Bring back our fathers, if ye speak the truth!"' Behold, what foolish evidences they sought from these Embodiments of an all-encompassing mercy! They scoffed at the verses, a single letter of which is greater than the creation of heavens and earth, and which quickeneth the dead of the valley of self and desire with the spirit of faith; and clamoured saying: 'Cause our fathers to speed out of their sepulchres.' Such was the perversity and pride of that people 209
and likewise, He saith: 'As for those who believe not in the verses of God, or that they shall ever meet Him, these of My mercy shall despair, and these doth a grievous chastisement await.' Also, 'And they say, "Shall we then abandon our gods for a crazed poet?"' The implication of this verse is manifest. Behold what they observed after the verses were revealed. They called Him a poet, scoffed at the verses of God, and exclaimed saying: 'These words of his are but tales of the Ancients!' By this they meant that those words which were spoken by the peoples of old Muḥammad hath compiled and called them the Word of God 211–12
and when Our clear verses are recited to them, they say, 'This is merely a man who would fain pervert you from your father's worship.' And they say, 'This is none other than a forged falsehood' *Knowledge* 214–15
this verse was revealed at a time when Islám was assailed by the infidels, and its followers were accused of misbelief, when the Companions of Muḥammad were denounced as repudiators of God and as followers of a lying sorcerer – re: Qur'án 5:59 *Islám* 217–18
'two verses have made Me old' *Steadfastness* 233
in like manner shouldst thou hearken unto the verses of the Bayán and acknowledge its truth, only then would the revealed verses of God profit thee *Bayán* SB 80–81
indeed, if any living creature were to pause to meditate he would undoubtedly realize that these verses are not the work of man, but are solely to be ascribed unto God, the One, the Peerless, Who causeth them 105

to flow forth from the tongue of whomsoever He willeth, and hath not revealed nor will He reveal them save through the Focal Point of God's Primal Will. He it is, through Whose dispensations divine Messengers are raised up and heavenly Books are sent down. Had human beings been able to accomplish this deed surely someone would have brought forth at least one verse during the period of twelve hundred and seventy years which hath elapsed since the revelation of the Qur'án until that of the Bayán. However, all men have proved themselves impotent and have utterly failed to do so, although they endeavoured, with their vehement might, to quench the flame of the Word of God

God hath made Him manifest invested with the proof wherewith the Apostle of God was invested, so that none of the believers in the Qur'án might entertain doubts about the validity of His Cause, for it is set down in the Qur'án that none but God is capable of revealing verses *Qá'im* 118

Virgin [see also *Mary*]

Birth of Jesus SAQ 87–8, 89–90

blessed are ye for attaining to that which was the greatest hope of Mary the Magdalene and Mary the mother of Jacob! This gift was shining on the face of the Virgin Mary like unto a brilliant gem glistening on the great crown of glory TAB 662

Vision

no vision taketh in Him, but He taketh in all vision *Seal* KI 170

Voice

and every attentive ear can recognize the Voice that was heard from the Burning Bush *Revelation* G 270

Zion – re: 'lift up Thy Voice with strength' ESW 144–5

thus in moments in which these Essences of being were deep immersed beneath the oceans of ancient and everlasting holiness, or when they soared to the loftiest summits of divine mysteries, they claimed their utterance to be the Voice of divinity, the Call of God Himself KI 179–80

by virtue of this station, they have claimed for themselves the Voice of Divinity and the like, whilst by virtue of their station of Messengership, they have declared themselves the Messengers of God. In every instance they have voiced an utterance that would conform to the requirements of the occasion, and have ascribed all these declarations to Themselves, declarations ranging from the realm of divine Revelation to the realm of creation, and from the domain of Divinity even unto the domain of earthly existence. Thus it is that whatsoever be their utterance, whether it pertain to the realm of Divinity, Lordship, Prophethood, Messengership, Guardianship, Apostleship or Servitude, all is true, beyond the shadow of a doubt 181

'the Breath hath been wafted, and the Breeze hath blown, and from Zion hath appeared that which was hidden, and from Jerusalem is heard the Voice of God, the One, the Incomparable, the Omniscient' [words of Bahá'u'lláh] PDC 77

Water

this is the flowing water ye were promised in the Qur'án, and later in the Bayán, as a recompense from your Lord, the God of Mercy. Blessed are they that quaff it *Qur'án* G 46

Baptism – re: not material water PT 82

when in the Gospels, Christ speaks of 'water', He means that which causes 82 life, for without water no worldly creature can live – mineral, vegetable, animal and man, one and all, depend upon water for their very being. Yes, the latest scientific discoveries prove to us that even mineral has some form of life, and that it also needs water for its existence [see also *Symbol*]

that is why, in the heavenly Books, the divine counsels and commands have been compared to water. So, in the Qur'án it is said, 'and we have caused a pure water to descend from heaven;' and in the Gospel, 'Except a man hath received the baptism of water and of the spirit, he cannot enter into the Kingdom of God' TAB 581

West

but nay! I swear by the Lord of the Easts and the Wests *Lord* KI 43

His Holiness Christ appeared in Palestine and his teachings were founded there. Although the doors of the Kingdom were opened in that country and the bestowals of divinity were spread broadcast from its center, the people of the West have embraced and promulgated Christianity more fully than those in the East. The Sun of Reality shone forth from the horizon of the East but its heat and ray are most resplendent in the West where the radiant standard of His Holiness Christ has been upraised FWU 72

the West has acquired illumination from the East but in some respects the reflection of the light has been greater in the Occident. This is especially true of Christianity *East* 72

Wilderness

this is the wilderness in which all the Messengers of God have wandered, from which they cry, 'Here am I, here am I, O my God' was raised *Holy Land* G 343

Witness

'and I will give power unto my two witnesses, and they shall prophesy a thousand two hundred and threescore days, clothed in sackcloth.' These two witnesses are Muḥammad the Messenger of God, and 'Alí, son of Abú Ṭálib. SAQ 48–9

In the Qur'án it is said that God addressed Muḥammad, the Messenger of God, saying: 'We made You a Witness, a Herald of good news, and a Warner' – that is to say, We have established Thee as the witness, the giver of good tidings, and as One bringing the wrath of God. The meaning of 'a witness' is one by whose testimony things may be verified. The commands of these two witnesses were to be performed for twelve hundred and sixty days, each day signifying a year. Now, Muḥammad was the root, and 'Alí the branch, like Moses and Joshua. It is said they 'are clothed in sackcloth,' meaning that they, apparently, were to be clothed in old raiment, not in new raiment; in other words, in the beginning they would possess no splendor in the eyes of the people, nor would their Cause appear new; for Muḥammad's spiritual Law corresponds to that of Christ in the Gospel, and most of His laws relating to material things correspond to those of the Pentateuch. This is the meaning of the old raiment

then it is said: 'They have power over water to turn it to blood,' meaning that the prophethood of Muḥammad was the same as that of Moses, and that the power of 'Alí was the same as that of Joshua: if they wished, they could turn the water of the Nile into blood, so far as the Egyptians and those who denied them were concerned – that is to say, that that which was the cause of their life, through their ignorance and pride, became the cause of their death. So the kingdom, wealth and power of Pharaoh and 50 his people, which were the causes of the life of the nation, became, through their opposition, denial and pride, the cause of death, destruction, dispersion, degradation and poverty. Hence these two witnesses have power to destroy the nations – re: Rev. 11 [see also *Power*]

Beast – re: 'the beast made war against these two witnesses' 51

Woe

and the second clarion hath sounded, there hath followed the second blast after the first, and the dread woe hath come, and every nursing mother hath forgot the infant at her breast – yet still the people, confused and distracted, heed it not SAB 14

'the second woe is past; and, behold, the third woe cometh quickly.' The first woe is the appearance of the Prophet, Muḥammad, the son of 'Abdu'lláh – peace be upon Him! The second woe is that of the Báb – to Him be glory and praise! The third woe is the great day of the manifestation of the Lord of Hosts and the radiance of the Beauty of the Promised One. The explanation of this subject, woe, is mentioned in the thirtieth chapter of Ezekiel, where it is said: 'The word of the Lord came again unto me, saying, Son of man, prophesy and say, Thus saith the Lord God; Howl ye, Woe worth the day! For the day is near, even the day of the Lord is near [see also *Lord*] SAQ 56

Wolf

Significance – re: prophecy of the wolf and the lamb KI 113

are metaphors and symbols for various nations, peoples, antagonistic sects and hostile races, who are as opposite and inimical as the wolf and lamb SAQ 63

strong and weak, rich and poor, antagonistic sects and hostile nations – which are like the wolf and the lamb, the leopard and kid, the lion and the calf – will act toward each other with the most complete love, friendship, justice and equity *Peace* 64

vicious people, like wolves, would destroy the sheep of God. The community has no ill-will and rancor in the infliction of punishment, and it does not desire to appease the anger of the heart; its purpose is by punishment to protect others so that no atrocious actions may be committed. 269–70

Thus when Christ said: 'Whosoever shall smite thee on the right cheek, turn to him the left one also,' it was for the purpose of teaching men not to take personal revenge. He did not mean that, if a wolf should fall upon a flock of sheep and wish to destroy it, the wolf should be encouraged to do so. No, if Christ had known that a wolf had entered the fold and was about to destroy the sheep, most certainly He would have prevented it

various peoples symbolized by the wolf and the lamb *Messiah* FWU 75

Woman

as to the woman in the Revelation of Saint John, chapter 12, who fled into the wilderness, and the great wonder appearing in the heavens – that woman clothed with the sun, with the moon under her feet: what is meant by the woman is the Law of God. For according to the terminology of the Holy Books, this reference is to the Law, the woman being its symbol here *John* SAB 172

and in chapter 12, verse 1, it is said: 'And there appeared a great wonder in heaven; a woman clothed with the sun, and the moon under her feet, and upon her head a crown of twelve stars.' This woman is that bride, the SAQ 68

Law of God that descended upon Muḥammad. The sun with which she was clothed, and the moon which was under her feet, are the two nations which are under the shadow of that Law, the Persian and Ottoman kingdoms; for the emblem of Persia is the sun, and that of the Ottoman Empire is the crescent moon. Thus the sun and moon are the emblems of two great kingdoms which are under the power of the Law of God. Afterward it is said: 'upon her head is a crown of twelve stars.' These twelve stars are the twelve Imáms, who were the promoters of the Law of Muḥammad and the educators of the people, shining like stars in the heaven of guidance [see also *Child*]

'and the dragon stood before the woman which was ready to be delivered, for to devour the child as soon as it was born.' As we have before explained, this woman is the Law of God. The dragon was standing near the woman to devour her child, and this child was the promised Manifestation, the offspring of the Law of Muḥammad. The Umayyads were always waiting to get possession of the Promised One, Who was to come from the line of Muḥammad, to destroy and annihilate Him; for they much feared the appearance of the promised Manifestation, and they sought to kill any of Muḥammad's descendants who might be highly esteemed – re: Rev. 12:11 70

'and the woman fled into the wilderness' – that is to say, the Law of God fled to the wilderness, meaning the vast desert of Ḥijáz, and the Arabian Peninsula. 70–71

Verse 6. 'Where she had a place prepared of God.' The Arabian Peninsula became the abode and dwelling place, and the center of the Law of God.

Verse 6. 'That they should feed her there a thousand two hundred and threescore days.' In the terminology of the Holy Book these twelve hundred and sixty days mean the twelve hundred and sixty years that the Law of God was set up in the wilderness of Arabia, the great desert: from it the Promised One has come. After twelve hundred and sixty years that Law will have no more influence, for the fruit of that tree will have appeared, and the result will have been produced – re: Rev. 12:6

Word

this is the Word which the Son concealed, when to those around Him He said: 'Ye cannot bear it now' *Father* TB 11

and yet they bear witness to this well-known tradition: 'Verily Our Word is abstruse, bewilderingly abstruse' *Tradition* KI 82

in yet another instance, He saith: 'A part of them heard the Word of God, and then, after they had understood it, distorted it, and knew that they did so.' This verse, too, doth indicate that the meaning of the Word of God hath been perverted, not that the actual words have been effaced 87

nor ceased to cling to those words of men, not one letter of which they that have spoken them comprehend *Verse* 105

those words uttered by the Luminaries of Truth must needs be pondered, and should their significance not be grasped, enlightenment should be sought from the Trustees of the depositories of Knowledge, that these may expound their meaning, and unravel their mystery. For it behooveth no man to interpret the holy words according to his own imperfect understanding, nor, having found them to be contrary to his inclination and desires, to reject and repudiate their truth. For such, today, is the manner of the divines and doctors of the age, who occupy the seats of knowledge and learning, and who have named ignorance knowledge, and called oppression justice 181–2 that City is none other than the Word of God revealed in every age and dispensation. In the days of Moses it was the Pentateuch; in the days of Jesus, the Gospel; in the days of Muḥammad, the Messenger of God, the Qur'án; in this day, the Bayán; and in the Dispensation of Him Whom God will make manifest, His own Book – the Book unto which all the Books of former Dispensations must needs be referred, the Book that standeth amongst them all transcendent and supreme (G 268–9) 199–200

the understanding of His words and the comprehension of the utterances of the Birds of Heaven are in no wise dependent upon human learning. They depend solely upon purity of heart, chastity of soul, and freedom of spirit. This is evidenced by those who, today, though without a single letter of the accepted standard of learning, are occupying the loftiest seats of knowledge; and the garden of their hearts is adorned, through the showers of divine grace, with the roses of wisdom and the tulips of understanding. Well is it with the sincere in heart for their share of the light of a mighty Day 211

Verse – re: these words of his are but tales of the Ancients 211–12

how vast the number of people who are well versed in every science, yet it is their adherence to the holy Word of God which will determine their faith, inasmuch as the fruit of every science is none other than the knowledge of divine precepts and submission unto His good-pleasure SB 88

only the keenest insight will detect the fact that if the hearts of these individuals were really impelled by righteousness and the fear of God, the fragrance of it would, like musk, be spreading everywhere. Nothing in the world can ever be supported by words alone SDC 57–8

it is evident that the Letter is a member of the Word, and this membership in the Word signifieth that the Letter is dependent for its value on the Word, that is, it deriveth its grace from the Word; it has a spiritual kinship with the Word, and is accounted an integral part of the Word. The Apostles were even as Letters, and Christ was the essence of the Word Itself; and the meaning of the Word, which is grace everlasting, cast a splendour on those Letters. Again, since the Letter is a member of the Word, it therefore, in its inner meaning, is consonant with the Word SAB 60

the Reality of Christ, Who is the Word of God, with regard to essence, attributes and glory *Jesus Christ* SAQ 116–17

but the proceeding through manifestation (if by this is meant the divine appearance, and not division into parts), we have said, is the proceeding and the appearance of the Holy Spirit and the Word, which is from God. As it is said in the Gospel of John, 'In the beginning was the Word, and the Word was with God'; then the Holy Spirit and the Word are the appearance of God. The Spirit and the Word mean the divine perfections that appeared in the Reality of Christ, and these perfections were with God; so the sun manifests all its glory in the mirror. For the Word does not signify the body of Christ, no, but the divine perfections manifested in Him 206

'I am the Word which the Qá'im is to utter' *Ṭáhirih* GPB 32–3

it proffered to mankind the 'Choice Sealed Wine,' whose seal is of 'musk,' and broke the 'seals' of the 'Book' referred to by Daniel, and disclosed the meaning of the 'words' destined to remain 'closed up' till the 'time of the end' – re: Kitáb-i-Íqán 139

'the Word which the Son concealed is made manifest. It hath been sent down in the form of the human temple in this day. Blessed be the Lord Who is the Father! He, verily, is come unto the nations in His most great majesty' [words of Bahá'u'lláh] PDC 32

Worship

among the Ten Commandments is one which says: 'Do not worship any picture or image.' At present in some of the Christian churches many pictures and images exist — SAQ 165

the Buddhists and Confucianists now worship images and statues. They are entirely heedless of the Oneness of God and believe in imaginary gods like the ancient Greeks. But in the beginning it was not so; there were different principles and other ordinances — 166

all the people have formed a god in the world of thought, and that form of their own imagination they worship; when the fact is that the imagined form is finite and the human mind is infinite. Surely the infinite is greater than the finite, for imagination is accidental while the mind is essential; surely the essential is greater than the accidental. — BWF 381–2

Therefore consider: All the sects and peoples worship their own thought; they create a god in their own minds and acknowledge him to be the creator of all things, when that form is a superstition – thus people adore and worship imagination

Likeness – re: worship of likenesses and pictures — 394

Writings

if the Muslim divines have cause for pride in understanding the meaning of the Holy Writings, His glory is in revealing the Writings, that none of them may hesitate to believe in His Words. So great is the celestial might and power which God hath revealed in Him that if it were His will and no break should intervene He could, within the space of five days and nights, reveal the equivalent of the Qur'án which was sent down in twenty-three years. Ponder thou and reflect. Hath anyone like unto Him ever appeared in former times, or is this characteristic strictly confined unto Him? [see also *Promised One*] — SB 118–19

Year [see also *Daniel, Prophecy*]

all have been enjoined to follow the precepts of that Book until 'the year sixty' – the year of the advent of God's wondrous Manifestation – re: Qur'án *Book* — KI 201

each day, according to the text of the Holy Book, is a year. For in the Bible it is said: 'The day of the Lord is one year' – re: explanation of 70 weeks, 62 weeks — SAQ 40

let us now explain the date of the manifestation of Bahá'u'lláh from the Bible. The date of Bahá'u'lláh is calculated according to lunar years from the mission and the Hejira of Muḥammad; for in the religion of Muḥammad the lunar year is in use, as also it is the lunar year which is employed concerning all commands of worship . . . each day of the Father counts as a year, and in each year there are twelve months. Thus three years and a half make forty-two months, and forty-two months are twelve hundred and sixty days. The Báb, the precursor of Bahá'u'lláh, appeared in the year 1260 from the Hejira of Muḥammad, by the reckoning of Islám *Daniel* — 43

each day signifying a year *Witness* [see also *Child* 68–9] — 48–9

in the Qur'án a day is reckoned as one thousand years *Day* (Letter 7.8.34) — LG 353

Youth

Proof – re: this flamelike-Youth — KI 147

'a Youth from Baní-Há<u>sh</u>im shall be made manifest, Who will reveal a new Book and promulgate a new Law' *'Aválim* — 241

'there shall appear a Youth from Baní-Há<u>sh</u>im, Who will bid the people plight fealty unto Him' *Ṣádiq* — 241 in 'Arba'in' it is recorded: 'Out of Baní-Háshim there shall come forth a Youth Who shall reveal new laws *Tradition* 242–3

Zawrá'

even as it hath been recorded in the 'Rawḍiy-i-Káfí,' concerning 'Zawrá'.' In the 'Rawḍiy-i-Káfí' it is related of Mu'áviyih, son of Vahháb, that Abú-'Abdi'lláh hath spoken: '"Knowest thou Zawrá?"' I said: "May my life be a sacrifice unto thee! They say it is Baghdád." "Nay," he answered. And then added: "Hast thou entered the city of Rayy?", to which I made reply: "Yea, I have entered it." Whereupon, He enquired: "Didst thou visit the cattle-market?" "Yea," I answered. He said: "Hast thou seen the black mountain on the right hand side of the road? The same is Zawrá'. There shall eighty men, of the children of certain ones, be slain, all of whom are worthy to be called caliphs." "Who will slay them?" I asked. He made reply: "The children of Persia"' KI 246–7

Zion

peruse that which Isaiah hath spoken in His Book. He saith: 'Get thee up into the high mountain, O Zion, that bringest good tidings; lift up Thy Voice with strength, O Jerusalem, that bringest good tidings. Lift it up, be not afraid; say unto the cities of Judah: "Behold your God! Behold the Lord God will come with strong hand, and His arm shall rule for Him."' This Day all the signs have appeared. A Great City hath descended from heaven, and Zion trembleth and exulteth with joy at the Revelation of God, for it hath heard the Voice of God on every side *Jerusalem* ESW 144–5

Amos saith: 'The Lord will roar from Zion, and utter His Voice from Jerusalem; and the habitations of the shepherds shall mourn, and the top of Carmel shall wither.' Carmel, in the Book of God, hath been designated as the Hill of God, and His Vineyard. It is here that, by the grace of the Lord of Revelation, the Tabernacle of Glory hath been raised. Happy are they that attain thereunto; happy they that set their faces towards it. And likewise He saith: 'Our God will come, and He will not be silent' [see also *Tabernacle* GPB 194; *Voice* PDC 77] 145

Zíyárat

He hath, likewise, revealed in the Zíyárat: 'Peace be upon the Truth made new' – re: Visiting Tablet revealed by 'Alí KI 240

Zoroaster [see also *High Priest*]

the 'Úshídar-Máh' referred to in the Zoroastrian scriptures – re: the Báb GPB 58

of Zoroaster when awakened to His mission by a succession of seven visions 93

to the Zoroastrians the promised Sháh-Bahrám – re: Bahá'u'lláh 94

to His Dispensation the sacred books of the followers of Zoroaster had referred as that in which the sun must needs be brought to a standstill for no less than one whole month. To Him Zoroaster must have alluded when, according to tradition, He foretold that a period of three thousand years of conflict and contention must needs precede the advent of the World-Saviour Sháh-Bahrám, Who would triumph over Ahriman and usher in an era of blessedness and peace 95

and as the place where Zoroaster, according to 'Abdu'l-Bahá's testimony, had 'held converse with some of the Prophets of Israel' 183

and that 'whatsoever hath been announced in the Books (Zoroastrian Holy Writ) hath been revealed and made clear' *Book* 230

the gradual infiltration into Christian doctrine of the . . . precepts of Zoroastrianism WOB 57 as a further testimony to the greatness of the Revelation identified with Bahá'u'lláh may be cited the following extracts from a Tablet addressed by 'Abdu'l-Bahá to an eminent Zoroastrian follower of the Faith: 'Thou hast written that in the sacred books of the followers of Zoroaster it is written that in the latter days, in three separate Dispensations, the sun must needs be brought to a standstill. In the first Dispensation, it is predicted, the sun will remain motionless for ten days; in the second for twice that time; in the third for no less than one whole month. The interpretation of this prophecy is this: the first Dispensation to which it refers is the Muḥammadan Dispensation during which the Sun of Truth stood still for ten days. Each day is reckoned as one century. The Muḥammadan Dispensation must have, therefore, lasted no less than one thousand years, which is precisely the period that has elapsed from the setting of the Star of the Imámate to the advent of the Dispensation proclaimed by the Báb. The second Dispensation referred to in this prophecy is the one inaugurated by the Báb Himself, which began in the year 1260 A.H. and was brought to a close in the year 1280 A.H. As to the third Dispensation – the Revelation proclaimed by Bahá'u'lláh – inasmuch as the Sun of Truth when attaining that station shineth in the plenitude of its meridian splendor its duration hath been fixed for a period of one whole month, which is the maximum time taken by the sun to pass through a sign of the Zodiac. From this thou canst imagine the magnitude of the Bahá'í cycle – a cycle that must extend over a period of at least five hundred thousand years' [see also *Prophecy* LG 353] 101–2

Appendix

Selections from the Holy Qur'án: Translations and Emendations by Shoghi Effendi

compiled by Burl Barer

The best known English translations of the Qur'án extant when Shoghi Effendi became Guardian of the Bahá'í Faith in 1921 were those of George Sale (1734) and J. M. Rodwell (1861). While Shoghi Effendi praised Sale's version for its accuracy, Rodwell's more poetic and literary rendering became the Guardian's preferred translation.

It is in Shoghi Effendi's translation of Bahá'u'lláh's *Kitáb-i-Íqán* that Rodwell for the first time replaces Sale as the source of English Qur'ánic quotations in a major work by the Author of the Bahá'í Revelation. The Guardian does not simply extract the appropriate verse from Rodwell, but alters and improves the translation through subtle yet consistent emendations. Some verses are translated anew by Shoghi Effendi, giving us glimpses of what an English Qur'án could have been if rendered in its entirety by the 'Sign of God on Earth'.

This collection has been compiled from Shoghi Effendi's translations of the *Kitáb-i-Íqán, Epistle to the Son of the Wolf, Gleanings from the Writings of Bahá'u'lláh* and other writings. The numbering of the verses has been standardized to that of the Arabic Qur'án.

Acknowledgement and gratitude for their support during the completion of the compilation are due Britt Barer and Lee Goldberg, with special thanks to Marzieh Gail for her encouragement and contributions.

This compilation is not intended to be a guide to major themes of the Qur'án, nor does it contain even all Qur'ánic verses quoted in the Bahá'í Writings. Its purpose is simply to highlight those verses translated or emended by Shoghi Effendi – verses that resonate with a new poetry and accuracy by virtue of the Guardian's brilliant mind and God-given insight.

2:1–2 Alif, Lám, Mím. No doubt is there about this Book: It is a guidance unto the God-Fearing.

2:46 They who bear in mind that they shall attain unto the Presence of their Lord, and that unto Him shall they return.

2:75 A part of them heard the Word of God, and then, after they had understood it, distorted it, and knew that they did so.

2:87 As oft as an Apostle cometh unto you with that which your souls desire not, ye swell with pride, accusing some of being imposters and slaying others.

2:89 Although they had before prayed for victory over those who believed not, yet when there came unto them, He of Whom they had knowledge, they disbelieved in Him. The curse of God on the infidels!

2:94 Wish for death, if ye are men of truth.

2:115 The East and the West are God's: therefore whichever way ye turn, there is the face of God.

2:136 No distinction do We make between any of them. (i.e. the Messengers of God)

2:143 We did not appoint that which Thou wouldst have be the Qiblih, but that We might know him who followeth the Apostle from him who turneth on his heels.

2:144 We behold Thee from above, turning Thy face to heaven; but We will have Thee turn to a Qiblih which shall please Thee.

2:148 All have a quarter of the Heavens to which they turn.

2:149 Turn Thou Thy face towards the sacred Mosque.

2:177 There is no piety in turning your faces toward the east or toward the west, but he is pious who believeth in God and the Last Day.

2:253 Some of the Apostles We have caused to excel the others. To some God hath spoken, some He hath raised and exalted. And to Jesus, Son of Mary, We gave manifest signs, and We strengthened Him with the Holy Spirit.

2:285 No distinction do We make between any of His Messengers!

3:7 None knoweth the meaning thereof (i.e. the Book) except God and them that are well-grounded in knowledge.

3:39 God announceth Yaḥyá to thee, who shall bear witness unto the Word from God, and a great one and chaste.

3:70 O People of the Book! Why disbelieve the signs of God to which ye yourselves have been witnesses?

3:183 To those who say: 'Verily, God hath entered into a covenant with us that we are not to credit an apostle until he present us a sacrifice which fire out of heaven shall devour', Say: 'Already have Apostles before me come to you with sure testimonies, and with that of which ye speak. Wherefore slew ye them? Tell me, if ye are men of truth.'

4:46 They pervert the text of the Word of God.

5:64 'The hand of God,' say the Jews, 'is chained up.' Chained up be their own hands! And for that which they have said, they were accursed. Nay, outstretched are both His hands!

5:114 Lord, send down upon us Thy bread from heaven.

6:7 And had We sent down unto Thee a book written on parchment, and they had touched it with their hands, the infidels would surely have said 'This is naught but palpable sorcery.'

6:35 But if their opposition be grievous to Thee – if Thou canst, seek out an opening into the earth or a ladder into heaven.

6:59 There is neither a thing green nor sere but it is noted in the unerring Book.

6:91 Say: It is God; then leave them to entertain themselves with their cavillings.

6:103 No vision taketh in Him, but He taketh in all vision; He is the Subtile, the All-Perceiving.

6:127 For them is an Abode of Peace with their Lord! and He shall be their Protector because of their works.

6:154 Then gave We the Book to Moses – complete for Him who should do right, and a decision for all matters, and a guidance, and a mercy, that they might believe in the Presence of their Lord.

7:58 In a rich soil, its plants spring forth abundantly by permission of its Lord, and in that soil which is bad, they spring forth but scantily.

7:146 And if they see the path of righteousness, they will not take it for their path; but if they see the path of error, for their path will they take it. This because they treated Our signs as lies, and were heedless of them.

9:32 Fain would they put out God's light with their mouths; But God hath willed to perfect His light, albeit the infidels abhor it.

9:32 Fain would they put out the light of God with their mouths! But though the infidels hate it, God will perfect His light.

10:15 But when Our clear signs are recited to them, they who look not forward to attain Our Presence, say, 'Bring a different Qur'án from this, or make some change in it.' Say: It is not for Me to change it as Mine own soul prompteth. I follow only what is revealed to Me: verily, I fear, if I rebel against My Lord, the punishment of a great day.

10:25 And God calleth to the Abode of Peace; and He guideth whom He will into the right way.

11:7 And if thou shouldst say, 'After death ye shall surely be raised again,' the infidels will certainly exclaim, 'This is nothing but manifest sorcery.'

11:27 Then said the chiefs of His people who believed not, 'We see in Thee but a man like ourselves; and we see not any who have followed Thee except our meanest ones of hasty judgement, nor see we any excellence in you above ourselves; nay, we deem you liars.'

11:38 And as often as a company of His people passed by Him, they derided Him. To them He said: 'Though ye scoff at us now, we will scoff at you hereafter even as ye scoff at us. In the end ye shall know.'

11:61 And unto the tribe of Th͟amúd We sent their brother Ṣáliḥ. 'O my people,' said He, 'Worship God, ye have none other God beside Him . . .'

11:62 They made reply: 'O Ṣáliḥ, our hopes were fixed on thee until now; forbiddest thou us to worship that which our fathers worshipped? Truly we misdoubt that whereunto thou callest us as suspicious.'

11:112 Be thou steadfast as thou hast been bidden.

13:2 It is God Who hath reared the heavens without pillars thou canst behold; then mounted His throne, and imposed laws on the sun and moon: each travelleth to its appointed goal. He ordereth all things. He maketh His signs clear, that ye may have firm faith in the Presence of your Lord.

14:24–5 Seest thou not to what God likeneth a good word? To a good tree; its root firmly fixed, and its branches reaching unto heaven: yielding its fruit in all seasons.

15:72 As Thou livest, O Muḥammad! they are seized by the frenzy of their vain fancies.

16:43 Ask ye, therefore, of them that have the custody of the Scriptures, if ye know it not.

16:61 If God should chastise men for their perverse doings, He would not leave upon the earth a moving thing! But to an appointed time doth He respite them.

17:51 Erelong will they wag their heads at Thee, and say, 'When shall this be?' Say: 'Perchance it is nigh.'

18:110 Let him then who hopeth to attain the presence of his Lord work a righteous work.

20:9–14 Hath the history of Moses reached thee? When He saw a fire, and said to His family, 'Tarry ye here, for I perceive a fire; haply I may bring you a brand from it, or find at the fire a guide.' And when He came to it, He was called to, 'O Moses! Verily, I am Thy Lord; therefore pull off Thy shoes, for Thou art in the holy vale of Ṭowá. And I have chosen Thee; hearken then to what shall be revealed. Verily, I am God, there is no God but Me. Therefore, worship Me.'

20:124 And whoso turneth away from My remembrance, truly his shall be a life of misery.

25:7 And they have said: 'What manner of apostle is this? He eateth food, and walketh the streets. Unless an angel be sent down and take part in His warnings, we will not believe.'

25:25 On that day shall the heaven be cloven by the clouds.

25:44 Thinkest thou that the greater part of them hear or understand? They are even like unto the brutes! yea, they stray even further from the path!

26:227 And they who act unjustly shall soon know what lot awaiteth them!

28:5 And We desire to show favour to those who were brought low in the land, and to make them spiritual leaders among men, and to make of them Our heirs.

28:19 O Moses! Dost Thou desire to slay me, as thou slewest a man yesterday?

28:20 O Moses! of a truth, the chiefs take counsel to slay Thee.

28:30 And when He came up to it, a Voice cried to Him out of the Bush from the right side of the Vale in the sacred Spot: 'O Moses, I truly am God, the Lord of the worlds!'

29:2 Do men think when they say 'We believe' they shall be let alone and not be put to proof?

29:23 As for those who believe not in the signs of God, or that they shall ever meet Him, these of My mercy shall despair, and for them doth a grievous chastisement await.

29:51 Is it not enough for them that We have sent down unto Thee the Book?

29:69 Whoso maketh efforts for Us, in Our ways shall We assuredly guide him.

30:7 Have they not considered within themselves that God hath not created the heavens and the earth and all that is between them but for a serious end, and for a fixed term? But truly most men believe not that they shall attain the Presence of their Lord.

32:9 And they say, 'What! when we shall have lain hidden in the earth, shall we become a new creation?' Yea, they deny that they shall attain the Presence of their Lord.

33:40 Muḥammad is the Apostle of God and the Seal of the Prophets.

34:13 And few of My servants are the thankful.

34:43 And when Our clear verses are recited to them, they say, 'This is merely a man who would fain pervert you from your father's worship.' And they say, 'This is none other than a forged falsehood.'

35:15 O men! Ye are but paupers in need of God; but God is the Rich, the Self-Sufficing.

36:20 Follow ye, O people! the Messengers of God.

36:30 O the misery of men! No Messenger cometh unto them but they laugh Him to scorn.

37:36 And they say, 'Shall we then abandon our gods for a crazed poet?'

38:67–8 Say: it is a weighty Message, from which ye turn aside!

39:67 The whole earth shall on the Resurrection Day be but His handful, and in His right hand shall the heavens be folded together.

40:5 Each nation hath plotted darkly against their Messenger to lay violent hold on Him, and disputed with vain words to invalidate the truth.

40:28 And a man of the family of Pharaoh who was a believer and concealed his faith said: 'Will ye slay a man because he saith my Lord is God, when He hath already come to you with signs from your Lord? If he be a liar, on him will be his lie, but if he be a man of truth, part of what he threateneth will fall upon you. In truth God guideth not him who is a transgressor, a liar.'

40:34 And Joseph came to you aforetime with clear tokens, but ye ceased not to doubt of the message with which He came to you, until, when He died, ye said, 'God will by no means raise up a Messenger after Him.' Thus God misleadeth him who is the transgressor, the doubter.

41:30 They that say 'Our Lord is God,' and continue steadfast in His way, upon them, verily, shall the angels descend.

41:53 We will surely show them Our signs in the world and within themselves.

43:22 Verily we found our fathers with a faith, and verily, in their footsteps we follow.

44:43 Verily, the tree of Zaqqúm shall be the food of the Athím. (Zaqqúm is 'Infernal tree', Athím is 'sinner' or 'sinful'.)

44:49 Taste this, for thou forsooth art the mighty Karím! (Karím is 'honourable'.)

45:6 Such are the verses of God: with truth do We recite them to Thee. But in what revelation will they believe, if they reject God and His verses?

45:7–8 Woe to every lying sinner, who heareth the verses of God recited to him, and then, as though he heard them not, persisteth in proud disdain! Apprise him of a painful punishment.

45:9 And when he becometh acquainted with any of Our verses he turneth them to ridicule. There is a shameful punishment for them!

45:23 What thinkest thou? He who hath made a God of his passions, and whom God causeth to err through a knowledge, and whose ears and whose heart He hath sealed up, and over whose sight He hath cast a veil – who, after his rejection by God, shall guide such a one? Will ye not then be warned?

45:25 And when Our clear verses are recited to them, their only argument is to say, 'Bring back our fathers, if ye speak the truth!'

48:10 The hand of God is above their hands.

50:20–21 And there was a blast on the trumpet, – lo! it is the threatened Day! And every soul is summoned to a reckoning, – with him an impeller and a witness.

51:21 And also in your own selves: will ye not then behold the signs of God?

54:50 Our Cause is but one.

55:5 Verily, the sun and the moon are both condemned to the torment of infernal fire.*

55:29 Verily, His ways differ every day.

55:56 whom no man nor spirit hath touched before.

59:2 Wherefore, take ye good heed ye who are men of insight!

59:19 And be ye not like those who forget God, and whom He hath caused to forget their own selves.

67:2 That He might prove you, which of you excel in deeds.

* Rodwell: 'The Sun and the Moon have each their times.'

70:40 But nay! I swear by the Lord of the Easts and the Wests.

71:26 Lord! Leave not upon the land a single dweller from among the unbelievers.

76:5 The righteous shall drink of a cup tempered at the camphor fountain.

76:9 We nourish your souls for the sake of God; we seek from you neither recompense nor thanks.

78:29 We noted all things and wrote them down.

82:1 When the heaven shall be cloven asunder.

Complete English Translations of the Qur'án

1. Alexander Ross 1649. Translated from Du Ryer's French rendering.
2. George Sale 1734
3. J. M. Rodwell 1861. First rendering into poetic prose.
4. E. H. Palmer 1880
5. Abdul Hakim 1905
6. Mírzá Abu'l Fazl 1910. First chronological presentation by a Muslim; First translation in English with Arabic text.
7. Muhammad Ali 1917
8. Ghulam Sarwar 1929
9. M. Pickthall 1930
10. Abdullah Yusuf Ali 1934
11. Richard Bell 1937
12. A. J. Arberry 1955
13. Sher Ali 1955
14. N. J. Dawood 1956
15. Abdul Majid Daryabadi 1957
16. Mir Ahmed Ali 1964. With a Shí'ih commentary.
17. Syed Abdul Lateef 1968
18. Zafarullah Khan 1971
19. Hashim Amir-Ali 1974

Page Conversion Tables

Gleanings from the Writings of Bahá'u'lláh

The American edition used in this book is about one page longer than the British edition. By about page 85 of the American edition, there is half a page between the two; therefore subtract half a page from the reference given in this book to get to the British edition. By about page 200 of the American edition, there is a full page difference between the two; therefore subtract one page from the reference given in this book to get to the British edition, and also for the rest of the book.

Kitáb-i-Íqán

There are 257 pages of text in the American edition used in this book, by comparison with 164 pages in the British edition. The first figure in this table is the number in the American edition, the second figure is for the British edition. This table shows where the beginning of any page in the American edition is to be found in the British edition. Thus the beginning of page 53 of the American edition is on page 34 of the British edition. This rule is followed exactly, even if most of the page of the American edition is on the following page of the British edition.

3	3	26	17	49	32	72	46	98	63	121	78
4	3	27	18	50	32	73	47	99	64	122	78
5	4	28	18	51	33	74	47	100	64	123	79
6	4	29	19	52	33	75	48	101	65	124	80
7	5	30	20	53	34	76	49	102	66	125	80
8	6	31	20	54	34	77	49	103	66	126	81
9	6	32	21	55	35	78	50	104	67	127	81
10	7	33	22	56	36	79	50	105	68	128	82
11	8	34	22	57	37	80	51	106	68	129	83
12	8	35	23	58	37	81	52	107	69	130	83
13	9	36	23	59	38	82	52	108	69	131	84
14	9	37	24	60	38	83	53	109	70	132	85
15	10	38	25	61	39	84	54	110	71	133	85
16	11	39	25	62	40	85	54	111	71	134	86
17	11	40	26	63	40	86	55	112	72	135	86
18	12	41	27	64	41	87	56	113	73	136	87
19	13	42	27	65	42	88	56	114	73	137	88
20	13	43	28	66	42	89	57	115	74	138	88
21	14	44	28	67	43	90	58	116	75	139	89
22	15	45	29	68	43	91	58	117	75	140	90
23	15	46	30	69	44	92	59	118	76	141	90
24	16	47	30	70	45	93	59	119	76	142	91
25	16	48	31	71	45	97	63	120	77	143	92

144	92	163	104	182	116	201	128	220	140	239	152
145	93	164	105	183	117	202	129	221	141	240	153
146	93	165	106	184	118	203	129	222	141	241	154
147	94	166	106	185	118	204	130	223	142	242	154
148	95	167	107	186	119	205	131	224	143	243	155
149	95	168	107	187	119	206	131	225	144	244	155
150	96	169	108	188	120	207	132	226	144	245	156
151	97	170	109	189	121	208	133	227	145	246	157
152	97	171	109	190	121	209	133	228	145	247	157
153	98	172	110	191	122	210	134	229	146	248	158
154	98	173	111	192	123	211	135	230	147	249	159
155	99	174	111	193	123	212	135	231	147	250	159
156	100	175	112	194	124	213	136	232	148	251	160
157	100	176	113	195	124	214	136	233	149	252	161
158	101	177	113	196	125	215	137	234	149	253	161
159	102	178	114	197	126	216	138	235	150	254	162
160	102	179	114	198	126	217	138	236	150	255	162
161	103	180	115	199	127	218	139	237	151	256	163
162	104	181	116	200	128	219	140	238	152	257	164

Some Answered Questions

There are 305 pages of text in the 1981 edition used in this book, by comparison with 350 pages in earlier editions. The same rules for use of this table apply as for the **Kitáb-i-Íqán** above.

3	3	24	29	45	53	66	76	89	102	110	126
4	4	25	30	46	54	67	77	90	103	111	127
5	5	26	31	47	55	68	78	91	104	112	128
6	6	27	32	48	56	69	79	92	105	113	129
7	8	28	33	49	57	70	80	93	107	114	130
8	9	29	34	50	58	71	81	94	108	115	131
9	10	30	35	51	60	72	82	95	109	116	132
10	11	31	36	52	61	73	83	96	110	117	133
11	12	32	37	53	62	74	84	97	112	118	134
12	14	33	38	54	63	75	85	98	113	119	135
13	15	34	40	55	64	76	86	99	114	120	136
14	17	35	41	56	65	77	87	100	115	121	137
15	18	36	43	57	66	78	89	101	116	122	139
16	20	37	44	58	67	79	90	102	117	123	140
17	21	38	45	59	69	80	91	103	119	124	141
18	22	39	46	60	70	83	95	104	120	125	142
19	23	40	47	61	71	84	96	105	121	126	143
20	24	41	48	62	72	85	97	106	122	127	145
21	25	42	50	63	73	86	98	107	123	128	146
22	26	43	51	64	74	87	99	108	124	129	148
23	27	44	52	65	75	88	100	109	125	130	149

131	150	163	185	194	225	223	259	252	291	284	326
132	151	164	186	195	227	224	260	253	292	285	327
133	152	165	188	196	228	225	261	254	293	286	328
134	153	166	190	197	229	226	262	255	294	287	330
135	154	167	192	198	230	227	263	256	295	288	331
136	155	168	193	199	231	228	264	257	296	289	332
137	156	169	194	200	233	229	265	258	297	290	333
138	158	170	195	201	234	230	267	259	298	291	334
139	159	171	197	202	236	231	268	263	301	292	335
143	163	172	198	203	237	232	269	264	302	293	336
144	164	173	199	204	238	233	270	265	303	294	337
145	165	174	200	205	239	234	271	266	304	295	338
146	167	177	205	206	240	235	272	267	305	296	339
147	168	178	206	207	241	236	273	268	307	297	341
148	169	179	207	208	243	237	274	269	308	298	342
149	170	180	209	209	244	238	275	270	309	299	343
150	171	181	210	210	245	239	277	271	310	300	344
151	173	182	211	211	246	240	278	272	311	301	345
152	174	183	212	212	247	241	280	273	313	302	346
153	175	184	213	213	248	242	281	274	314	303	347
154	177	185	215	214	249	243	282	275	315	304	348
155	178	186	216	215	250	244	283	276	316	305	349
156	179	187	217	216	251	245	284	277	317		
157	180	188	218	217	252	246	285	278	319		
158	181	189	219	218	253	247	286	279	320		
159	182	190	221	219	254	248	287	280	321		
160	183	191	222	220	255	249	288	281	322		
161	184	192	223	221	256	250	289	282	324		
162	185	193	224	222	257	251	290	283	325		

The Promised Day Is Come

There are 124 pages of text in the 1980 edition used in this book, by comparison with 129 pages in the previous editions. The 1980 edition is the left-hand column.

3	1	13	11	23	21	33	32	43	43	53	53
4	2	14	12	24	23	34	33	44	44	54	54
5	3	15	13	25	24	35	34	45	45	55	56
6	4	16	14	26	25	36	35	46	46	56	57
7	5	17	15	27	26	37	36	47	47	57	58
8	6	18	16	28	27	38	37	48	48	58	59
9	7	19	17	29	28	39	38	49	49	59	60
10	8	20	18	30	29	40	40	50	50	60	61
1	9	21	19	31	30	41	41	51	51	61	62
12	10	22	20	32	31	42	42	52	52	62	63

Page Conversion Tables

63	64	74	75	85	87	96	99	107	110	118	122
64	65	75	76	86	88	97	100	108	111	119	123
65	66	76	78	87	89	98	101	109	112	120	124
66	67	77	79	88	90	99	102	110	114	121	125
67	68	78	80	89	92	100	103	111	115	122	126
68	69	79	81	90	93	101	104	112	116	123	127
69	70	80	82	91	94	102	105	113	117	124	128
70	71	81	83	92	95	103	106	114	118		
71	72	82	84	93	96	104	107	115	119		
72	73	83	85	94	97	105	108	116	120		
73	74	84	86	95	98	106	109	117	121		

List of Head Words

Abase
'Abdu'lláh Ubayy
'Abdu'ṣ-Ṣáḥib
Abel
Abí-'Abdi'lláh
Abject
Abode
Abolish
Abomination of Desolation *see* Daniel
Abraham
Abú-Jahl
Accept
Access
Adam
Ádhirbáyján
Admittance
Admonition
Advent
Affliction
'Akká
'Alí
Alpha and Omega
Amos
Ancient of Days
Angel
Annas *see* Caiaphas
Announcement
Annul
Apocalypse *see* John, Beast, Bride, Child *and various headings*
Apostle of God
Apostles of Christ
Ark
Ascendancy
Ascension
Ásíyih
Ask
Assemblage
Astray
Atonement
Attain
Authority
'Aválim

Báb
Babel
Baghdád
Bahá'u'lláh
Balál
Balance
Banquet-Hall of God
Baptism
Barter
Bayán
Beast
Beginning
Belief
Beloved
Bible
Biḥár
Birth of Jesus
Blind
Blood
Body
Book
Branch
Bread
Bride
Bridge
Brother
Buddha
Bugle
Burning Bush

Caiaphas
Cain
Calamity
Caliphate
Call
Calumny
Canaan
Canons
Carmel
Catastrophe
Cause
Cavil
Ceremony
Chain
Champion
Change
Character
Chastise
Child
Chosen
Christ *see* Jesus Christ
Christianity
Christmas
Church
City
Clean
Cleaving of the Heaven
Clerics
Cloud
Comforter
Commentary on the Súrih of Joseph *see* Qur'án
Communion *see* Lord's Supper
Community
Companions
Conduct
Confederates
Confucius
Congregations
Consummation
Contrary
Corruption of the Text
Countenance
Covenant
Creation
Cross
Crown
Crucifixion
Cult
Customs
Cycle *see* Adam, Prophetic Cycle

Daniel
David
Day
Dead
Deaf
Death
Deed
Degradation
Deluge
Deny
Deprive
Descent
Disaster
Disavow
Disbelieve
Disciple
Divine Physician
Divines
Divinity
Divorce
Dogma
Dove
Dragon
Earth

List of Head Words

East
Educator
Egypt
Elders
Elias
Elijah
Emmanuel
End
Enemy
Error
Essence
Evangel
Eve
Evolution
Existence
Exponent
Extinguish

Face
Faith
Father
Fealty
Fidelity
Fire
First
Follow
Food
Footsteps
Forerunner
Foundation
Frequented Fane

Gabriel
Garden
Gate
Gems of Holiness
Glad-Tidings
God
Good-Pleasure
Gospel
Grace
Guard

Hamzih
Heart
Heaven
Hebrew
Heir
Hezekiah
Hidden Words
High Priest
Histories
Holy Books
Holy City
Holy of Holies
Holy Land
Holy Spirit
Hour
Ḥusayn

Ibn-i-Súríyá
Idol
Ignorance
Imám
Imitation
Infidel
Interpret
Isaiah
Ishmael
Islám
Israel

Jacob
Jehovah
Jeremiah
Jerusalem
Jesse
Jesus Christ
Jews
Job
Joel
John
John the Baptist
Joseph
Joshua
Judah
Judaism *see* Israel, Jew
Judas Iscariot
Judge
Judgment

Ka'bah
Káfí
Karím
King
Kingdom
Kitáb-i-Aqdas
Kitáb-i-Íqán
Knowledge
Krishna

Lament
Lamp
Language
Latter Days
Law
Lazarus
Leaders
Learned
Leper
Life
Light
Likeness
Literal
Lord
Lord of Hosts
Lord's Supper
Lot
Luminaries

Ma'ání
Magi
Malediction
Man
Man Child *see* Child
Manifestation
Manna
Mary
Mary Magdalene
Meaning
Mecca
Medina
Message
Messenger
Messiah
Mihdí
Millennium
Miracle
Mi'ráj
Mirror
Mission
Mithras
Monarch
Monk
Moon
Moses
Most Great Remembrance
Most Great Spirit
Mother
Mountain
Muḥammad

Names
Nation
Nazarene
Near Ones
Nebuchadnezzar
Neglect
New
Night
Nimrod
Noah

Obey
Old
Old Testament

One
Oppression
Orchard

Pagan
Paraclete
Paradise
Path
Paul
Peace
Pentateuch
Pentecost
People
Persecution
Person
Personal
Peter
Pharaoh
Pharisees
Philosophy
Piety
Poet
Point
Pope
Poverty
Power
Prayer
Prelates
Presence
Priests
Primacy
Primal Point
Primal Tree
Primal Will
Primal Word
Prince
Principle
Progressive
Revelation
Promise
Promised Land
Promised One
Proof
Prophecy
Prophet
Prophetic Cycle
Providence
Purpose

Qá'im
Qiblih
Qur'án

Rebirth
Reckoning
Redeemer
Reformation
Rehoboam
Religion
Remembrance
Repentance
Resurrection
Retribution
Return
Revealer
Revelation
Revelation, Book of, *see* John, Beast, Bride, Child *and various headings*
Ridicule
Right
Rod
Rúz-bih

Sabbath
Sackcloth
Sacraments
Sacrifice
Ṣádiq
Saint
Salmán
Salvation
Sanctuary
Satan
Science
Scripture
Sea
Seal
Seclusion
Second Coming
Seed
Seek
Seir
Self
Seraph
Serpent
Servant
Seven Martyrs of Ṭihrán
Seven Valleys
Sháh-Bahrám
Sharí'ah Law
Shí'ih
Shimr
Sign
Significance
Sin
Sinai
Smoke
Socrates
Sodom
Solomon
Son
Sorcery
Soul
Sovereignty
Spirit
Spiritual
Staff *see* Rod
Standard
Star
Station
Steadfastness
Storm
Succession
Suffer
Summon
Sun
Sunní
Superstition
Súrih
Sword
Symbol

Tabernacle
Tale
Ṭáhirih
Teachings
Temple
Ten Commandments
Test
Testament
Testimony
Text *see* Corruption of the Text
Theosophy
Times
Torah
Torment
Touchstone
Tradition
Traditor
Transfiguration
Transform
Tree
Trial
Tribes
Trinity
Trumpet
Truth
Turn

'Umar
Umayyads
Union
Unity
Unjust

List of Head Words

'Urvatu'l-Vuthqa
Utterance

Value
Vanity
Veil
Verse
Virgin
Vision
Voice

Water
West
Wilderness
Witness
Woe
Wolf
Woman
Word
Worship
Writings

Year
Youth

Zawrá'
Zion
Zíyárat
Zoroaster